£5.25p

Two week

CONTROL IN ORGANIZATIONS

McGRAW-HILL SERIES IN MANAGEMENT

Keith Davis, consulting editor

CONTROL IN ORGANIZATIONS

Arnold S. Tannenbaum
survey research center
institute for social research
and department of psychology
the university of michigan

McGraw-Hill Book Company

New York   St. Louis   San Francisco   Toronto   London   Sydney

CONTROL IN ORGANIZATIONS

Institutions, as many have said, are tools for "building civilization"; but they do not, like most tools, lie wholly outside and apart from the individuals who use them. They are, on the contrary, our own habits which, entering into our vital organization, exert upon other phases of our personalities an effect which we cannot safely ignore. Institutions are not merely our instruments; they are a part of ourselves.

Floyd H. Allport
Institutional Behavior, p. 471.

to Carol, Peter, Michael, and Rachel

FOREWORD

This book is a major contribution to organizational theory and to organizational operation. It is the first research-based volume dealing with a fundamental aspect of organization: the process by which members determine or influence how things get done in an organization. This process of control has been subject to a great deal of confusion and misconception, which this book does much to allay. The concept of control offered in this volume provides a framework for understanding a wide variety of issues, such as leadership, interpersonal relations, group processes, communication, conflict and cooperation, along with the central problems of authority and power in organizations. Control is thus seen as a general and underlying process that helps bring together many issues that are sometimes treated as discrete topics.

The methodological and substantive research along with the conceptualizations reported here represents an exciting departure from earlier approaches to understanding the control process. The application of the research findings can improve the performance of a great variety of enterprises of a business, governmental, educational, international, professional, or voluntary nature. Although the focus is on organizations, the insights that are provided apply to all social systems where control in one form or another plays an essential part. The reader will therefore see in this work implications for small social groups and families as well as for national and international systems.

The value of programmatic research is nicely demonstrated by this volume. The role of an overall conceptualization guiding a series of related studies yields a cumulative body of significant and integrated findings. The research therefore offers far more than can be obtained from a comparable series of separate investigations.

This book, and especially the introductory and summary chapters, are required reading for all persons concerned with improving the effectiveness of any kind of organization. The new insights that will be obtained will correct some serious conceptual errors that now adversely affect organizational performance. A sound understanding of the control process, to which this volume contributes, will be of great assistance in improving the day-to-day operations of every kind of organization.

Rensis Likert

PREFACE

This book presents the work of a number of persons, most of whom were joined in a programmatic effort to explore the problem of control in organizations. The explorations reported here concern questions of theory and practice, and they employ some of the tools of empirical social research in a large number and wide variety of organizations, including unions, voluntary associations, colleges, and business and industrial organizations of many kinds. Several industrial enterprises in Yugoslavia are included. The papers thus illustrate a comparative approach to the study of organizations, and the relatively recent development of research design in which the units of analysis are organizations as well as individuals. Most of the papers in this volume are technical, and most have been published earlier. The original sources—journals of sociology, psychology, and administration—illustrate the interdisciplinary nature of the behavioral science of organizations to which this book is intended as a contribution.

The book is divided into four parts. Part 1 presents the main concepts and illustrates their application through research in a variety of organizations. The second part delves into relationships between aspects of control and performance suggested in the earlier chapters. We treat in detail in this section some questions of methodological as well as substantive import. The articles here are concerned with reactions and adjustments of members as well as indices of organizational effectiveness. However, we reserve for a third part of the book several analyses that focus on the effects of control on the satisfactions, personalities, and conformity behavior of members. In a fourth part we discuss data that help explain what union members mean by control when they respond to questions about this subject. A second study in this section evaluates empirically several concepts and measures of control, including one measure, like that employed in this text, based on the judgment of organization members. A final chapter summarizes some of what we have learned about the effects of control on the reactions and adjustments of organization members and on the performance of organizations.

A good deal of the work reported here was made possible by a grant from the Carnegie Corporation of New York. This grant was most generous, not only in its amount, but in its conditions; because of the understanding of the corporation's officers we enjoyed the combination of freedom and support that most researchers covet.

The work described in this book required the direct collaboration of a number of persons, most of whom share authorship of the articles that follow. However, we relied on a number of others whose contributions proved highly significant. Robert Kahn helped launch me on this progammatic effort, and he, along with Jack French and Dorwin Cartwright, agreed to serve as consultants. I have not heretofore expressed my full appreciation to them for their great help in discussing with me their ideas about the concepts of power and control; I should like to express that appreciation now. I should also like to express thanks to my secretary, Mrs. Margaret Simpson, who has been a most tolerant and sympathetic coworker. She took on many tasks that lightened the burden for me.

Little of the work reported in this volume could have been carried out without the facilities and expert consultation provided by colleagues in the sampling, field, coding, data processing, and services sections of the Survey Research Center and the Institute for Social Research. We took for granted, during the course of our work, the help accorded us by our colleagues, benefitting from an atmosphere of support and cooperativeness that characterizes the Institute. Studying organizations, we ourselves were the beneficiaries of an unusual and highly effective organization.

These acknowledgments would not be complete without mentioning my good fortune in having been at Syracuse University while Floyd H. Allport held the chair of Social and Political Psychology there. I hope it is not a source of embarrassment for him to see his mark, however inadequately reflected, in some of what follows.

Arnold S. Tannenbaum

CONTENTS

This section presents the main concepts and illustrates their application through research in a variety of organizations. In the first chapter we define control and offer an analysis of the control process. The character of control in organizations has changed through the years, and classical conceptions, being based on experience of the past, are limited in their capacity to explain control in contemporary organizations. We therefore advocate assumptions about control that seem to us more general and more realistic than some that have prevailed. A simple descriptive model called the "control graph" illustrates several of these assumptions. This model also makes apparent a basic but little considered distinction, that between the distribution and the total amount of control in an organization. The meaning of this distinction is explored extensively in this and in subsequent chapters.

The following three chapters represent early attempts to apply the control graph in a number of organizations. Chapter 2 describes research in four union locals. This exploratory study supports some and rejects other current hypotheses concerning the relationships of control to interorganizational conflict, to the loyalty and activity of members, and to organizational effectiveness. But more significantly, this study illustrates how the control graph might offer a fresh view of current arguments about control and how the graph might therefore provide a basis for resolving some of these arguments. Chapter 3 extends application of the model into an industrial service organization, and Chapter 4 describes research concerning organizational control and effectiveness in a large voluntary organization. This study represents a methodological advance over its predecessors because of the relatively large probability sample of organizational units included.

Chapter 5 summarizes and integrates the results from the above studies along with a number of studies not reported here. Different types of organizations are compared with respect to their patterns of control as perceived by members and by officers, and analyses are described relating indices of control to criteria of performance. This chapter illustrates some of the potentialities and limitations of the control graph as a comparative approach to the study of organizations. The final chapter of this section further illustrates these potentialities and limitations by carrying the approach into a number of Yugoslav organizations.

1

CONTROL IN ORGANIZATION*

Arnold S. Tannenbaum[1]

Man's life in contemporary society can be characterized largely as one of organizational memberships. Man commits a major portion of his waking hours to participation in at least one, and more often several, social organizations. His motivation, his aspirations, his general way of life, are tied inextricably to the organizations of which he is a part, and even to some of which he is not.

Organizations are of vital interest to the social scientist, because one finds within them an important juncture between the individual and the collectivity. Out of this juncture comes much in our pattern of living that has been the subject of both eulogy and derogation. That man derives a great deal from organizational membership leaves little to be argued; that he often pays heavily for the benefits of organizational membership seems an argument equally compelling. At the heart of this exchange lies the process of control.

Characterizing an organization in terms of its pattern of control is to describe an essential and universal aspect of organization which every member must face and to which he must adjust. Organization implies control. A social organization is an ordered arrangement of individual human interactions. Control processes help circumscribe idiosyncratic behaviors and keep them conformant to the rational plan of the organization. Organizations require a certain amount of conformity as well as the integration of diverse activities. It is the function of control to bring about conformance to organizational requirements and achievement of the ultimate purposes of the organization. The coordination and order created out of the diverse interests and potentially diffuse behaviors of members is largely a function of control. It is at this point that many of the problems of organizational functioning and of individual adjustment arise.

Control is an inevitable correlate of organization. But it is more than this. It is concerned with aspects of social life that are of the utmost importance to everyone. It is concerned with questions of the common will and the common weal. It is related, not only to what goes on within the organization,

* This chapter, written in large measure expressly for the present work, includes excerpts from the author's articles, Control in organizations: individual adjustment and organizational performance, *Administrative Sci. quart.*, 7 (2), 1962, 236–257, with permission of the publisher; and Leadership: Sociological Aspects, adapted by permission of the Publisher from Tannenbaum, "Leadership: Sociological Aspects" in (Vol. 9, pp. 101–107) INTERNATIONAL ENCYCLOPEDIA OF THE SOCIAL SCIENCES, Sills, ed. Copyright © 1968 by Crowell Collier and Macmillan, Inc.

[1] I should like to express my appreciation to Lutz Erbring, Amitai Etzioni, Michael Inbar, Rensis Likert, Raymond Miles, and Josip Zupanov for helpful suggestions.

but also to what the organization does in its external relations. It touches on the questions of democracy and autocracy, centralization and decentralization, "flat" and "tall" organizational structures, workers' councils and joint management.

The problems of control and conformity in organizations contribute to a serious dilemma. Organization provides order—a condition necessary for man to produce abundantly and live securely. Abundance and security in turn create opportunities and choice—conditions that form the basis for human freedom. Yet social order itself requires conformity and imposes limitations. Furthermore, the responsibility for creating and sustaining order tends to be distributed unevenly within organizations. Often it is the few who decide on the kind of order to which the many must conform. But regardless of how order is created, it requires the conformity of all or nearly all to organizational norms.

The magnitude of this problem as it applies to our economic institutions has been indicated by Berle and Means (1952):

> To the dozen or so men who are in control there is room for . . . [individual] initiative. For the tens of thousands and even hundreds of thousands of workers and of owners in a single enterprise, [individual] initiative no longer exists. Their activity is group activity on a scale so large that the individual, except he be in a position of control, has dropped into relative insignificance.

And the trend, according to Barnard (1951, pp. 109–110) is in the direction of greater concentration of control in the hands of fewer persons:

> There has been a greater and greater acceleration of centralization in this country, not merely in government, and not merely in the organization of great corporations, but also a great concentration on the part of labor unions and other organizations. There has been a social disintegration going along with this material development, and this formulation of organized activities implies payment of a price, the amount of which we are not yet able to assess.

This, perhaps, is one of the most crucial problems of social morality that we face in the age of massive organization, although the problem is not an entirely new one. We see it in Rousseau's *Social Contract*, Marx's *Capital*, Freud's *Civilization and Its Discontents*, Huxley's *Brave New World*, and Whyte's *The Organization Man*. Social and administrative scientists have become increasingly interested in this question, and as a result social researchers are applying themselves to the study of control and its relationship to individual adjustment and organizational functioning. Consequently a body of facts and hypotheses concerning control in organizations is growing. This book describes research concerned with some of these facts and hypotheses.

SOME CONCEPTIONS OF CONTROL

Control has been variously defined, and different terms (for example, power, authority, influence) are sometimes used synonymously with it. Its original application in business organizations derives from the French usage meaning to check. It is now commonly used in a broader sense synonymously with the notions of influence and power. We shall use the term in this way to refer to any process in which a person or group of persons or organization of persons determines, that is, intentionally affects, the behavior of another person, group, or organization.

Although our definition conforms essentially to what many authors mean by control, power, or influence (see, for example, Dahl, 1957), there certainly are differences of opinion regarding the definition of these terms (Cartwright, 1965; Schopler, 1965). For example, some writers prefer to think of power as an exclusively coercive form of control. Weber was the first of the classic authors on organization to reject this limited notion of power, and many contemporary social scientists, including the authors of this volume, are inclined to think of power as having bases in addition to, although by no means excluding, coercive ones. Some authors like to think of power in terms of differentials or ratios that describe the relative "strengths" of persons in a system. In this view power is essentially the effect that one person has on a second compared with that which the second has on the first. This is an important index of power relations, but we see it conceptually as a derivative of the more general definition that we propose. A number of authors prefer to distinguish power from control by defining power essentially as the ability or capacity to exercise control, that is, as "potential control." Compare, for example, Goldhamer and Shils's (1939) definition with that of Etzioni (1961a). According to the former, "a person may be said to have power to the extent that he influences the behavior of others in accordance with his own intentions" (p. 171); according to the second, "power is an actor's ability to induce or influence another actor to carry out his directives or any other norms he supports" (p. 4). Both these definitions are consistent in essential respects with our own, although Etzioni's statement implies what we should prefer to call potential control. For most authors the term *authority* usually refers to the formal right to exercise control, and we follow this general convention in the articles that follow.

The meaning of control, as we define it, can be seen in the simple prototype in Figure 1, which represents control as a cycle beginning with an intent on the part of one person, followed by an influence attempt addressed to another person, who then acts in some way that fulfills the intent of the first.[2] Figure 1 presents the control process in its simplest form. There are, of course, many elements in addition to those indicated that are important in under-

---

[2] The notion of control as a cycle of events is suggested by F. H. Allport's (1955, 1962) event-structure theory.

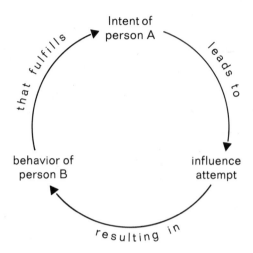

FIGURE 1   *The control process.*

standing this process (Cartwright, 1965). These include the assumptions and values of the actors, the "bases of power" that help explain B's response, and the great variety of means by which A attempts to influence B. Such means may be direct or indirect (through a chain of command, through the use of groups, through written communications, or through the intervention of technological devices); they may include orders or requests, threats or promises, and so forth. The behavior of B may involve relationships with other persons or it may involve actions in relation to technological elements, such as tools, computers, or production lines. Thus technology may enter into the cycle at various points, creating what has been called a "sociotechnical" system (Emery and Trist, 1959; and Trist et al., 1963). For example, computers may provide A with information that leads him to request B to do one thing rather than another. Or A may simply use the computer to tell B. A may also speed up a production line, which illustrates another form of influence attempt on B.[3]

The intentions of A may be initiated by him, or they may be the intentions of others that are acquired by A (Etzioni, 1961a, p. 4). These intentions may imply quite specific actions for B, as when a supervisor gives detailed instructions to a subordinate; or they may be very general, although no less real, as in the formulation of organizational policy.[4] The behavior of B, which is the

[3] Although machines may play an important role in the control process, we do not attribute control to machines. Machines are used by men (A's) as instruments of control. Machines may have important effects quite unintended by those who employ them, but such effects do not represent social control, as we define the term. This is not to belittle such "unintended effects," but simply to distinguish them from social control. Our definition thus has moral, in addition to conceptual, implications, because it calls attention to the intentions of persons as the initial component of the control process. The difficulties and the benefits of industrial life hinge ultimately on these intentions.

[4] This raises the difficult problem of "power comparability" (Dahl, 1957), for which a theoretical solution is proposed by Tannenbaum (1962b).

object of A's intentions, may, in our definition, be covert as well as overt. A, for example, may have intentions regarding the intentions of B, and vice versa.

When we say that A determines B's behavior, we mean that A "causes" B to behave in an intended way. Control, then, is a special case of social causation (March, 1955; Simon, 1957b). Dahl (1957) has provided a useful conceptualization of this point by defining the control of A over B as the probability that B does what A requests minus the probability that B would have done it in the absence of the request. In an elaboration of Dahl's definition, Tannenbaum (1962b) has proposed that the amount of control be understood as a function of the importance to B of the changes in behavior affected by the control cycle. Thus control is greater when important behaviors are affected than when unimportant ones are affected.[5]

Thus the cycle in Figure 1, although simplified, represents the essence of the control process, as we define it. Such a cycle includes essentially what Etzioni refers to as "compliance" (1961a). The control cycle is a basic unit of organization structure; organizations are composed of large numbers of such cycles in interrelationship.[6] If a cycle breaks down at any point, for whatever reason, control cannot be said to exist. For example, A may have conflicting intents that lead to confusing influence attempts and hence to a breakdown in the cycle; or B may be incapable of fulfilling A's request, even though B may wish to; or B may dislike A and so refuse to do A's bidding; or B may be included in two or more cycles that involve contradictory influence attempts; and so on. Chronic breakdowns of such cycles imply a breakdown in the organization itself.

TRADITIONAL ANALYSES OF CONTROL

Although the theoretical analysis of control in social systems has a long and venerable history, empirical research on this subject has been initiated only recently in organizations. The "human-relations" approach that inspired a great deal of research in organizations avoided explicit reference to social power or control, partly because these terms carried connotations that were inconsistent with the ideal of the harmonious, conflict-free organization.[7] Traditionally, the concept of power has been associated with forms of tyranny, elitism or authoritarianism, or with conflict and struggle. Almost all the literature on the power of leadership, according to Bell (1950), stems from the

---

[5] This brief statement does not do justice to the arguments of Dahl (1957) and of Tannenbaum (1962b), which the interested reader should see in the original.

[6] See Allport (1955, 1962) for a discussion of the relationship among cycles in a collective system.

[7] Nonetheless, much of the human-relations research was concerned implicitly with enhancing the control exercised by management, for example, through devising more effective techniques of supervision and through reducing "resistances" on the part of workers to managerial policies. Thus, some advocates of human relations were committed, implicitly at least, to enhancing control within organizations while denying its importance—a contradiction that may have contributed to the charge that human relations was manipulative. See, for example, Bendix and Fisher (1961). See also Crozier (1964, pp. 145–150) for a discussion of the changing treatment accorded power in organizational theory and research through the years. Pugh (1966) also describes the development of a concern among psychologists for power as a variable in studies of organizational behavior.

works of Aristotle and Machiavelli and is committed to "the image of the mindless masses and the image of the strong-willed leader." Historically, ideologies of management have grown up, according to Bendix (1956), specifically to justify the employers' exercise of authority, which was associated in one way or another with the subordination or exploitation of workers.

According to Michels's (1962) classic conception, control in organizations must inevitably become oligarchic. Michels's "iron law of oligarchy" applies even to political organizations that begin democratically and are committed to a democratic ideology. Leaders themselves are incapable of deflecting this historic process; democratic and idealistic leaders succumb eventually to the corruption inherent in power. Michels cites a number of arguments in support of the tendency toward oligarchy in organizations. First, the rank and file, through incompetence and apathy, cannot and do not wish to exercise control; the masses prefer to be led. Second, democracy is structurally impossible in large and complex social systems; there is no way of arranging the system so that the views of the many individual members can be heard and taken into account. The impracticality of democracy is especially apparent in organizations undergoing conflict with others. Especially during periods of crisis, organizations need firm leadership and precise adherence to orders. Finally, the tendency toward oligarchy results from the character of leaders and the role that they must play. Because of their cultural and educational superiority over the masses, leaders form a distinct elite. The status, perquisites, and privileges associated with the leadership role serve further to separate the leaders from the masses. In labor unions and socialist parties, for example, the life of the leaders becomes that of the petite bourgeoisie. Leaders therefore develop a vested interest in their position, which they must protect. Furthermore, a personal lust for power, which is characteristic of leaders, intensifies their efforts to enhance their power, and leaders resort to ulterior devices toward this end. In "democratic" parties leaders employ emotional and demagogic appeals to manipulate the gullible masses. They control the party press, using it to describe themselves in the most favorable light, while deriding their opposition within the party. They exploit their special information and knowledge of the organization to outmaneuver opponents. And, if despite these tactics, the leaders are overthrown, the new office holders, in turn, undergo the inevitable "transformation which renders them in every respect similar to the dethroned tyrants. . . . The revolutionaries of today become the reactionaries of tomorrow" (p. 195).

SOME CHANGES IN THE CONCEPTION OF CONTROL

Michels's pessimism about democracy in organizations is reflected, in one form or another, in the work of a number of contemporary organization theorists. Gouldner (1955) has wondered why these theorists focus so tenaciously on the constraints inherent in organization that thwart democracy, while failing to consider the constraints that may contribute to the realization of democratic aspirations. "Why is it that 'unanticipated consequences' are always tacitly assumed to be destructive of democratic values and 'bad'; why can't they sometimes be 'good?' Are there no constraints which *force* men to adhere valorously to their democratic beliefs, which *compel* them to be intelligent rather than blind, which leave them *no choice* but to be men of good will rather than predators?" (p. 505). The failure by some organization theorists to consider the "positive" as well as "negative" constraints in organizations suggests to Gouldner (p. 507) a distorting "pathos of pessimism":

> *Wrapping themselves in the shrouds of nineteenth-century political economy, some social scientists appear to be bent on resurrecting a dismal science. For the iron law of wages which maintained that workers could never improve their material standards of life, some sociologists have substituted the iron law of oligarchy, which declares that men cannot improve their political standards of life. Woven to a great extent out of theoretical whole cloth, much of the discussion of bureaucracy and of organizational needs seems to have provided a screen onto which some intellectuals have projected their own despair and pessimism, reinforcing the despair of others.*[8]

Although many of the classical conceptions of control, including those of Weber in bureaucracies and Michels in political organizations, have proved valuable in analyses of contemporary organizations, the changing character of societies and organizations over the years is making apparent some of the limitations of those older conceptions. The emphasis in contemporary social science on quantitative research has also contributed to changes in interpretations of the control process because of the need to develop conceptions that are operational as well as theoretically meaningful. At the same time, research findings themselves have led to reinterpretations of older conceptions.

The increasing numbers and complexity of organizations in modern industrial societies require large numbers of persons with a high level of technical and administrative expertise to play leadership roles. The demand for expert leaders reduces the suitability of those recruited on the basis of social status or family connections. Achievement replaces ascription as the basis for placing leaders, and their recruitment spreads to all strata of society. Similarly, political criteria, prevalent as the basis of recruitment during early stages in newly independent and in revolutionary societies, become less important. At the same time, training centers for leaders are established in universities, business schools, and training institutes, and the possibility for careers in industrial leadership is opened to large numbers of persons. Management becomes professionalized. Although these developments are most apparent in business and industrial organizations and in some agencies of government, they are

---

[8] For an "optimistic" analysis that defines some of the constraints contributing to the development of more democratic organizational forms, see Bennis (1966), especially Chap. 2.

also occurring in other organizations, including the military and labor unions (Kerr et al., 1962).

Most of these changes imply a rationalization of the control process in organizations consistent with Weber's (1947) bureaucratic model. However, further changes in the way leaders exercise control are likely to accompany this rationalization, and these represent a divergence from the classical bureaucratic model. Leaders may rely on discussion and persuasion rather than on command exclusively. Attempts may be made to elicit cooperation, sometimes by having organization members participate in the making of decisions that affect them in the work place. The rising level of education of the work force represents an important "constraint" that contributes to this trend. In addition the specialized skills that are frequently required of persons at all levels in modern organizations may sometimes mean that subordinates are more expert in a particular specialization than their superiors, thus modifying the classical supervisory-subordinate relationships (Thompson, 1961). Furthermore, professional managers are more inclined than their predecessors to consider the results of social research, such as that described in this book, which have supported the growth of human-relations approaches to control in organizations. At the same time, political developments, particularly in some European countries, have led to the introduction of schemes of comanagement and of workers' councils, with varying degrees of success (Emery and Thorsrud, 1965; Kolaja, 1965; Meister, 1964; Sturmthal, 1964; Zupanov and Tannenbaum, 1967). These developments may not be fully consolidated in any contemporary society, but incipient support, at least, can be found in many organizations for less autocratic control than was customary in the past. A survey in fourteen industrialized and developing nations, for example, shows that managers overwhelmingly subscribe at least to the idea of participation by workers in decision making, although managers express skepticism about the capacity of workers to assume the responsibilities consonant with democratic leadership (Haire et al., 1966).

Taken together, these developments imply the growth—actual in some places, potential in others—of new kinds of control in addition to those prevalent in the past. Partly as a consequence of this and of developments in research, conceptions of the control process have been broadened.

First, a change has taken place in analyses of the bases of power. Coercion has played a prominent role in traditional analyses, consistent with the presumed conflict between leaders and followers. Leaders are obeyed out of fear of punishment or hope for reward. Weber (1961), however, argues that the stability of social systems depends on acceptance by followers of the right of leaders to exercise control. This implied legitimate authority, and Weber defines three types: (1) "Charismatic" authority, according to which leaders are thought to be endowed with extraordinary, sometimes magical powers. Charisma on the part of a leader elicits obedience out of awe. It is illustrated in its pure form by "the prophet, the warrior hero, the great demagogue" (p. 10).

(2) "Traditional" authority, which appertains to those who have the right to rule by virtue of birth or class. The traditional leader is obeyed because he or members of his class or family have always been followed. Its pure type is illustrated by certain patriarchs, monarchs, and feudal lords. (3) "Legal" authority, which applies to those who hold leadership positions because of demonstrated technical competence. Legal authorities act impersonally as instruments of the law, and they are obeyed impersonally out of a sense of duty to the law. Leadership in the ideal bureaucracy is based exclusively on legal authority.

The character of authority envisioned within this framework is consistent with many of the traditional analyses: Weber's authority figures are prophets, warriors, demagogues, patriarchs, lords, and bureaucrats. More recent analyses have stressed bases of power in addition to those outlined by Weber.

Simon (1957a), for example, points to the importance of social approval. Approval and disapproval represent forms of reward and punishment, but they deserve special consideration because they are frequently dispensed, not only by the designated leader, but also by others. Thus, a subordinate may obey a supervisor, not so much because of the rewards and punishments meted out by the supervisor, as because of the approval and disapproval by the subordinate's own peers. Confidence may represent a further basis for acceptance of leaders' authority. A subordinate may trust the judgment and therefore accept the authority of a leader in areas where the leader has great technical competence. French and Raven (1960) make a further distinction between the influence of a leader based on confidence by subordinates in the leaders' expert knowledge and "informational influence" based on acceptance by subordinates of the logic of the arguments that the leader offers. An expert leader, then, may exercise control, not simply because he is an acknowledged authority, but because his decisions, being based on expertise, are manifestly logical, appropriate, and convincing. Subordinates are persuaded that the decisions are correct. This is related to some human-relations approaches that stress control by facts as opposed to control by men. Such "fact control" relies on understanding, and is illustrated by the participative leader who influences the behavior of subordinates by helping them understand the facts of a situation so that they may jointly arrive at a course of action consistent with their own interests and that of the collectivity. Some of these conceptions represent radical departures from many traditional ones; assuming, as they do, an overriding community of interests among all members of the organization.

A further change in the conception of power relates to assumptions concerning the mutuality-unilaterality of control. A view common to traditional analyses argues that the control process is unilateral; one either leads or is led, is strong or weak, controls or is controlled. Simmel, in spite of his general adherence to the traditional conflict view of power, noted a more subtle interaction underlying the appearance of "pure superiority" on the part of one person and the "purely passive being led" of another: "All leaders are also led; in innumerable cases the master is the slave of his slaves" (Wolff, 1950, pp. 185–186). Contemporary analyses are more likely than earlier ones to consider relationships of mutual as well as unilateral power, of followers influencing leaders, as well as vice versa.

Finally, traditional analyses of social power assume that the total amount of power in a social system is a fixed quantity and that leaders and followers are engaged in a "zero sum game": increasing the power of one party must be accompanied by a corresponding decrease in the power of the other. Some social scientists are now inclined to question the generality of this assumption (Deutsch, 1966; Lammers, 1967; Likert, 1961; Parsons, 1963; Tannenbaum and Kahn, 1957). The total amount of power in a social system may grow, and leaders and followers may therefore enhance their power jointly. Total power may also decline, and all groups within the system may suffer corresponding decreases.

THE VIEWPOINT OF THIS BOOK

Some of our assumptions regarding control in organizations can be illustrated through the hypothetical control graph in Figure 2. Such a graph was first applied by Tannenbaum and Kahn (1958) to a study of four trade-union locals. If the horizontal base of this graph is taken to represent the hierarchical scale in an organization, and the vertical axis the amount of control exercised by the respective hierarchical echelons, then a curve drawn on this graph represents the hierarchical distribution of control. Like many abstractions this one is a simplification, but it has certain methodological and conceptual advantages, as we hope to illustrate in this book.

It is clear from this graph that an infinite number of curves of widely varying shapes are possible. (This variety is not easily accommodated by the traditional typologies—democratic, autocratic, and the like—that are simplifications in their own right.) It is also apparent that these curves may differ from one another, not only in their shape, but also in their average height, suggesting theoretically that organizations may differ in their total amount of control, as well as in the relative amount of control exercised by the respective hierarchical echelons. The control graph thus takes issue with what Parsons (1963) refers to as "the dominant [and erroneous] tendency in the literature . . . that there is a fixed 'quantity' of power in any relational system. . . ."

The assumption of a variable amount of control in organizations represents, we believe, an assumption of basic theoretical and practical importance. Theoretically, this assumption opens up a number of possibilities that would not otherwise be apparent. Consequently it allows us to resolve what might otherwise appear to be opposing and irreconcilable arguments concerning the implications of control in organizations. For example, one argument holds that the enhancement of control by rank-and-file members is essential for increasing organizational effectiveness, because involvement in decision making by these persons, especially in the context of a "democratic society," is necessary

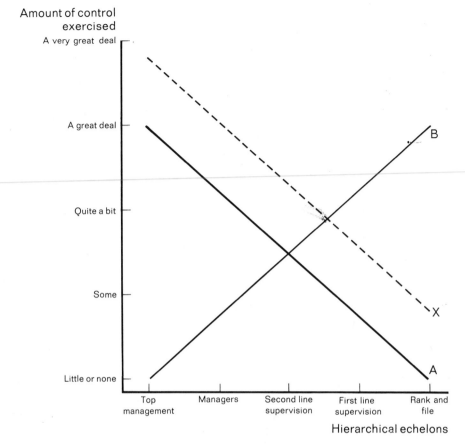

FIGURE 2   *Some hypothetical distributions of control.*

to foster conditions of identification, motivation, and loyalty. On the other hand, the conflicting argument goes, a high degree of control by leaders is necessary for the efficient direction and administration of organizations. Our use of the control graph has led us to question the "fixed-pie" assumption underlying this controversy and has raised the question of why increased control exercised by both leaders and members does not create conditions for more effective organizational performance. Curve X illustrates this possibility. By comparison with curve A, curve X is both more "democratic," in the sense of greater control by lower echelons, and more "oligarchic," in the sense of greater control by upper echelons—which, in traditional terms, is a contradiction.[9]

[9] It is amusing to think of this controversy in terms of a dialectic in which curve A represents the thesis of oligarchy and the antithesis, curve B, the dictatorship of the proletariat. Figure 2 portrays revolution graphically, because one gets from "oligarchy" to "dictatorship of the proletariat" through a revolution of curve A around its center point. Many organization leaders, indeed, have seen a haunting specter in participative schemes, because, committed as they have been to a fixed-pie, conflict view of power, these leaders could envision such schemes only as implying some degree of "revolution." A possible synthesis in the dialectic, curve X, has therefore been overlooked by most managerial persons, as well as by many organization theorists.

Assumptions about control in organizations also have practical consequences, because organizational leaders who hold these assumptions are likely to act on the basis of them. The practical importance of these assumptions is compounded by the fact that the choice of assumptions may lead to self-fulfilling prophecies. For example, the assumption by organization members of a fixed amount of control may lead to attempts by some members to restrict the powers of others, thus in fact limiting the amount of control within the system. Furthermore, it seems reasonable to think that the fixed-pie assumption and its self-fulfilling consequences contribute to an assumption of basic and prevailing conflict within the organization and to attempts by leaders to exercise unilateral control, just as the assumption of prevailing conflict is likely to lead to attempts by some parties to limit the power of others.[10] Thus the choice of some assumptions is likely to affect the choice of others, partly because the assumptions may seem logically to be related, but also because actions based on some assumptions have effects that verify others. Ultimately the choice of assumptions can have a bearing on the effectiveness of the system. For example, Likert (1961) suggests that the effective social organization is characterized by supportive relations, mutual respect, confidence and trust, and a substantial system of interaction and influence among members and between members and leaders. Such an effective system is not likely to develop where leaders believe that increased influence by members can be achieved only by a decline in the leaders' influence.

THE TOTAL AMOUNT OF CONTROL IN AN ORGANIZATION

The issue of total amount of control in a system has been of concern to social scientists more implicitly than explicitly.[11] Most analyses of control have been concerned with the relative control exercised by groups within organizations rather than with the total amount. The literature, therefore, provides little guidance concerning the conditions under which the amount of control in a system may expand.

In principle this expansion may occur under either of two classes of conditions. The first is that of an external expansion of power into the organization's environment. The second concerns a number of internal conditions that subsume (1) structural conditions expediting interaction and influence among members and (2) motivational conditions implying increased interest by members in exercising control and a greater amenability by members to

---

[10] It is important to distinguish between the belief in underlying conflict of interests among members and the overt manifestation of conflict. The former may sometimes lead to the latter and to one of several possible outcomes, including (1) dominance by one side over the other, (2) some form of compromise, or (3) a new synthesis or resolution of differences. A belief in underlying conflict may also lead to withdrawal or disengagement by one or both parties as a means of avoiding overt conflict. Such withdrawal can be more dysfunctional for the organization than an overt conflict that implies involvement and commitment by members in the organization.

[11] For a dialogue on this subject see Dahrendorf (1959) and Parsons (1963).

being controlled. These conditions may sometimes be related. For example, extending control by the organization into its environment may bring more decisions within the purview of the organization that are subject to the control of its members, thus increasing the possibility of a greater total amount of control. At the same time such increased opportunities to exercise control within the organization may increase the members' involvement in and identification with the organization and hence increase their interest in exercising control and their amenability to being controlled. Members, then, as possible control agents, engage in more frequent influence attempts, and as possible objects of control, provide new opportunities to one another to exercise control. Thus external developments may affect social and psychological processes within the organization conducive to a high level of internal control, just as conditions of a high level of involvement by members and of a high level of control within the organization may contribute to the strength of the organization and hence to its power in its environment (see Chapter 2). Several general concepts in current use are helpful in describing how the above conditions may contribute to the expansion of control within a social system.

Control and exchange

The first concept is that of "exchange of resources," as discussed by Blau (1964), Deutsch (1966), Homans (1961), Lasswell and Kaplan (1950), and Thibaut and Kelley (1959). For example, Homans suggests that a "sense of justice" (that may prevail within some groups at least) demands that a person who has received much from another should also give much to him. The exercise of control may be viewed as an exchange of some valued resource dispensed by one person in return for compliance on the part of another. The total amount of control or power in a system may therefore be seen as a function of the amount of exchange involving compliance. This amount may change, because the quantity of resources among members changes or because of a change in the rules (implicit or explicit) regarding exchange. For example, an increase in affectional ties among members may lead to the growth of social approval as a resource, because approval is valued more from liked persons than from those not liked. Hence social systems composed of persons who like one another can, in principle, engage in a greater amount of exchange of approval for compliance than systems composed of persons who are indifferent to one another.[12] In simplest terms, A does what B requests, because A values B's approval, and B does what A requests, because he values A's approval. Or A does what B requests, because he values B's approval, and B does what A requests because "justice demands" that B reciprocate.

---

[12] See, for example, Homan's (1961, pp. 85–89) discussion of research by Festinger and his colleagues.

Traditional managerial approaches can be distinguished from participative by the rules (implicit or explicit) regarding the quality and quantity of exchange within them. In some traditional systems employees exchange compliance for pay; in participative systems they do so for some managerial compliance (plus pay), thus increasing the total amount of compliance (that is, control). The possibility of such an expanding exchange relies heavily on the assumption of broad areas of common interest (rather than conflict) between members and leaders of the organization (Simon, 1957a).

Control and partial inclusion

A second concept that may be helpful in describing how control expands within a system is that of "partial inclusion," suggested by Allport (1933b). Organizational behavior involves only a limited segment of the many needs and the potential repertory of behavior that define the total make-up of members as individuals. In their role as organization members individuals do not express the full range of their personalities; they are thus only "partially included" in the organization. Because only a part of the member is included, only a part of him is at the disposal, so to speak, of the organization. Thus there are limitations to the range of activities that are subject to influence; excluded from influence is that large segment of the person that does not belong to the organization. Bureaucracy was designed precisely to exclude this segment, not as a means of restricting members, but as a means of protecting them from undue and illegitimate control.

Including members more fully in the organization can be viewed as an expansion of the organization into its environment, because the newly included segments of the individual were heretofore outside the organization. More things to be controlled now fall within the purview of the organization, and hence there is opportunity for some members at least to increase their control without necessarily reducing that exercised by others.

Anything that enhances members' personal commitment to or identification with the organization is implicitly including them more fully within the organization and hence is increasing the possibility of an expanded total amount of control. Human-relations approaches that are designed to increase the identification of members may therefore result in greater inclusion and greater control. Similarly, giving members some influence in the organization generally has the effect of increasing their identification with the organization and their inclusion in it. Hence increasing members' influence may also increase their influenceability, and so contributing to a higher level of control in the system.

Control and negative entropy

A third concept that may help describe the meaning of the total amount of control in an organization is that of "negative entropy," which is an index of order (Allport, 1955; Katz and Kahn, 1966; Wiener, 1950). Order is the essence of organization; organizational behavior is ordered behavior. This order applies to what goes on within the organization at a particular moment as well as to the regularity of the organization through time. However, the natural tendency of all systems is toward disorder, or entropy. "This tending toward entropy (maximum disorganization or disorder) is, so far as we know, a universal law of nature" (Allport, 1955, p. 475). Hence in social organizations, as in all systems that are to maintain their orderliness, there is a need for some means of negating the entropic tendency. Control is part of the means for meeting this essential requirement. For this reason organization is inconceivable without some system of control.

The function of control in reducing the amount of entropy in organizations can be seen through a comparison of the actions of persons who are behaving on the basis of their purely individualistic inclinations without regard for organizational requirements and persons who are behaving in organizational roles. The former tend, as a group, to show in their behavior a considerable degree of randomness. For example, persons arise at widely disparate hours and come and go according to their many diverse, personal, and idiosyncratic interests. Their behavior along given dimensions (for example, time of awaking) thus tends to be distributed according to the normal probability curve, following the usual distribution of personality traits (Allport, 1933a). This randomness, in the "collective" behavior of persons displays a high degree of entropy. As organization members, however, their collective behavior is more controlled and less entropic. One, although not the only, manifestation of this reduced entropy can be found in the uniformities that characterize some of the behavior of organization members. Allport provides a graphic illustration, through the hypothetical curves in Figure 3, of the uniformity and orderliness of behavior implied by organization. "The narrow, more uniform distribution

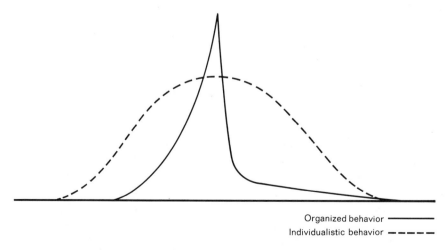

Organized behavior ——————
Individualistic behavior — — — — —

FIGURE 3 *Hypothetical distribution of organized and individualistic behavior. (Adapted from Allport, 1933a.)*

demonstrates the effects of social control, adherence or conformity by members to some organizational rule or standard. It also illustrates one aspect of the order and predictability essential to organization; we know or can predict within a relatively narrow margin of error, where a particular person is likely to fall on the scale if he is a member of a group whose behaviors distribute according to the solid-line curve. Most persons in this group fall within a very narrow range. In the case of the dashed-line curve, however, our prediction would be less certain and less reliable—as would an organization built on distributions of this kind" (Tannenbaum, 1966, pp. 4–5).

The second law of thermodynamics states that a system tends toward its most probable state, which, for the hypothetical groups portrayed in the above curves, is the normal probability distribution—unless a reduction of entropy is achieved and maintained to forestall the inevitable deterioration into randomness. Since control is a means of creating order, organizations that differ in their orderliness (degree of negative entropy) may be expected to differ in the amounts of control within them. The limiting case of the laissez-faire, anarchic organization, characterized by a high degree of entropy, is relatively little controlled. The move away from *laissez faire*, whether toward a more democratic, autocratic, or polyarchic system of control, is a move toward more orderliness and more control. This is consistent with the argument that organizations should be viewed, not simply as all-or-none phenomena, but as variable states. The total amount of control, like negative entropy, may be taken as one index of degree of organization (Tannenbaum and Kahn, 1958).

Control and graph theory

The notions of graph theory may also be helpful in conceptualizing the total amount of control as a variable in a group or organization (Harary et al., 1966). Graph theory calls attention to the "connections" between points (individuals) in a network. A limiting case is a set of points that are not connected at all. This may represent a social "network" in which the individuals are isolated socially from one another; hence there is no control within this system. Figure 4, taken from French (1956), illustrates hypothetical networks that differ in their connectedness and total amounts of control. Set A, a "weakly connected" set, manifests little change through time in the attitudes of members. Set B, a "completely connected" set, shows a great deal of change toward a single, uniform attitude position. This set has a high total amount of control within it—and less entropy. (Note that sets A and B in Figure 4 offer a type of "dynamic" explanation for the dashed and solid curves respectively in Figure 3.)

Graph theory is helpful in describing many kinds of social relations. For example, an acquaintanceship between two persons is weakly connected; hence it manifests little internal control in comparison with an intimate friendship, which is strongly connected and hence high in control. Some relationships may vary through time in their connectedness. For example, an acquain-

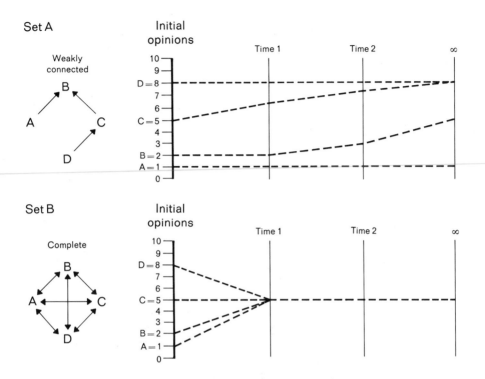

FIGURE 4   *The effects of connectedness on opinion changes in the group. (Adapted from French, 1956.)*

tanceship may evolve into a more intimate relationship. Or particular classes of relationships, such as families, may include cases that differ in their connectedness and the amounts of control within them. For example, some families are more tightly knit than others. In the former, members engage in more activities together, and they interact and influence one another more substantially. There is more to the family in this case and hence more to be controlled. Similarly, the cohesive group is characterized by more connectedness and hence more control than the noncohesive group. Furthermore such groups may themselves be conceived graph-theoretically as points that can be connected. An organization represented by strong connections between such points, each of which itself represents a set of strongly connected points, is an organization high in total amount of control in comparison with one that is weakly connected.

SOME APPROACHES TO ENHANCING THE TOTAL AMOUNT OF CONTROL

Several authors illustrate, through a number of relatively specific "mechanisms," the possibility of increasing the total amount of control in organizations. For example, Selznick's cooptation principle (1953, pp. 13–16 and 259–

261) implies, at least under some circumstances, a degree of influence exercised within the organization by the coopted element, which it did not exercise before cooptation, as well as an increased control by the "hierarchy" over the coopted element. Aspects of "participative management" share some features with cooptation. For example, the more complete inclusion through participation of "partially included" members may be viewed as a form of cooptation. Similarly, through participation, cohesive informal groups may be coopted by the formal organization. March and Simon (1958, p. 54) are explicit in describing the control-enhancing character of the participative system:

> Where there is participation, alternatives are suggested in a setting that permits the organizational hierarchy to control (at least in part) what is evoked. "Participative management" can be viewed as a device for permitting management to participate more fully in the making of decisions as well as a means for expanding the influence of lower echelons in the organization.[13]

Some of the control-enhancing features of the participative approach can be seen with respect to the supervisor-subordinate relationship. One can easily picture the laissez-faire leader who exercises little control over his subordinates and who at the same time may be indifferent to their wishes. He neither influences nor is influenced by his men. A second, more participative supervisor interacts and communicates often, welcomes opinions, and elicits influence attempts. Suggestions that subordinates offer make a difference to him, and his subordinates are responsive, in turn, to his requests. To the extent that the organizational hierarchy from top to bottom is characterized in this way, we have a highly integrated, tightly knit social system. We have, in the terms of Likert (1961), a more substantial interaction influence system—and a greater total amount of control.

Participative systems of management that conform to what Miles (1965) calls the "human-resources" model imply a more active involvement of members in the organization and a higher total amount of control than is typical of most bureaucracies. The human-resources model, which Miles sees emerging in the writings of McGregor (1960), Likert (1961), Haire (1962), and others, assumes that members have capabilities (resources) that are not ordinarily exploited in the organization. Some of these capabilities can be used by the organization, just as the organization can be used by these capabilities, in the sense that the organization is a means through which the capabilities can be realized. Hence there is a greater identification, objectively as well as subjectively, between the member and the collectivity; the actions that represent fulfillment of the heretofore excluded capabilities of members are, in the human-resources model, an integral part of the organization. Furthermore, these capabilities, and the needs associated with them, are active and, in some

---

[13] See also Hofstede (1967), especially p. 175.

degree, directing elements in the system; they help define "intents" (see Figure 1) in the cycles of actions and interactions of members that *are* the organization.

"Mechanistic" and "organic" models of organization, described by Burns and Stalker (1961) and by Shepard and Blake (1961), imply differences in the total amount of control. The mechanistic organization is characterized by a hierarchic structure of control and "precise definition of rights and obligations" of members, as in the traditional bureaucracy (Burns and Stalker, p. 120). The organic system, which is more like the human resources model has a network structure of control. The effectiveness of control in this type of organization derives more from the member's deep involvement and "presumed community of interest with the rest of the working organization in the survival and growth of the firm, . . . [rather than] from a contractual relationship between himself and a non-personal corporation . . ." (p. 121). The network system of control and the involvement of members in their organizational roles implies a highly integrated system. As a consequence the organic organization is more flexible, or adaptable, than the mechanistic. For example, the mechanistic organization may adapt to an environmental change by creating a special group within the organization to protect it from change. This group may be relatively isolated from the rest of the organization. In the organic organization, on the other hand, members respond and adjust mutually and integratively to change. The reaction here is holistic; adaptation is a "concerted response of the firm" in which all members play a part. The highly coordinated response of the organic system implies a relatively high level of control by as well as over all organization members. The total amount of control in the organic system is therefore relatively high compared with the mechanistic.[14]

Organizations constructed on the basis of overlapping "organizational families," as proposed by Likert (1961) and Mann (1957) conform, in a number of respects, to the organic model. To achieve this type of organization, Likert proposes that each supervisor must form his subordinates into a highly cohesive work group, called an organizational family, in which he is a member. Supervisors, in turn, are members of a second set of highly cohesive groups with their superiors, who are members of a third set, and so on, up the organizational hierarchy. Most supervisors, therefore, are members of two groups, one in which they act as supervisors with their subordinates and one in which they are subordinates along with their own peers. Thus the effects of the high level of control generated within the tightly knit organizational families are coordinated by the supervisors, who act as "linking pins" between groups.

Likert's model clearly implies the network system of control, which is characteristic of the organic model. Control is more mutual rather than exclusively

---

[14] Burns and Stalker (1961) stress the especially high degree of control over (rather than by) members in the organic system. They therefore see the adaptive advantages of the organic system being "paid for by the increased constraint on the individuals . . . . Such submission is all the more absolute when it is made voluntarily, even enthusiastically" (p. 11). For a further treatment of the relationship between total control and adaptability, see Bunker and Allen (in press).

unilateral. Peers play an important role in maintaining adherence to organizational standards that they have helped to establish. The cohesive group is an integral part of the system. Such groups, which might otherwise oppose the organization, are given formal status within it. Supervisory and managerial personnel are integrated into the groups and help establish the groups' norms. Thus the power of the group is exercised on behalf of the organization rather than in opposition to it.

An analysis by Likert (1961) of some departments that conform to this model led to the conclusion that the "managers have actually increased the size of the 'influence pie' by means of the leadership processes which they use. They listen more to their men, are more interested in their men's ideas, and have more confidence and trust in their men." There is a greater give-and-take and supportiveness by superiors and a higher level of effective communication upward, downward, and sideward. This all contributes to a greater sensitivity and receptivity on the part of each organization member to the influence of others—superiors relative to subordinates and subordinates relative to superiors. There is in these departments a higher level of mutual control and a more likely integration of the interests of workers, supervisors, and managers.

The participative system distinguishes itself from the traditional bureaucracy by the extent to which members are personally involved. The deeper, personal commitment of members is one of the bases for the success of the participative approach, but it is also the basis for interpersonal complications and possible conflicts that are precisely what Weber hoped, through bureaucracy, to avoid. Participative models, therefore, require interpersonal skills and sophistication of members, as well as acceptance of values and assumptions that are not called for in more traditional models. Training laboratory techniques, including sensitivity training, the T group, and the managerial grid, represent approaches to meeting this requirement (Argyris, 1964; Bennis, 1963; Blake, Mouton, et al., 1962 and 1964; Bradford et al., 1964; R. Tannenbaum et al., 1961). Such training, when associated with appropriate structural changes and delegations of authority in an organization, may contribute to the total enhancement of control through contributing to competencies that permit persons to interrelate more "sensitively" and thus to resolve conflicts and reduce resistances that otherwise would stand in the way of effective interaction and influence. If it is effective, laboratory training may also foster confidence and trust that lead to acceptance by each member of the intents, rather than simply the orders, of others. Sensitivity to and acceptance of intents reduces "noise," for example, misunderstandings or defensive reactions, that otherwise might enter into and impede the control cycles.

The relatively high level of control in many participative models does not fit common stereotypes that assume participation to be a vaguely permissive or laissez-faire system—or some kind of dictatorship of the proletariat. Participative models that conform to such stereotypes justify the arguments of opponents who maintain that participation is not feasible in a work organization.

There is no escaping the need for some system of control in organizations, including participative organizations. These organizations are not practical unless they have an effective system of control through which the potentially diverse interests and actions of members are integrated into concerted, that is, organized, behavior. The relative success of participative approaches, therefore, hinges, not on reducing control, but on achieving a system of control that is more effective than that of other systems. In some organizations there may be a lot of order giving but relatively little control because of structural and motivational breakdowns in the control cycles. (Informal organization, which may itself be characterized by a relatively high level of control, may contribute to such breakdowns.) The participative model is designed to overcome these obstacles. Thus, there may be relatively little order giving, as such, in the participative system, but the influence attempts that are made are effective; that is, they eventuate in control.

The high level of control implicit in organic, participative models can be understood in terms of the general concepts previously described. Participative models imply strong connectedness through structural arrangements, such as overlapping organizational families; high total, as opposed to partial, inclusion of members by utilizing more of their capacities and fostering their identification with the organization; a large stock of resources, such as social approval or skills of various kinds, that are exchanged for compliance; and low entropy ("noise") through reduction of misunderstandings, conflicts, and resistances.

THE MEASUREMENT OF CONTROL IN ORGANIZATIONS

A serious problem in studies of control is that of measurement. In general, researchers have obtained data about control either from available records describing the legal or structural characteristics of organizations or from informants who respond to questions concerning how or where in the organization decisions are made or how influence is exercised.

Evan (1963) has reviewed a number of indices that illustrate the measurement of control in industrial organizations.[15] These include, span of control; the number of levels of hierarchy; the ratio of administrative to production personnel (Melman, 1958); "time-span of discretion," which is defined as "the maximum length of time an employee is authorized to make decisions on his own initiative which commit a given amount of the resources of the organization" (Evan, 1963, p. 472; Jaques, 1956); the hierarchical level at which given classes of decisions are made; and the formal limitations that apply to the decision-making authority of management (for example, workers may use the grievance procedure to appeal decisions of superiors). Some of these mea-

---

[15] See Pugh et al. (1963) for further illustrations and Tannenbaum (1965, pp. 743–744) for a review of approaches to conceptualization and measurement of control in unions. In Chap. 20, Whisler et al. compare several concepts and measures of centralization of control.

sures have been formulated to meet the requirements of particular conceptual schemes; others have been chosen for research, because they are readily available.

The work described in the following articles relies for measures of control largely on the averaged judgments by organization members in response to questionnaire items dealing with the amount of influence or control exercised by various groups in their organization. This approach to measurement has limitations; yet it seems to us more suitable than the available alternatives for the measurement of the particular concepts with which we are concerned.

In adopting this approach to the measurement of control, we have made the assumption that organization members as a group are able to provide reasonably valid and reliable data. It is apparent, however, that organization members differ in their judgment about control and these differences may sometimes call our assumption into question. However, it is important to bear in mind that the reliability of the measures, which are intended as organizational indices, is a function of the number of respondents chosen from each of the organizations studied. Thus, although the reliability of scores based on an individual's responses may be low (in the sense that one person's responses per organization correlate poorly with those of other persons in the respective organizations), averaged responses may be quite stable. In most cases, reliability can be improved by increasing the number of informants. (This is analogous to increasing the reliability of a psychological test by increasing the number of items.) The fact that individual respondents may be unsure of their answers and that they may be in error does not in itself vitiate the method, provided that respondents give better than chance answers, that the errors are random, and that a sufficient number of respondents are available. (Experience with the method suggests that in most cases a minimum of twenty-five to fifty respondents per organizational unit are necessary.) To the extent that errors of measurement are not random, we are probably moving from a measure of organizational control to a measure of perceived organizational control. Chapters 12 to 14 are concerned in part with this problem.[16]

Direct tests of validity for measures of control are difficult to obtain, because precise criteria have not been established. Our first application of the method in four union locals was encouraging because the data corresponded

[16] Correlations reported in this text between measures of control and independently measured criteria of organizational performance are one indication of reliability. The interested reader may also wish to see analyses by Patchen (1963) in two organizational sites where low and mainly insignificant correlations are found between measures of control based on responses of rank-and-file members and responses of supervisors. However, in one of Patchen's analyses the organizational units were closely situated departments in the same plant, and some of the referents of the control questions were officers common to all departments; hence only small (if any) differences among departments are likely to exist. The measure is more likely to work where there are real differences in control patterns, as in the comparison of distinct organizations. A further problem is the very small number of supervisory respondents per organization in Patchen's analyses (one per organizational unit). This represents a serious limitation, as we indicated. However, Patchen did find that an index based on a number of parallel questions dealing with control in specific areas of decision making may be more reliable than an index based on a single, global question. See, for example, Chap. 11. See also Hofstede (1967) for analyses relevant to the measurement of control.

in general to our own observations, although this impressionistic analysis was *post hoc*. Subsequent applications of the measures in a variety of organizations also revealed differences that seemed realistic to us. For example, measures in union locals, voluntary associations, business and industrial organizations (see Chapter 5), including some in Yugoslavia (see Chapter 6), yielded differences, as well as certain general constancies that seemed reasonable, although again, this evidence is only a rough indication of validity.

Perhaps the strongest support for the measures comes from what we believe are meaningful relationships between patterns of control as measured and other aspects of organizational structure and functioning independently measured. Ultimately our case for the validity of the measures hinges on the extent to which the meaning that we claim for them fits meaningfully the predictions that we have made and the substantiation for these predictions that we find. Some of the articles in this text report research concerning such predictions. Although the correlations in these studies are not usually high, they yield a reasonably consistent picture and one that we take to represent a form of construct validity.

CONCLUSION

The research reported in the following pages assumes that the interests of organization members may or may not be in conflict; that control may be unilateral or mutual; and that the total amount of control in an organization may grow or decline. Organizations in which conflicts of interest among members override mutual interest, where control is exclusively unilateral, and where the total amount of control is fixed (that is, organizations that fit traditional assumptions) represent, in our view, special, limiting cases. The prevalence of such cases is a matter for empirical documentation. But what happens to prevail should be of no more importance to organization theorists and practitioners than what happens to be possible. Progress in organizational theory and practice has in fact been marked by a growing awareness and an increasing actualization of new possibilities that derive in part from changing assumptions about the nature of conflict and control in organizations.

We have stressed the possibility of variations in the total amount of control —a possibility that has not been very much considered in the literature—and we have pointed to some approaches to enhancing this variable. Our emphasis does not imply a belief that the enhancement of control is necessarily desirable but that it is important, having implications for the adjustment and welfare of members, as well as for the performance of the organization. Our emphasis reflects a concern for the advantages to the organization and its members that appear to be associated with some "high-control" systems—and the costs that seem also to be associated with such systems. We think this exchange should be better understood.

REFERENCES

Allport, F. H. (1933a). Individuals and their human environment. *Proc. Ass. Res. nerv. Dis.*, **14**, 234–252.

———, (1933b). *Institutional behavior.* Chapel Hill, N.C.: The University of North Carolina Press.

———, (1955). *Theories of perception and the concept of structure.* New York: Wiley.

———, (1962). A structuronomic concept of behavior: individual and collective. I. Structural theory and the master problem of social psychology. *J. abnorm. soc. Psychol.*, **64**, 3–30.

———, (1967). A theory of enestruence (event-structure theory): report of progress. *Amer. Psychologist*, **22** (1), 1–24.

Argyris, C. (1964). *Integrating the individual and the organization.* New York: Wiley.

Barnard, C. I. (1951). As quoted in the *Harvard Business Review*, XXIX, No. 6, November, 1951, p. 59.

Bell, D. (1950). Notes on authoritarian and democratic leadership. In A. W. Gouldner (Ed.), *Studies in leadership.* New York: Harper & Row.

Bendix, R. (1956). *Work and authority in industry.* New York: Wiley.

———, and Fisher, L. H. (1961). The perspectives of Elton Mayo. In A. Etzioni (Ed.), *Complex organizations: a sociological reader.* New York: Holt.

Bennis, W. G. (1963). A new role for the behavioral sciences: effecting organizational change. *Admin. Sci. quart.*, **8** (2), 125–165.

———, (1966). *Changing organizations.* New York: McGraw-Hill.

Berle, A. A., and Means, G. C. (1952). The control of the modern corporation. In R. Merton, Ailsa P. Gray, Barbara Hockey, H. C. Selvin (Eds.), *Reader in bureaucracy.* New York: Free Press.

Blake, R. R., Mouton, J. S., Barnes, L. B., and Greiner, L. E. (1964). Breakthrough in organization development. *Harvard Business Rev.*, **42** (6), 133–135.

———, ———, and Bidwell, A. C. (1962). The managerial grid. *Advanced Mgmt. Office Executive*, **36**.

Blau, P. M. (1964). *Exchange and power in social life.* New York: Wiley.

Bradford, L. P., Gibb, J. R., and Benne, K. D. (Eds.) (1964). *T-group theory and laboratory method.* New York: Wiley.

Bunker, Douglas R. with S. Allen III (in press). *The Adaptable Organization.* Boston: Harvard Business School, Division of Research.

Burns, T., and Stalker, G. M. (1961). *The management of innovation.* London: Tavistock.

Cartwright, D. (1965). Influence, leadership, control. In James March (Ed.), *Handbook of organizations.* Chicago: Rand McNally.

Crozier, M. (1964). *The Bureaucratic phenomenon.* Chicago: The University of Chicago Press.

Dahl, R. A. (1957). The concept of power. *Behavioral Sci.*, **2**, 201–218.

Dahrendorf, R. (1959). *Class and class conflict in industrial society.* Stanford, Calif.: Stanford University Press. (Originally published under the title *Soziale Klassen und Klassenkonflict in der industriellen Gesellschaft.*)

Deutsch, K. W. (1966). Some quantitative constraints on value allocation in society and politics. *Behavioral Sci.*, **11** (4), 245–252.

Emery, F. E., and Trist, E. L. (September, 1959). Socio-technical systems. Paper presented at the 6th Annual International Meeting of the Institute of Management Sciences, Paris.

———, and Thorsrud, E. (1965). *Industrial democracy*. London: Tavistock. (First published as *Industrielt demokrati*. Oslo Universitetsforlaget, 1964.)

Etzioni, A. (1961a). *A comparative analysis of complex organizations*. New York: Free Press.

———, (1961b). *Complex organizations: a sociological reader*. New York: Holt.

Evan, W. M. (1963). Indices of hierarchical structure of industrial organizations. *Mgmt. Sci.*, **9** (3), 468–477.

Festinger, L., Schachter, S., and Back, K. (1950). *Social pressures in informal groups: a study of a housing project*. New York: Harper & Row.

French, J. R. P., Jr. (1956). A formal theory of social power. *Psychol. Rev.*, **63** (3), 41–52.

———, and Raven, B. (1960). The bases of social power. In D. Cartwright (Ed.), *Studies in social power*. Ann Arbor: Institute for Social Research.

Goldhamer, H., and Shils, E. A. (1939). Types of power and status. *Amer. J. Sociol.*, **45**, 171–182.

Gouldner, A. W. (1955). Metaphysical pathos and the theory of bureaucracy. *Amer. pol. Sci. Rev.*, **49**, 496–507.

Haire, M. (1962). The concept of power and the concept of man. In G. Strother (Ed.), *Social science approaches to business behavior*. Homewood, Ill.: Dorsey Press.

———, Ghiselli, E., and Porter, L. (1966). *Managerial thinking*. New York: Wiley.

Harary, F., Norman, R. Z., and Cartwright, D. (1966). *Structural models*. New York: Wiley.

Hartmann, H. (1959). *Authority and organization in German management*. Princeton, N.J.: Princeton University Press.

Hofstede, G. H. (1967). *The game of budget control*. Assen, The Netherlands: Van Gorcum and Company.

Homans, G. C. (1961). *Social behavior: its elementary forms*. New York: Harcourt, Brace & World.

Jaques, E. (1956). *Measurement of responsibility*. Cambridge, Mass.: Harvard.

Katz, D., and Kahn, R. L. (1966). *The social psychology of organizations*. New York: Wiley.

Kerr, C., Harbison, F., Dunlop, J. T., and Myers, C. A. (1962). *Industrialism and industrial man*. London: Heinemann.

Kolaja, J. (1965). *Workers' councils: the Yugoslav experience*. London: Tavistock.

Lammers, C. J. (1967). Power and participation in decision-making in formal organizations. *Amer. J. Sociol.*, **73** (2), 201–216.

Lasswell, H. D., and Kaplan, A. (1950). *Power and society*. New Haven: Yale.

Likert, R. (1961). *New patterns of management*. New York: McGraw-Hill.

Mann, F. G. (1957). Studying and creating change: a means to understanding social organization. In *Research in industrial human relations*. Madison, Wis.: Industrial Relations Research Association, 146–167.

March, J. G. (1955). An introduction to the theory and measurement of influence. *Amer. pol. Sci. Rev.*, **49**, 431–451.

————, and Simon, H. A. (1958). *Organizations*. New York: Wiley.

Meister, A. (1964). *Socialisme et autogestion: l'expérience yugoslav*. Paris. L'édition du Seuil.

Melman, S. (1958). *Decision making and productivity*. Oxford: Blackwell.

Michels, R. (1962). *Political parties*. New York: Crowell.

Miles, R. E. (1965). Human relations or human resources? *Harvard Business Rev.*, **43** (4), 148–154.

McGregor, D. (1960). *The human side of enterprise*. New York: McGraw-Hill.

Parsons, T. (1963). On the concept of political power. *Proc. Amer. Phil. Soc.*, **107**, 232–262.

Patchen, M. (1963). Alternative questionnaire approaches to the measurement of influence in organizations. *Amer. J. Sociol.*, **69** (1), 41–52.

Pugh, D. S. (1966). Modern organization theory: a psychological and sociological study. *Psychol. Bull.*, **66** (4), 235–251.

————, Hickson, D. F., Hinings, C. R., Macdonald, K. M., Turner, C., and Lupton, T. (1963). A conceptual scheme for organizational analysis. *Administrative Sci. quart.*, **8** (3), 289–315.

Schopler, J. (1965). Social power. In L. Berkowitz (Ed.), *Advances in experimental social psychology*. Vol. II. New York: Academic.

Selznick, P. (1953). *TVA and the grass roots*. Berkeley: University of California Press.

Shepard, H., and Blake, R. R. (1961). Changing behavior through cognitive change. *Human Organization*, **21**, 88–96.

Simon, H. A. (1957a). Authority. In C. M. Arensberg, S. Barkin, W. E. Chalmers, H. L. Wilensky, J. C. Worthy, and Barbara Dennis (Eds.), *Research in industrial relations*. New York: Harper & Row.

————, (1957b). *Models of man*. New York: Wiley.

Sturmthal, A. (1964). *Workers' councils*. Cambridge, Mass.: Harvard.

Tannenbaum, A. S. (1956). Control structure and union functions. *Amer. J. Sociol.*, **61** (2), 127–140 (in this book, Chapter 2).

————, (1962b). An event-structure approach to power and to the problem of power comparability. *Behav. Sci.*, **7** (3), 315–331.

————, (1965). Unions. In J. March (Ed.), *Handbook of organizations*. Chicago: Rand McNally.

————, (1966). *Social psychology of the work organization*. Belmont, Calif.: Wadsworth.

————, and Kahn, R. L. (1957). Organizational control structure. *Human Relat.*, **10** (2), 127–140.

————, and ———— (1958). *Participation in union locals*. New York: Harper & Row.

Tannenbaum, R., Weschler, I. R., and Massarik, F. (1961). *Leadership and organization: a behavioral science approach*. New York: McGraw-Hill.

Thibaut, J. W., and Kelley, H. H. (1959). *The social psychology of groups*. New York: Wiley.

Thompson, V. A. (1961). *Modern organization*. New York: Knopf.

Trist, F. E., Higgin, G. W., Murray, H., and Pollock, A. B. (1963). *Organizational choice*. London: Tavistock.

Weber, M. (1947). *The theory of social and economic organizations.* Fair Lawn, N.J.: Oxford. (Translated by A. M. Henderson and Talcott Parsons.)

———, (1961). The three types of legitimate rule. In A. Etzioni (Ed.), *Complex organizations: a sociological reader.* New York: Holt.

Wiener, N. (1950). *The human use of human beings.* New York: Harper & Row.

Wolff, K. H. (Ed. and Trans.) (1950). *The Sociology of Georg Simmel.* New York: Free Press.

Zupanov, J., and Tannenbaum, A. S. (1967). Distribucija jutjecaja u nekim jugo-slavenskim industryskim organizacijama kako je vide clanovi tih organizacija (The distribution of control in some Yugoslav industrial organizations as perceived by members). *Ekonomski Pregled,* 1966, God. XVII, Broj. 2–3, Str. 115–132 (in this book, Chapter 6).

2

CONTROL STRUCTURE AND UNION FUNCTIONS*

Arnold S. Tannenbaum[1]

The importance of control in organizations has led to the development of a number of hypotheses relating it to other aspects of functioning. Relationships have been suggested, for example, between the goals of a union and the form which control will take within it. The "business union," devoted primarily to the enhancement of wages and other specific benefits from management, is predicted to develop strong leadership and an autocratic government.[2] A union's commitment to large social goals, on the other hand, is often considered to be associated with internal democratic procedures.[3] The relationship between union-management conflict and control has also been the subject of some thought and speculation. Militant conflict with management is said to contribute to membership interest and the maintenance of democracy within the union.[4] A related view suggests that unions may be led into undemocratic procedures in an effort to achieve a harmonious relationship with management. Autocratic control is seen as a correlate of "union responsibility."[5] These hypotheses are consistent with the general notion that the form or structure of a union is related to its functions or goals. Furthermore, they imply that the relationship goes one way; the functions determine the structure.

Social psychologists have been interested in control from another point of view: as an independent variable. Interest in the effects of control is reflected in a number of studies from the early research in laboratory groups to the more recent experimental studies in large organizations. Control has been shown to have implications for group cohesiveness, morale, and productivity;[6] it seems of importance as both a cause and an effect.

*Reprinted from *American Journal of Sociology*, Vol. LXI, No. 6 (May 1956), with permission of The University of Chicago Press. (This article has been edited to eliminate overlap and to bring it into a consistent format with the other articles in this book. Certain portions have therefore been deleted or reworded. Ed.)

[1] The material presented here is adapted in part from a larger report written by the present author in collaboration with Robert L. Kahn and subsidized by the Rockefeller Foundation. I would like to thank Irving Goffman and Joan Lohmann for their contributions to the design and execution of this study, as well as Elizabeth Douvan, Basil Georgopoulos, and Ernest Lilienstein for their helpful comments concerning this paper.

[2] R. F. Hoxie, *Trade Unionism in the United States* (2d ed.; New York: D. Appleton & Co., 1923), p. 46.

[3] Irving Howe and B. J. Widick, *The UAW and Walter Reuther* (New York: Random House, 1949), p. 244.

[4] *Ibid.*, p. 259.

[5] Seymour Martin Lipset, "The Political Process in Trade Unions: A Theoretical Statement" in *Freedom and Control in Modern Society*, ed. Morroe Berger, Theodore Abel, and Charles H. Page (New York: D. Van Nostrand Co., Inc., 1954), pp. 82–124.

[6] See, e.g., Kurt Lewin, Ronald Lippitt, and Ralph K. White, "Patterns of Aggressive Behavior in Experimentally Created 'Social Climates,' " *Journal of Social Psychology*, X (May, 1939), 5–40; James C. Worthy, "Factors Influencing Employee Morale," *Harvard Business Review*, XXVIII (January, 1950), 61–73; and Nancy Morse and Everett Reimer, "The Experimental Change of a Major Organizational Variable," *Journal of Abnormal and Social Psychology*, Vol. LII (January, 1956), 120–129.

The study of control in unions is especially fruitful because of the great variety of practices encountered among the local and international unions in America. One can easily point to unions which exemplify democratic or, if one wishes, autocratic procedures. This great diversity of structural form offers a field for unlimited exploration and comparison. It also poses a serious problem, that of developing descriptive techniques which are capable of capturing some of the essential qualities of union organizations and which at the same time are amenable to standardization and replication.

We have attempted to meet this problem by developing a method of description which is both quantitative and conceptually meaningful. We have called it the "control graph." This scheme characterizes the control structure of an organization in terms of two axes.[7] The horizontal axis is based on a universal characteristic of formal organizations: the system of hierarchically defined ranks. This axis is designed to represent the various hierarchical levels, from low to high, in the organization. The vertical axis of the graph represents the amount of control over the organization's policies and actions that is exercised by each of the hierarchical levels. For example, a given level, conceivably, could have very little control in determining the policies and actions of the organization. This might be true of the rank and file in some locals or of the president in others. On the other hand, certain levels might be extremely influential in controlling the affairs of the organization. Again, this might be true of the rank and file, the president, *or* any combination of hierarchical levels. One can see that varying shapes of curve might be generated from these axes, depending on how much control is exercised by each of the hierarchical groups. Four simple prototypes will serve to illustrate the numerous possibilities. These are a few ideal types but by no means the most important theoretically. The graph as a descriptive technique subsumes them all while accounting at the same time for the many variations from these extremes.

1. *The democratic model.* This is a curve which rises (i.e., control increases) as one goes down the hierarchy. Groups at lower levels in the hierarchy (such as the rank and file) have more power than groups at higher levels (such as the executive board or the president).
2. *The autocratic or oligarchic model.* This is a curve which falls (i.e., control decreases) as one goes down the hierarchy.
3. *The laissez faire or anarchic model.* This is a curve which remains low (i.e., control is low) for all hierarchical levels. No one exercises much control.
4. *The polyarchic model.* This is a curve which remains high (i.e., control is high) for all hierarchical levels. All hierarchical groups have important influence in this type of organization.

[7] A more detailed discussion of the control graph as a descriptive technique is presented in an article by Arnold S. Tannenbaum and Robert L. Kahn, "Organizational Control Structure: A General Descriptive Technique as Applied to Four Local Unions," *Human Relations*, **10**, No. 2 (1957), 127–140.

The foregoing examples help illustrate the importance of two distinct aspects of control in organizations: *the distribution of control*, i.e., who or what hierarchically defined groups exercise control over the affairs of the organization, and the *total amount of control*, i.e., how much control is exercised within the organization, from all sources. The first is represented by the shape of the curve, the second by its average height. The one emphasizes the relative power of individuals and groups within the organization, while the other considers its absolute amount. Discussion of control in organizations has more often recognized the former. However, an understanding of control in unions requires an accounting not only of where control resides but of how much it all amounts to. Unions vary much more than do their industrial counterparts as to both these dimensions. Furthermore, locals which have the same distribution of control may differ markedly in total amount of control. Similarly, in unions with the same total amount of control, the control may be distributed in quite different ways.

Several hypotheses are discussed later relating these dimensions of control to membership participation, to the ideology of the union, and to the extent to which the union engages in militant conflict with management. An organizational syndrome is suggested which relates control in the union to a larger pattern of variables, including organizational power, inter- and intraorganizational conflict, participation, loyalty, and conformity. While the limited sample of locals does not permit a definitive test of any of the hypotheses, the data are sufficiently suggestive to justify reporting.

SAMPLE

This article is based on a study of four local unions, all of the industrial type. They are located in Michigan and include between 350 and 850 members. None of the officers is employed full time by the union. Since the study was initiated as an investigation of the factors affecting membership participation, locals were chosen which differ on this variable. Two locals, one high and one low in participation, are in each of two internationals. Differences in participation among the locals as judged by international officers were found to agree with our own measures, which include measures of meeting attendance (both regular and special), member activities at meetings (such as raising and seconding motions, asking questions, etc.), work on committees, and voting in union elections. The locals are assigned fictitious names and, in the order of their level of membership participation, are National, Sergeant, Ensign, and Walker. Sergeant is the largest of the locals, while Ensign is the smallest. The major findings reported here were obtained through paper-and-pencil questionnaires administered to a representative sample of about 150 members in each local. The rate of questionnaire returns averaged over 90 per cent.

CONTROL IN THE FOUR LOCALS

What picture do the control graphs present of the four locals? Four hierarchical levels were chosen to represent the possible loci of control within each
of the locals. The horizontal axis was constructed by employing these hierarchical levels in the following order: (1) the president, (2) the executive
board, (3) the plant bargaining committee, and (4) the rank-and-file membership. The amount of control exercised by each of these levels was ascertained through a series of parallel questions. In determining the amount of
control exercised by the president, for example, the following question was
employed: "In general, how much do you think the president has to say about
how things are decided in this local?" Answers were checked on a five-point
scale from 1, "He has no say at all," to 5, "He has a great deal of say." This
question was repeated for the executive board, the plant bargaining committee, and the rank-and-file membership.[8]

Figure 1 presents the control curves based on the mean responses to these
questions in each of the locals. Three of the curves approximate the prototypes
discussed previously. National resembles the democratic model most closely,
while Sergeant and Walker approach the polyarchic and laissez faire models,
respectively. Ensign does not conform closely to any of the previously discussed prototypes, although the general slope of this curve is positive, with
the membership having a relatively high level of control.[9]

Walker and Sergeant, both characterized by relatively flat curves, represent
locals differing sharply in their total amounts of control. As we shall see, this
difference helps explain a number of other variations. On the other hand, while
National and Sergeant are similar in total amount of control, the sources of
power differ. In National the rank and file is the single most powerful group.
In Sergeant the bargaining committee ranks above the membership (although
this difference is not statistically significant), and the other levels follow close
behind. When acting as a concerted group, the officers in Sergeant are extremely influential and can seriously challenge the members on many issues.
This is unlikely in National.

In discussing some of the hypotheses suggested in the literature, we shall
assume that the distribution of control, as represented in the control graph,
provides an index of "democratic control." National is the most democratic
local of the four, having a curve with the steepest average slope. The rank and
file exercises more control in it than in any of the other locals. Ensign is second,
having the next most positively sloped curve. The control exercised by its
membership ranks second to that in National. Sergeant follows, having a less

---

[8] The ratings receive some support from observations of the locals as well as from statements of international
officers. Further validation of the control graphs as a descriptive technique comes from their recent application
in a study of industrial organizations. The curves found in these organizations differ markedly from those in the
locals of the present study and, as expected, tend much more in the oligarchic direction.

[9] Statistical tests were performed to determine the significance of the differences in control between the various
levels in each local. For example, in National, where the curve is steep, the membership has a significantly
greater amount of control than each of the other groups; in Walker, where the curve is flat, none of the differences is significant (see Tannenbaum and Kahn, *op. cit.*).

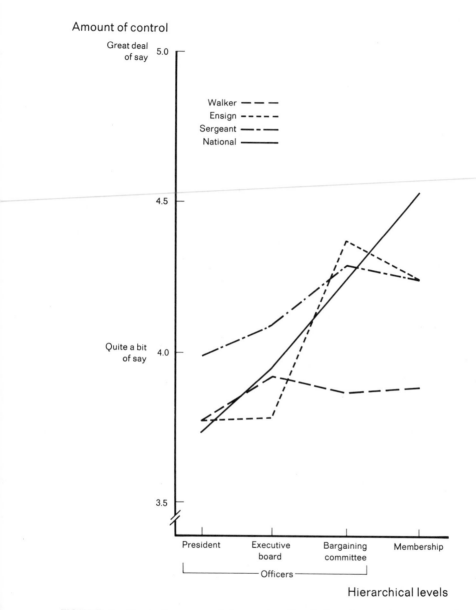

FIGURE 1 *Control curves of four union locals based on mean scores of ratings on how much say various persons and groups have in how things are decided in the local. The means are based on N's of about 150 in each local.*

positively sloped curve. The amount of control exercised by the membership in this local is about equal to that in Ensign, but both the president and the executive board are relatively powerful there. Walker is ranked fourth, with a practically flat curve, and the members are the least powerful among the four locals. In terms of their total amount of control, the locals are ranked as follows: Sergeant, National, Ensign, and Walker. This index, reflecting the average height of curve, was obtained by simply adding the amount of control exercised by the four levels in each local.

Considering these rankings and the level of membership participation in the four locals, two facts become evident. Participation and democratic control, though not synonymous, appear to be correlated. National, the most democratic local, is characterized by the highest level of participation, while in Walker, the least democratic local, it is correspondingly low. Although this relationship seems obvious, another fact emerges which is perhaps of greater interest. Strong leadership control, per se, does not appear to be inimical to membership participation. Sergeant, with a powerful president (described by one international officer as an "autocrat") and with a relatively strong executive board (described as part of a "tight political machine"), is significantly higher than Ensign and Walker in membership participation.

It would seem that the total amount of control as well as the distribution of control may be related in important ways to participation. Control reflects an active interest on the part of the controllers in the affairs of the local. Furthermore, control itself, if properly oriented, may be instrumental in mobilizing participation and conformity to union norms. In both National and Sergeant, the members are subject to greater pressures toward participation than are the members in either Ensign or Walker. If a member fails to attend a meeting, vote in a union election, or help out during a strike, he is more likely to hear about it in these relatively active locals. However, in Sergeant such pressures are more likely to originate with the leaders, while in National it is with the members themselves. In either event, whether administered by leaders or members, sanctions for failure to participate constitute a significant force in the direction of membership activity. The relationship of control to participation is illustrated by the relative rankings of the four locals in Table 1.

TABLE 1 Rank Order of Locals on Participation and Control

| | Membership participation | Democratic control | Total control | Officer control | | |
				President	Executive board	Bargaining committee
National	1	1	2	4	2	3
Sergeant	2	3	1	1	1	2
Ensign	3	2	3	3	4	1
Walker	4	4	4	2	3	4

CONTROL AND IDEOLOGY

Two hypotheses relating control to the goals or ideology of the union were suggested previously: (1) the greater the members' interest in broad and general social goals, the more democratic the union; and (2) the greater the members' interest in narrow and specific ("bread-and-butter") goals, the less democratic the union.

A number of questions were asked to determine the extent of member support for union goals of a relatively general social nature and those of a relatively narrow, bread-and-butter-type. The former include a desire for the union to "work to improve the general welfare of all the people in the community," "increase its political action," and "support the international and other unions in organizing workers." The latter include a desire for the union to "try to get higher wages for the workers," "try to get better working conditions in the shop," and "work for better health, pension, and insurance benefits." In addition, two questions were asked concerning the extent to which the international union should spend time and money organizing non-union places and getting things for people already in the union. The former is included among the items representing an interest in relatively broad issues. The latter is treated with the bread-and-butter issues. Table 2 presents the rank order of the four locals as to democratic control and as to each of the items used to measure member support for "broad and general" goals.

National ranks first on all items, and, with one exception, Walker ranks fourth. The summary rank order appears to be correlated (though imperfectly) with the level of democratic control, thus lending tentative support to the hypothesis that democratic control will be related to member interest in broad social goals. It is of further interest to note that support for broad union goals corresponds perfectly in these locals with the level of membership participation. Although these data provide some support for the hypothesis as

TABLE 2   Rank Order of Locals as to Support by Members of Broad and General Goals and Level of Democratic Control

	Democratic control	Union should work to improve welfare of community	Union should increase political action	Union should support international in unionizing	International should spend money unionizing nonunion places	Summary rank for all broad and general items
National	1	1	1	1	1	1
Ensign	2	2	4	3	3	3
Sergeant	3	3	3	2	2	2
Walker	4	4	2	4	4	4

stated, two qualifications appear in order. A general social orientation or ideology will be associated with strong internal democracy in a local union, provided that (1) the ideology itself is not undemocratic (an ideology, however broad and general, however socially or politically oriented, will not be associated with democratic procedures if it emphasizes autocratic ideals); and (2) the ideology is not held as an absolute desideratum (absolute adherence to a set of ideals may be the basis for justifying undemocratic means; these ideals may conceivably become so important as to override all other considerations—including the maintenance of democratic procedures).[10]

Generally, however, if the ideology expresses a broad social responsibility and a general interest in the welfare of the larger society, it is very likely to exert an influence in the direction of increased membership control within the local. Such an ideological orientation may be particularly important for the officers. A philosophy or ideology may be necessary to sustain them, to enable them to sacrifice immediate goals for long-range ideals, to resist materialistic temptations, and to think in terms of altruistic purposes. Lack of social ideology on the part of persons in power may make them especially vulnerable to appeals to personal interests, to possible racketeering and corruption.

In contrast to the foregoing data, no relationship is evident between members' orientation toward immediate and specific goals for the union and democratic (or autocratic) control. Sergeant ranks first on a summary measure of these specific issues, while both Walker and National rank next. Ensign is last. These data suggest that while members of more democratic locals may tend to have a somewhat greater interest in broad and general union goals, they need not be less interested in bread-and-butter issues.

UNION-MANAGEMENT CONFLICT AND CONTROL

In addition to the ideology of the union, the extent of aggressive, union-management conflict is often considered a correlate of democratic control within the union. While we do not have a measure in the questionnaire of the unions' actual militancy toward management, personal observations of the four locals have been sufficiently intensive to permit a clear ranking of them in the following order: Sergeant, National, Ensign, and Walker. This ordering, however, does not correspond with the index of democratic control and does not support the original hypothesis. There is little indication in these data that militancy on the part of the union is related to the practice in that union of democratic control. However, another hypothesis is suggested: that connecting union-management conflict to the *total amount of control* exercised within the local. This relationship appears explicable in terms of two contrasting and perhaps contravening implications of union-management conflict. On the one

---

[10] See Merton's discussion of aberrant behavior as a function of overemphasis upon specific goals without a corresponding emphasis on institutional means (Robert K. Merton, *Social Theory and Social Structure* [Glencoe, Ill.: Free Press, 1949], chap. iv).

hand, we have the suggestion that "continued . . . antagonism between corporations and unions prevents the latter from sinking into bureaucratic sloth. Merely to survive, the union must remain vital, democratic and militant."[11] Conflict will often activate an otherwise apathetic membership. On the other hand, conflict between social groups frequently leads to the restriction and not the expansion of internal freedom. In some instances the fact of external conflict is more rationalization than cause, and the abandonment of democratic procedures within an organization undergoing conflict may be justified "as a desperate measure to unify the union in time of economic distress and organizational disorder."[12] Nor is it completely unlikely that conflict may be manufactured by leaders as a means of consolidating power within an organization. Democratic control is sometimes seen as "inefficient" and as impeding the effectiveness of an organization in crisis, while control by the leaders is often explained as an expedient necessary to pull the union through periods of conflict and difficulty:

> It is a question of whether you desire your organization to be the most effective instrumentality . . . or whether you prefer to sacrifice the efficiency of your organization in some respect for a litle more academic freedom in the selection of some local representative. . . . What do you want? Do you want an efficient organization or do you want merely a political instrumentality?[13]

Conformity within the union is considered a requirement of success in its struggle with management. The truth of this assertion might be questioned, but it is nevertheless believed by many; an international president observed: ". . . democracy does not come cheap: the price is a certain amount of confusion and disunity."[14] But "confusion and disunity" cannot always be tolerated during times of strife, and conflict with an outside enemy often has the effect of banishing them. Lines are drawn, a common purpose is accepted, and control is very likely to be increased. An organization under these conditions must be more highly regulated in order to survive. Common acceptance of this notion increases the amenability of members to the regulations of the organization.

However, viewing the issue in terms of the control graphs suggests that increased control need not be autocratic any more than it need be democratic. Interorganizational conflict may serve as an incentive for concentrating control in the hands of a few *or* for increasing the total amount of control in the organization in other ways. The important thing is that the organization be more tightly controlled. We are therefore led to the hypothesis that interor-

---

[11] Howe and Widick, *op. cit.*, p. 259.

[12] James A. Wechsler, *Labor Baron: A Portrait of John L. Lewis* (New York: William Morrow & Co., 1944), p. 80.

[13] John L. Lewis, quoted *ibid.*, p. 79.

[14] Paul L. Phillips, "Unions and Politics, Anglo American Contrasts," *Nation*, CLXXIX (October 30, 1954), 382–84.

ganizational strife will create an increase in total control—but not necessarily exerted at the top or at the bottom of the organization. The increased control may come primarily from the rank and file, it may come relatively more from the officers, or it may come from *both*. The distribution of this increased control is determined by other factors, among them, perhaps, the ideological orientation of the participants. We are suggesting, therefore, that while conflict may have a bearing on the shape of the control curve, its most predictable effect will be on the average height of this curve: conflict may be associated with a high degree of control either by members or by leaders, but it will almost invariably be associated with an increase in total control. The data of the present study, which reveal a direct correspondence between the extent of aggressiveness toward management and total control, provide support for this notion.

THE ORGANIZATIONAL POWER SYNDROME

The data discussed here have given tentative support to the hypotheses that the level of democratic control in a local is related to the members' interest in broad and general goals for the union and that the total amount of control is related to the extent of union-management conflict. We are led, however, to the further view that control in a union is part of a larger syndrome. A high level of control within the local and militant conflict with management is part of an organizational pattern characteristic of many strong and vital labor unions. Among the correlates of this syndrome we would expect the following variables: organizational power, total control, inter- and intraorganizational conflict, participation, loyalty, and conformity (see Table 3). The connections among these variables, of course, are not rigid and inexorable, but we would predict their association as a pattern. Furthermore, the effects of these variables may be reciprocal in some cases. This becomes evident when we consider further the union in conflict with its management. The union's success in achieving its goals is often contingent on its power—its ability to impose, or threaten the imposition of, sanctions. This power in

TABLE 3 Rank Order of Locals on Variables in Organizational Power Syndrome

	Union power	Total control	Union-management conflict	Intralocal conflict	Loyalty	Conformity	Participation
Sergeant	1	1	1	1	1	1	2
National	2	2	2	2	2	2	1
Ensign	3	3	3	4	3	3	3
Walker	4	4	4	3	4	4	4

turn depends partly on concerted member action and member readiness to "stand behind" their organization in the face of adversity, on conformity to union norms and loyalty to its goals. The increased control created by conflict is an adjustment, instrumental to mobilization. It becomes directed partly toward co-ordinating member action and partly toward the internal administration of sanctions for breaches in union policy. It is an internal mechanism designed in part to bolster external power.

This increased control serves other functions for unions engaging in conflict with management: in a very real sense, there is *more to be controlled* during such periods. The repertory of union actions increases, committees become activated, decisions must be made concerning the dispensation of benefits anticipated or achieved from management. All this stimulates the interest and participation of the members—and they, too, may have to be controlled. Union policy becomes a day-to-day affair, changing with the tide of battle. New issues arise which require regulation; and, although the leaders are not likely to relinquish power during such periods, the members may increase theirs. They now want a say on issues which are of vital importance to them.

The loyalty of members is associated with this syndrome in a number of ways. Conflict creates, or at least arouses, the members' loyalty.[15] During times of conflict, danger to the union is more imminent and awareness of the union's importance to the members more apparent. Furthermore, a union "carrying on aggressive struggles" may be demonstrating its value to the members: it is attempting to derive benefits for them, and its success in this endeavor is likely to be a cause for satisfaction and loyalty. Thus the results of organizational power return ultimately to enhance this power. The adage that "nothing succeeds like success" is especially apparent in unions. To this extent, power can become its own mainstay.

Intra-organizational conflict is also expected as part of this syndrome.[16] The fact that there is greater involvement and activity and a correspondingly greater interest in control of the organization is likely to lead to some element of conflict within the local through which different interests and points of view are reconciled. In the extreme case of the "power centers," for example, "internal political rivalries between factional machines are likely to be intense because the stakes in the struggle over power are so large."[17] Furthermore, this internal conflict may contribute to the intensity of the conflict between the union and its management. Under these circumstances "each

---

[15] See, e.g., William Becker, "Conflict as a Source of Solidarity," *Journal of Social Issues,* IX, No. 1 (1953), 25–27.

[16] Although factionalization or intra-organizational conflict may imply special subgroup loyalties within the union, these need not contravene the loyalty of the members to the union itself. On the contrary, such intra-union affiliations may serve to arouse greater loyalty among the participants to the larger organization. Lipset has observed this phenomenon in the ITU (personal communication).

[17] F. H. Harbison and R. Dubin, *Patterns of Union Management Relations* (New York: Science Research Associates, 1947), pp. 185–86.

side may be committed before the bargaining starts to programs which stem from protracted discussions and expedient compromises of conflicting viewpoints within its own group. There is usually an absence of flexibility, therefore, in the joint union-management decision making process. This fact makes agreement much more difficult."[18]

Finally, we might consider the relation of member conformity to some of the other elements of the syndrome. The existence of conformity is contingent upon the (formal and informal) definitions of rules and policies around which uniformity is to take place. Control implies the formulation of such rules (legislative control) and the regulation of behavior in accord with these rules (administrative and sanctions control).[19] The possible receipt of criticism or punishment for failure to adhere to the rules of an organization is an effective force toward uniformity. A high level of total control, therefore, leads to a greater degree of order and uniformity in an organization. Control creates conformity. Second, external conflict develops an ostensible need for unity. Members are willing to sacrifice and conform in a crisis who otherwise might be less subject to the influence of the union. Conflict justifies uniformity. Third, loyalty motivates the member to support the rules, standards, and policies of the organization. The loyal member *wants* to adhere to organizational norms. He wants to do what is "right" for the organization. Loyalty fortifies uniformity. Finally, participation has a bearing on conformity. It is through participation that the member comes into contact with organizational norms, sees what is "right" and what is "wrong," and learns what is required of him. He himself may also help set the norms. Participation thus expedites uniformity.

In the preceding material are outlined briefly some of the interconnections among the variables in the organizational power syndrome. The dimension of total control is one aspect of this larger pattern. Table 3 presents the rank order of the four locals on each of the items discussed. Measures are available in the questionnaire for each, exclusive of union-management conflict and organizational power.[20] For measures of these, reliance is

---

[18] *Ibid.*, p. 186.

[19] Nancy C. Morse, Everett Reimer, and Arnold S. Tannenbaum, "Regulation and Control in Hierarchical Organizations," *Journal of Social Issues*, VII, No. 3 (1951), 41–48.

[20] Intra-organizational conflict was measured through an index of three questions: "Do these [groups within the local] disagree on most matters or only a few?" "Do these groups have leaders who speak up for them?" "When these groups disagree, how much do you find yourself taking sides?"

Loyalty, similarly, was measured by three items: "Suppose the union went through a strike which so weakened it that it was in real danger of folding up. How much would you be willing to do about it?" "Suppose that there was so much disagreement within the local that it was in real danger of folding up. How much would you be willing to do about it?" "If the local went out on strike, how willing would you be to do picket duty?"

Uniformity of behavior within the local was measured as the inverse of variance on a number of items chosen a priori to reflect union norms. These items include perceived norms about voting, attending meetings, and helping out on strikes; the likelihood of sanctions against members for failure to perform these functions; the intensity of member involvement in the union; and the alacrity with which members utilize union channels for the expression of grievances.

For a more detailed discussion of these measures, see A. S. Tannenbaum and R. L. Kahn, *Participation in Union Locals* (Evanston: Row, Peterson, 1958).

placed on personal observations of the locals, in addition to general com ments of international and company officials as well as comments of members. For example, Sergeant, which is ranked first in power, is widely recognized as "carrying a hell of a lot of weight," as one regional director of another international described it. The personnel manager at the Sergeant plant also recognized its power and militancy when he pointed out, philosophically, that the union "keeps management on its toes."

In contrast, the weakness of Walker, the least powerful among the four locals, is evident to all who know it; a field representative commented: "If the company wanted to take advantage, they could make the people live hard here." An old-timer expressed his disillusionment with the effectiveness of this local: "We feel that it's not what it used to be. . . . Nothing happens to grievances. You can't find out what happens to them—they get lost . . . . The [bargaining] committee doesn't fight any more."

SUMMARY

The control graph illustrates the importance of two distinct aspects of control in organizations: the distribution of control and the total amount of control. Variations on these dimensions are hypothesized to relate to other aspects of union functioning, including membership participation, the expressed ideology of the members, and conflict with management. A broader syndrome of variables is suggested, including a number of determinants and implications of control. These include union power, intra- as well as interorganizational conflict, membership loyalty, participation, and conformity.

3

THE DISTRIBUTION OF CONTROL
IN FORMAL ORGANIZATIONS*

Arnold S. Tannenbaum
Basil S. Georgopoulos[1]

An elementary and fairly general proposition concerning organizational life states that individuals at different levels in an organizational hierarchy exercise different degrees of control. It is not uncommon to find, for example, that influence within an organization increases with hierarchical ascent. Higher echelons exercise more control within the organization than lower echelons. However, while certain individuals may be relatively powerful and others uninfluential, the distinction between those who control and those who are controlled is not clear cut. This is especially apparent for individuals at intermediate hierarchical levels who may exercise control over lower echelons and who are subject in turn to the control of higher levels. Equally important is the fact that control may flow *up* the hierarchy. Subordinates may exercise a degree of control over their superiors. This is an important facet of control structure, and social systems differ in the extent to which leading is the exclusive prerogative of the "leaders" and following the exclusive obligation of "followers."

Moreover, these differences occur not only among social systems, but also within a given system over time. Riesman, for example, contrasts the American political scene during the age of McKinley when "the obvious job of the leaders was to lead, of the led to follow" with that of contemporary America.[2] Studies aiming at representation of control in organizations ought to take into account both of these aspects. For convenience, we shall refer to them as the "active" and "passive" aspects of the control process. By "active control" we mean the extent to which the actor (either an individual or a group) *exercises control* in the organization. By "passive control" we mean the extent to which the actor *is controlled* within the organization.

We shall present in this paper an extension of a model discussed in earlier articles concerning organizational control. More specifically, we shall discuss a model for the analysis of the hierarchical distribution of active

* Reprinted from *Social Forces*, Vol. 36, No. 1 (October 1957), with permission of the publisher and the authors. (This article has been edited to eliminate overlap and to bring it into a consistent format with the other articles in this book. Certain portions have therefore been deleted or reworded. Ed.)

[1] The authors wish to thank Howard Baumgartel, Nan Donald, Robert Kahn, Floyd Mann, and Stanley Seashore for their help.

[2] D. Riesman, with N. Glazer and R. Denney, *The Lonely Crowd* (Garden City: Doubleday and Company, Inc., 1953), p. 241.

and passive control. We present this model primarily as a conceptual tool; as a technique for helping analyze and better understand certain aspects of organizational control. This technique shall be illustrated with data from two plants of a large industrial service organization. These plants are located in the Midwest and are among a number of units within a larger parent organization. The management of this central organization is referred to as "Higher Management." Each plant is headed by a manager and is subdivided into a number of stations, or departments, headed by station managers. The first-line supervisors fall immediately below the station managers in the hierarchy. One, Plant A, employs about one hundred and fifty, and the other, Plant B, about one hundred men.

ACTIVE AND PASSIVE CONTROL

The curves discussed in the previous articles describe control in the active sense, i.e., the extent to which hierarchically defined groups *exercise control* in the organization. A passive control curve can also be drawn according to the same principles. The vertical axis in this case represents the degree to which each of the hierarchical levels *is controlled*. While the former tells us how much control is exercised by each level, the latter describes the extent to which each level is subjected to control within the organization. The superimposition of the active and passive control curves provides an important comparison: the extent to which each level exercises control compared with the extent to which it is being controlled. Figure 1 presents such a comparison for the industrial plants under study.

The data for Figure 1 were obtained through a series of questions asked of all supervisors up to but not including the plant manager (i.e., all station managers and first-line supervisors), a total of 15 persons in Plant A and 7 persons in Plant B. The questions, a series of five, were tabular in form and were presented in terms of "how much say or influence" each of the five hierarchical levels has with respect to what each level does in the company. For example, one such question was "In general, how much say or influence does the manager of your station have on what the following groups do in the company?"[3] The "following groups" referred to in the question are: higher (central) management, top management of the plant, the first-line supervisors, the nonsupervisory employees, and the station manager himself. In each case, the respondent could answer in terms of a five-point scale ranging from "little or no influence" to "a very great deal of influence."

The total amount of control which any given level exercises in the organization (active control) is inferred from the sum of control which the respondents judge it to have over all levels, including the level in question.

[3] The same respondents answered all five questions. Each of the other four questions had as their subject, in place of "the manager of your station," one of the remaining hierarchical levels: the Higher Management; the plant manager; the first-line supervisors; and the nonsupervisory employees in the station.

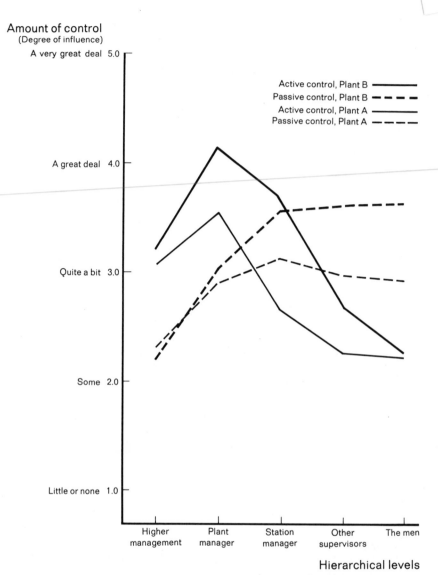

FIGURE 1   *Active vs. passive control: Extent to which each level exercises control compared with the extent to which it is being controlled, in two plants.*

It is computed as follows: On the basis of a five-point scale, the several respondents judge a particular level, e.g., the station manager, to exercise a certain amount of control over level x, over level p, etc. For each of these levels, the mean of responses is computed. Since there are five levels in all, five different means are thus derived. These means are then summed up, and the result is divided by 5 to obtain the final score. This score represents the total amount of control which the hierarchical level under consideration exercises in the organization. The same procedure is repeated for each of the remaining four levels. Similarly, the total amount of control to which any given hierarchical level is subject (passive control) is inferred from the sum of control which the respondents judge all levels to have over it. It is computed from the same data used in the case of active control, as follows: The respondents judge level x to have so much control over a particular level, e.g., the station manager; they also judge level y to have so much control over the station manager, etc. In each case, the mean of responses is computed. Since there are five levels in all which exercise control over the station manager, five different means are thus derived. These means are then summed and the result is divided by 5 to obtain the final score. This score represents the total amount of control to which the station manager is subject in the organization. The same procedure is next repeated with respect to each of the other four hierarchical levels.

Figure 1 helps to illustrate some analyses possible through the use of this technique. Let us take Plant A: First, the curve conforms to the oligarchic model. Active control increases with hierarchical ascent. This, however, does not apply to higher management, since this level lies outside the plant boundaries. Second, the increase of control is not uniform from one level to the next. Major increments occur between the upper levels, while the increments between lower levels are relatively small. The men are considered to have about as much control as the first-line supervisors—a fact of importance in understanding the plight of the first-line supervisors.[4] Third, the drop in control at the higher management level reflects the physical separation of central, "higher management" from the individual plants, as well as the decentralization which characterizes the relationship between the plants and higher management. Finally, disregarding for these reasons that part of the curve which represents higher management, the passive control curve is relatively flat. Each level is being controlled about equally. However, the plant manager exercises more control than he is subject to himself, while lower levels, particularly the men and first-line supervisors, are subject to more control than they exercise. Consequently, the plant manager's role in the control structure is primarily one of active control. That of the men and first-line supervisors is primarily on the receiving end of the control process.[5]

The discrepancy between the active and passive control curves in this plant suggests what may be a general characteristic of formal organizations.

[4] Donald E. Wray, "Marginal Men of Industry," *The American Journal of Sociology*, LIV (January 1949), 298–301.

[5] The preliminary application of this device in a large voluntary organization presents an expected but contrasting picture to that found in the present industrial situation: both active and passive control were found to increase with hierarchical ascent. Upper levels in the voluntary group are judged to exercise more control than the rank and file, but they are also subject in turn to a greater amount of control within the organization. This suggests one possible difference between certain voluntary and industrial types of organizations.

One might predict for organizations generally that, while the amount of active control will often vary markedly with hierarchical level, the amounts of control to which differing hierarchical groups are subject may remain fairly similar. Nearly everyone is subject to the influence of his organizational role, i.e., is subject to control within the organization (in some cases by their peers as control agents). In this sense, the *receipt* of control in organizations is probably a more universal principle than the *exercise* of control. Everyone, from the highest executive to the lowest employee, must conform to role requirements and hence be subject to some minimum level of control. It is probable, in fact, that, if a person's behavior is not controlled to some degree within the organization, he is not an integrated member. This generalization, however, cannot be extended to the distribution of active control. In this case, it is more likely that certain levels exercise a great deal of control while others may be relatively powerless. As a result, on the dimension of passive control, the executive and the rank and file are more nearly equal than on the dimension of active control.[6]

Additional facts of importance are suggested from a comparison of the corresponding curves of the two plants. The active control curve is more negatively sloped, while the passive control curve is more positively sloped, for Plant B than for Plant A. While the men in Plant B do not have less control than those in Plant A, the various supervisory levels do have *more*. Furthermore, the discrepancy between active and passive control for the men in Plant B is almost twice as great as that of Plant A. The men are controlled more in the former plant. As a matter of fact, this is true of all levels here, since the total amount of control (the average height of the curve) in this plant is higher. This increased control, however, originates exclusively from levels above the rank and file.

Although a number of interesting differences are suggested by the comparison of the above curves, it is of equal importance to observe some of the basic similarities among them. Both conform generally to the oligarchic pattern of control. Active control is highest for the upper hierarchical levels (with the exception of higher management, which is physically distant from the plant), while passive control is greatest in the lowest levels. In both cases, the passive control curves are relatively flatter than the active control curves, a characteristic which we hypothesize to be general to most organizations.

ORIENTATIONS AND SOURCES OF CONTROL

Figure 1 presents a general picture of the distribution of control, both active and passive, among the hierarchical levels in the two plants. However, it tells us nothing about where any given level orients its control or from

---

[6] Results obtained in a large voluntary organization tend to be consistent with this hypothesized characteristic of formal organizations. As in the industrial plants, the slope of the passive control curve is *less* than that of the active control curve. *Exercising* control varies more with hierarchical position than does *being controlled*.

whence its passive control comes. It shows that the plant manager exercises a great deal of control, but toward what hierarchical level does he exert it? Does he mainly exercise control over the station manager, the first-line supervisors, or the men? Then, what about the station manager? How does he orient his control? Questions of this nature refer to one particular aspect of the sociometry of control. We call it the orientations of control to distinguish it from another, and complementary, aspect—the origins of the control which is being exercised over any given level. We refer to this latter aspect of control as the *sources of control*, since it indicates the sources from which control over any given level originates.

The curves of orientation of control and of sources of control present the same information, but in different ways. While we can infer one from a total picture of the other, there are advantages of convenience and clarity to presenting each in its own way. Figure 2 presents the *orientations of control* curves for Plant A. For clarity and simplicity, in Figures 2 and 3, we present only the curves of Plant A.

Each curve in Figure 2 indicates the average amount of control which a given level, according to the judgment of the respondents, exercises over each of the other hierarchical levels as well as over itself. For example, the plant manager (solid line curve) has a broad span of control, including "a great deal of influence" over the station managers and the first-line supervisors, as well as "quite a bit of influence" over what the men do in the organization. He also has a great deal of say over what he himself does. The station manager, on the other hand, has "some influence" over the plant manager, "quite a bit of influence" over the men, and so on. The remaining curves provide comparable information for each of the other hierarchical groups. In each case, the same data utilized for the presentation of the active and passive control graphs are used. For example, the curve for the plant manager is plotted from data obtained through a question dealing with the amount of influence which the plant manager exercises over each of the five levels in the organization.

The *sources of control* curves for Plant A are presented in Figure 3. Again, the data are obtained from the same series of five tabular questions but are plotted differently. Each of these curves represents the extent to which a particular level *is controlled* by each of the groups appearing along the horizontal axis as judged by the respondents. For example, the curve for the men (dotted line) indicates that they are controlled by a fairly broad array of hierarchical levels, including the plant manager, the station manager, and the first-line supervisors. The men are not controlled to a very high degree by any single group but rather by a number of groups sharing control. In contrast, the plant manager (solid line curve) is controlled primarily by one person within the plant—himself (as well as by higher management from outside the plant). The station managers, supervisors, and men have only "some" control over the plant manager.

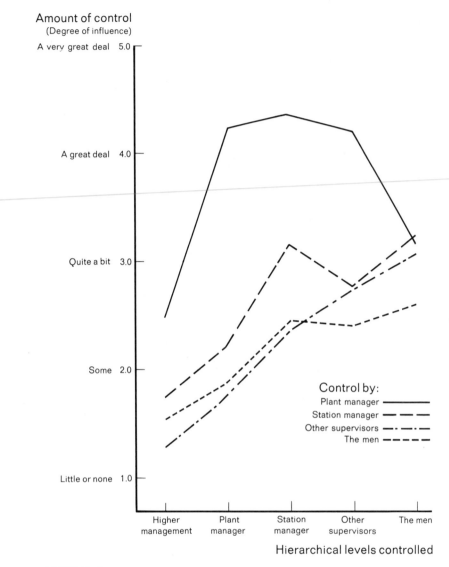

FIGURE 2   *Orientations of control: Amount of control exercised by each of four hierarchical levels over each level, for Plant A.*

DISCUSSION

The control graphs provide a convenient device for characterizing and thinking about control in social systems. Organizations differ with respect to distribution of control (shape of curve) and total amount of control exercised within them (average height of curve). The distributions of active and passive control reveal the extent to which hierarchical levels (1) exercise

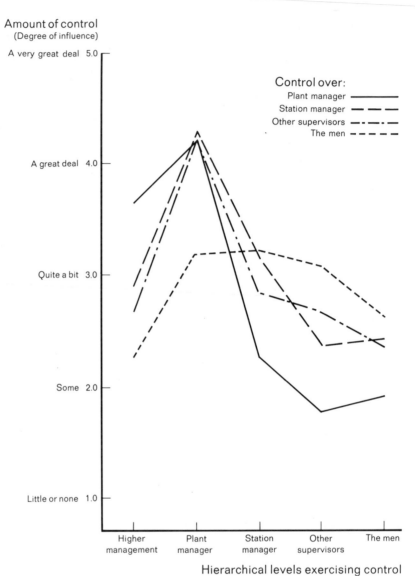

FIGURE 3   *Sources of control: Amount of control over each of four hierarchical levels exercised by each level, for Plant A.*

control and (2) are subject to control within the organization. Information thus derived will go a long way toward answering such important questions as: How sharply is the leadership process differentiated from the follower-ship process? To what extent does the control process involve reciprocity? To what extent are the "leaders" led by the "followers"?

The orientation and sources of control curves provide more detailed information about which hierarchically defined groups exercise control over which other groups. From these curves information regarding the span of control, in both the active and passive sense, is available: How widespread is the control which any given level exercises, and to what extent does the control exercised by a number of hierarchical groups converge on any one level? Are the increments of control from one hierarchical level to the next regular, or do sudden increases or gaps occur in the curve? There may be some indication from Figure 2, for example, to the effect that the station managers by-pass the first-line supervisors in their control over the men. These are some of the questions of descriptive, analytical interest which may be answered through the control graphs.

Descriptive analysis is the first step in the application of the above curves. Such indices as are available from the graphs can be utilized profitably in the study of phenomena of organizational growth and change. The height as well as the shape of the control curve would be expected to differ for different developmental phases within an organization. Early organizational phases of unions, for example, are remarked to be more "democratic" than later, more stable phases of union growth. It may be possible, however, that the shift from "pure democracy" to "bureaucracy," where it occurs, is marked, not by an increase, but rather by a decrease in the total amount of active and passive control within the organization. It is not so much that officers increase their control but that the members decrease theirs. The oligarchic form need not imply a greater amount of control than the democratic; oligarchy is not synonymous with a high level any more than democracy is synonymous with a low level of control. The "democracy" of early organizational phases may be a highly controlled organizational form, and in some cases may resemble the polyarchic rather than the democratic model discussed above.

Military organizations during times of peace and war provide another example of how changes in control are brought about by changes in the functions of the organization. We would venture the hypothesis that the most significant change in the shift to a war footing is an increase in the general height of the control curve rather than a change in the general slope of the curve. Armies on the battlefield are no more autocratic in this sense than they are in peacetime camps. In certain respects they may even be more democratic. They are, however, subject to a greater amount of control. Feedback from lower to higher levels is important, and this may serve as one mechanism of control by lower over higher levels.

The relationship between control and other organizational variables is also of interest, and a number of important questions might be answered through the application of these graphs: Do social systems with clear and unambiguous goals tend to be more oligarchic (as Riesman implies) than systems with a more complicated and perhaps ambiguous set of goals? There is some evidence, for example, that unions with a membership avowing broad and general social goals tend to be more democratic than unions with members supporting primarily narrow and specific goals.[7] Similarly, does the routinization of functions performed by the organization have implications for the distribution and amount of control? In this connection, we would suggest the hypothesis that predominantly routine operations will be associated with an oligarchically sloped curve of moderate height, i.e., with moderate total control, while less routine functions will be associated with a less oligarchically shaped curve *but with a higher degree of total control.*

Further questions concerning the internal operations of an organization suggest themselves within the framework of the distribution of control. Is the span of control by one level over others related to conflict between these levels? For example, is conflict more likely between the plant manager and other supervisory levels in the present organization than in one in which the span of control of the manager is less broad? Is there any optimum ratio of active to passive control for the proper fulfillment of the supervisor's role? Answers to questions of this nature would be of practical as well as theoretical interest.

SUMMARY

In this article we have used the term control as coextensive with the concepts of social influence and power. Briefly, we have presented an analytical framework for the study of the distribution of control in formal organizations, illustrated with data from recent research, and have indicated some of the issues involved as well as some of the directions which further research may follow. Beginning with the "control graph," we have elaborated on four major concepts pertaining to the distribution of control: (1) active control, (2) passive control, (3) orientations of control, and (4) sources of control. In each case, we have proposed some hypotheses which could be fruitfully investigated within a distribution of control approach to the study of formal organization.

[7] A. Tannenbaum, "Control Structure and Union Functions," *The American Journal of Sociology*, LXI (1956), 536–545 (in this book, Chap. 2).

4

CONTROL AND EFFECTIVENESS
IN A VOLUNTARY ORGANIZATION*

Arnold S. Tannenbaum[1]

While the literature of social science is rich in provocative ideas concerning the causes and effects of varying patterns of control, much remains to be done in testing empirically some of the many hypotheses formulated around this concept. The classic research of Lewin, Lippitt, and White is an early attempt to study in the laboratory the effects of varying patterns of control on children in groups.[2] A number of studies have since been performed in laboratory as well as in field settings. The experiment by Coch and French in a textile manufacturing plant and that of Morse and Reimer in a large clerical organization illustrate the extension of this work into organizations.[3] The study to be reported here, conducted among a number of local Leagues within the League of Women Voters of the United States, has been designed to extend some implications of the earlier research.

Two aspects of organizational control structure are indicated by the control curve: the hierarchical distribution of control, represented by the shape or slope of the curve, and the total amount of control exercised by all levels in the organization, represented by the general height of the curve. The fact that these dimensions may vary independently emphasizes the importance of distinguishing them. Organizations, for example, might have the same general distribution of control, while the total amount of control exercised within them differs sharply. On the other hand, organizations, though equal in the amount of control exercised within them, might differ markedly in the way it is distributed. Such variations have been found among the organizations to which the control graph has been applied, and it is in terms of these dimensions that the hypotheses of the present study are formulated:

> *Hypothesis 1.* Organizational effectiveness will be related directly to degree of positive slope of the control curve.

*Reprinted from *American Journal of Sociology*, Vol. LXVII, No. 1, July 1961, with permission of The University of Chicago Press. (This article has been edited to eliminate overlap and to bring it into a consistent format with the other articles in this book. Certain portions have therefore been deleted or reworded. Ed.)

[1] I acknowledge the valuable contribution of Marjorie N. Donald and Robert L. Kahn in the research and would also like to thank Rensis Likert, Carol Livingstone, Donald Pelz, and Clagett Smith for their helpful suggestions.

[2] Ronald Lippitt and Ralph K. White, "An Experimental Study of Leadership and Group Life," in G. E. Swanson, T. M. Newcomb, and E. L. Hartley (eds.), *Readings in Social Psychology* (2d ed.; New York: Henry Holt & Co., 1953), pp. 340–54.

[3] Lester Coch and John R. P. French, Jr., "Overcoming Resistance to Change," *Human Relations*, I (November, 1948), 512–32; and Nancy C. Morse and Everett Reimer, "The Experimental Change of a Major Organizational Variable," *Journal of Abnormal and Social Psychology*, LII (January, 1956), 120–29.

Hypothesis 2. Organizational effectiveness will be related directly to the average height of the control curve.

Organizational effectiveness is defined in terms of the means and ends of the organization. It is the extent to which an organization fulfils its objectives and preserves its means and resources.[4]

The first hypothesis is a recasting, in terms of the control graph, of the conviction that in our society the "democratic" type of organization will work more effectively than will the "autocratic." There are two kinds of reasons for making such a prediction under certain circumstances: those which apply to the maintenance of organizational resources and means and those which refer to the attainment of organizational goals.

1. In a culture where democratic values are extolled, rank-and-file influence is desired by a large proportion of members of organizations. Since relatively high rank-and-file influence is desired by many as an end in itself, organizational control characterized by a positively sloped curve would be expected to contribute to the members' morale. Furthermore, having a say in determining the policies and actions of an organization may permit members to move the organization in directions which satisfy the needs of a fairly broad segment of them rather than the needs of the leaders.[5] This assumes that the members have some understanding of the implications of the control they exercise and the skill and desire to exercise it effectively.

While a high degree of satisfaction among the members in itself is not considered a criterion of effectiveness, an organization with high morale will attract and retain members—a characteristic especially important to the maintenance of voluntary groups.

2. The exercise of control by lower echelons is likely to bring with it greater acceptance of jointly made decisions as well as an increased sense of responsibility and motivation to further the goals of the organization.[6] It may also provide, according to Likert, the means for effective coordination of the members' activity through the process of mutual influence.[7] Some authors point out the detrimental effects of control from above. "Hierarchical authority" has been said, in a democratic society, to reduce initiative, inhibit identification with the organization, and to create conflict and hostility among members.[8]

---

[4] Basil Georgopoulos and Arnold S. Tannenbaum, "A Study of Organizational Effectiveness," *American Sociological Review*, XXII (October, 1957), 534–40.

[5] See, e.g., Morse and Reimer, *op. cit.*; and David L. Sills, *The Volunteers: Means and Ends in a National Organization* (Glencoe, Ill.: Free Press, 1957), p. 4.

[6] See, e.g., John R. P. French, Jr., Joachim Israel, and Dagfinn Ås, "An Experiment on Participation in a Norwegian Factory," *Human Relations*, XIII (February, 1960), 3–19; James G. March and Herbert A. Simon, *Organizations* (New York: John Wiley & Sons, 1958), p. 54; and Morse and Reimer, *op. cit.*

[7] For a more detailed discussion of this point see Rensis Likert, "A Motivational Approach to a Modified Theory of Organization and Management," in Mason Haire (ed.), *Modern Organization Theory* (New York: John Wiley & Sons, 1959), pp. 184–217.

[8] See, e.g., *ibid.*, and Peter M. Blau, *Bureaucracy in Modern Society* (New York: Random House, 1956), p. 80.

While control from above has detrimental effects, it also seems, to some authors, to be necessary for efficient functioning. The detrimental effects can be mitigated under certain circumstances. Blau, for example, suggests the importance of minimizing the disruptive inequalities created by hierarchical authority.[9] Sills sees the necessity of centralized control in the National Foundation for Infantile Paralysis but points to the importance of members' perception as a mitigating factor. Continued interest and participation in the Foundation by volunteers can be explained by the fact that nearly half the members believe that the organization is democratic, even though it is not.[10]

Another approach to this dilemma—the necessity of control from above together with the favorable effects of control from below—would consider the possibility of increasing the influence of lower levels in an organization without decreasing that of upper-echelon personnel—of increasing the average height as well as the degree of positive slope of the control curve. This leads to Hypothesis 2.[11]

Two aspects of this relationship should be considered: one in which total control can be seen as an effect and one in which it is a cause of (or "intervening variable" in relation to) effectiveness.

1. The hypothesis that total control is a cause of organizational effectiveness is based on an elementary assumption regarding organization: Organized behavior is predicated on the co-ordination of individual behavior into some form of concerted action toward a goal or set of goals. This requires adherence to rules, conformity to organizational law, formal and informal: in other words, it requires control. Discussions of control in organizations, however, often assume a reciprocal relationship between the control exercised by upper and that exercised by lower levels of the hierarchy. Increasing the influence of one group implies decreasing the influence of another. The weakness of this view, however, becomes apparent when one considers the laissez faire organization, which represents the limiting case in which little or no control is exercised and in which little external direction or internal co-ordination will be manifest.

One can readily imagine moving in any of several possible directions away from the laissez faire condition: by increasing the control exercised by upper-echelon personnel, by increasing that of lower-level personnel, or by increasing the influence of both. If, as some authors contend, a high degree of control by the leaders is necessary for the efficient administration of organizations, and if, on the other hand, a high degree of control by the members is also necessary to foster identification, motivation, and loyalty, why would not sub-

[9] Blau, *op. cit.*, pp. 82–83.

[10] Sills, *op. cit.*, p. 219; see also March and Simon, *op. cit.*, p. 54.

[11] Aspects of Hypothesis 2 have been elaborated in earlier publications; e.g., Rensis Likert, "Influence and National Sovereignty," in John G. Peatman and Eugene L. Hartley (eds.), *Festschrift for Gardner Murphy* (New York: Henry Holt & Co., 1960); Arnold S. Tannenbaum, "Control Structure and Union Functions," *American Journal of Sociology*, LXI (May, 1956) (in this book, Chap. 2); Arnold S. Tannenbaum and Robert L. Kahn, *Participation in Union Locals* (Evanston, Ill.: Row, Peterson & Co., 1958).

stantial control exercised by both create conditions for more effective performance? Likert has suggested the importance of high "mutual influence" at all levels within organizations as the basis of the effective co-ordination of organizational activity as well as for the integration of the goals of individual members and of the organization.[12] This condition, leading to effective performance, entails significant control exercised by persons at all levels, the leaders as well as the rank and file. Furthermore, employing the control-graph method, Likert has found a direct relationship between effectiveness (measured in terms of productivity and other criteria) and height of control curve among thirty-one plants of an industrial organization.[13]

2. The hypothesis that a high degree of total control may be a result of organizational effectiveness follows from the assumption that all organizations have functions to perform, and rewards (of one kind or another) to dispense. The effective organization, by definition, is more likely to achieve its goals. It is also likely to have a greater stock of disposable rewards. Both organizational goals and rewards are likely to be relevant to the interests, if not the welfare, of members as well as leaders, and the amount of control which they try to exercise may be affected accordingly. Control in the effective organization is attractive to members and leaders alike because it is instrumental to the achievement of important satisfactions. The ineffective organization, on the other hand, has relatively little to offer. The rewards of control, and, consequently, the motivation to exercise control, are correspondingly less.

THE LEAGUE OF WOMEN VOTERS OF THE UNITED STATES, IN 1956

The League of Women Voters of the United States includes over 100,000 members organized into about one thousand relatively autonomous local Leagues around the country. These local Leagues, which vary in size from about 25 to 3,000 members, form the units of the present study.

The League is a non-partisan political organization. Its general purpose is "to promote political responsibility through informed and active participation of citizens in government." Its activities include selecting and studying public issues, declaring a position on some of them, bringing them to the attention of the public, and supporting legislation in line with their stand. In addition, the organization informs the public about the mechanics of voting and supplies information on issues on which the League may not have taken an official stand, as well as information about (but never in support of, or in opposition to) political candidates. Members also prepare publications, make occasional

---

[2] Likert, "A Motivational Approach . . . ," *op. cit.*, "Influence and National Sovereignty," *op. cit.*

[13] Some of these data are reported by Rensis Likert ("Influence and National Sovereignty," *op. cit.*). We would suspect that too much control may be as dysfunctional as too little, and a hypothesis more general than that offered above would specify an optimum level of control above or below which the organization would function below its potential. We are not yet in a position to specify the optimum for specific organizations. We can safely assume, however, that many, and particularly voluntary organizations, are operating at a level considerably below it.

presentations to public groups, and conduct fund-raising campaigns and membership drives.

The business of the local League is carried out in part through several kinds of meetings, the most frequent of which are discussion groups. It is here that most of the study, discussion, and participation by members take place and that many decisions are made regarding policies and actions.

Members are strongly committed to the ideals of democratic government: they often refer to their organization as a kind of workshop in democracy. Its formally established decision-making machinery provides, in theory, ample opportunity for the members to exercise control over the affairs of their local organization. Many members and leaders are aware, however, that the actual local decision-making does not always conform to the ideal.

League members are an unusual group in several respects. About 50 per cent have completed college. In joining and participating, many feel they are doing something of real value in helping extend the spirit of responsible citizenship and good government. In addition, many join for personal or social reasons; they find it a welcome change from their regular household routine; they enjoy meeting other women and find the discussions interesting and edifying.

The hierarchical scale of the local League consists of an elected president at the top, a partly elected and partly appointed board of directors at an intermediate level, and the rank and file at the bottom. These three hierarchical levels form the basis for the horizontal axis of the control graph.

THE LEAGUE AS A FORMAL ORGANIZATION

The League has all of the characteristics of a formal organization. As a voluntary organization, however, it differs in certain respects from many other formal organizations: (1) The League's governmental structure is partly representational in nature, including elected as well as appointed leaders. Many aspects of policy-making are formally decentralized and in the hands of the rank and file. (2) League action follows a long process of interpersonal action; discussion and agreement are necessary and important in it. (3) Much of the League's effort is psychic rather than physical (to use the distinction of Ross).[14] (4) The League's primary function involves working on and through people external to the organization and, to some extent, interacting and influencing other organizations, as is the case in unions and political organizations. (5) Membership in the League is open to all female citizens of voting age in the community. However, women who join tend to be educated, middle-income women, interested in public affairs. (6) Unlike some voluntary groups, the League de-emphasizes social interaction as an objective. Formally, the League is primarily a "social influence" rather than an "expressive" group (to

---

[14] Edward A. Ross, "The Organization of Effort," *American Journal of Sociology,* XXII (1916), 1–18; reprinted in Edgar F. Borgatta and Henry J. Meyer (eds.), *Sociological Theory* (New York: Alfred A. Knopf, Inc., 1956).

use the distinction of Rose).[15] (7) The forms of sanctions, coercion, or pressure which can be applied to members to achieve conformity and activity are much more limited than they are in other organizations. (8) The League's ability to survive is largely a function of the members' willingness to do its work. It does not have to maintain a competitive advantage vis-à-vis other groups, as do profit-making organizations.

PROCEDURE

A probability sample of 104 local Leagues was drawn from a complete list of all Leagues in the country. A stratification procedure by state and by size of League was employed so as to increase the accuracy of the sample. Each League was assigned a probability of falling into the sample proportional to its size. While 104 different Leagues fell into the sample, several of the very large Leagues were chosen more than once, and they therefore enter into the data more than once, making our total N of sample choices 112. Ignoring these duplicate choices would have created some bias. The stratification procedures employed added accuracy to the sample, and they make our use of $N = 112$ a good approximation.[16] We are thus projecting to a hypothetical population of Leagues which includes a somewhat greater proportion of large and a somewhat smaller proportion of small Leagues than exist in the population.[17]

Three basic sets of measures were employed:

1. Measures of local League effectiveness

A score for each of the 104 Leagues was obtained through rating forms filled out by twenty-nine persons assigned by national headquarters. These persons qualified as experts through their experience in the organization at state or national levels and their familiarity with the work of many of the local Leagues.

In judging the over-all effectiveness of each of the Leagues, raters were asked to consider several criteria of effective functioning. These were based on a number of objectives established for Leagues by the national organization. They include the primary objectives of all Leagues: high quality and quantity of League publications and significant impact of the League in its community. Also included are a number of objectives stated by the national organization which might be considered instrumental in nature: success of the League in fund-raising campaigns, the growth of the League and its size rela-

---

[15] Arnold Rose, *Theory and Method in the Social Sciences* (Minneapolis: University of Minnesota Press, 1954), p. 52.

[16] I am indebted to Dr. Leslie Kish and Miss Irene Hess for the technical design of the sample.

[17] Choosing a sample in this way is justified on the grounds that very large Leagues are rare, and a simple random sample would not be likely to include any very large ones, and that a kind of proportional representation of Leagues in the results is achieved. Each League in the sample represents the same number of members. The greater weight and importance attached to the larger Leagues reflect the correspondingly larger proportion of members in these Leagues.

tive to the community, and the amount of activity of members and their knowledge of League activities.

A rating scale with landmark statements was provided as follows:

100   This is an excellent League—among the very best. It is outstanding and exemplary of what I think Leagues should be like. It is probably unlikely that we can get many Leagues to operate as well as this one.

75   This is a good League. It is generally above average in the various standards which I feel apply to the evaluation of Leagues. If all locals were this good, the League of Women Voters of the United States would be much improved as an organization.

50   This is a fair League—about average in the various standards of effective League operation. It does not stand out, however.

25   This is only moderate (mediocre) in that it meets most of the standards of League operation but falls below the average. It needs improvement more than most Leagues.

0   This is a very poor League—as poor as one can get and still remain within the organization. It barely meets standards and falls below on most. It is considerably below average and would require drastic changes to bring it up to par.

Scores of effectiveness were computed for each League by averaging the ratings of each by all the judges who rated them. Some of the raters were not sufficiently familiar with all 104 Leagues to provide a rating of each; however, each League was rated by at least two raters, and many were rated by all. The scores derived in this way range from a low of 8 to a high of 100. Their split-half reliability is .82. The product-moment correlation between League effectiveness and size of League is .55. However, the relationship is not linear, and, when size of League is transformed logarithmically, the correlation becomes .74. Size, then, is an important component of League effectiveness. This is to be explained in terms of the greater impact which a large League is able to make within its community and within the national organization. It also reflects the ability of the League to get and hold members—an important criterion of effectiveness. However, size itself is likely to create important effects of its own quite apart from the question of effectiveness. In testing our hypotheses then, we shall control for the logarithm of size through partial correlation.

It might be argued that the raters of effectiveness are, in effect, judging aspects of control in the various Leagues, thus creating a spurious correlation between effectiveness and control. We shall therefore employ a supplementary and quite independent measure of League effectiveness, discussed below.

2. Measures of control in the Leagues

A questionnaire was mailed to approximately twenty-five randomly chosen members in each of the sample Leagues, with the exception of the few large Leagues which were sampled more than once. Here, fifty or seventy-five questionnaires were administered according to the number of times these Leagues might have been chosen in the sample. A final response rate of 77 per cent was obtained.[18] The total N of respondents who returned questionnaires is 2,847, but of this group about 15 per cent did not answer the relevant questions. This sample of respondents includes only rank-and-file members. The N of organizational units, serving as the basis for the correlational tests employed, however, remains 112.

Each respondent was asked a set of questions concerning control in the local League. The question upon which the control graph is based was asked in tabular form (Table 1).

The amount of control exercised by each of the hierarchical levels in a given League is computed by averaging the judgments of all respondents regarding each of the levels. The independent-variable index for each League is obtained on the basis of these scores. A measure of the independent variable of Hypothesis 1 is derived by computing the slope of a best-fit straight line for the data of each League. This requires the admittedly crude but workable assumption of equal scale intervals along both the horizontal and vertical axes. Total control, the independent variable of Hypothesis 2, is obtained simply by adding the amounts of control exercised by the three hierarchical levels in each League as reported in response to the question (Table 1).

It might be argued that the predicted correlations obtained through the use of the above measures really reflect greater subjective feeling for "democratic" control among members of effective Leagues than there is among members of ineffective Leagues, rather than accurate appraisals of the objective situation in each League. We shall therefore employ the question: "In your opinion, how much influence do you think each of these groups *should have* in determining the policies and actions of your local League?" This is intended as a measure of the possible halo or response set in effective as compared to ineffective Leagues. The curves derived from this question are referred to as the "ideal control curves" as contrasted with the "actual control curves" based on the earlier question. The "ideal" question was asked immediately after the "actual" control question.

The response categories are precisely the same as those for the previous question. If a certain halo or response set in relation to control exists in effective as compared to ineffective Leagues, we would expect such differences to be reflected in the responses to the above question. We shall therefore be interested in the extent to which slope and height of control curve derived from this question correlate with effectiveness. Zero correlations would be most favorable to the original hypotheses.

In addition to the sample of rank-and-file members who serve as informants regarding control within each League, a sample of six board members in each

[18] After an elaborate set of follow-up procedures including letters and telephone calls by members of the research staff. I am indebted to Dr. Charles Cannell and to Miss Sharon Summers for their contribution to this phase of the research.

TABLE 1   In General, How Much Influence Do You Think the Following Groups or Persons Actually Have in Determining the Policies and Actions of Your Local League?

	No influence	A little influence	Some influence	A great deal of influence	A very great deal of influence
Your local president	□	□	□	□	□
Your local board as a group (excluding the president)	□	□	□	□	□
Your local membership as a whole (excluding the board)	□	□	□	□	□

League was also questioned. The correlations between the responses of these groups are smaller than was hoped, although they are all significant beyond the .05 level. The judgments of the rank and file and of board members regarding the control exercised by the president correlate .50; of the control exercised by the board, .18; and of the control by the membership, .25. Our measures are thus subject to some unreliability, and we shall therefore be interested in the extent to which our hypotheses are substantiated by using the judgments of board members as well as those of rank-and-file members.

Finally, one might argue that the measures of control and of effectiveness are really measures of amount of activity by members and that the hypotheses are, in effect, tautologous. We shall evaluate the strength of this contention through the use of a direct measure of members' participation based on two questions dealing with the amount of time members spend in the activities of the organization and the number of meetings (of several kinds) which they attend. These questions were formed into an index with a split-half reliability of .87.

3. Supplementary measure of League effectiveness

The ratings of effectiveness described above are subject to some of the limitations inherent in any measure based on judgment. We shall therefore retest our hypotheses, using an independent and behavioristic criterion of one aspect of effective League functioning: the proportion of sampled members in each League who filled out and returned the survey questionnaire. Although the job of completing the questionnaires was assigned by ourselves, this was clearly a task relevant to the organization, since the research was designed to be of use to the League, and was officially endorsed by the national organization and the local Leagues. General appeals for co-operation were made at the outset by the national president through the national publication and by local officers through their own organs. The rate of returns is an especially interesting index of unit performance, since it represents, in the terms of Lewin, Lippitt, and White, a type of "leader-out" behavior—a task performed by members away from the direct supervision of leaders.[19]

We would expect that, if both the rate of questionnaire returns and the ratings of effectiveness are valid measures, they would be correlated positively. On the other hand, we would be concerned about differences in rate of response between effective and ineffective Leagues as creating a possible contamination of the other relationships studied. The method of administration of the questionnaire and the follow-up procedures were designed to minimize this relationship. Two correlations are therefore of importance here: the correlation between the League's effectiveness and rate of return of questionnaires immediately before the follow-up procedures were initiated, and the correlation between effectiveness and final rate of returns. The former, if positive and significant, reflects the validity of the scores of effectiveness; the latter provides some indication of the success (or lack thereof) of the follow-up procedures, as well as the extent to which differential response rate may enter as a possible contamination in the relationships studied.

Prior to the follow-up procedures, 49.7 per cent of the questionnaires were returned. The partial correlation (holding the logarithm of size constant) between League effectiveness and rate of returns at this point is .33, which is significant beyond the .001 level of confidence. The correlation, after all follow-ups were terminated, is .24. Although the correlation decreases slightly, it is not as low as might be hoped. There is a somewhat higher response rate from effective than from ineffective Leagues. These correlations nevertheless provide evidence for the validity of the scores of effectiveness.

RESULTS

Figure 1 shows the control curves, actual and ideal, averaged for all Leagues in the sample. Curves based on the judgments of rank-and-file members and of board members are drawn separately. Both the "actual" curves tend to be negatively sloped.[20] By way of contrast, the "ideal" curves are positively sloped. This conforms to the generally recognized ideal for the organization. The sharp differences between the "ideal" and "actual" curves suggest that the respondents are making an important distinction in their responses to these questions between how, in their opinion, the organization should work and how it actually does.

Table 2 presents the partial correlations in a test of our hypotheses. The data support each. Effectiveness of the League is significantly related to the slope

[19] Lippitt and White, *op. cit.*

[20] Our hypotheses are thus to be tested among organizational units which have predominantly negatively sloped control curves. When we refer, then, to increases in degree of positive slope, we understand this to be equivalent to decreases in degree of negative slope.

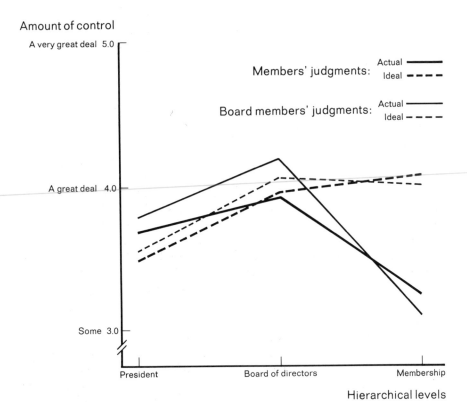

FIGURE 1   *Control curves, actual and ideal, averaged for all Leagues, based on the judgments of members and board members.*

TABLE 2   Partial Correlations between Effectiveness and Aspects of Control in Leagues, Holding Size of League Constant

| | Basis of data on control | | | |
| | Members' judgments | | Board members' judgments | |
	r_p	P	r_p	P
Actual				
Degree of + slope of control curve	.31	<.001	.19	<.03
Total amount of control	.29	<.002	.25	<.005
Ideal				
Degree of + slope of control curve	.12	>.10	.10	>.14
Total amount of control	.04	>.32	.10	>.14

The standard error of the z transformation for the partial correlation is $1\sqrt{(N-4)}$ (see Q. McNemar, *Psychological Statistics* [New York: John Wiley & Sons, 1949]). The one-tailed method, predicting positive correlations in each case, is employed.

($r_p = .31$) and average height ($r_p = .29$) of the control curve based on judgments of members. Furthermore, the correlations between effectiveness and the slope and height of the "ideal" control curve are not significantly different from zero. When the judgments of board members are employed as the basis for measuring the independent variables, the correlations are .19 between slope and effectiveness and .25 between total amount of control and effectiveness. Although modest in size, these correlations are statistically significant. The "ideal" data as reported by board members yield essentially the same results as that reported by the members.

The correlation between total control and slope (based on members' judgments) is only .14, indicating that we are testing two distinct hypotheses. This is further substantiated by second-order partial correlations. For example, the partial correlation between slope and effectiveness is .28, holding size and total control constant; the correlation between total control and effectiveness is .26, holding slope and size constant. Both are significant beyond the .005 level of confidence. An approximation of the multiple correlation using both slope and total control as the independent variables, and holding the logarithm of size constant, yields a value of .42, suggesting some advantage to predicting effectiveness from both slope and height of control curve rather than one or another separately.[21]

Nor are these results to be explained in terms of the differential rate of return of questionnaires in effective and ineffective Leagues. For example, the correlation between slope and effectiveness is .28, and that between total control and effectiveness, .24, when size and final rate of returns are partialed out. Both correlations are significant at beyond the .005 level of confidence.

Finally, let us consider the possibility that the measures of control and of effectiveness are really measures of members' participation and that the hypotheses are, for this reason, tautologous. The correlation between members' participation and effectiveness, holding League size constant, is .18. This is a relatively small but statistically significant relationship. Participation by members also correlates significantly with slope of control curve ($r_p = .38$) but not with height of control curve ($r_p = .05$).[22] However, partialing-out the effects of members' participation (as well as size) does not destroy the relationship between each of the two control indexes and effectiveness. These second-order partials yield values of .26 and .28 respectively for slope and height of control curve as independent variables ($p < .003$). On the other hand, partialing-out slope of control curve reduces the correlation between members' participation and effectiveness to .07. This argues against the contention that participation by members explains the relationship between slope and effectiveness, and it

---

[21] Frederic M. Lord, "Nomograph for Computing Multiple Correlation Coefficients," *Journal of the American Statistical Association*, L (December, 1955), 1073–77.

[22] The near zero correlation between total control and participation by members is not consistent with the results of an earlier study of four union locals (see Chap. 2, and Tannenbaum and Kahn, *Participation in Union Locals, op. cit.*).

TABLE 3 Per Cent of Leagues Which Are above Median in Effectiveness,* for Varying Combinations of Slope and Total Control

Degree of positive slope	Total control						
	High (11.2–12.2)		Medium (10.7–11.1)		Low (9.7–10.6)		
	N	Per cent	N	Per cent	N	Per cent	N
High (−.05–+.35)	14	78	13	69	8	50	35
Medium (−.06–−.25)	13	62	12	75	15	13	40
Low (−.26–−.85)	9	33	17	41	11	36	37
Total N	36		42		34		112

* Size of League is controlled by obtaining deviations of the effectiveness scores from the regression line of effectiveness on the logarithm of size of League.

suggests, on the contrary, that the small degree of association between participation and effectiveness is to be explained in terms of a certain degree of control by the membership implicit in some activities of members.

A further impression of the joint effects of slope and of total control can be obtained from Table 3, in which are presented the proportions of Leagues that are above median effectiveness under varying combinations of slope and total control (based on members' judgments).

In general, Leagues that are high or medium on both degree of positive slope and total control are likely also to be high in effectiveness. Furthermore, increasing the value of either one of the independent variables while decreasing the other does not seem to be accompanied predictably by increases in effectiveness. The effects of variations on one variable may be different when the second is held constant at a high level, as compared to when it is held low; for example, decreasing the total amount of control appears to be accompanied by decreasing effectiveness when degree of positive slope is relatively high, but not when it is low. Likewise, decreasing the degree of positive slope appears more predictably related to decreasing effectiveness when total control is high than when it is low. A type of threshold is suggested by these data: a minimum level of total control and of degree of positive slope may be necessary for effective performance. If the appropriate threshold is not met by one of these variables, increasing the other does not seem to help. For example, the performance of laissez faire (low total control) Leagues may not be much improved by making them more "democratic" (positively sloped) without at the same time making them less laissez faire.

Table 4 presents the correlations between initial rate of questionnaire returns as a criterion of the effectiveness of the local League and the respective dimensions of the control curve. The results based on the responses of mem-

TABLE 4 Partial Correlations between Initial Rate of Questionnaire Returns (as a Criterion of Effectiveness) and Aspects of Control in Leagues, Holding Size of League Constant

| | Basis of data on control | | | |
| | Members' judgments | | Board members' judgments | |
	r_p	P	r_p	P
Actual				
Degree of + slope of control curve	.23	<.008	.20	<.03
Total amount of control	.10	<.15	.00	.50
Ideal				
Degree of + slope of control curve	.14	>.07	.02	>.49
Total amount of control	−.13	......	−.12	

bers and board members are quite similar. They both offer further support for Hypothesis 1 but not for Hypothesis 2. However, when the dependent variable is interpreted simply as a type of "leader-out behavior" (rather than as an adequate measure of League effectiveness) the results make sense. They are consistent with the early observation of Lewin, Lippitt, and White: the "democratic" organization is more productive than is the "autocratic" when the leader is absent. However, productivity under leader- (and member-)out conditions would appear to be no greater in an organization high in total control than in one which is low.

Partialing-out the effects of final rate of returns in addition to size lowers the correlation between slope (based on members' judgments) and initial rate of returns from .23 to .18.[23] This correlation is small, but it would seem that in partialing-out final rate of returns we are applying a rather conservative test of the hypothesis. We are, in effect, considerably restricting the variance of the dependent variable, since final rate of returns and initial rate of returns correlate at .56. Nevertheless, a correlation as large as .18 would occur only three times out of one hundred by chance, and we feel safe in rejecting the null hypothesis.

DISCUSSION

The average local League in the present study is characterized by a control curve with a negative slope; leaders tend to exercise more control than do the members as a group. While not universal, the negatively sloped curve is probably typical of the formal organizations which make up the fabric of American society. Industrial organizations are more extreme in this characteristic than

---

[23] Variations among Leagues in rate of questionnaire returns from Board members is negligible, since 95 per cent of sampled Board members completed and returned their questionnaires.

are the voluntary Leagues of the present study. But many voluntary organizations, no doubt, conform to this pattern.[24] The negative slope exists in the League in spite of the apparent desire of most members and leaders for a more positive distribution. Directing and sustaining the local League is a complex and difficult task. Translating the expressed wish for greater control by the members into the actual exercise of that control is fraught with problems, some of which can be seen as contributing to the development of an "oligarchic" (negatively sloped) distribution of control, and others to a laissez faire (low total control) pattern.

A number of circumstances may lead to the development of an "oligarchic" distribution of control. The president, for example, in an effort to get things done, may feel it necessary to make decisions herself rather than to put into motion a more cumbersome decision-making machinery. Or leaders may simply fail to communicate relevant information, thus depriving members of the necessary bases for decision-making. In some cases presidents may not sense clearly the distinction between those decisions which are appropriate to them and those which belong to the members, and they may unwittingly overstep their jurisdiction. Or leaders may assume too much regarding the directives they have from the members. They may act as if certain decisions have been made which, in fact, have not been made.

A number of conditions may contribute to the development of a laissez faire control structure. The loci of responsibility for exercising control may not be sufficiently well defined and responsibility may consequently fall between roles. The failure of mutual understandings relative to the appropriate loci of control may also lead to conflicts in which the efforts of one group cancel those of another; neither exercises much control. This implies the importance of a system of communication and interaction permitting the development of mutual understanding and influence. The success of attempts at influence may also depend upon the "bases of power"[25] and the attitudes of members toward each other—whether or not members accept, trust, or like the persons exercising control, or whether or not the members exercising control have "expertness" or "legitimacy" or resources of reward or punishment at their disposal.

[24] For control curves characterizing industrial organizations, see "The Distribution of Control in Formal Organizations" (Chap. 3); Likert, "Influence and National Sovereignty," op. cit.; Floyd C. Mann and L. Richard Hoffman, Automation and the Worker: A Study of Social Change in Power Plants (New York: Henry Holt and Co., 1960); Arnold S. Tannenbaum, "The Concept of Organizational Control," Journal of Social Issues, XII (1956), 50–60; and Lawrence K. Williams, L. Richard Hoffman, and Floyd C. Mann, "An Investigation of the Control Graph: Influence in a Staff Organization," Social Forces, XXXVII (March, 1959), 189–95. The League probably has a more active and influential membership than does the typical voluntary organization described by Blau (op. cit., p. 117) and by Philip Selznick (The Organization Weapon [New York: McGraw-Hill Book Co., 1952], p. 96). See also Sills, op. cit., and Paul M. Harrison, "Weber's Categories of Authority and Voluntary Associations," American Sociological Review, XXV (April, 1960), 232–37. It is interesting to consider this general appraisal of voluntary organizations (other than the League) in the context of the hypothesis that voluntary associations in America have the function of providing "a sense of satisfaction with modern democratic processes because they help the ordinary citizen see how the processes function in limited circumstances" (Rose, op. cit., p. 51).

[25] John R. P. French, Jr., and Burtram Raven, "The Bases of Social Power," in D. Cartwright (ed.), Studies in Social Power (Ann Arbor: Institute for Social Research, 1959), 150–67.

The exercise of control is not likely to be widespread in an organization unless some of these characteristics are.

The data of this study support the hypothesis that local Leagues with less negatively sloped control curves tend to be more effective in their operations than are those with more negatively sloped curves. We have found some support for this hypothesis within the limits of a culture in which democratic values are extolled, among members who are interested in and somewhat sophisticated about the control of their organization, and within a voluntary organization which is not engaged in strenuous competition with other organizations and whose goals and products are relatively diffuse and intangible rather than specific and material. While these limits to generalization are implicit in the design of the study, the present results, together with those of earlier research in industrial settings, suggest a somewhat wider generality.[26]

Hypothesis 2 is partially supported by the data. It should be considered a corollary of a more general hypothesis concerning the optimal amount of control necessary for effective organizational functioning. Although its generality was initially assumed to be limited to voluntary organizations and labor unions, an analysis of thirty-one industrial plants provides further support for the hypothesis and suggests broader generality.[27] This hypothesis, however, may not apply to criteria of effectiveness in which the member is functioning away from the direct influence of other members or leaders.

An interesting question concerning the possible effects of differing combinations of height and slope of control curve is raised by the facts that each is related separately to effectiveness, that each can vary independently of the other, and that together they yield a somewhat higher degree of association with effectiveness. For example, while we would expect to find increases in the effectiveness of our Leagues corresponding to increases in positive slope, we would not expect effectiveness to go up if the increased slope is accompanied by a decrease in the height of the control curve. The more effective Leagues of our sample appear to be those characterized by a relatively high degree of positive slope and height of control curve.

While we have taken the data of this study as partially supportive of the original hypotheses, several limitations of design must be borne in mind. We cannot rule out the possibility that members and board members may "see" patterns of control in their Leagues which do not exist in reality. Although we are inclined to doubt this possibility, members in effective Leagues may believe that their Leagues are more "democratic" than members of ineffective Leagues believe theirs to be when, in reality, no such difference exists. Nor can we answer with certainty the question of causality. It is clear, further-

---

[26] See Coch and French, *op. cit.*; and Morse and Reimer, *op. cit.* While Morse's and Reimer's experiment showed an increase in production under conditions of centralized control, it is doubtful that the increased productivity could have been maintained (see Rensis Likert, "Measuring Organizational Performance," *Harvard Business Review*, XXXVI [March–April, 1958], 41–50).

[27] Likert, "Influence and National Sovereignty," *op. cit.*

more, that the independent-variable measures are not as reliable as we would like. But this fact operated against finding verification for our hypotheses. It should also be noted that the hierarchy within each League includes only three levels and that slope, under this condition, is equivalent to the difference in control exercised by the highest and lowest levels. Finally, the ranges of variation of our independent-variable measures are relatively narrow, and one might question the extent to which the hypothesized relationships would hold for more extreme values of slope and height of control curve. The data suggest, furthermore, that the effects of variations of one independent variable may be conditioned by the value of the other. Thus, increases in height of control curve among the Leagues of our sample appear to be associated with increases in effectiveness when degree of positive slope is relatively high, but not when it is low. Methodological refinement is called for, in addition to the retesting of the above hypotheses under varying organizational conditions.

5

ORGANIZATIONAL CONTROL STRUCTURE: A COMPARATIVE ANALYSIS*

Clagett G. Smith
Arnold S. Tannenbaum[1]

Several writers have recently attempted conceptual categorizations of organizations based partly on differences in control which suggest the fruitfulness of comparative analytic approaches in understanding this phenomenon (Blau, 1956; Blau & Scott, 1962; Etzioni, 1961; Gouldner, 1954; and Likert, 1961). This study presents comparisons among a number of organizations, including a voluntary association, unions, and business and industrial organizations, in terms of the "control graph." Control curves have been drawn on the basis of responses to questions asked of members regarding the amount of control which various echelons exercise. In addition to providing a description of the situation as members see it, the graph has also been used to characterize the pattern of control which members desire. In order to distinguish between these, we refer to the former as "actual" and the latter as "ideal" control.

This analysis is intended to explore the following general questions: First, what are the similarities and differences among the voluntary association, unions, and business-industrial organizations with respect to their actual and ideal patterns of control, as these are inferred from members' responses? Second, what are the similarities and differences between members and officers in the actual and ideal control curves which are derived from their responses and how do these differences vary in the three types of organization examined? The third general question is concerned with the relationships between aspects of control, measures of organizational effectiveness, and member attitudes toward the organization.

Relationships between control, organizational effectiveness, and member attitudes have been suggested in a number of studies.[2] Morse and Reimer (1956), for example, offer the hypothesis that an increased role in the decision-making processes for the rank-and-file groups (relative to supervisory and managerial groups) increases their satisfaction and productivity. While much

---

* Reprinted from *Human Relations*, Fall 1963, Vol. 16, pp. 299–316, with permission of the publisher and the authors. (This article has been edited to eliminate overlap and to bring it into a consistent format with the other articles in this book. Certain portions have therefore been deleted or reworded. Ed.)

[1] This analysis draws upon some of the findings obtained during the past ten years from a program of research on organizational behavior conducted by members of the Organizational Behavior and Change Program of the Survey Research Center. We gratefully acknowledge the valuable suggestions of Dorwin Cartwright, John R. P. French, Jr., Robert L. Kahn, Stanley E. Seashore, Jonathan A. Slesinger, Martin Patchen, and David G. Bowers, and the assistance of Dora Cafagna and Michael E. Brown.

[2] March & Simon (1958) provide a review of some of these studies.

attention has been focused on the distribution of control, the relevance of total control for organizational effectiveness has only recently been investigated.

In the first study in which the control graph was employed, Tannenbaum & Kahn (1958, Chapter 7) provide a rationale for the relationships which they note between measures of total control, effectiveness, and member loyalty in four local unions. Likert (1960) has suggested the importance of high mutual influence, or control by all levels within an organization, as the basis for the effective co-ordination of organizational activity as well as for the integration of the goals of individual members and of the organization—this co-ordination and integration being conducive to high organizational effectiveness. The exercise of control may also be a *result* of organizational effectiveness in certain circumstances. An effective organization as compared to an ineffective one is likely to have a greater stock of disposable rewards relevant to the interests of all members. Consequently, the exercise of control in the effective organization may be relatively more attractive to both leaders and members, because it is instrumental to the achievement of important satisfactions, and the amount of control which all groups try to exercise will be greater in this type of organization (Tannenbaum, 1961).

French, Israel & As (1960) present experimental data to show that discrepancies between the influence which members perceive to exist in an organization and that which they feel should exist (i.e. which they consider "legitimate") are related to aspects of worker-management relations and to member satisfaction. Finally, March & Simon (1958) argue that disagreements between members and leaders regarding organizational facts and ideals (including facts and ideals about control) are among the conditions contributing to intergroup conflict within organizations, and one might also expect these discrepancies to have some bearing on member satisfaction and productivity.

Specifically, then, one phase of the analysis will investigate the relationships between organizational effectiveness and member attitudes on the one hand, and variations in patterns of actual control, correspondences between actual and ideal patterns, and agreement between members and officers regarding different aspects of control on the other.

PROCEDURE

A. Organizations

The following analysis concerns approximately 200 geographically separate organizational units from a number of larger organizations. They include 32 geographically separate stations within a nationally organized delivery company (Georgopoulos, 1957, Georgopoulos & Tannenbaum, 1957; Likert, 1961; and Indik, Georgopoulos & Seashore, 1961); 36 geographically separate dealerships of an automotive sales organization (Patchen, Seashore & Eckerman, 1961); a department within a large clerical organization (Morse & Reimer, 1956; Morse, Reimer & Tannenbaum, 1951); a manufacturing plant (Seashore

& Bowers, 1962); the line organizations of two power plants varying in extent of automation (Mann & Hoffman, 1960); and the staff organization of a power plant (Williams, Hoffman & Mann, 1959). In addition to these business-industrial organizations, a weighted sample of 112 local leagues of the League of Women Voters of the United States (Tannenbaum, 1961) and five union locals (Tannenbaum & Kahn, 1958; Tannenbaum, 1956; Greenstone, 1960) are included. The interested reader is referred to the reports cited for a more detailed description of each organizational setting.

The organizations selected for inclusion in the present analysis are those in which reasonably comparable measures of control are available. They do not, however, comprise a sample, and we cannot know how representative they are of organizations on a nation-wide level. Nevertheless, in summarizing results, we shall perform some elementary statistical operations, such as the computations of means and percentages, and we shall apply several non-parametric tests. We hope, by summarizing in this way, to provide a basis for the development of hypotheses which can be tested among other groups of organizations and, ultimately, in representative samples.

B. Measurement of variables

1. Control   Employing the survey method, similar questions were asked of members in each of the organizations studied. Respondents were asked to rate on a five-point scale the amount of influence that each of several hierarchical groups (or persons) within the organization has upon what goes on within the organization. For example, in the delivery organization, respondents were asked the following question:

In general, how much say or influence do you feel each of the following groups *has* on what goes on in your station?

	Little or no influence	*Some influence*	*Quite a bit of influence*	*A great deal of influence*	*A very great deal of influence*
Your station manager	————	————	————	————	————
The other supervisors in your station	————	————	————	————	————
The men in your station	————	————	————	————	————

Respondents in most of the organizations studied were also asked a parallel set of questions concerning control as they desire it to be. For example, in the ideal question, parallel to the one illustrated above, respondents were asked:

In general, how much say or influence do you think each of the following groups *should have* on what goes on in your station?

In the majority of organizations studied, officers, as well as rank-and-file members, were asked these pairs of questions.

The amounts of actual and ideal control exercised by each of the hierarchical levels in a given organizational unit were computed by averaging the judgments of respondents (members and officers separately) regarding each of the levels. Indices obtained include the degree of actual and ideal slope, and the level of actual and ideal total control. Measures of the slope of the control curve were derived by computing, for each organizational unit, the average of the algebraic differences between the amounts of influence reported to be exercised by successive hierarchical levels. This requires the admittedly crude but workable assumption of equal scale intervals along both the horizontal and the vertical axes. The same operation was employed in deriving measures of the ideal as was employed for the actual slope of the control curve. Actual and ideal total control were computed for each organizational unit simply by summing the amount of control reported to be exercised by or 'desired' for the various hierarchical levels. The magnitude of these scores is, of course, a function of the amount of influence attributed to each level and the number of organizational levels in the unit considered.

2. *Effectiveness*   Organizational effectiveness is generally defined as the extent to which an organization achieves its goals or objectives. Scores of effectiveness are available in only four of the organizations studied, and these were obtained differently in each of them. Measures of effectiveness in the 112 units of the voluntary association are based on ratings of 29 experts who were familiar, as a group, with all of the local leagues studied. They were not, however, members of the local leagues in question. Raters were asked to consider, in making their judgements, several criteria of effective functioning based on the formal objectives established for local leagues by the national organization, such as high quality and quantity of publications and impact in the community (Tannenbaum, 1961). Organizational effectiveness in each of the 32 units of the delivery company is operationalized in terms of objective productivity measures provided by the company (Likert, 1960; Georgopoulos & Tannenbaum, 1957). These are based on the total time required to accomplish standard units of work. Measures of effectiveness in the sales organization represent the extent to which the actual sales volume met assigned sales quotas in each of the 36 dealerships (Patchen, Seashore & Eckerman, 1961). Measures of the effectiveness of the four union locals are based on judgements by the original researchers of the unions' power *vis-à-vis* their managements (Tannenbaum & Kahn, 1957). These judgments are based partly on the researchers' observations of the unions and on the statements of international and company officials.

3. *Member attitudes toward the organization*   Data regarding members' attitudes toward their organizations are based on responses to different questions in each of the four organizations. In the voluntary association, member atti-

tudes are measured in terms of two questions asked of members concerning their willingness to expend effort to prevent their local leagues from ceasing to function as a result of community opposition or member apathy. An index derived from these two questions is referred to as "member loyalty." The measure of member attitudes in the delivery company is based on members' ratings of the level of morale which they judge to exist in their respective stations. In the sales organization, member attitudes are measured in terms of their preference for remaining in their particular dealership given the possibility of moving to another. We refer to this as a measure of "attraction to the dealership." The measure of member attitudes in the union locals is similar to that in the voluntary association, viz. an index of member loyalty. This is measured in terms of members' ratings of willingness to expend effort on behalf of their union in the event that its existence were threatened owing to a serious strike or intra-union conflict.

The question of strict comparability of the indices of control, effectiveness, and member attitudes for different organizations must be considered. A problem may exist in the control measures owing to some differences of wording and response sets which might affect the indices of control differently in different organizations. Consequently, organizational comparisons are made cautiously with these possible sources of error in mind. Furthermore, our measures of control are subject to several interpretations, since they are based on judgments of members and officers. One might argue, for example, that we are dealing essentially with perceptions of control and that these do not correspond to the realities of control. Or one might interpret the measures as providing reasonably valid data of existing control patterns, although it is clear that the measures are subject to error.[3] The measures of organizational effectiveness and attitudes are perhaps more variable than those dealing with control. Organizational effectiveness is measured differently in each of the organizations studied, but each of the measures is reasonably consistent with the conceptual definition of effectiveness.[4] The measures of member attitudes do not, strictly speaking, represent the same attitudinal reactions in each of the organizations studied, but they are probably closely related. We nevertheless offer the following results as suggestive of important hypotheses which can be tested through further research employing more refined and standardized measures.

RESULTS

For purposes of illustration, the control curves for the 32 organizational units of the delivery company are presented in Figure 1. The "actual" curves are negatively sloped as reported by both supervisory and non-supervisory personnel. Members and supervisors are in fairly close agreement regarding the

---

[3] An analysis by Tannenbaum and Smith (1964) supports the tenability of this interpretation.

[4] See Georgopoulos & Tannenbaum (1957) for a discussion of the concept of organizational effectiveness.

Amount of control

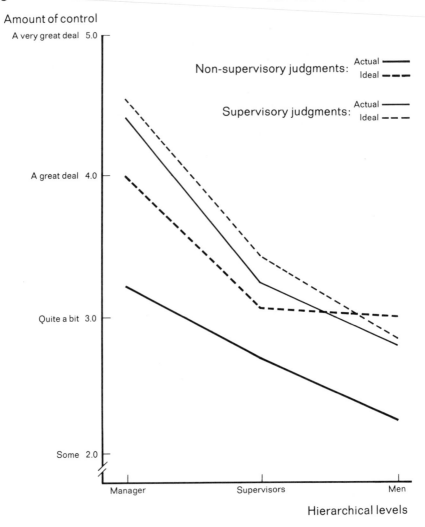

FIGURE 1 *Average control curves for 32 stations of a delivery company:*
Actual and ideal control—non-supervisors and supervisors.

relative amounts of control which the three hierarchical levels exercise. However, the supervisors report a higher amount of total control than do the men;
supervisors ascribe a greater degree of control to each hierarchical level. Furthermore, the ideal and actual curves correspond relatively closely as reported
by the supervisors but differ sharply for the men. The latter desire a considerably higher degree of control than they perceive to exist for themselves as a
group, although they do not view this ideal as lowering the control to be exercised by the manager and supervisors. In the case of both supervisors and
men, the ideal pattern implies a higher degree of total control than the actual.

For purposes of comparison, consider the data from the voluntary units shown in Figure 1, page 65. Both members and board members report, on the average, negatively sloped control curves. However, these curves diverge sharply from those which members and board members consider ideal. Both ideal curves are positively sloped and, furthermore, they are practically identical. It is interesting to see that the degree of ideological consensus among leaders and members in the voluntary organization does not exist in the industrial organization represented in Figure 1, page 78.

Table 1 summarizes the findings concerning similarities and differences among organizations in their patterns of control, as well as the results of member-officer comparisons.

Organizational type comparisons

Certain similarities among organizations are indicated from an examination of Table 1 (comparisons I(a)–(d)). A negatively sloped distribution of control occurs in a large majority of the organizational units studied. It is also apparent that the ideals which members have concerning the pattern of control differ from the actual pattern in almost all cases. The ideal distribution of control is more positively sloped than the actual, and the ideal level of total control is higher than the actual level in a large percentage of the organizational units. While members desire a more positively sloped distribution of control than they perceive exists, they do not wish to achieve this by reducing the control exercised by other levels. They are more inclined to increase the control exercised by most groups, especially their own. (Members desire an increase in the control exercised by the rank-and-file group in 99 per cent of the organizational units examined.) This results in a higher level of ideal than actual total control in most organizations. It also results in the actual curve approaching most closely that of the ideal near the upper levels of the organization. It is at the level of the rank-and-file member that the greatest discrepancy between actual and ideal control, as reported by members, occurs.

Differences in patterns of control as a function of organizational type are also suggested (see I(a)–(d)). All of the business-industrial organizations are characterized by negatively sloped curves. The units of the voluntary association represented here are less negatively sloped than the business-industrial organizations, although 88 per cent of the voluntary units studied have negative slopes. Four of the five unions studied are positively sloped.

Organizational differences are also seen with regard to the ideal distribution of control. Members of the voluntary units desire, in general, a positively sloped distribution, whereas participants in business-industrial organizations desire, perhaps with some sense of 'realism', a negatively sloped distribution of control (although less negatively sloped than the situation they judge to exist.) The distribution which industrial members propose, unlike that proposed by voluntary members, does not deviate radically from the distribution which

TABLE 1   Organizational and Member-Officer Comparisons of Actual and Ideal Patterns of Control

	Type of organization		
	Voluntary association	Business-industrial	Unions[2]
I. **Organizational type comparisons**[1]	% ($N=112$)	% (73)	% (5)
(a) % of organization units having actual negative slope	88	100	20
(b) % of organization units having ideal negative slope	10	99	
(c) % of organization units in which ideal slope is more positive than actual slope	100	83	
(d) % of organization units in which ideal total control is greater than actual total control	89	94	
II. **Member-officer comparisons**[3]	($N=112$)	(70)	(4)
(a) % of organization units in which actual slope members is more positive than actual slope officers	68*	47	0
(b) % of organization units in which ideal slope members is more positive than ideal slope officers	55	72*	
(c) % of organization units in which actual total control officers is greater than actual total control members	62*	72*	50
(d) % of organization units in which ideal total control officers is greater than ideal total control members	44	61	
(e) % of organization units in which members more often than officers indicate a more positive ideal than actual slope	41	77*	
(f) % of organization units in which members more often than officers indicate a higher level of ideal than actual total control	58	70*	

[1] Analysis based on responses of members.
[2] Measures of ideal control not obtained in the union studies.
[3] The null hypothesis in the member-officer comparisons is that $p = 50\%$.
* Significant at .01 level, 2-tailed test.

is seen to exist. Their response is probably determined, in part, by what seems possible under existing conditions of American industrial life.[5] Furthermore, the somewhat greater degree of 'democratization' which members propose as ideal does not imply a lowering of the control to be exercised by levels in the

[5] Note contrast with ideals expressed by organization members in Yugoslavia (see Chap. 6). Ed.

hierarchy above their own. On the contrary, the increased control proposed for the rank and file is often accompanied by an increase in the control proposed for upper levels too (see, for example, Figure 1). In the great majority or organizational units in both the voluntary and the business-industrial organizations, the ideal total control exceeds the actual.

Member-officer comparisons

Table 1 also compares members and officers in their judgements and ideals concerning different aspects of control (II (a)–(f)). In all the unions studied, officers judge the actual distribution of control to be more positively sloped than do members. This suggests some systematic bias in the judgements of the union respondents. This may be due to the special sense of pressure officers feel, as external representatives of the union *vis-à-vis* management and the community, to portray the union in a socially favorable way. However, in none of the unions observed is the sign of the slope different between members and officers. A positively sloped curve is, of course, consistent with a formal organization structure which is representational in nature. But in the voluntary organization a different result is apparent. Officers here are less inclined than members to represent their local leagues as democratic. Officers report on the average a more *negative* slope than members in 68 per cent of the branches. A systematic bias may be operating here, too, but in a different direction than that in the local unions. While officers and members share common ideals regarding control in the League, officers may be more sensitive to aspects of League functioning which fall short of these ideals and may therefore be inclined to represent their leagues as having a less democratic distribution of control than do the members. Still another pattern of findings exists in the business-industrial organizations. Members and supervisors, on the average, do not differ consistently in the slope of the control curve which they portray. In about half of the organizational units studied the supervisors represent their organizations as more negatively sloped than do rank-and-file members, whereas in the other half supervisors represent their organizations as more positively sloped.

When it comes to the ideal pattern of control, supervisors and members in the business organizations differ markedly, while, in the voluntary organization, members and officers do not, on the average, differ very much, if at all. In 72 per cent of the units of the business organizations studied, members desire a more positively sloped distribution of control than do supervisors. The proportion of voluntary units in which members desire a more positively sloped curve than do officers is close to 50 per cent, and very much what is to be expected by chance under the null hypothesis. This ideological consensus regarding how their leagues should be controlled probably reflects the common values of the population from which the league draws its membership, and the shared interests between members and officers which participation in the league promotes. That members report more democratic ideals than do supervisors in the units of the business-industrial organization perhaps indicates a conflict or difference of interests between rank-and-file and leadership groups in these organizations.

In both the voluntary units and the business organizations, officers are likely to see more control in general in their organizations than do members. Officers may be more inclined than members to err on the side of over-stating the control exercised by various groups in their organizations, or they may, through greater familiarity with the details of control at all levels, see and report manifestations of control which are not apparent to rank-and-file members.

The last two comparisons in Table 1 (II(e) and II(f)) make explicit several comparisons already implicitly made (comparisons II (a)–(d)). In the business organizations studied, members more often than officers desire a more positively sloped distribution of control than they judge to exist. This difference does not occur in the voluntary groups, i.e. officers here want, as much as do the members, a more positively sloped distribution of control than they judge to exist. Furthermore, in the business organizations, members more often than officers desire a greater amount of total control than they judge to exist, i.e. ideal total control is greater than actual total control more often for members than for officers. This difference does not occur in the units of the voluntary association, i.e. officers as often as members indicate a higher level of ideal total control than actual total control.

Relationships of aspects of control
with organizational effectiveness and member attitudes

Table 2 presents correlations between measures of control and organizational effectiveness and member attitudes in four organizations. The correlations summarize, in part, results that are presented elsewhere. They are based on analyses done separately among the 112 leagues of the voluntary association, the 32 stations of the delivery company, the 36 dealerships of the automobile sales organization, and four local unions.[6]

The general significance of total control for organizational effectiveness and member attitudes is noteworthy. A relationship between amount of total control and organizational effectiveness is indicated by the data in the voluntary association, the unions, and the delivery company. Total control is also related to positive member attitudes in these organizations. On the other hand, degree of positive slope is related to effectiveness only in the sample of local leagues. It is also related to member loyalty in the voluntary association and to member morale in the delivery company. Relationships between the discrepancy between the actual and the ideal patterns of control and effectiveness and mem-

[6] The studies referred to include Tannenbaum (1961); Likert (1960); Patchen, Seashore, and Eckerman (1961); and Tannenbaum and Kahn (1957) respectively.

TABLE 2 Correlations of Aspects of Control with Organizational Effectiveness and Member Attitudes[1]

Independent variables	Voluntary association[2] N=112		Delivery[3] N=32		Automobile sales N=33		Unions[4] N=4	
	Effectiveness (expert rater judgments)	Member loyalty	Effectiveness (company time standard records)	Member morale	Effectiveness (company sales records)	Member attraction	Effectiveness (researcher judgments)	Member loyalty
Degree of actual+slope (members)	.31***	.26***	.14	.55***	−.18	.03	R = .40	R = .40
Degree of actual total control (members)	.29***	.23**	.43***	.72***	.00	.21	R = 1.00†	R = 1.00†
Ideal minus actual slope (members)	−.13	−.21**	−.24	−.35**	−.08	−.05		
Ideal minus actual total control (members)	−.26***	−.25***	−.31**	−.26	.05	−.22		
Member-officer agreement actual slope	−.03	−.16	.00	−.09	−.09	.19	R = .20	R = .20
Member-officer agreement ideal slope	.01	−.02	.49***	.06	.03	.13		
Member-officer agreement actual total control	.15*	.05	.34**	.11	.27*	.03	R = 1.00**	R = 1.00**
Member-officer agreement ideal total control	.08	−.05	.38**	−.12	−.14	.12		

Dependent variables

[1] Hypotheses relating total control and slope to effectiveness and member loyalty were first suggested in the union study, and two-tailed tests are employed to assess the significance of these relationships. Directional predictions were made in the subsequent studies and one-tailed tests are employed here.

[2] Since log size is highly related to the measures of control and of effectiveness and member loyalty in the League, but not in the other organizations studied, the relationships in question were computed with log size partialled out.

[3] Total control and degree of positive slope are highly related among the stations in the delivery organization, but not in the other organizations studied. To assess the independent effects of total control and of degree of positive slope on the dependent variables, the correlations with slope are partial correlations holding total control constant, while the correlations with total control hold slope constant.

[4] Measures of ideal total control were not obtained.

* Significant at .10 level, 1-tailed test;   ** Significant at .05 level, 1-tailed test;   *** Significant at .01 level, 1-tailed test;   † Significant at .10 level, 2-tailed test.

ber attitudes are also indicated in the voluntary association and the delivery organization. The discrepancy between ideal and actual slope is negatively related to member attitudes but not to organizational effectiveness in these organizations. The discrepancy between ideal and actual total control is negatively related to organizational effectiveness in both organizations and to member loyalty in the voluntary association. The extent of member-officer agreement (with the exception of agreement regarding actual slope) seems relevant to organizational effectiveness only in the delivery company. Member-officer agreement with respect to the amount of actual total control is related to effectiveness and to member loyalty in the unions.

DISCUSSION

Similarities and differences in organizational control

The great majority of organizational units is characterized by negatively sloped control curves. All of these organizations require concerted member effort in performing tasks. The usual response to such a requirement is the employment of hierarchical control, and the finding of a preponderance of negatively sloped control curves is not surprising. However, the pattern of control reported by members in these organizations does not, for one reason or another, conform to what members consider ideal. It is perhaps to be expected that members will express a desire for the exercise of greater control of their organizations in a society where democratic values are extolled. And, of course, the exercise of control may bring certain pragmatic rewards and satisfactions.

It is interesting to consider why organizations are not reported to conform more closely to the ideal patterns of control as expressed by members in response to our questions. In some cases members are not able to increase the control which they exercise even though they may want to do so. They do not have the "bases of power" (legitimate or other), or they do not have the knowledge necessary for the effective exercise of control. Or the organization may not be formally structured in ways to expedite control by rank-and-file groups. The League, for example, provides a structure permitting high membership control, but most industrial organizations do not. On the other hand, members may not be prepared to expend the effort that the exercise of control implies, even though they express the wish for greater control. The discrepancy between actual and ideal control within organizations nevertheless represents, we believe, an important fact of life for large numbers of persons.

It is notable that the ideal pattern proposed by most members does not often imply radical or dysfunctional aspirations regarding control. On the contrary, it implies a higher degree of total control, and, as we have seen, this is related to organizational effectiveness as well as to member attitudes in three of four organizations examined. Most members in the business-industrial organizations studied appear to accept the legitimacy of an effectively functioning system of control, rather than want a less highly controlled organization or any radical change in the pattern itself.

The differences obtained among the types of organization in actual and ideal patterns of control are of equal interest and are probably related to important differences in structure, functions, objectives, and member expectations. The more negatively sloped distributions of control in the business-industrial organizations, as compared to the voluntary association and the labor unions, probably reflect the greater emphasis upon productive efficiency than on member welfare, and the traditional reliance upon a centralized system of authority for achieving this objective. In addition, the upper levels in these organizations have more extensive bases of power than the rank and file, including coercive, expert, and reward bases as well as legitimate bases. Furthermore, most members in business-industrial organizations expect and accept a hierarchical system of authority. This does not seem to be the case in the voluntary association or the labor unions.

Member-officer differences

The effect which rank has on the perceptions of control and the ideals one holds regarding control would seem to depend on the nature of the organization as well as on the population from which it draws its members. Business and industrial organizations have relatively well-defined formal patterns of authority, and the actual distribution of control is not likely to vary very much from this pattern. The relative amounts of control exercised by different echelons are therefore fairly clear to workers and supervisors, and are likely to be a fairly well-accepted fact of life. Voluntary agencies and labor unions have less clearly defined patterns of authority, and the actual distribution of control is more fluid and hence more ambiguous. In addition, a democratic pattern of control is an important (if sometimes unrealized) value to both members and leaders. One might therefore expect greater differences between officers and members in their perceptions of slope in the voluntary agencies and labor unions than in industrial organizations.

Supervisors and workers in industrial organizations, however, do differ significantly in their perceptions of total control as do officers and members of the voluntary association. Total control is not formally defined in organizations as slope implicitly is and therefore may be subject to more variation than slope. It may vary with the nature of leadership and other factors (Likert, 1961). Consequently, perceptions of total control may be more subject to variation, particularly between members and officers, in part owing to their differential familiarity with the control exercised by the various echelons.

The differences between members and officers regarding the ideal pattern of control in the business-industrial organizations may reflect conflicts created by objectives which are not primarily oriented toward furthering the interests of most members, by different positions with respect to a hierarchically distributed control structure, and by a relatively unequal share of the rewards of these organizations. The ideological consensus between members and officers in the voluntary association not only reflects their shared values concerning democratic process, but may also be a function of the formal structure of the local league, including the committee and membership meetings, the election of officers, and the broad decision-making rights of the membership.

The implications of organizational control

The relevance of total control for organizational effectiveness and positive member attitudes seems especially noteworthy. Substantial control exercised by both leaders and members appears to be a correlate of high organizational performance in the majority of organizations examined. This apparently occurs because the motivations and contributions of the rank-and-file members are utilized, as well as those of the leaders. This conclusion is substantiated by the positive relationships obtained between amount of total control and member loyalty or morale. However, this pattern of control may be conducive to high organizational performance through different processes such as participative management as described by March & Simon (1958, page 54) or cooptation as discussed by Selznick (1953), or as a system of high interaction and mutual influence as suggested by Likert (1961). This pattern of influence provides one of the major bases for concerted, integrated activity underlying effective organizational performance.

It is interesting to find that the League is the only organization among the four in which slope relates to effectiveness. The ideals of League members, as well as the formal structure of the local league, including its system of authority and decision-making, are potentially consistent with a positively sloped distribution of control. Those leagues which come closest to fulfilling this potential, i.e. which have less negatively sloped curves, tend to be relatively high in effectiveness and member loyalty. However, while slope is significantly related to effectiveness in the League, total control is not unrelated to effectiveness. Each of these variables independently is related to effectiveness, the most effective leagues being those high both in degree of positive slope and in total control (Tannenbaum, 1961).

Many of the formal characteristics of the League apply to unions, too, but there are differences. Perhaps the most significant concern the conflict in which unions engage with their managements, and the pragmatic or "bread-and-butter" orientation which most members have toward their unions. Members are not unconcerned with how their unions are controlled, but they are probably more interested in the material benefits with which their unions may be able to provide them (Lipset, Trow & Coleman, 1956). We thus find that while four of the five unions are indicated by their members and officers to have positively sloped curves, slope, *per se*, is not related to effectiveness or member loyalty. Both of these dependent variables are connected with what the union is doing for its members, and the hypothesis has been proposed that this is a function of total control (Tannenbaum, 1956).

In the units of the delivery organization, amount of total control is highly related to member morale, as well as to organizational effectiveness. Slope is also related to member morale in the delivery organization. This is consistent with the hypothesis that some conflict of interest is felt by rank-and-file members between themselves and the manager, and that under this condition workers are likely to be happier if the discrepancy between their power and that of the manager is not so great. Having control relative to the manager then seems to boost morale in the delivery organization, as reported by members, even though it does not lead to greater productivity.

Moreover, member-officer agreement regarding several aspects of control is related to effectiveness only in the delivery organization. This may be attributable, in part, to the greater degree of disagreement concerning control in this organization than exists in the League or the sales organization (see, for example, pages 65 and 78). It may be that disagreements must reach a certain magnitude before they contribute to conflict and impede organizational performance. Member-officer agreement concerning control may also be more important in the delivery organization than in the League, since the latter organization is set up to resolve disagreements through meetings and discussion, while the former is not. Disagreements in the delivery organization remain disagreements. We thus find larger disagreements in this organization than in the League, and a possible negative effect of these upon the performance of the delivery units.

The sales organization does not show the relationships which are found in the other organizations. This may be attributable to the inappropriateness of the dependent variable measures here. For example, sales volume may fluctuate widely owing to conditions external to the organization, and these fluctuations may not have been adequately taken into account in the ratio of actual to expected sales volumes employed as our measure of effectiveness. A second interpretation suggests that the nature and importance of control depend upon the integration and coordination required in an organization. Dealerships are characterized in large measure by independent, individual performance of salesmen; little coordination and interdependent activity are required. Furthermore, the rewards which salesmen achieve depend upon the success of individual, if not competitive, performance.

CONCLUSION

This paper has attempted to provide some information concerning aspects of organizational control through a comparative analysis of a number of organizations. The need for comparative approaches is great, but comparative studies are beset with serious conceptual as well as methodological problems. There is especially the difficulty of defining and measuring dimensions of organizational structure which are general and conceptually meaningful, and which are, at the same time, amenable to standardization and replication.[7] The control graph method has been offered as one approach to the comparative study of organizations. It has been claimed to have the advantages of being a general, quantitative technique with conceptual as well as operational potentialities (Tannenbaum & Kahn, 1957). The data of the present article help to illustrate the potential of this method in comparative analyses of organizations. They also suggest some of its limitations as it has been applied so far. Perhaps the most serious of these is the reliance placed on the judgments of organization members for the measures of control. Yet, some of the meaningful differences between organizational types, and some of the significant and meaningful correlations between indices of control and independent criteria of organizational functioning (e.g. productivity) suggest that the data are reasonably reliable and that they may even have some validity as objective measures. In any event, this is an area in which methodological refinement is called for and we would hope to make some progress here through further research. In the meantime, we offer the data of the present study as illustrative of the potential of the method and as suggestive of a number of hypotheses about organizational control ("perceived," "real," or "ideal") which are amenable to empirical tests.

REFERENCES

Barton, A. (1961). *Organizational measurement.* New York: College Entrance Examination Board.

Blau, P. (1956). *Bureaucracy in modern society.* New York: Random House.

Blau, P., & Scott, W. (1962). *Formal organizations.* San Francisco: Chandler Publishing Co.

Etzioni, A. (1961). *A comparative analysis of complex organizations.* Glencoe, Ill.: The Free Press.

French, J., Israel, J., & Ås. D. (1960). An experiment in participation in a Norwegian factory. *Hum. Relat.* **13,** 3–19.

French, J., & Raven, B. (1959). The bases of social power. In D. Cartwright (Ed.), *Studies in social power.* Ann Arbor, Mich.: Institute for Social Research.

Georgopoulos, B. (1957). The normative structure of social systems: A study of organizational effectiveness. Ann Arbor, Mich.: Unpublished doctoral dissertation, University of Michigan.

Georgopoulos, B., & Tannenbaum, A. (1957). A study of organizational effectiveness. *Amer. sociol. Rev.* **22,** 534–40.

Gouldner, A. (1954). *Patterns of industrial bureaucracy.* Glencoe, Ill.: The Free Press.

Greenstone, D. (1960). Local union government: A case study of social and political determinants. Chicago, Ill.: Unpublished master's thesis, University of Chicago.

---

[7] For a summary of measurements of organizational structure, see the extensive review by Barton (1961).

Indik, B., Georgopoulos, B., & Seashore, S. (1961). Superior-subordinate relationships and performance. *Pers. Psychol.* **14,** 357–74.

Likert, R. (1960). Influence and national sovereignty. In J. Peatman & E. Hartley (Eds.), *Festschrift for Gardner Murphy.* New York: Harper. Pp. 214–27.

Likert, R. (1961). *New patterns of management.* New York: McGraw-Hill.

Lipset, S., Trow, M. & Coleman, J. (1956). *Union democracy.* Glencoe, Ill.: The Free Press.

Mann, F., & Hoffman, R. (1960). *Automation and the worker.* New York: Henry Holt.

March, J., & Simon, H. (1958). *Organizations.* New York: John Wiley.

Morse, Nancy, & Reimer, E. (1956). The experimental change of a major organizational variable. *J. abnorm. soc. Psychol.* **52,** 120–9.

Morse, Nancy, Reimer, E., & Tannenbaum, A. (1951). Regulation and control in hierarchical organizations. *J. soc. Issues* **7,** 41–8.

Patchen, M., Seashore, S., & Eckerman, W. (1961). Some dealership characteristics related to change in new car sales volume. Ann Arbor, Mich.: Unpublished report, Institute for Social Research.

Seashore, S., & Bowers, D. (1962). Communication and decision processes as determinants of organizational effectiveness. Ann Arbor, Mich.: Unpublished report, Institute for Social Research.

Selznick, P. (1953). *T.V.A. and the grass roots.* Berkeley, Calif.: University of California Press.

Tannenbaum, A. (1956). Control structure and union functions. *Amer. J. Sociol.* **61,** 536–45 (in this book, Chapter 2).

Tannenbaum, A. (1961). Control and effectiveness in a voluntary organization. *Amer. J. Sociol.* **67,** 33–46 (in this book, Chapter 4).

Tannenbaum, A. (1962). Control in organizations: Individual adjustment and organizational performance. *Admin. Sci. Quart.* **7,** 236–57 (in this book, partly reproduced in Chapters 1 and 21).

Tannenbaum, A., & Georgopoulos, B. (1957). The distribution of control in formal organizations. *Soc. Forces* **36,** 44–50 (in this book, Chapter 3).

Tannenbaum, A., & Kahn, R. (1957). Organizational control structure: A general descriptive technique as applied to four local unions. *Hum. Relat.* **10,** 127–40.

Tannenbaum, A., & Kahn, R. (1958). *Participation in union locals.* Evanston, Ill.: Row Peterson.

Tannenbaum, A., & Smith, C. (1964). The effects of member influence in an organization: Phenomenology versus organizational structure. *J. abnorm. Soc. Psych.* **69,** 401–410 (in this book, Chapter 13).

Williams, L., Hoffman, R., & Mann, F. (1959). An investigation of the control graph: Influence in a staff organization. *Soc. Forces* **37,** 189–95.

6

THE DISTRIBUTION OF CONTROL IN
SOME YUGOSLAV INDUSTRIAL ORGANIZATIONS
AS PERCEIVED BY MEMBERS*

Josip Županov
Arnold S. Tannenbaum[1]

Organizations in all societies share common characteristics. They all imply some form of concerted effort on the part of members and they all include a more or less stable pattern of authority relations designed to assure this co-ordinated behavior. However, the character of authority or control may vary widely among organizations, even among those which are similar in all other respects. These differences may reflect differences in formal plans or they may have evolved out of the particular circumstances within which the organizations function. The universality and centrality of control in organizations, however, suggest it as an important area for study and particularly as an area within which comparative research may profitably be conducted.

Several models concerned with organizational control have been described in the literature.[2] Smith and Tannenbaum, employing the control-graph model have presented comparative data from more than 200 organizational units in the United States, including business and industrial organizations, labor unions, and voluntary groups.[3] The present research is designed to extend this

* Previously published as Distribucija utjecaja u nekim jugoslavenskim industrijskim organizacijama kako je vide clanovi tih organizacija, *Ekonomski Pregled*, 1966, God. XVII, Broj. 2–3. Str. 115–132; and as La distribution du controle dans quelques organisations industrielles yougoslaves, *Sociologie du Travail*, Jan.–March, 1967, pp. 1–23. Printed here with permission of *Ekonomski Pregled* and the authors.

[1] This research is part of a more extensive program of studies undertaken by the Economics Institute of Zagreb concerning the behavior of the business firm. The present study was conducted under the direction of the first author, who would like to thank the following persons who gave him their assistance: Dr. I. Kuvacic, Assistant Professor, Faculty of Philosophy, Department of Sociology, Zagreb University; Dr. P. Novosel, Assistant Professor, Faculty of Political Sciences, Zagreb University; Mr. I. Zavrski, the Workers' University of Zagreb; and Miss Cemalovic, the former director of a department of the Workers' University, where part of the survey was carried out. The second author provided consultation at the beginning and worked with the study director in interpreting the results and writing this paper. He would like to thank the Carnegie Corporation of New York, which, through a grant to the Survey Research Center, Institute for Social Research, the University of Michigan, permitted him to engage in this collaborative work. He would also like to thank the Tavistock Institute of Human Relations, where he was in residence while part of this paper was being written. The authors appreciate the suggestions of Miso Jezernik, although they alone are responsible for the interpretations presented in this paper.

[2] See, for example, Peter M. Blau, *Bureaucracy in modern society*, New York: Random House, 1956; Michel Crozier, *The bureaucratic phenomenon*, London: Tavistock Publications, 1964; Amitai Etzioni, *A comparative analysis of complex organizations.* New York: Free Press, 1961; Alvin W. Gouldner, *Patterns of industrial bureaucracy*, New York: Free Press, 1954; Rensis Likert, *New patterns of management*, New York: McGraw-Hill, 1961; Max Weber, *The theory of social and economic organization*, A. M. Henderson and Talcott Parsons (Trans.), New York: Oxford, 1947.

[3] Clagett G. Smith and Arnold S. Tannenbaum, Organizational control structure: a comparative analysis, *Human Relat.* 16 (4), 1963, 299–316 (in this book, Chap. 5).

line of inquiry by attempting to ascertain whether the control-graph method may be applicable in Yugoslavia. Are members of some Yugoslav business and industrial organizations able to respond meaningfully to questions like those asked of members of American organizations about the distribution of control in their organization? The present research is therefore exploratory and methodological in character. However, the data to be presented seem reasonably encouraging from a methodological point of view, and we are led to raise several questions of a more substantive, although entirely exploratory, nature. How do members of some Yugoslav industrial firms perceive aspects of control in their organization? How do these perceptions compare with the ideals that members express? How do supervisors and workers, Party members and nonmembers, differ in their perceptions and ideals regarding control? What meaningful comparisons can be made between these Yugoslav data and the American data presented by Smith and Tannenbaum? What possible implications do these data have for understanding the development and functioning of Yugoslav industrial organizations?

RESEARCH SITES AND METHOD

General

We cannot present here details of the social, political, and legal factors that are relevant to an understanding of the Yugoslav industrial organization. The reader is referred to a number of books and articles that provide some background to this question.[4] We sketch a few of these factors briefly.

Prior to World War II Yugoslavia was largely an agricultural, peasant society. However, some industries existed. We describe the two most common.[5]

First are industries organized as big handicraft shops, with some elements of modern technology, such as large machines, but with no mass production. Skilled craftsmen were the center of the production process. Holding all basic functions, the skilled worker blocked the development of staff organization. These industries, therefore, had practically no staff. After World War II an attempt was made to improve these organizations largely through capital in-

---

[4] The legal and institutional framework of the system of workers' self-management is thoroughly and accurately described in the B.I.T. study *La qestion ouvriere des entreprises en Yugoslavie*, Genève, 1962. See also Aser Deleon, *33 questions, 33 answers on workers' self-government in Yugoslavia*, Belgrade: Publicity Enterprise, 1956, and Oleg Mandic, Yugoslavia, in Arnold M. Rose (Ed.), *The institutions of advanced societies*, Minneapolis: The University of Minnesota Press, 1958. Social values and philosophies underlying the Yugoslav system of workers' councils are stated in the program of the League of Communists, *Yugoslavia's way: the program of the league*, New York: All Nations Press, 1958. For social studies see Adolf Sturmthal, *Workers' councils*, Cambridge, Mass.: Harvard, 1964; Jiri Kolaja, *Workers' councils: the Yugoslav experience*, London: Tavistock Publications, 1965; John T. Dunlop, *Industrial relations systems*, New York: Holt, 1959, chap. 8. For general background information and views see George W. Hoffman and F. W. Neal, *Yugoslavia and the new communism*, Fund for the Republic, 1962; Fitzroy Maclean, *Tito*, New York: Ballantine Books, Inc., 1957; and Charles P. McVicker, *Titoism: pattern for international communism*, London: Macmillan, 1957.

[5] Ing. S. Nesek, Reorganizacija poduzeca radi poboljsanja odnosa prema radu i povecanja produktivnosti rada, *Ekonomske Jedinice U Praksi*, Zagreb: Savezni Centar, 1961.

vestments designed to enlarge plants and increase the number and sizes of machines. Some staff services that are characteristically found in modern organizations were introduced, not without considerable resistance. However, the essential structure of the firms was not changed. Firms of this type can survive in modern times only in centralized economies where high production costs are permitted and where products can be sold at high fixed prices. The decentralization of the Yugoslav economy, which began with the strengthening of market forces as an important determinant of organizational survival, exerted pressure against the maintenance of this kind of structure.

The second most important form of industry in prewar Yugoslavia included branches of foreign companies some of which were engaged in *montage*. These were established largely as a means of overcoming customs obstacles. Parts were imported with low duty, assembled into finished products, and sold domestically. These plants had great difficulty after the war, because the *montage* function depended on foreign parts. Now, however, some are producing their own parts and are managing to survive.

The character of authority differed somewhat in these enterprises. In the domestically owned, handicraft plants, the basis of authority was largely traditional. Industrial organizations inherited patterns of authority that had been part of the handicraft system of production established during feudal times. The authority relationship was essentially that of master to servant. Status distinctions and personal deference by subordinates toward supervisors were strongly emphasized. Within broad limits, decisions by managers were nonbureaucratic; they were personal, arbitrary, and sometimes harsh.

Foreign-owned plants did not usually have either a traditional or a legal rational basis of authority. Some foreign managements tried to establish legitimate control through paternalistic devices. Others, as in the coal-mining industry, resorted to coercive techniques of control.

Plants organized as big handicraft shops were the most prevalent in the Zagreb area, where most of the organizations included in this research are located. These handicraft shops set the stage for most new industry in this region. Persons from old plants of this kind transferred to the new ones created after the war, and they brought with them their old ideas and habits, including their traditional attitudes toward authority. These habits, however, were not in direct conflict with the postwar nationalization. Nationalization simply brought centralization through special government agencies set up to manage business firms. The Party, and to some extent trade unions, were employed as a means of expediting centralized control. Very little autonomy was given the business firm. Production plans, prices, distribution, and other business arrangements were fixed. This did not change the handicraft method of production, with its rigid hierarchy, its traditional approach to authority, and the important role of the craft worker. On the contrary, the old form was frozen.

In 1950 the system of workers' self-management was introduced through a law passed by the Federal Parliament.[6] This law had a number of important stipulations. The centralized agencies were disbanded, and broad areas of policy-making authority were delegated to the workers' collectives (that is, to all members of the firm). The government was thus deprived of its managerial function within firms. It did, however, exercise some important (or "regulating") control through taxation, dispensation of credit, regulations concerning imports and exports, and general laws regarding the distribution of profits. Although great authority was officially delegated to the workers' collectives, the control that plant managers could exercise was not lessened. On the contrary, plant managers now had greater freedom of action and were probably able, through their strategic position within the firm, to exercise more control than formerly.

The 1950 law implied two authority structures within firms: one concerned with the determination of general policies, including basic decisions like setting prices, and one concerned with technical, administrative, and operative decisions, including advising, consulting, and preparing proposals; making subsidiary decisions in implementing approved policies; and exercising management prerogatives given by law directly to managers, for example, making business contracts and some personnel decisions.

Two related hierarchical axes might therefore be said to exist. They are joined at one end by the general manager, who plays a role in both. The first includes workers as producers at one end, followed by supervisors, heads of economic units (which are roughly equivalent to department heads), and the manager at the other. The second includes the workers' council at one end, followed by the managing board and the manager at the other. Theoretically, the first is concerned with operative, and the second with general policy decisions.

Workers' councils and managing boards are elected bodies composed of the employees of an enterprise. The workers' council may include as many as 120 members, depending on the size of the enterprise. It meets at least once every six weeks. The managing board consists of three to eleven persons elected by the council but the general manager is a member by law. Prior to the 1950 law the function of the council was solely advisory, suggestive, and consultative. Its function has subsequently been strengthened. The workers' council is now delegated by law as the most authoritative of the three groups in the second hierarchy described above. "If one were to pose the question thus: who is senior—the workers' council, the managing board, or the director of an enterprise—in the sense of who was accountable to whom, then the answer would be that the workers' council was superior over the rest, since the director accounts to the managing board for his work and must abide by its decisions, while the managing board is accountable to the workers' council. . . ."[7] The

---

[6] The following is a brief and simplified description. The reader should recognize that the system is in a state of flux.

[7] Deleon, *op. cit.*

manager is formally appointed to his job by the workers' council. All other managers and supervisors are appointed by the managing board.

Economic units are a relatively recent innovation designed to expedite decentralization within the firm. They are functional groups, in many respects like sociotechnical units[8] and organizational families.[9] They may, however, include a number of supervisors and a larger number of workers than is typical of the organizational family. Economic units have, theoretically, a high degree of autonomy and a number of economic and social prerogatives, such as deciding how wages and work might be distributed among members or whether a new worker should be permitted into the group.

Organizations and workers studied

The respondents in the present study include fifty-six workers attending a two-year course at the Workers' University in Zagreb. They come from a number of Zagreb industries, ranging in size from 200 to 10,000 members. They attend the university part time while working four hours a day. This group does not comprise a sample in the technical sense of the term. It includes a relatively high proportion of formally educated, highly skilled and aspiring workers. Approximately 89 percent hold membership in the Communist Party as compared with 10.6 percent of workers in the district of Zagreb.[10] Thirty-nine percent are first-line supervisors. This group includes members who are probably more aware of the processes of control than the average worker. Furthermore, being at a university and away from work part time, they may be in a better position psychologically to think about, and answer freely, questions about control in their organizations; they were probably in a good frame of mind as respondents for a study of this kind. These respondents, then, comprise a special group.

Despite the special character of this sample, the data presented below are similar in general to results obtained from questionnaires administered as pretests in several plants and to an earlier sample from the Workers' University. They are also consistent in large measure with results obtained from questionnaires in which variations in phraseology were tried. Furthermore, an independently conducted study in Slovenia and a recent investigation employing similar methods in Serbia, which we describe below, provide additional data within which the results of the present study can be interpreted.[11] We there-

---

[8] Eric L. Trist, Gurth W. Higgin, Hugh Murray, and Alec B. Pollock, *Organizational Choice*, London: Tavistock Publications, 1963.

[9] Likert, *op. cit.*

[10] Official data, 1958.

[11] For further research in Yugoslavia employing the method of the control graph see Veljko Rus, *Status vodstvenega kadra v pogojih samoupravljanja*, Kranj: Zavod az organizacijo dela v Kranju, 1964; and J. Zupanov, *Grafikon utjecaja kao analiticko orudje za izucavanje strukturalne promjene socijalne organizacije poduzeca*, Zagreb: Ekonomski Institut, 1964; unpublished doctoral dissertation, University of Ljubljana, 1964.

fore present these data as illustrative of those from a larger number of respondents in a variety of locations. Where our experience with these other samples suggests qualifications, they are indicated in our discussion of results.

Questionnaire method

Each respondent was given a paper-and-pencil questionnaire in which questions employed in connection with the control-graph method were included. An attempt was made to use questions as close as possible in meaning to those employed in American studies. These include questions concerning the amount of influence that various hierarchical groups in the organizations are perceived to have, as well as questions concerning the amount of influence that these groups should have. For the sake of simplicity, the results of the former are referred to as "actual" control and the latter as "ideal" control. The questions were asked in tabular form as follows:

How much influence do the following groups have on what happens in the firm?

	A very great deal	A great deal	Some	A little	None
Workers' council					
Managing board					
Managers					
Heads of economic units					
Supervisors					
Workers					

This is the actual control question. A second question in which the word *should* was substituted for *do* formed the ideal question.

In addition to these questions a series of parallel actual questions was asked concerning the following thirteen areas of decision making:

    1. Approving annual production plan
    2. Fixing prices
    3. Investments (purchasing new machines)
    4. Investments (building new shop)
    5. Allocation of the net profit
    6. Use of funds for "collective consumption" (welfare, housing, cafeteria, and the like)

7. Wages and salaries
8. Assigning employees to jobs
9. Assigning particular tasks to employees
10. Fixing work standards
11. Hiring
12. Firing
13. Disciplining employees

All respondents were questioned during class hours at the Workers' University. The questionnaires were strictly anonymous, and all respondents were assured that their individual answers would be kept confidential. Respondents were told that the survey was designed for the purpose of gaining scientific knowledge. There is reason to think that most respondents accepted the good faith of the researchers, although some of them may have been skeptical about the stated objectives and some workers may have been reticent to respond frankly to the questions. Some respondents of this type eliminated themselves by not responding. Approximately 5 percent of the total of fifty-six respondents were eliminated in this way. The data themselves, as the reader will see below, seem to indicate a willingness on the part of many respondents to answer frankly.

RESULTS

Figure 1 shows the control curves, actual and ideal distributed along the two hierarchies described above. Figure 1a shows curves for hierarchy 1; Figure 1b for hierarchy 2. Both actual curves are negatively sloped. Managers, in other words, are considered the most influential group, followed by heads of economic units, supervisors, and workers in hierarchy 1 and by the workers' council and managing board in hierarchy 2. However, the difference between the managers and workers' council is very small in this sample, and actual curve 2 tends to be flatter than 1. Both ideal curves, on the other hand, tend to be positively sloped. In curve 1 the workers as a group are desired to be most influential, and in curve 2 it is the workers' council. The discrepancy between the actual and ideal curves along hierarchy 2 is relatively small compared with that of hierarchy 1. The largest discrepancy between ideal and actual occurs for the workers as a group. The respondents clearly feel that the workers should have more control than they do. The managers are the only group among those cited above for which respondents feel a decrease in influence would be appropriate. Despite this decrease, the ideal curves tend to be higher on the average than the actual. Respondents are more inclined to increase than to decrease the influence of most groups. These results are, in a number of respects, strikingly similar to those collected in American organizations; yet some important differences are apparent too, as we shall see below.

The workers' council is perceived to have a reasonably high degree of control, and the discrepancy between actual and ideal for this group is not so

Amount of control

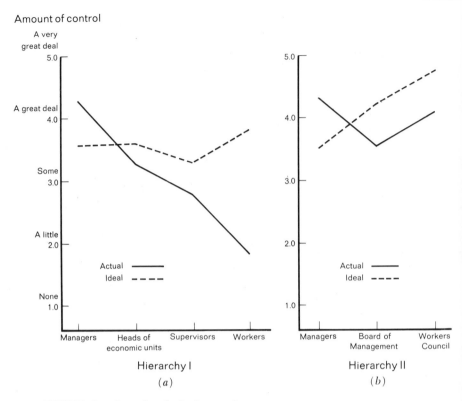

FIGURE 1   *Actual and ideal control curves.*

large as that for the workers as a group. The large discrepancy for the latter occurs despite the fact that the workers' council is elected by the workers and is comprised in large part of workers. This discrepancy seems to suggest that the workers' council as a representative of workers does not give workers a sense of control in their enterprises.[12]

A possible explanation for this breakdown is suggested by the data in Table 1. Here we see the influence that various groups in the enterprises have within the workers' councils as reported by the Workers' University sample. Workers' councils, according to these data, are influenced most by managers and relatively little by workers, although the councils are created expressly to represent the latter. But differences among the various categories of workers are

[12] This discrepancy may be a more general problem for representative systems of comanagement than advocates of such systems believe. Note, for example, a similar breakdown in a Norwegian enterprise: Fred E. Emery, and Einar Thorsrud, *Industrial democracy*, London: Tavistock Publications, 1965. The general conception in Yugoslavia of workers' self-management is not limited to representative forms of worker participation. The shortcomings of a purely representative system are becoming apparent to political and administrative leaders in Yugoslavia, and attempts are being made to supplement the purely representative system with more direct forms of participation. The system of economic units is one such approach (see below).

TABLE 1   Perceptions by Workers' University Sample of the Influence of Various Groups within the Workers' Council*

Group	Influence ($N = 50$–53)
Managers	4.7
Staff	4.1
Heads of economic units	3.4
Supervisors	2.7
White-collar workers	2.7
Highly skilled workers	2.5
Skilled workers	2.2
Semiskilled workers	1.6
Unskilled laborers	1.5

* Question: "How much influence do the following groups have on what goes on in the workers' council?" Answers checked on a scale from 1, "none," to 5, "a very great deal."

worth noting. White-collar and skilled workers have more influence than laborers. This suggests that an educated and skilled work force is likely to provide conditions more favorable to the effective functioning of a workers'-council system. Thus, although councils may be a means through which workers can exercise control, they need not be. Councils may, on the other hand, provide means through which managers and some other groups exercise control. One need not expect that high influence by the council of elected representatives is necessarily felt as such by the electors themselves.[13]

We did not ask questions about the influence of the Party or of trade unions within the organizations, although these groups unquestionably have influence too. The influence of trade unions, for example, is especially pertinent to the workers' councils, because unions are usually important in choosing slates of candidates for election to the councils. The influence of the Party operates primarily through its members in the enterprise. The Party can exercise significant influence, despite relatively low rates of membership, because membership in the Party is more likely for persons at higher levels in the organization. Thus the influence of managers, who are very likely to be Party members, reflects, to some extent, the influence of the Party. However, it would probably be incorrect to assume that Party influence through the manager or through other lines is absolute. The Party is only one among a number of sources of control over the enterprise. As an open system the organization is subject to many influences both internal and external.

[13] See also Emery and Thorsrud, *ibid.*

The results concerning the thirteen areas of decision making provide an interesting comparison with the "global" results presented above. Managers are perceived to exercise more control than any other group in twelve of the thirteen areas. The exception occurs in the assignment of tasks to employees, where the head of the economic unit is perceived to be most influential, followed closely by supervisors.

Table 2 is an attempt to systematize some of the differences among control patterns in the thirteen areas. These areas were chosen to fall roughly into two

TABLE 2 Amount of Control by Six Hierarchical Groups That Is Above (+) and Below (−) Median for the Respective Groups in Thirteen Areas of Decision Making

	Hierarchical groups					
	1	2	3	4	5	6
	Managers	Managing board	Workers' council	Heads of economic units	Supervisors	Workers
Business policy						
1. Approving annual production plan	+	+	+	−	−	−
2. Fixing prices	−	+	+	−	−	−
3. Purchasing new machines	+	+	+	−	+	+
4. Building new shop	−	+	+	−	−	+
5. Allocation of net profit	+	+	+	−	−	+
6. Use of funds for collective consumption	−	+	+	−	−	−
7. Wages and salaries	+	+	+	+	+	+
Administration						
8. Assigning employees to jobs	+	−	−	+	+	−
9. Assigning tasks to employees	−	−	−	+	+	+
10. Fixing work standards	−	−	−	+	+	+
11. Hiring	+	−	−	+	−	−
12. Firing	−	−	−	+	+	+
13. Disciplining workers	+	−	−	+	+	−

categories. The first seven rows in the table refer to areas of business policy; the rest concern administrative issues. A plus sign signifies that the amount of influence by a hierarchical group (columns) in a particular area (rows) is above the median influence by that group in all areas. Thus we see in column 1 that the relatively great control that managers exercise is diversified among the two categories, policy and administration. This is consistent with the managers' roles in the two hierarchies, although one might question the advisability of managers concerning themselves to such a high degree with questions of hiring, disciplining, and assigning employees to jobs. This appears to be a continuation by managers of their traditional approach to control. On the other hand, managing boards and workers' councils stress policy areas, and heads of economic units and supervisors exercise most of their control in administration. These facts are consistent with the formal roles of these groups. The workers as a group, like the managers, have a more diversified pattern of influence, although, as we have seen, their influence is relatively slight. All groups exercise a relatively high degree of control over wage determination (item 7), and this is an area of obvious interest to all organization members.

Table 3 presents perceptions by supervisors and nonsupervisors. Differences between these groups are not very great in the sample under investigation;

TABLE 3   Distribution of Actual and Ideal Control as Reported by Supervisors and Non-supervisors, Workers' University Sample, Zagreb

	Actual control perceptions by		Ideal control perceptions by	
	Supervisors (N = 20–21)	Nonsupervisors (N = 30–32)	Supervisors (N = 20–21)	Nonsupervisors (N = 31–33)
Managers	4.2	4.4	3.6	3.6
Managing board	3.4	3.6	4.3	4.4
Workers' council	3.7	3.9	4.8	5.0
Heads of economic units	3.0*	3.6	3.4	3.7
Supervisors	2.5	2.9	3.2	3.3
Workers	1.7	1.8	3.9	3.9

* $p < .05$.

there is a slight tendency for nonsupervisory personnel to report greater control by all levels, but only the difference relative to heads of economic units is found to be statistically significant ($p < .05$). Similarly, differences in ideals expressed by the supervisory and nonsupervisory respondents are slight and in the direction of greater control for most groups being proposed by nonsupervisory employees. However, none of these differences proves significant statistically. By and large the patterns perceived and desired by supervisors and nonsupervisors in this sample of respondents are quite similar. At the same time, differences between the actual and ideal distribution of control are striking, as reported by both groups. The absence of differences between supervisors and nonsupervisors should probably be interpreted with special caution, because these groups at the Workers' University may be more alike in education, skill, and other background characteristics than is ordinarily the case.

We can also take a look at differences between the perceptions of Party and non-Party members. We must, however, turn to a second sample, in which sufficient numbers of Party and non-Party members are available to permit comparison.[14] Data of this kind are available from a study of two departments, an old and a modern one, in a Serbian glass factory. The results of the comparisons in the new department (first half of Table 4) are similar to those between supervisors and nonsupervisors (Table 3). Both Party and non-Party members report an "oligarchic" distribution of control like those shown in Figure 1. Nonmembers, however, seem to report a slightly higher level of control by all levels, but none of the differences proves statistically significant ($p < .05$). Again, the ideal distribution reported by the respondents, Party and non-Party members alike, is more positively sloped than the actual distribution. Differences between these two groups in their expressed ideals are minimal.

The results in the old department (second half of Table 4) differ in some respects from those already discussed. The discrepancies between Party and non-Party members in this department appear sharper than those between Party and non-Party members in the new department and between supervisors and workers attending the Workers' University. We cannot be certain about the explanation for these discrepancies in the old department, although several facts about this department suggest themselves. The workers here are primarily glass blowers and blowers' helpers (as contrasted with machine operators in the modern department) who have learned their craft from their fathers in the traditional manner. The education level of these workers is lower than that in the new department—most are semiliterate—and they probably do not have a background of experience that gives them an adequate basis for responding to the questions. Party members in this department, on the other hand, are likely to have more formal education, and they are therefore better able to respond to questions of the kind posed here. Furthermore, they are likely to be more perceptive about the distribution of control in the plant, because, among other things, they tend more than non-Party members to have relationships with others outside the department. This is especially important in the old department, which is relatively self-contained and isolated. Non-Party members here are limited in their extradepartmental contacts and perceptions, and they may not, for these reasons, be able to provide valid judgments about control. At the same time, Party members in the old department do not offer a more presentable picture, politically, than non-Party members—

---

[14] In the Workers' University sample, only five respondents are non-Party members.

TABLE 4 Distribution of Actual and Ideal Control as Reported by Party and Non-Party Members in Two Departments, Serbian Glass Factory Samples

	Modern department				Old department			
	Actual control perceptions by		Ideal control perceptions by		Actual control perceptions by		Ideal control perceptions by	
	Party members ($N = 23$–24)	Non-Party members ($N = 27$–28)	Party members ($N = 23$–24)	Non-Party members ($N = 27$–28)	Party members ($N = 17$)	Non-Party members ($N = 33$–35)	Party members ($N = 17$)	Non-Party members ($N = 33$–36)
Managers	4.0	4.3	3.9	3.6	4.2*	3.3	3.9	3.8
Managing board	3.7	3.8	4.4	4.3	3.7	3.3	4.8*	4.1
Workers' council	3.5	3.8	4.6	4.6	3.6	3.2	4.7*	4.1
Heads of economic units	†	†	†	†	†	†	†	†
Supervisors	2.8	3.4	2.9	3.0	3.7	3.6	3.7	3.6
Workers	2.4	2.6	4.4	4.5	2.7	3.2	4.0*	4.5

* $p < .05$.
† No data available.

quite the contrary. This contributes to our belief that Party members in the old department are not only more knowledgeable about the control pattern in the plant, but that they are also prepared to report their perceptions with reasonable frankness.

DISCUSSION

Methodological implications

The Workers' University respondents in this study are a select group. They have relatively high skills, education, and aspirations. In all probability, a majority have been members of workers' councils and are reasonably knowledgeable about the processes of control in their plants. Most of them are therefore able to understand questions of the kind posed here, and they seem prepared, furthermore, to give meaningful answers. Some workers, however, especially those who have little formal education, are unable to answer these questions. This is apparent in the old department of the Serbian glass factory, where a number of such persons were questioned.[15] At the same time some respondents who are able to answer these questions may be reticent to do so or may answer in stereotyped ways.

The high proportion of Party members and supervisors in our sample may raise questions about possible biases of our respondents and their likelihood to answer questions wishfully or to distort responses intentionally so as to present a more acceptable picture. However, the rough comparisons that are possible between Party and non-Party respondents and between supervisors and nonsupervisors provide little support for this hypothesis, although we cannot reject it with certainty. The general character of the results, particularly the discrepancies between actual and ideal distribution, suggests that our respondents, by and large, answered the questions thoughtfully and frankly. In addition, our own observations of Yugoslav enterprises lead us to believe that the respondents, as a group, are providing a reasonably accurate picture of reality. Furthermore, the similarities between some of these data and those collected in the United States suggest that we are dealing with measures which have some stability and which are concerned with important and fairly universal organizational phenomena.

Yugoslav-American comparisons

We cannot know how well the data of this study apply to the Yugoslav industrial scene in general. Yet, consistencies within these data, and between these data and those collected in American organizations do provide a basis for the formulation of some tentative hypotheses that might be tested through

---

[15] A survey in an industrial plant in Slovenia with a large proportion of skilled and educated workers proved more encouraging in this respect, probably because the education level of workers and their sophistication about organizations is relatively high. Rus, *op. cit.*

further research. It is interesting to find for example, that the following quotation from the study by Smith and Tannenbaum of a large number of American organizations applies perfectly to our Yugoslav data:

> A *negatively sloped distribution of control occurs* [*in all the industrial*] *organizational units studied. It is also apparent that the ideals which members have concerning the pattern of control differ from the actual pattern in almost all cases. The ideal distribution of control is more positively sloped than the actual and the ideal level of total control is higher than the actual level in a large percentage of the organizational units. While members desire a more positively sloped distribution of control than they perceive, they do not wish to achieve this by reducing the control exercised by other levels. They are more inclined to increase the control exercised by most groups, especially their own. (Members desire an increase in the control exercised by the rank-and-file group in 99 percent of the organizational units examined.) This results in a higher level of ideal than actual total control in most organizations. It also results in the actual curve approaching most closely that of the ideal near the upper levels of the organization. It is at the level of the rank-and-file member that the greatest discrepancy between actual and ideal control, as reported by members, occurs.*

Some interesting differences are also apparent between the Yugoslav and American data. Ideal control is negatively sloped in all the American industrial organizations studied, although less so than the actual distribution, but it is positively sloped in the Yugoslav organizations studied. This difference becomes amplified when supervisory respondents are considered along with nonsupervisory. The supervisory groups studied in Yugoslavia indicate, along with the workers, a more positive ideal than actual slope. This is not true of the American data. Here officers indicate ideal distribution more positive than the actual in only 20 percent of the organizational units studied.[16] Doubtless the political emphasis placed on workers' control through the system of workers' self-management has an important effect on the responses of the Yugoslav supervisory personnel. On the other hand, the reluctance of supervisors in American industrial organizations to suggest more control for workers no doubt reflects the industrial-relations climate in this society. Table 5 summarizes, for purposes of comparison, some of the characteristics of the Yugoslav and American data.

Implications for the functioning of the Yugoslav enterprise

The ideal curves illustrated in this research represent, at least in one respect, a pattern of control that has been found in several American studies to be associated with criteria of organizational effectiveness. The ideal tends to be more polyarchic, to represent a higher degree of total control than the actual.

---

[16] Smith and Tannenbaum, unpublished report. By way of contrast these authors report that officers in 97 percent of Leagues in the League of Women Voters indicate ideal slopes more positive than the actual (Smith and Tannenbaum, *op. cit.*).

TABLE 5　Summary of Some Characteristics of Yugoslav and American Data*

	Yugoslav data	U.S. data
Sign of actual slope, hierarchy 1:		
Perceived by workers	Negative	Negative
Perceived by officers	Negative	Negative
Sign of actual slope, hierarchy 2:		
Perceived by workers	Negative	†
Perceived by officers	Negative	
Sign of ideal slope 1:		
Perceived by workers	Positive	Negative
Perceived by officers	Positive	Negative
Sign of ideal slope 2:		
Perceived by workers	Positive	†
Perceived by officers	Positive	
Ideal slope 1 more positive than actual:		
Perceived by workers	Yes	Yes
Perceived by officers	Yes	No
Ideal slope 2 more positive than actual:		
Perceived by workers	Yes	†
Perceived by officers	Yes	
Ideal total control 1 greater than actual:		
Perceived by workers	Yes	Yes
Perceived by officers	Yes	No
Ideal total control 2 greater than actual:		
Perceived by workers	Yes	†
Perceived by officers	Yes	
Actual slope 1 perceived by officers more negative than actual slope 1 perceived by workers	No	No
Ideal slope 1 reported by officers more negative than ideal slope 1 reported by workers	No	Yes

* U.S. data obtained from Smith and Tannenbaum, *op. cit.*, and from an unpublished report by these authors. The general trends of the U.S. data are dichotomized in this table.
† No comparable data available.

Although it is not possible to develop, on the basis of a few American studies, principles that apply to industrial organizations in Yugoslavia, it seems a reasonable hypothesis that a realization of the ideal, more polyarchic pattern would be associated with an increase in organizational effectiveness. It is interesting in any event to find that the ideal, and more or less ideologically sanctioned distribution of control, conforms in certain important respects to what is found empirically in the United States to be associated with effective performance. It is interesting to find too, that, for whatever reasons, our respondents are taking a "constructive" approach to control. They see the desirability of change, but it is change in the direction of "more organization," not less.

The achievement of more organization in Yugoslav enterprises is beset with serious obstacles, not least of which are the agricultural and, to some extent, feudal traditions that have existed there. An industrial work force is only now being created. It is not, by American or Western European standards highly trained, educated, or sophisticated. One might expect that a system of workers' self-management would be more successful with a work force better equipped and more highly disposed toward it. However, the education level of the country will rise, and this should contribute to a more sophisticated work force.[17] In addition, workers' universities are providing training to limited numbers of workers that may help them better understand the technical, economic, and administrative problems of their organizations. These developments may in time provide better circumstances for the effective functioning of workers' self-management and for the movement of the actual curves closer to the ideal. We have seen, for example, that skilled workers are likely to be more influential than unskilled.

The "economic unit" has been introduced into Yugoslav plants as one attempt to reduce the discrepancy between actual and ideal control. This functional unit, with its prerogatives and autonomy, was intended as a means for workers to exercise more direct control over some of the circumstances of their work lives. However, the immediate effect of this system, like that of workers' councils themselves, may have been to increase workers' aspirations regarding control and hence to increase the ideal control by workers more than the actual. A change in the latter may require more time.

An alternate approach to increasing control by workers was tried earlier by reducing some management prerogatives. This assumed that decreasing the control by managers would increase that by workers. However, this proved a mistaken assumption. Nonetheless, it is reasonable to think that some adjustment on the part of managers may be necessary in expediting greater control by workers. We have seen that managers comprise a crucial group in the Yugoslav enterprise. Our data also point to particular aspects of the manager's role, as he now plays it, that may represent an impediment to the development of a more polyarchic and effective system, and we should like to speculate briefly about this point.

Managers may not have fully accepted the redefinition of their functions that the new industrial system requires. Many managers are still playing, to some extent, the traditional role of "master," holding on to prerogatives of interpersonal control—hiring, disciplining, and assigning employees to jobs—that really should not be part of their job description. These are administrative

---

[17] Although the education level of the population as a whole is rising, that of the industrial work force is probably standing still at the moment. This is due to growth in industrialization and to the movement of poorly educated rural persons into factories. Education will probably catch up with the work force as this influx slows down.

details that are best left to others. Managers might move in the direction of a more appropriate role definition that could include, first, greater concentration in the area of business policy rather than administration, opening up opportunities for subordinates to exercise control in the latter area. But this move might be extended by broadening, not reducing, the scope of managerial power in the direction of what Selznick calls "organizational statesmanship."[18] Managers would think in broad value terms; in terms of the "mission" of their organization, of its long-range future and of its general impact in the larger society. Managers would devote themselves to problems of formulating general policy objectives and plans. They would help guide their organizations, as Selznick suggests, by embodying policy values into the structures of their organizations. This is a role quite different from that in which managers dissipate their energies disciplining workers. But it does not mean that managers are to be less influential—quite the contrary. It means extending the scope of management power and that of the organization itself into the community and into the larger society. It implies a more powerful organization externally and a more integrated polyarchic system within.[19] This conversion of enterprises into "institutions," to use Selznick's term, or into "associations," to use a term in current usage in Yugoslavia, has implications for the character of the larger society as much as for organizations themselves. It implies a polycentric society in which its many institutions are important centers of power through which members can have influence extending beyond their immediate work lives.[20]

CONCLUSIONS

The Yugoslav industrial scene is in a state of flux. New laws are being introduced that bear directly on the control structure of firms, and workers, who are only now being introduced into industrial life, together with old hands, must adjust to these changing conditions. It seems a reasonable hypothesis that, when the workers'-council system was introduced fifteen years ago, the discrepancies between the ideal (indicated in this paper) and the actual distributions (then existent) in the plants studied were greater than they are now, because the actual distributions were more negative than they are

---

[18] Philip Selznick, *Leadership in administration*, New York: Harper & Row, 1957.

[19] The growth of internal organization power assumes a variable total amount of power or control in a system, although we recognize this as a controversial assumption: "The dominant tendency in the literature, for example, in Lasswell and Wright Mills, is to maintain explicitly or implicitly that power is a zero-sum phenomenon, which is to say that there is a fixed quantity of power in any relational system and hence any gain of power on the part of A must by definition occur by diminishing the power at the disposal of other units B, C, D. . . . There are, of course, restricted contexts in which this condition holds, but I shall argue that it does not hold for total systems of a sufficient level of complexity" (pp. 232–233)—Talcott Parsons, On the concept of political power, *Proc. Amer. Phil. Soc.*, **107** (3), 1963, 232–262. See Chap. 1 of this book for a detailed discussion.

[20] This is consistent with the notion, expressed by some Yugoslav sociologists, that the system of workers self-management is the central institution of Yugoslav society. Jose Goricar, Radnicko samoupravljanje kao drustvena institucija, *Sociologija*, no. 1, 1965, pp. 5–17. Paper presented at the symposium of the Yugoslav Sociological Association on Social Self-government, Split, Feb. 11–13, 1965.

now. Although it is impossible to document this interpretation within the framework of the present data, we probably see a reflection in them of some change in the direction of meeting the ideal.

However, the ideal still is beyond the actuality as our respondents and probably as most organization members see it. This is true particularly along the first hierarchy. This discrepancy between the ideal and the actual is attributable in part to the rather high ideals expressed by the respondents. For example, discrepancies are smaller in the American industrial organizations studied, not because the actual curves are more positive, but because the ideal are more negative. These high positive ideals expressed in the data reflect new social values emerging in contemporary Yugoslavia. Although it is difficult to know how large a segment of the work force is represented by the sample, it seems reasonable to think that it represents an important segment and that many organization members are no doubt aware of these large discrepancies and feel some sense of disillusionment and frustration. For example, one of the authors discussed with a clerical worker her dislike of the control distribution in her firm and particularly the relatively high control exercised by the manager. When it was suggested to her that managers might have relatively high influence in American plants too, she replied: "Yes, but there's a difference. It was that way once here too, but we didn't claim to be a socialist society." The image of Yugoslavia as a socialist society probably has a bearing on the ideals and aspirations that organization members express regarding control.

The results of this study seem to us an encouraging first step in the development of research tools designed to measure a vital aspect of the functioning of Yugoslav organizations. Research of this kind can be extended to trace changes in the character of Yugoslav enterprises as they evolve from their present stage of development. This kind of data can provide one index of the success of attempts to introduce and expedite workers' self-management. Further research on the relationship between perceived patterns of control and criteria of organizational effectiveness is also called for, and we have reason to predict that some of the relationships found in American organizations will hold up in Yugoslav organizations too. We see this research, not only as a means of acquiring some knowledge about the functioning of Yugoslav organizations, but also as part of the process of broadening the basis for scientific generalization through research in widely differing cultures and political systems.

PART *2*
————————

This section delves into relationships between aspects of control and perform-ance suggested in the previous chapters. In Chapter 7, Bowers investigates, in insurance agencies, the relationships between aspects of control and each of seven criteria of performance defined factor-analytically. In Chapter 8, Yuchtman correlates indices of control with criteria of performance measured at two points in time in order to determine whether variations in control pre-cede those in performance. Analyses of this kind may be helpful in determin-ing whether the statistical associations found between control and perform-ance imply that control causes performance or vice versa. Smith and Brown consider, in Chapter 9, how control and communication may jointly affect criteria of organizational performance, and, in Chapter 10, Smith and Ari attempt to explain how control affects performance through the norms, or uniformities of behavior, that control creates. Chapter 11 presents the results of a field experiment in which Smith and Jones attempt to test aspects of Likert's model of participative management. In this model, patterns of control are part of a set of intervening variables that help explain organizational performance.

The next three chapters pursue a question of methodological and concep-tual significance. Do the correlations observed when employing measures based on responses of organization members truly represent the effects of control as an aspect of organizational structure, or do they simply represent relationships among the perceptions of organization members? In Chapter 12,

Tannenbaum and Bachman, building on the work of Blau and others, offer several statistical approaches for determining the existence of such "structural" as opposed to "individual" effects. Analyzing data from a voluntary organization, Tannenbaum and Smith, in Chapter 13, find evidence for the existence of both structural and individual effects, and they suggest a number of conditions under which each is more likely to be manifest. In Chapter 14, Bachman, Smith, and Slesinger present similar results from a study of sales organizations. They also introduce measures of bases of power (reasons why subordinates comply with the requests of their superiors) into their analyses, and they show how they relate to the total amount of control and to criteria of performance. In Chapter 14, Bachman, Bowers, and Marcus extend the analysis of bases of power into five groups of organizations, including colleges, a utility company, and industrial and clerical organizations, showing how these organizations differ in the prevalence of the bases of power employed and how such prevalence relates, in some of the organizations, to the total amount of control and to criteria of performance.

7

ORGANIZATIONAL CONTROL IN AN INSURANCE COMPANY*

David G. Bowers

The results of a number of studies summarized by Smith and Tannenbaum[1] suggest the hypothesis that the total amount of control in an organization is related positively to organizational effectiveness. This finding is interpreted as confirming the notion that relatively high total control implies a more "tight knit" organization, one in which there is a greater degree of interaction and influence within and between hierarchical levels and greater mutual understanding and uniformity in relevant attitudes and behaviors. It has also been suggested that this is associated with better coordination of efforts, higher motivation and identification, and more efficient effort toward attaining organizational objectives. The findings thus interpreted are squarely in opposition to those who argue that the fund of influence is limited and that greatest coordination and effectiveness comes from greatest centralization of limited resources of control in the hands of a single person or level.

Another finding of these studies is a direct relationship between positive slope of control (less steep increases in control as one goes up the organizational hierarchy) and effectiveness in voluntary organizations, but no such relationship is found in data from business organizations. It may be, however, that this reflects some important difference in the way in which increased influence accrues to various levels in these two types of organizations. Furthermore, it may be that in both types of organizations the relationship to effectiveness of increased total control can be attributed to that portion of the total increase which accrues to one crucial managerial or leadership level. This problem constitutes one question for investigation: whether the increased effectiveness which is observed in organizations with greater control is associated only with that portion of the total possessed by some key level of management, with the greater control attributed to other levels superfluous so far as effectiveness is concerned.

In the single sales organization reported in these studies (a group of automobile dealerships), no relationships of the type described above were obtained. This raises a second question: whether sales organizations are, in the effects of control, inherently different from other types of organizations. In

* Reprinted from *Sociometry*, Vol. 27, No. 2, June 1964, 230–244, with permission of the publisher and the author. (This article has been edited to eliminate overlap and to bring it into a consistent format with the other articles in this book. Certain portions have therefore been deleted or reworded. Ed.)

[1] Clagett G. Smith and Arnold S. Tannenbaum, "Organizational Control Structure: A Comparative Analysis," *Human Relations*, 16 (4, 1963), pp. 299–316 (in this book, Chap. 5).

their discussion of this case, Smith and Tannenbaum raise the possibility that performance in sales organizations depends, not so much upon integration and coordination, but upon independent, individual performance that in many cases may actually reflect rivalry or competition. An alternate possibility, also raised by Smith and Tannenbaum, is that the criterion measure in the particular study was inappropriate to a study of control. It would be useful, therefore, to see whether in another sales organization, similarly subject to the conditions of independent, individual performance, competition, and rivalry which existed in the organization already studied, the relationships obtained in studies of organizations of other kinds are upheld.

A third question arises from the measures of effectiveness used in past studies. Is the finding that total control relates to organizational effectiveness when one or two measures are used to reflect the latter upheld when an integrated criterion system is used, involving sub-components, systematically derived, of overall effectiveness?

These problems, plus several additional tests of the generality of the findings reported by Smith and Tannenbaum, form the focus of the present investigation. They may be restated more formally in the following manner:

1. Is total control positively related to overall rankings of agency excellence?
2. In what way is total control related to systematically derived components of this excellence, as reflected in factorial measures of performance and questionnaire measures of satisfaction?
3. Is agency excellence positively related to all component attributions which make up the total control measure; that is, is it the total amount of control, or the amount attributed to selected levels, which is positively related to excellence?

In addition to these major questions, there are several findings which earlier results would lead us to expect (see Chapter 5):

4. The typical slope of actual control should be negative.
5. The ideal control slope should be less negative than the actual control slope.
6. The ideal total control mean should be higher than the actual total control mean.
7. There should be differences in the perceptions of control by managers and agents.

PROCEDURE

The present investigation is a portion of a larger study in a leading life insurance company, forty of whose agencies were selected for examination in such a manner that twenty represent the top-performing echelon, as ranked by company officials, and twenty represent the middle-and-bottom portion of these rankings. Each agency is directed by a regional manager, who has territorial exclusiveness for the area encompassed by his contract. He, in turn, is responsible for contracting with agents to sell policies and service the territory. Certain of these agents are responsible directly to him; others are responsible to district managers, whose contracts are with the regional manager and who are responsible for some defined sub-portion of his territory or for supervision of some subsection of his agency force. There are, therefore, four hierarchical levels for nearly all agencies: the Home Office, Regional Manager, District Managers, and Agents.

Questionnaires were mailed out to all regional and district managers and to all agents in 1961. Eighty-three per cent of those contacted, or 920 individuals, responded. The format used in asking for questionnaire ratings of control in the organization deviated from the format used in the studies by Tannenbaum. Instead of:

In general, how much say or influence do you think each of the following groups or persons *actually have* (or "should have") on what goes on in your agency as a whole?

the question was rephrased,

In general, how much say or influence do you think each of the following groups or persons *actually have* (or "should have") on matters affecting the performance of your agency as a whole?

This change was made in response to complaints of ambiguity on the part of subjects involved in the pretesting of the questionnaire. It was felt at the time that there was little or no change in meaning, but considerable reduction in ambiguity, for these particular subjects, by this rephrasing of the question.

Mean total control, whether actual or ideal, was computed for each agency by adding up subjects' mean attribution to each of the four levels in the hierarchy (Home Office, Regional Manager, District Manager, Agents) across all four levels, then dividing by four. Slope constants were obtained in a manner slightly different from that used by Tannenbaum: a process of successive "smoothings" was used. For example, if A, B, C, and D represented successive levels in the hierarchy, the attributions for A and B were averaged, as were the attributions for C and D. The latter figure was then subtracted from the former and divided by the number of slopes (or differences) in the hierarchy to obtain the slope constant.

Agency performance was measured in two different ways: the overall rankings by company officials, used in selecting the sample of agencies, constitute a judgment of overall effectiveness. In addition to this, some seventy actual performance measures, taken from company records, were factor analyzed, resulting in seven orthogonal factors which account for 95 per cent of the variance present in the original list of seventy. These seven factors are:

Factor I, Agency development, Factor A—this reflects development of younger men, with an emphasis on low-cost, high-protection sales;

Factor II, Growth of Business—this measures growth in dollar volume over the preceding few years;

Factor III, Business Costs—this loads principally on business unit costs, with minor loadings on measures of renewal business costs;

Factor IV, Agency Development, Factor B—this reflects development of younger men, but with an emphasis on high-equity sales;

Factor V, Volume of Business—this is a measure of dollar volume for the agency during the preceding year;

Factor VI, Manpower Turnover—this measures change in agency staff, both in terms of acquisitions of new men and in terms of terminations of older staff;

Factor VII, Regional Manager's Personal Performance—a factor reflecting the extent to which the regional manager is putting energy into agency maintenance and development.

Organizational effectiveness may also be evaluated in terms of member satisfaction. Five indices of satisfaction were available, covering the areas of satisfaction with the company, satisfaction with the regional manager, satisfaction with fellow agents, satisfaction with the job, and satisfaction with income.

Satisfaction with the company was measured through overall evaluations by respondents of how well they think the company is run, whether they have a feeling of pride and loyalty toward the company, and what, in general, they think of the company.

Satisfaction with the regional manager was tapped through questions asking whether he is the kind of man they feel like working hard for, whether they have confidence and trust in him, and, all in all, how satisfied they are with him.

Satisfaction with fellow agents was measured through questions asking how well they like their fellow agents and how this agency compares with other agencies in the company.

Satisfaction with the job was measured by averaging ratings by a respondent of how much he liked or disliked various aspects of his work.

Satisfaction with income was measured by a rating of whether this job provides agents with as good an income as they are entitled to in comparison with other companies or occupations that they might have gone into.

RESULTS AND DISCUSSION

Let us first consider the question of whether actual total control relates positively and significantly to overall agency rankings of excellence. Figure 1 presents results in graphic form: the actual control curve is higher at all points for the twenty top agencies than for the twenty medium-and-low ranked agencies. Confirming this, is a rank-order (rho) coefficient of correlation be-

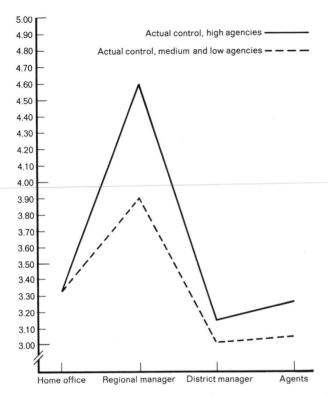

FIGURE 1 *Comparison of control distributions in high and low perfor-*
mance agencies.

tween these two measures of .46, which is significant beyond the .001 level
(two-tail test). The general proposition is again confirmed, therefore.

Turning to the second question, which suggests a refinement of the overall
finding, Table 1 presents product-moment (Pearson) correlation coefficients
of agents' estimates of total control with specific measures of effectiveness.

The data in Table 1 show that there is a significant, positive relationship of
agents' estimates of total actual control to every measure of satisfaction used.
There are, in addition, significant relationships to two performance factors,
such that a high level of actual control is associated with less development of
younger men through such techniques as handing them a rate book and telling
them to go sell term insurance (Agency Development, Factor A), and with a
lower level of business costs. None of the remaining performance factors show
significant relationships to ratings of total actual control. The conclusion,
therefore, in answer to the second question is that, so far as these data are in-
dicative, total actual control relates positively and generally to satisfaction,
and in a positive direction (although the coefficients are themselves negative)
to two factorial measures of performance.

The third question asks whether agency excellence is related positively to

TABLE 1   Correlation of Agents' Estimates of Total Actual Control with Measures of Organizational Effectiveness ($N = 40$ Agencies)

Measure of effectiveness	Coefficient
Factor I, agency development A	−.32*
Factor II, growth of business	.06
Factor III, business costs	−.55**
Factor IV, agency development B	−.25
Factor V, volume of business	−.20
Factor VI, manpower turnover	.05
Factor VII, regional mgr's personal perf.	−.15
Satisfaction with company	.36**
Satisfaction with regional manager	.53**
Satisfaction with fellow agents	.36**
Satisfaction with job	.46**
Satisfaction with income	.32*

* $P < .05$, 1-tail.   ** $P < .01$, 1-tail.

TABLE 2   Rank-order (Rho) Correlation of Overall Effectiveness with Amount of Control Attributed to Each Level by Agents

Attribution	Coefficient
Home office	.21
Regional manager	.59*
District manager	.13
Agents	.20

* $P < .001$, 2-tail test.

all of the component attributions which make up the total control measure. Table 2 presents the correlation of overall effectiveness with the amount of control which agents attribute to each of the four hierarchical levels. Only one of the coefficients is statistically significant: overall effectiveness relates even more strongly to the amount of control attributed to the regional manager that it does to the total amount of control.

Does this mean that total control as a concept is a statistic which conceals more fundamental, underlying relationships? Considering the data already presented, does this mean that the relationship of total control to overall effectiveness is nothing more than a reflection of a more basic relationship between the control of the regional manager and business costs?[2]

Tables 3 and 4 present data which indicate that this is not the case. From Table 3 it is apparent that overall effectiveness ratings reflect significantly only four of the subsidiary measures of effectiveness: in other words, in making these rankings company officials apparently considered principally volume of

TABLE 3   Rank-order (Rho) Correlation of Overall Effectiveness with Measures of Performance and Satisfaction

Effectiveness measure	Coefficient
Factor I, agency development A	.26
Factor II, growth of business	.04
Factor III, business costs	—.44*
Factor IV, agency development B	.00
Factor V, volume of business	.53*
Factor VI, manpower turnover	—.11
Factor VII, regional mgr.'s pers. perf.	.09
Satisfaction with company	.00
Satisfaction with regional manager	.53*
Satisfaction with fellow agents	.81*
Satisfaction with job	.13
Satisfaction with income	.32

* $P < .05$, 2-tail.

business, business costs, satisfaction with the regional manager, and satisfaction with fellow agents, the latter two measures probably constituting a rough "morale" estimation.

Table 4 shows that business costs, far from relating significantly only to the amount of control attributed to the regional manager, relate significantly to all attributions *except* that for the regional manager. Furthermore, the data suggest that a similar situation exists with regard to satisfaction with the regional manager and with satisfaction with fellow agents, since most of the other relationships are significant, even though the relationships to the regional manager's control are larger in size. In other words, in three of the four cases, it is the general level of total control, more than any specific attribution, which relates significantly to the subsidiary measures of effectiveness. In the

[2] The hypothesis relating total control to performance simply states that the total amount of control in an organization, *regardless of source*, is related to organizational performance. The question that Bowers raises therefore does not imply a questioning of the hypothesis as stated—although the question is certainly an interesting one. Ed.

TABLE 4 Correlation of Amount of Control Attributed to Each Level by Agents with Measures of Performance and Satisfaction

Effectiveness measure	Attribution			
	Home office	Reg. mgr.	Dist. mgr.	Agents
Factor I, agency development A	−.16	−.34*	−.27	−.09
Factor II, growth of business	.17	−.15	−.12	.28
Factor III, business costs	−.51*	−.26	−.32*	−.39*
Factor IV, agency development B	−.32*	−.13	−.06	−.19
Factor V, volume of business	−.31*	.18	−.28	−.13
Factor VI, manpower turnover	.28	−.09	−.11	.08
Factor VII, reg. mgr.'s pers. perf.	−.12	.15	−.23	−.15
Satisfaction with company	.32*	.13	.14	.42*
Satisfaction with regional manager	.39*	.62*	.11	.35*
Satisfaction with fellow agents	.20	.46*	−.02	.36*
Satisfaction with job	.56*	.23	.20	.23
Satisfaction with income	.31*	.17	.07	.35*

* $P < .05$, 2-tail.

fourth case, that of volume of business, nothing but a negative relationship of marginal significance with control attributed to the home office is generated.

It would appear, therefore, that overall effectiveness relates as strongly as it does to the control attributed by agents to the regional manager because both of these two variables relate to a third pair of variables, satisfaction with fellow agents and satisfaction with the regional manager.

TABLE 5 Control Curve Slopes as Perceived by Managers and Agents

Raters	Actual slope	Ideal slope	S.D.$_M$	t	p
Regional managers	+.15	+.21	.057	1.05	——
District managers	−.20	+.09	.049	2.24	<.05
Agents	−.32	−.15	.043	3.95	<.001

The answers to the fourth and fifth questions presented earlier are that the typical slope of actual control is negative, and that the ideal slope is in each of the three cases less negative (or more positive) than is the actual control slope, although the difference is statistically significant only for agents' and for district managers' perceptions, as indicated in Table 5.

Table 6 presents data relevant to the sixth question. These data indicate that, although all three differences between actual and ideal control ratings are in the predicted direction, only one difference, that for the perceptions of agents, is significantly larger than chance.

The last question deals with differences in perceptions of control among hierarchical levels. Tables 5, 6, and 7 contain data relevant to this hypothesis. Table 7 demonstrates that, although the three groups are relatively close together in their estimates of the actual control of upper hierarchical levels,

TABLE 6 Mean Actual and Ideal Total Control as Perceived by Managers and Agents

Raters	Mean actual	S.D.$_M$	Mean ideal
Regional managers	3.87	.42	4.01
District managers	3.47	.36	3.74
Agents	3.41	.29	3.93*

* .05 $> P >$ .025, 1-tail.

TABLE 7 Significance of the Difference between Perceptions by Managers and Agents of Amount of Control Attributed to Various Hierarchical Levels

Comparison	Home office		Reg. mgrs.		Dist. mgrs.		Agents	
	t or CR	df	t or CR	df	t or CR	df	t or CR	df
Regional mgrs. vs. dist. mgrs. (actual)	.08	177	.47	176	2.18*	147	4.69***	176
Regional mgrs. vs. agents (actual)	1.17	744	1.05	746	2.08*	360	4.68***	740
Dist. mgrs. vs. agents (actual)	2.00*		1.20		1.42		.41	
Regional mgrs. vs. dist. mgrs. (ideal)	.82	179	.58	179	1.31	151	4.30***	179
Regional mgrs. vs. agents (ideal)	2.65**	746	.17	749	1.30	366	2.76**	747
Dist. mgrs. vs. agents (ideal)	2.83**		.57		.09		3.61***	

* $P <$ .05, 2-tail.   ** $P <$ .01, 2-tail.   *** $P <$ .001, 2-tail.

they disagree markedly in their perceptions of actual control at the two lower levels. Agents tend to attribute more actual control to the home office than do the two groups of managers. On the other hand, regional managers tend to attribute more actual control to agents and district manager than these groups see themselves as having. These data suggest that respondents at one end of the hierarchy tend to overevaluate the amount of control attributable to groups at the other end.

On the other hand, more consensus exists at the two intermediate levels on ideal control than at either extreme: that is, respondents of all levels tend to agree in what they see as ideal for district managers and for regional managers, but to disagree in what they feel is desirable for the home office and for agents.

There are differences too in the perception of ideal control. Agents tend to desire more control for the home office than do managers; regional managers and agents tend to desire somewhat more control for agents than for district managers; in this expression of their wishes both groups differ from the district managers, who wish for themselves somewhat more control than they wish for agents.

In Table 5 it may be observed that both the actual and ideal slopes become increasingly negative as one goes down the hierarchy of respondents: the highest echelon, regional managers, actually evaluates the curve as positive, whereas the agents see it to be fairly negative.

Table 6 indicates that the mean amount of total control reported declines as we go down the hierarchy of respondents: regional managers see somewhat greater control than do agents. Ideal control shows a fairly similar pattern, with the exception that the intermediate level of respondents, district managers, prefer the least amount of control.

CONCLUSION

These results indicate that, far from disappearing in the context of a sales organization, the relationship of total control to overall organizational effectiveness can be found in at least some sales organizations. The fact that the hypothesis can be verified in even one sales organization which is dispersed geographically and tied closely to a commission system of reward, suggests that the negative finding related by Smith and Tannenbaum may be more reasonably explained as a problem in study design or criterion selection.

These additional findings confirm those from earlier studies employing the control graph and suggest that the generalizations inferred from these studies do apply at least to this sales organization: the typical slope of control in this business organization, as in those studied earlier, is negative, and the ideal slope as reported by all categories of respondents is, as it was in previous studies, less negative than the actual slope.

The present study also demonstrates that, at least in this one instance, total control as a variable does not relate equally to all possible organizational end-products. Instead, higher total control in this study is related positively to all forms of satisfaction measured, and to one style of organizational development, and is related negatively to business costs. It is not related to business growth, volume of business, or manpower turnover.

The last major point to consider is that the total control index, not any of its components singly, bears the crucial relation to effectiveness. This provides at least the beginning of an answer to those who would complain that "democratic" distribution of control is illusory, that it is only the portion given to certain individuals which is useful. Instead, it would appear that the better coordination, improved communication, and whatever other intermediate results are presumed to flow from greater total actual control depend upon a higher level of this control at all levels in the organization.

SUMMARY

The hypothesis that total control is related positively to overall organizational effectiveness is tested in a sample of forty agencies of a life insurance company. Evaluation of levels of control, obtained by mail-out questionnaire, are compared with questionnaire measures of satisfaction and with measures of performance derived from company records. Differences among various perceptions are also evaluated. The following conclusions may be drawn from the findings. 1) The general hypothesis is sustained: total actual control does relate positively to overall organizational effectiveness. 2) Total control does not, however, seem to relate positively (or negatively) to all measured aspects of organizational effectiveness. It relates to all forms of satisfaction measured, to cost performance, and to a particular style of organizational development. It does not relate significantly to growth of business, volume of business, or manpower turnover. 3) It is the total control figure, not any of its component attributions singly, which bears the crucial relation to effectiveness. 4) The typical slope of control, as in the studies reported by Smith and Tannenbaum (*op. cit.*) is negative. 5) The ideal slope is, for all three categories of respondents, less negative than the actual slope. 6) There is a slight tendency, significant only for the largest group of respondents, for the mean ideal total control to be higher than the mean actual total control. 7) There are differences in the perception of control by various hierarchical levels of respondents, with some suggestion that attributions from opposite ends of the hierarchy tend to be disproportionately high.

8

CONTROL IN AN INSURANCE COMPANY: CAUSE OR EFFECT*

Ephraim Yuchtman

The literature on organizations is relatively rich in data demonstrating statistical relationships between sociopsychological variables on the one hand and measures of organizational performance on the other. In their discussion of such relationships, behavioral scientists tend to assume, implicitly or explicitly, that variations in performance are causally determined by the organizational variables with which they are related. This assumption is also made in studies about organizational influence structure and control. Smith and Tannenbaum (1965), for example, conclude that "Research in labor unions and industrial and voluntary organizations suggests that concerted effort, and consequently the effectiveness of these organizations, may depend upon the manner in which control is distributed within them" (p. 265). However, the notion that performance is the "end result" of preceding sociopsychological processes cannot be taken for granted. This is evident from Farris's (1966) recent study of the scientific performance of engineers from three laboratories of a large industrial organization. Using a method for detecting causality from survey data, Farris found that several organizational factors cause at least one kind of scientific performance. His most striking finding is that "in every instance performance was found to cause the organizational factor with which it was associated" (p. 144); moreover, there was no case in which the causal impact of the sociopsychological factor was stronger than the influence of performance on that factor, and in several instances performance was the primary or even the sole cause. Thus, performance was found to cause influence (the extent to which the engineer can influence his work goals), but the converse did not hold.

Data from the study reported by Bowers in the preceding chapter provide a means by which inferences concerning the direction of causality in that study may be drawn. The data include measures of performance taken at two points in time: one at a time immediately preceding the measures of control and another at a time approximately one year later. If control causes performance, variations in control should precede, in time, variations in performance.[1] Hence the correlations between control structure measured at time 1 and measures of performance at time 2 should be greater than those measured at the same time.

---

* Unpublished paper.

[1] This assumes a time lag between control as a cause and its effect on performance.

For criteria of performance we have used the agencies' scores on ten orthogonal factors extracted from seventy-six performance measures taken from the company's records.[2] The ten factors, together with their "indicator" variables are listed in Table 1.

TABLE 1 Performance Factors: Insurance Agency Organizations

Factor	Assigned name	Indicator variables
1.	Business volume	Number of policies in force, year end New insurance sold, dollar volume Renewal premiums collected, dollars Number of lives insured, year end Agency manpower, number of agents
2.	Production cost	Production cost per new policy Production cost per $1,000 of insurance Production cost per $100 of premium
3.	New-member productivity	Average productivity per new agent Ratio of new agent (less than 5 years service) versus old agent productivity
4.	Youthfulness of members	Ratio of productivity of younger members to agency total Ratio of younger (under 35) to total membership
5.	Business mix	Average premium per $1,000 Percentage of new policies with quarterly payments Percentage of business in employee trust
6.	Manpower growth	Net change in manpower during year Ratio of net change to initial manpower
7.	Management emphasis	Manager's personal commissions
8.	Maintenance cost	Maintenance cost per collection Maintenance cost per $100 premium collected
9.	Member productivity	Average new business volume per agent
10.	Market penetration	Insurance in force per capita Number of lives covered per 1,000 insurables

Table 2 reveals that the measures of control tend to correlate more strongly with performance in the subsequent year than in the same year. More specifically, only one of the correlations between total control and factors of performance proves statistically significant when these variables are measured in 1961, but six correlations are significant when the performance factors are

[2] A detailed account of the factor-analytic procedure and the conceptual meaning of its outcomes is given in E. Yuchtman, "A Study of Organizational Effectiveness," unpublished doctoral dissertation, The University of Michigan, 1966. Because we employed a technique of factor analysis different from that of Bowers (1964), we found a somewhat different set of factors. Nonetheless the results of our correlational analyses are similar in their implications to those of Bowers.

TABLE 2   Relationship between Influence Variables and Criteria of Performance

Factor	Assigned name	Correlation between total control in 1961 and performance in		Correlation between slope* in 1961 and performance in	
		1961	1962	1961	1962
1.	Business volume	27	31†	−14	−16
2.	Production cost	−14	−30†	−11	−08
3.	New-member productivity	12	30†	28	39†
4.	Youthfulness of members	26	33†	−11	−01
5.	Business mix	22	28	03	27
6.	Manpower growth	18	34†	−23	−11
7.	Management emphasis	−16	−06	−50†	−54†
8.	Maintenance cost	−18	−13	05	02
9.	Member productivity	01	−11	−02	03
10.	Market penetration	50†	61‡	00	−02

* Negative slope scores imply greater control exercised by upper compared with lower levels.
† Significant at the .05 level (one-tailed).
‡ Significant at the .01 level (one-tailed).

measured a year later.[3] As in an unpublished analysis by Bowers, the correlations between "slope" and performance tend not to be clearly related to performance, either in 1961 or in 1962. The above results appear to be consistent with the argument that the influence structure is playing some causal role with respect to organizational performance. However, they do not rule out the possibility of a circular relationship, namely, that performance also has an effect on control. Thus, although control may be both a cause and an effect of performance, we feel reasonably confident that in these organizations it is at least a cause.

Studies of organizational control illustrate the general problem of understanding causation in organizational behavior. Our knowledge of causal relationships is very limited indeed. A number of researchers have conducted experimental studies, especially field experiments, to learn about the causal impacts of various organizational factors. The studies reported by Morse and Reimer (1956) and Marrow, Bowers, and Seashore (1967) illustrate the fruitfulness of the experimental method in this respect. A complementary research strategy, however, may be to obtain survey data that allow causal interpreta-

[3] Measures of performance during 1957 are available, and they allow correlations with measures of control in 1961. In general correlations between the 1957 performance scores and control measured in 1961 are lower than those shown in Table 2. However, the relatively long (four-year) interval between the measures, rather than the sequence (performance-control), may explain the lack of significant results here. Hence we cannot take the low correlations to provide very strong evidence against the possibility that performance may cause control.

tions. In recent years several nonexperimental models of causal inference have been developed (Blalock, 1961; Pelz and Andrews, 1964; Duncan, 1966). These methods need further elaboration in order to be usefully employed as working models; yet, organizational researchers can already obtain much help and guidance from studying such models and applying them to their data. It appears also that future research should be directed toward longitudinal studies, because data collected over time lend themselves more readily than cross-sectional studies to causal interpretations.

REFERENCES

Blalock, H. M. (1961). *Causal inferences in nonexperimental research.* Chapel Hill, N. C.: The University of North Carolina.

Bowers, D. G. (1964). Organizational control in an insurance company. *Sociometry,* **27** (2), 230–244 (in this book, Chap. 7).

Duncan, O. D. (1966). Path analysis: sociological examples. *Amer. J. Sociol.,* **72** (1), 1–16.

Farris, G. F. (1966). *A causal analysis of scientific performance.* Unpublished doctoral dissertation, The University of Michigan.

Marrow, A. J., Bowers, D. G., and Seashore, S. E. (1967). *Management by participation.* New York: Harper & Row.

Morse, N., and Reimer, E. (1956). The experimental change of a major organizational variable. *J. abnorm. Soc. Psychol.,* **52,** 120–129.

Pelz, D. C., and Andrews, F. M. (1964). Detecting causal priorities in panel study data. *Amer. Sociol. Rev.,* **29** (6), 836–848.

Smith, C. G., and Tannenbaum, A. S. (1965). Some implications of leadership and control for effectiveness in a voluntary association. *Human Relations,* **18** (3), 265–272.

9

COMMUNICATION STRUCTURE
AND CONTROL STRUCTURE
IN A VOLUNTARY ASSOCIATION*

Clagett G. Smith
Michael E. Brown[1]

The system of communication and control is of central importance for the functioning of organizations. To be effective, it requires adequate information transfer, high quality decision-making, and the implementation of decisions by motivated members. However, different investigators have focused upon different aspects of the control-communication system, and in doing so, have raised a number of important issues concerning the organization of communication and control as it affects member motivation and organizational performance.[2] This paper addresses itself to some of these issues by considering the effective organization of communication and control in a voluntary political organization.

BACKGROUND OF THE PROBLEM

The communication approach

One approach has emphasized the gathering, processing, and dissemination of information as the basic factor in organizational performance. For instance, Bavelas and Barrett state that "organizational effectiveness is closely related to its effectiveness in handling information."[3] Both the results of small group and organization research indicate the importance of a free flow of information for understanding and consensus, problem-solving and decision-making, and member satisfaction. There is also reason to believe that the flow of information must follow a pattern of a centralized nature, in order to avoid confusion, indecision, or problems of coordination. While many current writers have stressed the importance of "upward" communication in hierarchical organiza-

* Reprinted from *Sociometry*, December 1964, Vol. 27, No. 4, with permission of the publisher and the authors. (This article has been edited to eliminate overlap and to bring it into a consistent format with the other articles in this book. Certain portions have therefore been deleted or reworded. Ed.)

[1] We gratefully acknowledge the valuable suggestions of Jerald G. Bachman, David G. Bowers, Glenn Jones, Philip M. Marcus, Martin Patchen, and Arnold S. Tannenbaum, and the assistance of Roberta Ann Levenbach and Dora Cafagna.

[2] By "communication" we simply mean the transmission of information from a source to a recipient, whether these be individuals, groups or organizations.

[3] Alex Bavelas and Dermot Barrett, "An Experimental Approach to Organizational Communication," *Personnel*, 27 (March, 1951), p. 367.

tions, Donald's findings[4] indicate that, at least in a voluntary, political association, a high degree of communication among rank-and-file members is associated with member support of the organization but not with organizational
effectiveness. Instead, frequent and reciprocal communication among officers
and between members and officers is the important correlate of organizational
effectiveness.

The power or control approach

A second approach has emphasized the structure and process of decision-
making and the motivational variables translating decisions into effective action. The basic factor is thought to be power, influence, or control. For instance, Mulder,[5] prompted by the apparently inconsistent findings in the
experimental studies of communication networks, asserts that it is the "decision structure" (the pattern of influence on decision-making) and not the
communication structure which determines the task performance of the group.

Traditional emphasis has been placed upon centralized control, or hierarchical structure, as crucial to the effective coordination of action and administration of organizations. Morse and Reimer, however, present evidence in support
of the hypothesis that an increased role in decision-making for the rank-and-
file (relative to the supervisory and managerial levels) leads to an increase
in their satisfaction and productivity.[6] Similar results have been observed in a
voluntary association.[7] More generally, the findings indicate that substantial
influence exercised by members or by leaders *and* members creates conditions
which contribute to more effective organization performance as well as higher
member satisfaction. The efficacy of this pattern of control apparently derives
from the fact that it facilitates contributions from all organization members
and helps to insure their coordination by a process of joint decision-making.[8]

Communication and control as an integrated process: the consistency hypothesis

A third approach implicit in the literature presupposes a recognition of the
complex problem of eliciting contributions from members through communicative exchange, and, at the same time, coordinating those contributions

---

[4] Marjorie N. Donald, "Some Concomitants of Varying Patterns of Communication in a Large Organization,"
unpublished doctoral dissertation, The University of Michigan, 1958.

[5] Mauk Mulder, "Communication Structure, Decision Structure, and Group Performance," *Sociometry*, 23
(March, 1960), pp. 1–14.

[6] Nancy C. Morse and Everett Reimer, "The Experimental Change of a Major Organizational Variable,"
Journal of Abnormal and Social Psychology, 52 (January, 1956), pp. 120–129. The hypothesis is based on the
rationale that the exercise of control by lower echelons is likely to bring with it greater acceptance of jointly
made decisions as well as an increased sense of responsibility and motivation to further the goals of the organization.

[7] Arnold S. Tannenbaum, "Control and Effectiveness in a Voluntary Organization," *American Journal of
Sociology*, 67 (July, 1961), pp. 33–46 (in this book, Chap. 4).

[8] Clagett G. Smith and Arnold S. Tannenbaum, "Organizational Control Structure: A Comparative Analysis,"
Human Relations, 16 (November, 1963), pp. 299–316 (in this book, Chap. 5); and Arnold S. Tannenbaum,

through effective control. According to this approach, the solution to the problem lies in the manner in which communication and control are interrelated. Simon has suggested that this interrelationship must take a particular form: "Decision centers must of necessity either coincide with or be in conjunction with communication centers."[9] This implies that there are two important processes involved: first, information must be transmitted to the control centers; and second, control must be exercised in making and implementing decisions. These joint requirements may be met when the communication structure and the control structure are consistent with one another.

One type of consistency might be represented by an arrangement in which there is a high level of member communication flowing to the hierarchical control centers. In turn, such control could provide effective coordination. The converse is also implied, *viz.*, that an organization in which control is decentralized must also develop a decentralized communication structure, i.e., a downward flow of information. We have already noted that decentralized control seems efficacious, in some instances, for eliciting member involvement and responsibility in implementing decisions. It is often under these circumstances that appropriate information is available for making decisions. If such information is coupled with adequate contributions by the formal leadership, it is likely to provide the basis for high quality and acceptance of decisions, as well as for efficient coordination of member effort at the appropriate level. On the other hand, an inconsistency between the communication and control structures, i.e., a centralized control structure and a downward flow of information or a decentralized control structure and an upward flow of information, would imply both decision-making in the absence of sufficient information, and, even if such information were available, a failure to coordinate it into effective decisions.

However, there are certain limitations to the consistency hypothesis as stated. A centralized control structure coupled with an upward flow of information, while permitting coordination of whatever member contributions there are, may lessen the free flow of information, discourage member contributions, and result in decisions made by the leaders which are not acceptable to the rank-and-file members. Similarly, a decentralized control structure with a downward flow of information may limit the use of information available within the organization, may impose difficult problems of coordination, and may result in decisions which do not reflect the interests of the leaders and/or the policies of the organization.

Likert and Maier have suggested that communication and control can be organized in a way which would maximize the contributions of all organization members and still achieve effective, coordinated, effort.[10] This is based on

---

"Control in Organizations: Individual Adjustment and Organizational Performance," *Administrative Science Quarterly*, 7 (September, 1962), pp. 236–257 (in this book, Chaps. 1 and 21).

[9] Herbert A. Simon, *Administrative Behavior*, New York: Macmillan, 1957, p. 306.

[10] Rensis Likert, *New Patterns of Management*, New York: McGraw-Hill, 1961; and Norman R. F. Maier, *Principles of Human Relations*, New York: Wiley and Sons, 1955.

the general principle that we have already discussed: the pattern of communication must be consistent with the pattern of control. However, their solution requires a *multi-directional* flow of information throughout the organization coupled with influence by members at *all* levels, the rank-and-file as well as the leaders. Decisions would be based on information and contributions of members at all levels within the organization. The free flow of information would provide the basis for more effective decisions and promote high member satisfaction. In turn, high mutual influence would tend to encourage the free flow of information and its use in decision-making. At the same time, mutual influence and joint decision-making would furnish a necessary basis for integrating the contributions and interests of all membershp levels and for coordinating action in implementing decisions. Despite the obvious advantages, the actual importance of this scheme for high organization performance is not altogether clear. A particular disadvantage is the fact that coordination of communication and control, i.e., feeding information from multiple sources to multiple control centers, may be difficult and in many instances inefficient.

HYPOTHESES

The specific hypotheses suggested by these alternative approaches may be summarized as follows:[11]

    I. *Communication Approach:* The basic variable in organizational functioning is the pattern of communication:
        a. Upward communication will be positively related to organizational effectiveness.
        b. Downward and/or multi-directional communication will be positively related to member satisfaction.
    II. *Control Approach:* The basic variable in organizational functioning is the structure of control:
        a. A high amount of control exercised by both leaders and members will be positively related to organizational effectiveness and member satisfaction.
        b. Decentralized control will be positively related to organizational effectiveness and member satisfaction.
    III. *Communication and Control, the Integrative Approach:* Communication and control are both important for effective organization functioning, particularly when they are consistent with one another.
        a. Consistency Hypothesis, Version I

---

[11] The hypotheses are formulated, furthermore, with reference to the specific nature of the organization to be examined, *viz.*, the League of Women Voters (to be discussed in the following section), and in terms of the findings previously obtained in this organization. See Tannenbaum, "Control and Effectiveness in a Voluntary Association," *op. cit.*; Smith and Tannenbaum, *op. cit.*; and Arnold S. Tannenbaum and Clagett G. Smith, "The Effects of Member Influence in an Organization: Phenomenology versus Organizational Structure," *Journal of Abnormal and Social Psychology*, 69 (October, 1964), pp. 401–410 (in this book, Chap. 13).

1. Centralized control coupled with upward communication or decentralized control coupled with downward communication will
   be more highly related to organization effectiveness than when
   communication does not flow to the control centers.
2. Decentralized control coupled with downward communication
   will be associated with the highest member satisfaction; centralized control coupled with upward communication will be associated with the lowest member satisfaction; communication which
   does not flow to the control centers will be associated with an
   intermediate degree of member satisfaction.

b. Consistency Hypothesis, Version II
1. Multi-directional communication coupled with a high amount
   of control exercised by both leaders and members will be associated with high organizational effectiveness and member satisfaction. Where this confluence of communication and control is
   lacking, there will be a corresponding lowering of effectiveness
   and satisfaction.

Research design

The organizational setting, research design, and measures of control and effectiveness are described in Chapter 4, pp. 60–64. The measure of slope described there is taken as an index of decentralization. Measures of communication in each league were based upon responses to questions ascertaining
how frequently the respondent transmitted information to members at various
hierarchical levels, including her own. The general question asked was:

How often do you give information (facts and ideas) concerning League
matters to the following persons? (Consider in your answer the information
which you give through discussions, at meetings, in private, by letter and
telephone.)

The persons in question included the league president, members of the board,
and other members of the local league. The alternatives ranged from "never"
to "several times a month or more often." Since members at all three levels in
the league answered this question, it was possible to measure the frequency of
communication in all directions from a given level. Judgments of respondents
at each level were averaged to form the following measures of communication:
the frequency of communication of the members to other members; of the
members to the board; of members to the president; of the president to the
members; of the board to the members. The validity of these measures is
attested to by the high correlations of each of these measures of information
transmission from a source to a recipient with corresponding measures of the
receipt of information by the recipient from the source.[12]

[12] See Donald, *op. cit.*

For each league, two measures of communication structure were derived from the basic measures, *viz.*, the distribution along a vertical dimension of communication between members and leaders, and the amount of multi-directional communication. The vertical distribution of communication was operationalized as the extent of upward communication *relative* to the extent of downward communication. This permitted the specification of the relative flow of information between members and leaders. This index was computed by determining the ratio of the amount of communication from the members to the president and from the members to the board members over the amount of communication from the president to the members and from the board members to the members. A high score would indicate a relatively high upward flow of information from the members to the leaders, while a low score would indicate a relatively high downward flow of information from the leaders to the members. The index of multi-directional communication in the local league, i.e., upward, downward, and sideward, was derived by summing the frequency of communication from the members to other members, from the members to the board, from the members to the president, from the president to the members, and from the board to the members.

Member satisfaction with the local league was measured by questions ascertaining members' willingness to support the league, i.e., to expend effort to prevent their local league from ceasing to function. This variable, essentially an index of member loyalty, was measured in terms of the following two questions, the responses to which were averaged to form an index.

1. "Suppose that as a result of strong opposition to the league within your community your local league was in real danger of folding up. How much effort would you be willing to spend in order to prevent this?"
2. "Suppose as a result of general member disinterest your local league were in real danger of folding up. How much effort would you be willing to spend in order to prevent this?"

Each of these questions is answered on a five-point scale from 1, "none," to 5, "a very great deal." The reliability of this index is .67.

RESULTS

Table 1 presents correlations of the measures of communication and control structure with league effectiveness and member loyalty. These results summarize, in part, those previously reported by Donald, Tannenbaum, and Smith and Tannenbaum.[13] Since size of the local league is significantly correlated with the measures of communication and control structure and is highly correlated with League effectiveness ($r = .74$), all correlations are partial correlations holding log size constant. In view of the effects of size, and, partic-

---

[13] Donald, *op. cit.*; Tannenbaum, *op. cit.*; Smith and Tannenbaum, *op. cit.*

ularly, the different types of organization of communication and control processes in different size leagues, the results are also presented for small and large leagues separately. (The small leagues range in size from 20 to 200 members; the large leagues are those having from 200 to 3,000 members.)

Considering league effectiveness as the dependent variable, it seems that the structure of control rather than communication is the significant correlate for the entire sample of leagues. Both the extent of decentralized control and the total amount of control are correlated with league effectiveness to a significant degree ($r = .31$, $p < .001$; $r = .29$, $p < .002$, respectively). Degree of upward (or, conversely, downward) communication is not correlated with league effectiveness. However, the amount of multi-directional communication is significantly, although only moderately, correlated with league effectiveness ($r = .15$).

In contrast, when the dependent variable considered is member loyalty, the communication structure appears to be the more important variable. Amount of multi-directional communication is significantly related to member loyalty ($r = .38$, $p < .001$). At the same time, it is clear that the distribution and amount of control are involved. Decentralized control and the total amount of control are significantly correlated with member loyalty ($r = .26$, $p < .004$, and $r = .23$, $p < .009$, respectively).

TABLE 1 Correlations of Aspects of Communication Structure and Control Structure with League Effectiveness and Member Loyalty*

	Dependent variable			
	Effectiveness		Loyalty	
Independent variables	r_p	p	r_p	p
Small leagues (N = 52)				
Upward communication	.129	>.05	.084	>.05
Multi-directional communication	.249	<.05	.371	<.006
Decentralized control	.121	>.05	.070	>.05
Total amount of control	.328	<.02	.240	<.05
Large leagues (N = 60)				
Upward communication	−.019	>.05	.035	>.05
Multi-directional communication	.099	>.05	.419	<.001
Decentralized control	.230	<.05	.493	<.001
Total amount of control	.201	<.06	.184	>.05
All leagues (N = 112)				
Upward communication	.036	>.05	.021	>.05
Multi-directional communication	.154	<.06	.379	<.001
Decentralized control	.310	<.001	.263	<.004
Total amount of control	.290	<.002	.231	<.009

* All correlations are partial correlations holding log size constant. Tests of significance are tests of first-order partials and are one-tailed tests.

When the sample is broken down into categories according to size, there are interesting differences in the patterns of relationships between the measures of communication and control on the one hand, and league effectiveness and member loyalty on the other. For the small leagues, the correlations show the importance of multi-directional communication coupled with a high total amount of control for both effectiveness and member loyalty. In the large leagues, the pattern of communication appears to be unimportant so far as league effectiveness is concerned. Instead, the results suggest that a high total amount of control which is relatively decentralized is the important correlate of effectiveness in these leagues. The picture is somewhat different in the large leagues with respect to member loyalty. Here, the relevant independent variables are multi-directional communication coupled with decentralized control.

In a more definitive test of the communication hypothesis, the two measures of communication structure, upward communication and multi-directional communication, were correlated with league effectiveness and member loyalty, holding the measures of control structure constant by means of partial correlation. Controlling in this way for either decentralized control or the total amount of control has no appreciable effect upon the relationships between communication structure and league effectiveness or member loyalty. They remain essentially the same, both for the entire sample of leagues, as well as for large and small leagues considered separately.

While the relationships of communication structure with league effectiveness and member loyalty cannot be interpreted simply in terms of aspects of control, it should be noted that the degree to which communication is unidirectional (upward or downward) and the amount of multi-directional communication are insignificantly, or, at most, moderately related to league effectiveness. However, when member loyalty is considered as the dependent variable, the communication structure, particularly the amount of multidirectional communication, appears to be an important factor. This furnishes still stronger support for the communication hypothesis.

In a more definitive test of the control hypothesis, the two measures of control structure were correlated with league effectiveness and member loyalty, using partial correlation to hold constant the measures of communication. Holding constant either upward communication or multi-directional communication has no effect upon the relationships between decentralized control or the total amount of control on the one hand, and league effectiveness and member loyalty on the other.

These relationships hold up whether small, large, or the entire sample of local leagues are considered. It seems then that the significant relationships between aspects of control structure and league effectiveness or member loyalty cannot be interpreted in terms of the variables of communication structure. Therefore, these results furnish definite support for the control hypothesis with respect to both league effectiveness and member loyalty.

Table 2 presents results of a test of the consistency hypothesis, version I. In this table are presented variations in league effectiveness as a function of combinations of upward or downward communication and centralized or de-centralized control.[14] By regression analysis, log size has been partialled out of the dependent variable scores. For the total sample of local leagues, the data point to a confirmation of the hypothesis. An interaction effect between

TABLE 2 Effectiveness as a Function of the Distribution of Communication and Control*

Distribution of communication	Distribution of control					
	Decentralized			Centralized		
	N	$\bar{X}$	S	N	$\bar{X}$	S
	Small leagues					
Downward	(a) 7	56.6	15.1	(b) 17	46.3	9.1
Upward	(c) 9	44.7	12.5	(d) 19	49.3	9.9

Tests of significance:
(a) vs. (b): t = 1.67, p = .06   (a) vs. (c): t = 1.68, p < .10 > .05
(a) vs. (d): t = 1.17, p > .05   (d) vs. (b): t = .96, p > .05
(d) vs. (c): t = .98, p > .05   (c) vs. (b): t = .46, p > .05
(a), (d) vs. (b), (c): t = 1.82, p < .05 > .01

	Large leagues					
Downward	(a) 19	49.6	9.6	(b) 13	44.1	17.1
Upward	(c) 10	49.6	17.7	(d) 18	48.8	12.3

Tests of significance:
(a) vs. (b): t = 1.05, p > .05   (a) vs. (c): t = .02, p > .05
(a) vs. (d): t =   .21, p > .05   (d) vs. (b): t = .86, p > .05
(d) vs. (c): t = −.77, p > .05   (c) vs. (b): t = .75, p > .05

	All leagues					
Downward	(a) 26	51.5	11.4	(b) 30	45.3	12.9
Upward	(c) 19	47.3	15.3	(d) 37	49.1	11.0

Tests of significance:
(a) vs. (b): t = 1.88, p < .05   (a) vs. (c): t = 1.01, p > .05
(a) vs. (d): t = .83, p > .05   (d) vs. (b): t = 1.26, p < .10 > .05
(d) vs. (c): t = .46, p > .05   (c) vs. (b): t = .45, p > .05
(a), (d) vs. (b), (c): t = 1.64, p = .05

* Effectiveness measures have log size partialled out.

[14] The division into upward or downward communication or into centralized or decentralized control was made by splitting the scores at the median in each case.

the distribution of communication and control in the predicted direction is suggested. Leagues in which communication and control are consistent with one another, i.e., either downward communication and decentralized control or upward communication and centralized control, are significantly higher in effectiveness than leagues in which communication does not flow to the control centers ($t = 1.64$, $p = .05$). However, this effect occurs primarily for the small leagues. For large leagues, the predicted interaction effect does not occur.

Table 3 presents a test of the consistency hypothesis, version I, with member loyalty as the dependent variable. For the entire sample of local leagues,

TABLE 3   Loyalty as a Function of the Distribution of Communication and Control*

Distribution of communication	Distribution of control					
	Decentralized			Centralized		
	N	$\bar{X}$	S	N	$\bar{X}$	S
			Small leagues			
Downward	(a) 7	50.7	5.9	(b) 17	49.7	7.3
Upward	(c) 9	49.7	7.1	(d) 19	49.5	4.8

Tests of significance:

(a) vs. (b): $t = -.37$, $p > .05$ (a) vs. (c): $t = -.32$, $p > .05$
(a) vs. (d): $t = -.50$, $p > .05$ (d) vs. (c): $t =$ $.08$, $p > .05$
(d) vs. (b): $t =$ $.08$, $p > .05$ (c) vs. (b): $t =$ $.01$, $p > .05$

			Large leagues			
Downward	(a) 19	48.7	3.8	(b) 13	53.1	6.5
Upward	(c) 10	50.4	4.9	(d) 18	51.5	5.6

Tests of significance:

(a) vs. (b): $t = 2.17$, $p < .05$ (a) vs. (c): $t =$ $.93$, $p > .05$
(a) vs. (d): $t = 1.74$, $p < .05$ (d) vs. (c): $t = -.54$, $p > .05$
(d) vs. (b): $t =$ $.71$, $p > .05$ (c) vs. (b): $t =$ 1.13, $p > .05$

			All leagues			
Downward	(a) 26	49.3	4.4	(b) 30	51.1	7.1
Upward	(c) 19	50.1	5.9	(d) 37	50.5	5.2

Tests of significance:

(a) vs. (b): $t = 1.19$, $p > .05$ (a) vs. (c): $t =$ $.49$, $p > .05$
(a) vs. (d): $t =$ $.98$, $p > .05$ (d) vs. (c): $t = -.26$, $p > .05$
(d) vs. (b): $t =$ $.43$, $p > .05$ (c) vs. (b): $t =$ $.58$, $p > .05$

* Loyalty scores are inverse scores, i.e., a low score designates high loyalty and vice versa.

member loyalty does not vary as a function of combinations of upward or downward communication and centralized or decentralized control. These results consequently fail to support the hypothesis for this dependent variable. However, when leagues are categorized according to size, the results are mixed. While no interaction effect is found in the small leagues, in the large leagues there is partial substantiation. Specifically, member loyalty is highest when there is decentralized control coupled with downward communication.

Tables 4 and 5 present the results of the test of the consistency hypothesis, version II, predicting that multi-directional communication coupled with high

TABLE 4 Effectiveness as a Function of Degree of Multi-directional Communication and Total Amount of Control*

Multi-directional communication	Total amount of control					
	Low			High		
	N	X̄	S	N	X̄	S
	Small leagues					
Low	(a) 9	43.1	20.1	(b) 8	51.5	6.4
High	(c) 19	46.8	8.4	(d) 16	52.1	8.2

Tests of significance:
  (d) vs. (b): t = .18, p > .05   (d) vs. (c): t = 1.87, p < .05
  (d) vs. (a): t = 1.27, p > .05   (b) vs. (c): t = 1.57, p < .10 > .05
  (b) vs. (a): t = 1.18, p > .05   (c) vs. (a): t = .53, p > .05

	Large leagues					
Low	(a) 25	45.3	13.7	(b) 16	52.9	13.6
High	(c) 11	48.2	13.5	(d) 8	47.6	13.1

Tests of significance:
  (d) vs. (b): t = −.19, p > .05   (d) vs. (c): t = −.09, p > .05
  (d) vs. (a): t = .43, p > .05   (b) vs. (c): t = .89, p > .05
  (b) vs. (a): t = .91, p > .05   (c) vs. (a): t = .58, p > .05

	All leagues					
Low	(a) 34	44.7	15.3	(b) 24	52.4	11.6
High	(c) 30	47.3	10.3	(d) 24	50.6	10.1

Tests of significance:
  (d) vs. (b): t = −.59, p > .05   (d) vs. (c): t = 1.18, p > .05
  (d) vs. (a): t = 1.75, p < .05   (b) vs. (c): t = 1.70, p < .05
  (b) vs. (a): t = 2.18, p < .05   (c) vs. (a): t = .79, p > .05

* Effectiveness measures have log size partialled out.

TABLE 5   Loyalty as a Function of Degree of Multi-directional Communication and Total Amount of Control*

Multi-directional communication	Total amount of control					
	Low			High		
	N	$\bar{X}$	S	N	$\bar{X}$	S
	Small leagues					
Low	(a) 9	55.2	5.5	(b) 8	49.4	4.2
High	(c) 19	49.3	5.6	(d) 16	47.3	6.3

Tests of significance:
  (d) vs. (b): t = .95, p > .05   (d) vs. (c): t = .99, p > .05
  (d) vs. (a): t = 3.28, p < .01   (b) vs. (c): t = .02, p > .05
  (b) vs. (a): t = 2.48, p < .05   (c) vs. (a): t = 2.64, p < .01

Multi-directional communication						
	Large leagues					
Low	(a) 25	52.9	5.1	(b) 16	50.9	4.6
High	(c) 11	49.0	5.8	(d) 8	46.5	3.8

Tests of significance:
  (d) vs. (b): t = 2.46, p < .05   (d) vs. (c): t = 1.14, p > .05
  (d) vs. (a): t = 3.73, p < .001   (b) vs. (c): t = .90, p > .05
  (b) vs. (a): t = 1.30, p = .10   (c) vs. (a): t = 1.93, p < .05

Multi-directional communication						
	All leagues					
Low	(a) 34	53.5	5.3	(b) 24	50.4	4.4
High	(c) 30	49.2	5.6	(d) 24	47.0	5.5

Tests of significance:
  (d) vs. (b): t = 2.32, p < .05   (d) vs. (c): t = 1.42, p < .10 > .05
  (d) vs. (a): t = 4.48, p < .001   (b) vs. (c): t = .87, p > .05
  (b) vs. (a): t = 1.63, p = .05   (c) vs. (a): t = 3.16, p < .01

* Loyalty scores are inverse scores, i.e., a low score designates high loyalty and vice versa.

total amount of control will be associated with high member loyalty and league effectiveness.[15] Table 4 presents a test of the hypothesis when league effectiveness is taken as the dependent variable. Again log size is partialled out of the effectiveness scores. For the total sample of leagues, the predicted

[15] The divisions into high or low multi-directional communication and high or low total amount of control were made by splitting the scores at the median in each case.

interaction effect does not occur. Rather, the results indicate that the total amount of control is important for league effectiveness regardless of the amount of multi-directional communication. It is particularly where there is a low amount of multi-directional communication and a low total amount of control that league effectiveness is impaired. Since this pattern of results occurs predominantly in the small leagues, it appears to be in those leagues that league effectiveness depends primarily on the existence of a high total amount of control. In the large leagues, the predicted interaction effect does not occur. There are no significant differences in effectiveness as a function of the amount of multi-directional communication and total amount of control. In fact, the data suggest a reversal from the predicted optimal organization of communication and control. That is, the highest effectiveness for the large leagues occurs where there is a high total amount of control coupled with a *low* amount of multi-directional communication. But this result is not statistically significant.

Table 5 presents results of the analysis of member loyalty as a function of the amount of multi-directional communication and total amount of control. With respect to this dependent variable, the consistency hypothesis is confirmed. For the entire sample of local leagues, member loyalty is highest when there is a large amount of multi-directional communication coupled with a high total amount of control. Intermediate values of loyalty occur when there is either high amount of multi-directional communication and low total amount of control, or the reverse. Member loyalty is low when there is a low amount of multi-directional communication and a low total amount of control. As is indicated in the table, essentially the same pattern of results occurs for both the small and large leagues. However, multi-directional communication seems to be the more important correlate of member loyalty in the large leagues. It is only where there is both a low amount of multi-directional communication and low total amount of control that significant decreases in member loyalty occur in the small leagues.

DISCUSSION

In general, the findings support the communication hypothesis when the dependent variable is member loyalty, and support the control hypothesis when the dependent variable is league effectiveness. There are a number of considerations relevant to understanding why control is the more important variable in predicting league effectiveness. The formal machinery of the local league, including committee meetings and small group discussions, may adequately provide the basis for procuring and disseminating information within the organization. Communication may be less of a problem than the integration and coordination of member contributions into an effective process of decision-making, one in which control is both adequate in degree and decentralized in distribution. When we also consider the fact that this structure of influence and decision-making is consistent with league ideology, member expectations, and the representational system of authority and formal decision-making which the league claims as its goal, it is not surprising that it is an important factor in league effectiveness.

The more difficult and complex the problem of successfully integrating information into high quality decisions and achieving coordinated, motivated, effort, the more pressing should be the need for an effective system of control. Because of their greater complexity, the larger leagues should be faced with these problems to a greater extent than the smaller leagues. This may explain why effectiveness in the large leagues is more singularly and importantly a function of the structure of control—specifically of a structure in which there is a high total amount of control which is relatively decentralized—than of the pattern and amount of communication. In contrast, the small leagues have more of a problem in optimizing the contributions of their more limited personnel. Furthermore, because of the fact that integration and coordination are less pressing in the small leagues, they are able to operate in a manner less characteristic of a large, complex, formal organization, and more in a manner characteristic of a small group. This may explain why both a high degree of multi-directional communication and a high total amount of control exercised by leaders and members should be important factors underlying high effectiveness and member loyalty in these leagues.

The support of the first consistency hypothesis suggests a provocative conclusion, viz., that it is not simply communication or simply control which is conducive to high organization performance, as either the control or communication hypotheses would imply, but is also the way in which these processes are interrelated. The findings suggest that when there is an adequate flow of information to the centers of control (whether these are organized hierarchically or not), and where this information is effectively used in formulating and implementing decisions, there will be higher organizational effectiveness. Similarly, the results support the claim that without integration and coordination of the information available within the organization, and/or without informed control, organization performance will be low.

Whether the communication and control structures are consistent or inconsistent with one another has no effect upon the loyalty of league members, i.e., upon their willingness to support their league. Rather, it is when the communication and control structures are consistent with the formal objectives and organization of the league and reflect the members' ideals concerning "democratic process," that significantly high member loyalty is achieved. As the results show, this occurs when the leaders stay in contact with members, promote free information exchange, and help them realize their ideals and interests through decentralized control. Understandably, this seems to be especially the case in the large leagues where sustaining member loyalty is a more pressing problem.

The lack of support for the second consistency hypothesis predicting the efficacy for organization performance of multi-directional communication coupled with a high total amount of control indicate that what is important is the amount of control exercised irrespective of the amount of multi-directional communication. However, multi-directional communication coupled with a high total amount of control is associated with high member loyalty. This relationship is probably a mutual one. The existence of this pattern of communication and control is probably a function of the willingness of the membership to support their organization. In turn, multi-directional communication and high total amount of control are likely to be conducive to high member loyalty. While this pattern may not be the most efficient in the short run as far as the performance of the league is concerned, it is likely to provide a very satisfying experience to the members and elicit their active support. Thus, it may be that the effects of this latter on league performance will be felt only in the long run.

In conclusion, the results afford partial support for our initial hypotheses. Nevertheless, the results should be interpreted with at least two limitations in mind: first, we have implied that there are certain causal relations between communication and control on the one hand and league effectiveness and member loyalty on the other. In view of our cross-sectional data we cannot ascertain with certainty the direction of the relationships—they may very well operate both ways. Second, we have grossly oversimplified the organization of communication and control in our analysis. What may be the optimal organization of communication and control in one area of decision-making or action may not be optimal in another. Also, we have not distinguished kinds of information-exchange, nor have we separated decision-making from control. Furthermore, we have not distinguished operationally between the different phases of formulating and implementing decisions. What may be the most effective organization of communication and control for the formulation of decisions may not be the most effective for their implementation. We hope through further research to investigate these and other matters in greater detail with an eye to their complexity and variety.

10

ORGANIZATIONAL CONTROL STRUCTURE AND MEMBER CONSENSUS*

Clagett G. Smith
Oğuz N. Ari[1]

Recent research in several organizations, including a clerical organization, several union locals, a service organization, and a voluntary association, has indicated that the manner in which control is structured, at least as reported by members, is related to organizational effectiveness. These studies suggest the importance in some organizations of high rank-and-file control relative to leadership control and, more generally, the importance of a high amount of control exercised by members at all echelons in the organization. The interpretations offered of these findings suggest that these patterns of control may be conducive to high organizational effectiveness, in part, through the uniformity with respect to organizational standards and policies which they promote. Likert, for example, has suggested that significant influence exercised by persons at all levels, the leaders as well as the rank and file, provides the basis of the effective co-ordination of organizational activity. Such co-ordination is derived, in part, from the shared goals and agreement on the means to these goals which this pattern of control promotes. Similarly, the exercise of control by lower echelons is likely to bring with it greater acceptance of jointly made decisions as well as an increased sense of responsibility and motivation to further the goals of the organization. Such motivational effects are very likely to be reflected in increased uniformity concerning the decisions and goals of the organization. A relationship between a high amount of control exercised by persons at all echelons ("high total control") and member uniformity (as a criterion of organizational norms) was suggested in a study of union locals.[2] Furthermore, amount of total control and member uniformity were related to "union power," that is, effectiveness. The hypothesis was offered that a high level of total control is part of an organizational power syndrome including uniformity and effectiveness.

These interpretations seem to suggest one particularly significant process explaining the efficacy of these patterns of control in promoting high organi-

* Reprinted from the *American Journal of Sociology*, May 1964, Vol. LXIX, No. 6, 623–638, with permission of the publisher and the authors. (This article has been edited to eliminate overlap and to bring it into a consistent format with the other articles in this book. Certain portions have therefore been deleted or reworded. Ed.)

[1] We acknowledge the valuable suggestions of Arnold S. Tannenbaum, Robert L. Kahn, Dorwin Cartwright, and Stanley E. Seashore, and the assistance of Roberta Ann Levenbach and Dora Cafagna.

[2] Tannenbaum, "Control Structure and Union Functions," *American Journal of Sociology*, LXI (1956), 536–45 (in this book, Chap. 2).

zational performance, namely, the co-ordination and regulation of member behavior with respect to organizational norms. The resulting uniformity derives its significance from the fact that it is basic to the concerted member effort underlying effective organizational performance.[3] It is the purpose of this paper to consider further the relationships of patterns of control to member uniformity and to evaluate their implications for organizational effectiveness.

THEORY AND HYPOTHESES

1. Control structure

"Control" refers to any process by which a person (or group or organization of persons) determines, i.e., intentionally affects what another person (or group, or organization) will do. In organizations this process may include formal aspects, such as formulating policy and making decisions, exercising authority in implementing decisions, and applying rewards and sanctions for conformity or deviance. It may also include informal mechanisms and techniques, such as non-legitimated pressures, informal discussion, and decision-making.

The "structure of control" designates the relatively enduring pattern of influence within an organization. Most generally, this consists of the pattern of influence of persons or groups upon the organization. This entails, in large part, influence *between* persons or groups of persons within the organization. We shall employ as a measure of aspects of control structure the technique of the "control graph."

Two aspects of organizational control described by the control curve are (1) the hierarchical distribution of control, represented by the shape or slope of the curve and (2) the total amount of control exercised by all levels in the organization, represented by the average height of the curve.[4] In addition to specifying the pattern of influence of the various levels upon the organization in general, the control graph approach permits a more specific description of organizational control in terms of patterns of influence existing between members of various levels. This pattern of influence may be specified both in terms of exercising control ("active control") and of being controlled ("passive

---

[3] The importance for organizational functioning of such variables as member consensus and reciprocal role expectations has been suggested in a number of studies. Basil Georgopoulos, e.g., found aspects of the "normative system of the organization" such as "normative complementarity" and "group consensus" to be significantly related to organizational productivity ("The Normative Structure of Social Systems: A Study of Organizational Effectiveness" [unpublished doctoral dissertation, University of Michigan, 1957]).

[4] It is important to distinguish between these two aspects of control since they are conceptually distinct variables. A high amount of total control could occur under conditions of either relatively high rank-and-file influence or relatively high leader influence. Conversely, relatively high rank-and-file influence or high leader influence could each imply either a high or low amount of total control. Furthermore, these two aspects of control have previously been found to vary independently (see, e.g., Tannenbaum, "Control and Effectiveness in a Voluntary Organization," *American Journal of Sociology*, LXVII [1961], 33–46 [(in this book, Chap. 4)].

control"). Thus the amount of control which persons at a given level exercise over those at other levels may be ascertained, as well as the extent to which persons at a given level are controlled by those at other levels. This permits a description of where in the hierarchy a given level directs its control, as well as the determination of the sources from which control over any given level originates.[5]

2. Control and uniformity

The relationship between control and member uniformity has been traditionally subsumed under the concept of social norm. This concept can be defined simply as the continuous uniformity in expectations, attitudes, or behavior within a group (or organization) regarding an activity developed and maintained by processes of control.[6] Central to this definition of norms is the premise that they are a function of control. While this constitutes the basic premise of the present formulation, the subject of our inquiry is more specifically the relationships of varying patterns of organizational control to member uniformity. We shall be concerned with uniformity in perceptions and attitudes which will be referred to as "consensus." The focus will be upon consensus within the work group and between members of the work group and those at higher echelons in the organization. Two general hypotheses can be stated:

> Hypothesis I: Consensus within the work group and between members and supervisors will be related directly to the degree to which the control curve is positively sloped.
> Hypothesis II: Consensus within the work group and between members and supervisors will be related directly to the total amount of control.

The first hypothesis is a restatement in terms of the control graph that "democratic control" will be conducive to a system of shared norms. The rationale for this hypothesis is based on several processes. Rank-and-file involvement in decision-making, especially in a society that extols democratic values, tends to foster conditions of identification, motivation, and loyalty to the organization. These conditions should give rise to increased uniformity with respect to organizational and work-group standards. They tend also to promote a high level of participation and a greater amount of accurate communication and influence, permitting members to see what the norms of the organization and the work group are, as well as facilitating their determination. Further, relatively high rank-and-file influence in decision-making may per-

---

[5] Arnold S. Tannenbaum and Basil Georgopoulos, "The Distribution of Control in Formal Organizations," *Social Forces*, XXXVI (1957), 44–50 (in this book, Chap. 3).

[6] This definition is similar in some respects to that offered by Georgopoulos, *op. cit.*, and is consistent with the interpretation of social norms presented by Floyd H. Allport ("A Structuro-nomic Conception of Behavior: Individual and Collective. 1. Structural Theory and the Master Problem of Social Psychology," *Journal of Abnormal and Social Psychology*, LXIV [1962], 3–30).

mit members to develop policies and practices which represent the interests of a fairly broad segment rather than merely the interests of the leaders, and thus may further enhance acceptance of these decisions by both the rank-and-file members and the leaders.

While high rank-and-file control relative to that of the leadership may have these positive consequences under certain conditions, some authors have pointed up the necessity of control from above to insure efficient organizational functioning. Despite its detrimental effects, "hierarchical control" (negative slope) is viewed as necessary to insure shared organizational norms, effective co-ordination, and concerted member effort. Indeed high rank-and-file control relative to that of the leaders (i.e., positive slope) may result in a lack of consensus and conflict between echelons, if the rank-and-file members act simply in terms of their own self-interests, do not possess the skill to exercise control effectively, or do not accept the contributions of members at higher echelons.[7] The hypothesis as formulated assumes that these circumstances are not present.

The second hypothesis offers an approach to the dilemma stated above by considering the necessity of control by upper echelons *together* with the favorable effects of control by the rank-and-file members. This hypothesis states that a high amount of control exercised by persons at all levels in the organization will contribute to high member consensus within the organization. The hypothesis is based on a set of interrelated processes accompanying a high amount of total control previously elaborated by Tannenbaum and Likert.[8] Part of these processes derive from the high rank-and-file influence per se inherent in a high level of total control, and thus the predicted effects in promoting high consensus are similar to those specified in Hypothesis I.

Likert suggests that the efficacy of a high amount of total control in an organization may be explained in terms of the existence of an "effective interaction-influence system," that is, a system in which there is high reciprocal influence and free communicative exchange throughout the organization. Such an interaction-influence system permits members to understand clearly what the norms of the organization are, as well as fostering their *joint* determination and enforcement. Furthermore, this process provides the basis of the effective co-ordination of organizational activity, in part, by facilitating the integration of the interests of both the rank-and-file members and the leaders. As a consequence, there is wider acceptance of policies and practices, and co-operative relations between members at different levels tend to be enhanced. This is

---

[7] For a further discussion of this dilemma of "democratic control" see Norman R. F. Maier, *Principles of Human Relations* (New York: John Wiley & Sons, 1952); Philip Selznick, "Foundations of the Theory of Organizations," *American Sociological Review*, XII (1948), 25–35; and Tannenbaum, "Control and Effectiveness . . . ," *op. cit.*

[8] Tannenbaum (in this book Chaps. 1 and 2); Likert, "Influence and National Sovereignty," in *Festschrift for Gardner Murphy*, ed., John G. Peatman and Eugene L. Hartley (New York: Harper & Bros., 1960), pp. 214–27, and his *New Patterns of Management* (New York: McGraw-Hill, 1961).

likely to be reflected in a set of shared norms, in the form of means and goals, adherence to which tends to be "promotively interdependent" for all the parties involved.[9]

PROCEDURE

1. Research site

The present study is based on a survey of a nationwide service organization having operations in several metropolitan areas of the United States.[10] The primary function of the organization is to transport and deliver articles from central locations to homes. Each area is organized as a "plant" with two or more major divisions, and each division has several operating units or "stations." A typical station has a station manager, a supervisor, an assistant supervisor, several leaders who work at night, and about twenty-five drivers who work days delivering packages on their respective routes. The stations are geographically separate from one another, each one serving an exclusive territory. They are quite similar in facilities, operating policies, work methods, and procedures, but differ considerably in performance and somewhat in size. Thirty-two such stations, representing five company plants, together including twelve hundred employees, comprise our population.

2. Description of variables

The measurements of control structure and consensus are based on questionnaire data obtained from supervisory and non-supervisory employees in each of the thirty-two stations. The average questionnaire return rate for supervisory personnel was 97 per cent and for non-supervisory 87 per cent. No station having a return rate lower than 75 per cent of its non-supervisory members is represented in the sample.

a) Control measures

The following operations were employed to obtain measures of the two independent variables, slope of the control curve and amount of total control. Respondents in each station were asked:

[9] However, Mayer N. Zald finds that correctional institutions which pursue mixed goals or treatment goals tend to have a power structure that is distributed among all staff members; this is not the case in the more custodial institutions. Furthermore, there is more conflict in the former type of institution than in the latter. In effect, his findings suggest that when each group has different basic interests high total control leads to low consensus ("Organizational Control Stuctures in Five Correctional Institutions," *American Journal of Sociology*, LXVIII [1962], 335–45; "Power and Conflict in Correctional Institutions," VII [1962], 22–49). Our hypothesis assumes the existence of unitary goals and an absence of basic conflict. The tenability of this assumption will be investigated in the subsequent analysis.

[10] For a more extensive description of the research site see Georgopoulos, *op. cit.*; Likert, *New Patterns of Management;* and Bernard P. Indik, Basil Georgopoulos, and Stanley E. Seashore, "Superior-Subordinate Relationships and Performance," *Personnel Psychology*, XIV (1961), 357–74.

"In general, how much say or influence do you feel each of the following groups *has* on what goes on in your station: (1) Your station manager? (2) The other supervisors in your station? (3) The men in your station?" Response categories were "little or no influence," "some influence," "quite a bit of influence," "a great deal of influence," and "a very great deal of influence."

The amount of control exercised by each level within a station was computed by averaging separately the judgments of members and officers regarding each of the levels. Measures of the slope of the control curve for each station were derived by computing the slope of a best-fit straight line of the control exercised by the three hierarchical levels. This consisted of computing the average of the algebraic differences between the amounts of influence reported to be exercised by successive levels. The split-half reliability of this index is 67.[11] The amount of total control for each station was simply the sum of the amounts of control reported to be exercised by the three hierarchical levels. The split-half reliability of this index is .84.

In order to illuminate the processes by which slope and amount of total control might have their hypothesized effects, the control *exercised by* the rank and file itself and the extent to which the rank-and-file members *were controlled by* other echelons were measured. The following question was employed to measure the control exercised by the rank-and-file members:

"In general, how much say or influence do the men in your station have on what the following groups do in the company: (1) On what your station manager does? (2) On what the other supervisors in your station do? (3) On what the men in your station themselves do?"

The influence of each level was rated by respondents, again members and officers separately, on a five-point scale ranging from "little or no influence" to "a very great deal of influence." The influence of the men upon station managers and upon the other supervisors in the station was summed to provide an index of the influence of the men upon the upper (supervisory) levels. The split-half reliability of this index is .54. The split-half reliability of the measure of the influence exercised upon the men by the rank-and-file members themselves is .53.

Respondents also rated the influence of the station manager and of the other supervisors upon "what the men do in the company," again on a five-point scale identical to the other control questions. The index of the combined influence of the upper levels upon the men has a split-half reliability of .80.

The various measures of control are subject to two interpretations since they are based on the judgments of organization members. One might interpret them as representing perceptions of control rather than objective descriptions of control structure. Or one might interpret them as providing reasonably valid

---

[11] The split-half reliability for this index, as for the others to be reported, is the reliability for group data. Respondents in each station were divided into two random groups, and a correlation was computed between the scores of each group on the index for the thirty-two stations. The Spearman-Brown formula was then applied to the correlation to correct for size of population.

data on existing control patterns even though it is clear that they are subject to error.[12] Previous research employing the control graph has shown meaningful differences in several types of organizations, as well as significant relationships between indexes of control structure and independent criteria of organizational functioning,[13] suggesting that the data do have some validity as measures of control structure.[14] Moreover, the significant relationships to be reported in the present investigation support this same conclusion.

b) Consensus measures

The organizational activities selected in measuring consensus pertained to work standards, member support of the organization, supervisory behavior, and control. These are activities concerning which norms might be expected to exist since they are relevant to the functioning of the organization and important to its members.[15] The following questions were used to derive measures of consensus:

1. How do you feel about the standards or time schedules set up for your job? [Five alternatives, from "they are very fair for my job," to "they are not at all fair for my job."]
2. How do you feel about the morale in your station? [Five alternatives, from "excellent" to "very poor."]
3. How good is your immediate supervisor in planning, organizing, and scheduling work ahead of time? [Five alternatives, from "excellent" to "very poor."]
4. To what extent do you have confidence and trust in the supervisors in your station? [Five alternatives, from "to a very great extent" to "I don't trust them at all."]

In addition, respondents were asked a fifth question about the amount of control which they felt should ideally be exercised in the station: "In general, how much say or influence do you think each of the following groups *should have* on what goes on in your station?" These groups included the station manager, the other supervisors, and the men, and the influence desired for each was rated on a five-point scale identical to the "actual" influence question previously described. With the exception of the two questions dealing with

---

[12] The split-half reliability of our various indexes of control is certainly not as high in every case as would be desired. Particularly, we cannot be sure that the relatively lower reliability of the three measures of rank-and-file control may not operate to limit their correlations with the consensus measures. However, as will become apparent from the results to be reported, there is not a general tendency in this direction.

[13] Clagett G. Smith and Arnold S. Tannenbaum, "Organizational Control Structure: A Comparative Analysis," *Human Relations*, XVI (1963), 299–316 (see this book, Chap. 5).

[14] For a fuller discussion of the measurement of organizational structure see the extensive review by Allen H. Barton, *Organizational Measurement* (New York: College Entrance Examination Board, 1961).

[15] The necessity of considering behavioral areas which have relevance to the organization and its members is emphasized by Allport, *op. cit.*, who contends that particular norms will develop which have consequences for operation of a structure (i.e., a group or organization) in which the members have some degree of involvement.

supervision, both non-supervisory and supervisory employees responded to these questions.

Consensus in the work group was determined by computing the inverse of the variance of responses of non-supervisory employees within each station for each of the five questions. The three measures of agreement for the fifth question were averaged to form a general measure of work-group consensus regarding the "ideal" pattern of control.

It is important to note that the mean responses of rank-and-file members to all the questions on which the consensus measures are based occur in all stations fairly well within the middle of the scale. (For most of the questions the ranges are from 2.00 to 3.60 on a five-point scale; the most extreme ranges on two questions are from 1.70 to 4.00.) Furthermore no standard deviation on any question for any station exceeds 0.5 of a scale point. Consequently, the possibility is slight that variations in consensus are attributable to a "ceiling effect," that is, that they artificially reflect the fact of extreme scale responses and simply represent average responses to these questions.

Measures of consensus between members at the rank-and-file and the supervisory levels were also derived, using the same set of questions as before with the exception of the two questions pertaining to supervision. Indexes computed for each station by determining the extent of agreement between the *average* responses of rank-and-file members on the one hand and those of the supervisors on the other to each of the three questions resulted in three measures of hierarchical consensus, regarding work standards, "morale," and the "ideal" pattern of control. The last of these measures was again an over-all measure arrived at by averaging the indexes for each of the three echelons. The measures of hierarchical consensus, as thus operationalized, not only permitted the determination of the extent of agreement between the lower and upper echelons in a station but also indirectly provided information concerning the direction or content of the norms of the work group relative to those at higher echelons.

Supervisors tend to be somewhat higher or more positive in their responses than non-supervisory employees. This tendency might operate to create a ceiling effect so that the measures of hierarchical consensus would simply reflect the average responses of the rank-and-file members. In turn, this would tend to inflate the relationships between the independent variables of control structure and the measures of hierarchical consensus since both sets of measures would be based, in effect, upon the averaged judgments of the same group of respondents. However, the measures of hierarchical consensus do not strongly reflect the average responses of the non-supervisory employees. The correlations of average rank-and-file responses with each of the measures of hierarchical consensus while positive are all insignificant. Nevertheless, in view of this possible ceiling effect and the fact of these positive correlations, we cannot entirely rule out the possibility that the relationships between the independent variables and the measures of hierarchical consensus might be interpreted in terms of such a statistical dependency.

In addition to the measures of actual consensus, measures of the consensus which the respondents perceived to exist in their station were also derived. Measures of perceived consensus were based on the following questions:

> To what extent do people in the different jobs in your station see eye-to-eye on things about the everyday operations of your station? [Five alternatives, from "complete agreement" to "no agreement."]
>
> On the whole, would you say that in your station there is any tension or conflict between the following pairs of groups? [The pairs of groups included "employees *and* supervisors," "employees *and* higher management," "supervisors *and* higher management," and "the union *and* the management." For each pair, alternatives ranged on a five-point scale from "a great deal of tension" to "no tension at all."]

For the second question, ratings for the four pairs of groups were summed together to provide a general index of conflict within the station. Ratings for the first question and the net ratings for the second question were each averaged, members and officers separately, to provide two measures of perceived consensus within the station.

Table 1 presents the intercorrelations among the ten consensus measures. As seen from the generally low intercorrelations, consensus as we have measured it is not a unitary phenomenon; rather, it has many specific components. The average of intercorrelations among the measures of work-group consensus is only .18; among the measures of hierarchical consensus, it is only .06. The measures of work-group consensus correlate on the average with the measures of hierarchical consensus only .18. Consensus in the work group and consensus between members at different echelons appear to be distinct phenomena. In effect, where work-group norms exist they are not consistently in agreement with those of upper echelons. Conversely, hierarchical consensus does not necessarily imply the presence of work-group norms complementing those

TABLE 1 Intercorrelations among Consensus Measures

	1	2	3	4	5	6	7	8	9
Work-group consensus:									
1. Work standards									
2. Morale	—.11								
3. Adequacy of supervisory planning	—.20	.53							
4. Trust and confidence in supervisors	—.21	.34	.41						
5. Influence desired for various levels	.05	.50	.40	.12					
Hierarchical consensus:									
6. Work standards	—.33	.10	.17	.29	.02				
7. Morale	—.15	.30	.06	.07	.05	.08			
8. Influence desired for various levels	—.25	.03	.14	—.06	.27	.19	.00		
Perceived consensus:									
9. Everyday operations	—.21	.71	.37	.55	.37	.20	.37	.05	
10. Absence of conflict	—.32	.66	.54	.60	.28	.22	.30	.03	.85

of higher echelons. The measures of perceived consensus largely reflect work-group consensus concerning morale and supervision and hierarchical consensus concerning morale.

As might be expected, the several measures of consensus are negatively associated with size of the station. In view of this confounding effect, the relations between control and consensus will be examined with size, specifically log size, held constant through partial correlation techniques. Any relationship obtained cannot therefore be attributable to the effects of size.

c) Effectiveness measures

As noted, the control-consensus relationship will be examined with reference to its implications for organizational effectiveness. Organizational effectiveness is defined as the extent to which an organization, given certain resources and means, achieves its objectives without incapacitating its means and resources and without placing undue strain upon its members.[16] Two measures of organizational effectiveness are employed, the first measuring achievement of organizational objectives and the second measuring member satisfaction. The first, "station productivity," was operationalized in terms of objective productivity measures provided by the company. These are based on the total time required to accomplish standard units of work. Specifically, the measure is expressed in units of time consumed by the worker below or above that specified by the standard. The average productivity of all drivers in a station during the month preceding the field study was taken to represent the organizational productivity of that station. An index of member satisfaction is based on the average of respondents' estimates of the "morale" of their station, using the same question regarding morale as was used in measuring consensus. It is taken as reflecting the absence of strain upon the members and the degree to which the human resources of the organization are being preserved.

RESULTS

The two hypotheses predicting relationships between degree of positive slope and amount of total control on the one hand and member consensus on the other assume that slope and total control are independent of each other. However, a high negative correlation ($r = -.67$) exists between degree of positive slope and amount of total control in the stations under study.[17] A high level of total control obtains in these stations through high managerial control relative to that of the rank and file; conversely high rank-and-file control relative to

---

[16] This definition follows that of Georgopoulos and Tannenbaum, who have considered the validity of the concept in the same organization as that in which the present investigation is conducted (Basil S. Georgopoulos and Arnold S. Tannenbaum, "A Study of Organizational Effectiveness," *American Sociological Review*, XXII [1957], 534–40).

[17] In a study of the League of Women Voters the correlation between degree of positive slope and amount of total control was insignificant, $r = .14$ (Tannenbaum, "Control and Effectiveness . . . ," *op. cit.*).

that of the supervisors is associated with the low amount of control exercised by the various levels in the station. In order to provide independent tests of Hypotheses I and II, partial correlations of degree of positive slope with work-group and hierarchical consensus were computed holding amount of total control constant; partial correlations of amount of total control with these measures of consensus hold degree of positive slope constant. These partial correlations are presented in Table 2.

Hypothesis I is not substantiated. Degree of positive slope is not generally associated with either work-group consensus or hierarchical consensus. The results suggest even that degree of positive slope may be associated in some instances with lack of consensus, specifically concerning ideal control. It is apparently under conditions of high influence of the managers relative to that of the rank-and-file members (i.e., negative slope) that norms regarding the control which members feel the various levels should exercise are likely to occur. High rank-and-file influence relative to that of the managers does have the effect of promoting the perception that people at different levels see "eye-to-eye" concerning the operation of the station irrespective of whether in fact they do.

TABLE 2 Partial Correlations of Degree of Positive Slope and Amount of Total Control with Member Consensus

	Control structure	
Member consensus	**Degree of positive slope***	**Amount of total control†**
Work-group consensus:		
Work standards	—.02	—.17
Morale	—.03	.50§
Adequacy of supervisory planning	—.27	.11
Trust and confidence in supervisor	.36‡	.65§
Influence desired for various levels	—.43	—.13
Hierarchical consensus:		
Work standards	.06	.38‡
Morale	.06	.23
Influence desired for various levels	—.37	—.17
Perceived consensus:		
Everyday operations	.37‡	.66§
Absence of conflict	.13	.53§

* Partial correlations between member consensus and degree of positive slope; log size and amount of total control held constant.
† Partial correlations between member consensus and amount of total control; log size and degree of positive slope held constant.
‡ Significant at .05 level of confidence, one-tailed test.
§ Significant at .01 level of confidence, one-tailed test.

The results suggest that a high amount of total control is the effective pattern conducive to both work-group and hierarchical consensus, furnishing partial support for Hypothesis II. Considered from the point of view of specific behavioral areas, the results by no means give unequivocal support for the hypothesis. Amount of total control is related to work-group consensus concerning morale and trust in the supervisor—areas of particular importance to the workers. It is related to hierarchical consensus concerning work standards—an issue of vital significance for the effectiveness of the station. And in part because of consensus with respect to so basic an issue as the fairness of work standards, high total control is associated with the perception of consensus regarding the everyday operation of the station and with a felt absence of conflict between people at various echelons.

Table 3 provides information illuminating the meaning of degree of positive slope and amount of total control. The influence of the various echelons upon the station and the specific influences existing between the work groups and other levels are correlated with degree of positive slope and amount of total control. Again, because of the significant negative correlation between degree of positive slope and amount of total control, partial correlations between slope and the measures of specific influence are computed holding total control constant; correlations involving total control hold slope constant. As expected, degree of positive slope is highly negatively related to the influence of the station manager and highly positively related to the influence of the men

TABLE 3   Correlations of Specific Influences with Degree of Positive Slope and Amount of Total Control

Specific influences	Control structure	
	Degree of positive slope* r_p	Amount of total control† r_p
Influence of station manager on station	—.85‡	.98‡
Influence of supervisor on station	.02	.67
Influence of men on station	.72‡	.94‡
Influence on men from upper levels	—.06	.55
Influence of men on upper levels	.21	.39§
Influence of men on men	.21	.72‡

* Partial correlations between specific influences and degree of positive slope; amount of total control held constant.
† Partial correlations between specific influences and amount of total control; degree of positive slope held constant.
‡ Significant at .01 level of confidence, two-tailed test.
§ Significant at .05 level of confidence, two-tailed test.

on the station.[18] However, degree of positive slope is related neither to the influence of the work group upon various levels, including the work group itself, nor to the influence upon the work group from upper levels. The fact that positive slope is not associated with a high degree of control *between* members at different levels may explain the absence of the predicted relationships between positive slope and the measures of consensus, that is, high positive slope is not associated with an effective pattern of mutual influence involving rank-and-file members and those at higher echelons which would be expected to facilitate consensus.

In contrast, amount of total control suggests a pattern of high influence within the station. Amount of total control is highly correlated with influence of all echelons upon the operation of the station. High degrees of influence by the men, the supervisors, and the station managers tend to go together in this situation.[19] The correlation between the influence of the station manager and that of the supervisors is .65; the influence of the station manager and that of the men correlate .83; however, the correlation between the influence of the supervisors and that of the men is .05.[20] Of particular significance for the achievement of consensus, amount of total control is associated with a system of high mutual influence between members at different echelons, and specifically with the extent to which the workers exercise control upon the work group itself ($r = .72$). In effect, high total control means high self-determination by the workers (but not at the expense of the supervisors).

In an attempt to further interpret the manner in which the pattern of organizational control is related to member consensus in these stations, the various measures of specific interlevel influences involving the work group were correlated with the measures of work-group and hierarchical consensus. The results are presented in Table 4. Consensus derives in part from the influence of the supervisors upon the workers. It is apparently in response to such "hierarchical control" that work-group norms develop concerning morale, supervision, and the control desired. Such hierarchical control also has the effect of promoting perceived consensus throughout the station, even though in fact it may not exist. However, the direct influence upon the men by the supervisors is not sufficient in itself to guarantee consensus between the workers and the supervisors. In contrast, and consistent with the findings obtained with regard to positive slope, the control of the men upon the upper level is not associated with either work-group or hierarchical consensus. Such influence may have

[18] This finding does not strictly derive from the operations defining slope. High control of one level *relative* to another does not necessarily imply high control of that level in an absolute sense; in fact *both* levels could be exercising a low amount of control.

[19] This would not be expected to occur invariably in all organizations. For example, in the League of Women Voters, the intercorrelations among the amounts of influence of the various levels upon the League are insignificant (see Tannenbaum, "Control and Effectiveness . . . ," *op. cit.*).

[20] The absence of a positive relationship between the influence of the "supervisors" and the men is understandable in terms of the formal role of the supervisors in these stations. The supervisors are assistants to the station manager and, in terms of formal authority, have a relatively ambiguous role vis-à-vis the rank-and-file members.

TABLE 4 Correlations of Specific Influences with Member Consensus*

| | Specific influences | | | |
| | Influence on men from upper levels | Influence of men on upper levels | Influence of men on men | Influence of men on station |
Member consensus				
Work-group consensus:				
Work standards	.16	−.15	−.12	−.26
Morale	.46†	.15	.62†	.59†
Adequacy of supervisory planning	.18	.07	.33‡	.22
Trust and confidence in supervisor	.40†	.43†	.57‡	.61†
Ideal influence desired for various levels	.33‡	.05	.33‡	.07
Hierarchical consensus:				
Work standards	.11	.09	.29‡	.32‡
Morale	.22	−.04	.14	.24
Ideal influence desired for various levels	.21	.05	.23	−.02
Perceived consensus:				
Everyday operations	.41†	.41†	.54†	.61†
Absence of conflict	.38‡	.37‡	.45†	.59†

* All correlations of specific influences with member consensus are partial correlations holding log size constant.
† Significant at the .01 level of confidence, two-tailed test.
‡ Significant at the .05 level of confidence, two-tailed test.

positive motivational effects for the workers, resulting in a feeling that consensus does exist in the station, but it is not sufficient to promote actual consensus. Rather, the results indicate that it is the extent to which the rank-and-file members exercise control upon the station and particularly upon the work group itself which facilitates the development of a high degree of consensus in these stations. When high mutual influence among the workers is coupled with some say by the workers concerning the operation of the station, it constitutes a partial basis for at least a minimum of agreement between the workers and the supervisors, namely, with respect to the critical issue of work standards.

Table 5 assesses the implication of the control-consensus relationship for organizational effectiveness. The results summarize, in part, those previously reported by Likert, Georgopoulos, and Smith and Tannenbaum.[21] As seen from the findings the control-consensus relationship that emerges is part of a larger pattern characteristic of the effective station. Not only are amount of

[21] Likert, "Influence and National Sovereignty," *op. cit.*; Georgopoulos, *op. cit.*; and Smith and Tannenbaum, *op. cit.*

TABLE 5 Intercorrelations among Measures of Control Structure, Consensus, and Organizational Effectiveness

Variable	1	2	3	4
1. Positive slope*				
2. Total control†	—.67‡			
3. General station consensus§	—.22	.35‖		
4. Member morale	.55#	.72#	.32‖	
5. Station productivity	.14	.43#	.45#	.34**

* All correlations involving positive slope are partial correlations, holding total control constant (with the exception of r_{12}).
† All correlations involving total control are partial correlations, holding positive slope constant (with the exception of r_{12}).
‡ Significant at the .01 level, two-tailed test.
§ The measure of general station consensus is based on an index derived by pooling the five measures of work-group consensus and the three measures of hierarchical consensus. All correlations involving general station consensus are partial correlations, holding log size constant.
‖ Significant at the .05 level, one-tailed test.
Significant at the .01 level, one-tailed test.
** Significant at the .05 level, two-tailed test.

total control and general consensus in the station related, but each factor also has significant implications for the effectiveness of the station. Amount of total control is highly correlated with both member morale ($r = .72$) and station productivity ($r = .43$). General station consensus is also significantly correlated with member morale ($r = .32$) and station productivity ($r = .45$).[22] Together, amount of total control and general station consensus yield a high prediction of station productivity; the multiple correlation is .54. The multiple correlation of total control and general station consensus with member morale is even higher, .72. The high-producing station, in contrast to the low-producing station, is characterized by high total control, high member consensus, and high member morale. In contrast, while positive slope may have significant implications for the morale of the members ($r = .55$), the findings have shown that it is unrelated to consensus in the station. It may be for this reason that positive slope is not related to the productivity of these stations. It is not conducive to a high level of order and uniformity which is associated with the high-producing station. The fact that high total control is associated with such uniformity may explain to a large degree its significant implications for the productivity of these stations.

[22] We cannot be entirely sure that the relationships between total control and positive slope on the one hand and member morale on the other are not inflated to some extent. The relationships may be somewhat spurious because they are based on the judgments of the same respondents and may to some degree reflect a "halo effect" or response set.

DISCUSSION

1. The control-consensus relationship

In general, the findings suggest that the pattern of control which tends to be associated with member consensus in this organization is that predicted by Hypothesis II: a high amount of control exercised by members at all echelons, leaders as well as rank-and-file members. High total control tends to be conducive to consensus both within the work group and between the rank-and-file and the supervisory levels. However, considered more specifically, the findings are not uniform in their support of the hypothesis. They suggest that high total control facilitates consensus among rank-and-file members with respect to particularly salient and significant aspects of the work situation such as morale or feelings about the supervisor, areas concerning which the workers could also most readily reach an understanding and obtain agreement. Furthermore, high total control tends to promote consensus between rank-and-file members and those at higher echelons with respect to those critical areas, particularly work standards, which are highly relevant to the operation of the station and concerning which procedures might be expected to exist for reaching consensus. Amount of total control is unrelated to either work-group or hierarchical consensus regarding ideal control. This may be due simply to the unreliability of the measure or to the fact that ideal control is not a pertinent area for the development of consensus. Or it may be that it is more difficult to reach consensus about such a controversial area despite its relevance to the operation of the station.[23] Moreover, consensus in the essential areas mentioned is reflected in the perception that people in different positions see eye-to-eye regarding the operation of the station and in a felt absence of conflict between members at various echelons. Thus amount of total control, in part because of the actual basic agreement that it establishes, tends also to foster the feeling of co-operative relations in the station. The latter, in turn, may act to reinforce such basic agreement.

The findings further suggest that high total control is efficacious in promoting member consensus in these stations because it is associated with significant influence by the rank-and-file members upon the operation of the station. They have a part in determining organizational norms and consequently may be expected to be more motivated to accept them. This is substantiated, in part, by the significant relationship between total control and the morale of the members and by the significant relationships between the influence of the rank and file upon the operation of the station and the measures of work-group and hierarchical consensus. Equally important, under conditions of high total control, the direction provided by an effective leadership is utilized in determining consensus as well as the control of the rank-and-file members.

[23] The relevance of consensus regarding control to organizational performance is demonstrated by the finding, previously reported, of significant positive correlations between member-officer agreement concerning ideal control and productivity in this organization (Smith and Tannenbaum, *op. cit.*).

Such *joint* control has the effect of facilitating an integration of interests and promoting a shared, acceptable system of norms.

Furthermore, a high amount of total control is conducive to member consensus because it is accompanied by an effective system of high mutual influence *within* the work group and *between* members at the rank-and-file and supervisory levels. The system of control is effective because it reflects *both* significant control by the supervisors upon the rank-and-file members and substantial control by the rank-and-file members upon the work group. The data suggest that it is the control of the rank-and-file members themselves within the work group which contributes to an important extent to work-group and hierarchical consensus. It is understandable that such control by workers themselves would particularly facilitate acceptance of the norms of the work group. When complemented by structure which the supervisors provide, there is the insurance that the control by the rank-and-file members within the work group also functions to enhance consensus between the rank-and-file and supervisory levels. In effect, given this system of control, promoting acceptance of the norms of the work group also has the result of reinforcing acceptance of the norms of upper echelons.

Finally, high total control is associated with the acceptance by the rank-and-file members of this pattern of organizational control as legitimate. A significant positive correlation exists between amount of total control and an index of the extent of correspondence between the actual control exercised by the various levels and that desired for these levels based on member responses ($r = .35$, $p < .05$). Such acceptance facilitates the exercise of effective leadership as well as encouraging the influence of the rank-and-file members in determining and enforcing consensus.

In contrast, while high control by the rank and file *relative* to that of higher echelons may have positive motivational effects for the former and promote the perception of consensus in these stations, it is not in itself a sufficient condition to promote consensus in the work group or to guarantee that the norms of the work group will actually complement those of higher echelons. The absence of the predicted relations between positive slope and member consensus may run counter to the argument of many observers who have discussed the positive effect of "democratic" control or "democratic" decision-making (if by these terms we mean relatively high rank-and-file as compared to leader influence) without considering their full implications in terms of *both* the distribution and amount of control exercised. The insignificant results obtain in these stations primarily because positive slope is not associated with an effective interaction-influence system. High rank-and-file control relative to that of the supervisors is not associated with a high level of control within the work group, which was found to be a highly significant determinant of member consensus, nor is it associated with any appreciable rank-and-file control upon the supervisors or manager. It is furthermore associated with a low amount of control by the supervisors upon the station and the work group.

Hence an effective leadership which might provide structure and direction to the relatively high rank-and-file control, and thereby promote and expedite consensus, is absent. This lack of effective leadership under conditions of positive slope is accentuated by the fact that relatively high rank-and-file control may be accompanied by a rejection of the existing pattern of control, that is, by work group norms regarding ideal control counter to those of the supervisory levels. This may have the effect of reducing the significance of the control exercised by either the rank-and-file or supervisory levels.

While the findings appear to support one of the two major hypotheses, a note of caution should be injected. In our conceptualization we have implied certain causal relationships between control structure and member consensus. However, in view of our cross-sectional data, we are unable to specify with certainty the direction of the relationship. It may be a reciprocal one. Not only may the system of control determine member consensus, but the nature and extent of member consensus may condition the type of organizational control.[24] It is readily conceivable that a system of work-group norms counter to those of a higher echelon might increase the tendency toward hierarchical control, that is, negative slope. Or lack of consensus within an organization may be so dysfunctional that a low amount of control is exercised by the various conflicting groups.

2. Control, consensus, and organizational effectiveness

The thesis of this investigation has been that the effects of certain patterns of control on organizational performance derive partially from the uniformity with respect to organizational standards and policies which these patterns of control promote. In turn, the regularity, orderliness, and predictability deriving from such uniformity were viewed as being essential to the concerted action underlying the highly effective organization.

Our findings indicate that this is indeed a tenable explanation for the effects of total control upon organizational performance which we have found in these stations. The significant exercise of control by both members and leaders leads to a high degree of identification and involvement in the organization. All organization members are more motivated to develop a set of shared policies and practices, to accept jointly made decisions, and to act on behalf of the organization. The system of high mutual influence which this pattern of control signifies provides an opportunity for members and leaders to reconcile their interests and facilitates an atmosphere of co-operation. This further bolsters common loyalties and promotes shared objectives which are reflected in the wider acceptance of organizational norms. The conditions thus

[24] This is suggested by James D. Thompson and Arthur Tuden, "Strategies and Processes of Organizational Decision," in *Comparative Studies in Administration*, ed. Pittsburgh University Administration Science Center (Pittsburgh: University of Pittsburgh Press, 1959), pp. 195–216. They hypothesize that agreement or lack of agreement about different types of issues in the decision process calls for different strategies of decision-making, which in turn dictates different patterns of control.

exist for effective decision-making and improved co-ordination in carrying out organizational objectives in a concerted manner. Finally, it may be inferred that the joint contributions of members and leaders facilitate better and more acceptable policies and decisions insuring their translation into concerted action of an adaptive nature characteristic of the highly effective organization.

The findings also suggest that "democratic" control (i.e., positive slope) does not have the predicted effect of promoting high organizational performance in these stations partially because it does not promote a system of shared organizational norms which we have found to be associated with the high-performing station. While this pattern of control may lead to high rank-and-file morale, it does not appear to promote basic identification with organizational objectives and practices or motivated action leading to high performance. It appears that in this organization high rank-and-file control relative to the leaders may have the effect of members' acting simply in terms of their own self-interests and not accepting the contributions of the leaders. Furthermore, this pattern of control is not associated with a system of high reciprocal influence in which structure is provided by the leaders. Such structure would help to insure a system of shared organizational norms. In the absence of shared organizational norms and a system of high mutual influence (i.e., high total control) to regulate and co-ordinate member action with respect to these norms, it is not surprising that democratic control is not conducive to high organizational performance.

It is conceivable that a positively sloped distribution of control might lead to a system of shared norms and consequently concerted action on behalf of the organization in a different type of organization with different organizational conditions.[25] This might occur in a "mutual benefit" type of organization, such as some voluntary associations, where the interests and objectives of members and leaders are more fully shared, and where decision-making is of a judgmental nature.[26] Other necessary conditions would include a prevailing ideology sanctioning "democratic" control and a formal structure, including authority and decision-making, that would facilitate the control of the rank-and-file members. If such a structure is also associated with high mutual influence between the members and the leaders, the basis is provided to achieve the necessary co-ordination and to translate rank-and-file control into effective action. In the present organization such conditions do not exist and their absence may account in large part for the lack of the predicted effects of positive slope.

---

[25] In the League of Women Voters, a significant positive relationship occurs between positive slope and organizational effectiveness (Tannenbaum, "Control and Effectiveness . . . ," *op. cit.*).

[26] See Thompson and Tuden, *op. cit.*

11

THE ROLE OF THE INTERACTION-INFLUENCE SYSTEM IN A PLANNED ORGANIZATIONAL CHANGE*

Clagett G. Smith
Glenn Jones[1]

This paper reports findings on one aspect of a field experiment involving the introduction of "participative-management" procedures into the production departments of a manufacturing company.[2] Likert's theory of participative management served as the conceptual framework for the design and execution of the field experiment.[3] This theory has been derived from a long series of small group laboratory studies and surveys of complex organizations; two field experiments, one small and one large, played crucial roles in its formulation (1, 6). It "is conceived to apply within the general framework of the classical line-and-staff, hierarchical organizational form, and is thought to be an enlargement upon, rather than a contradiction to, the familiar conceptions of scientific management and human relations mangement" (9, pp. 16–17). The theory is addressed to the "problem of achieving mutual compatibility and adaptation between the requirements of the organization and the requirements of the individual members" (9, p. 16).

In the formal statement of the theory, four "systems of organization" are specified: the "exploitative authoritative," the "benevolent authoritative," the "consultative," and the "participative group" (3, Ch. 14). As one proceeds from the exploitative-authoritative system to the participative-group system, the compatibility of organization and individual requirements increases. The theory hypothesizes that this increase in compatibility, in turn, increases pro-

* This paper has not been previously published.

[1] This report represents the efforts of a number of staff members of the Institute for Social Research, The University of Michigan, during a four-year period. The initial conception of the study and arrangements with the firm as well as part of the subsequent field work, were contributed by Rensis Likert and Robert L. Kahn. Robert Norman and John G. Hooven were major change agents, and their efforts and perseverance accounted in large part for the success of the change program. General study direction was provided successively by Dagfinn Ås, Donald C. Pelz, and Stanley E. Seashore, and Arnold S. Tannenbaum. They were assisted in measurement and analysis activities and in the preparation of client and professional reports by Martin Patchen, David Sirota, Mrs. Dora Marcus, and Joyce Stephens. The present article and the analysis on which it is based were made possible by a grant from the Carnegie Corporation of New York to the Survey Research Center, Institute for Social Research. We thank our colleagues who read and suggested revisions in earlier drafts of this paper; we are particularly grateful to Stanley E. Seashore, whose suggestions showed us the way to make it a more united presentation.

[2] The reader is referred to Seashore and Bowers (9) for a comprehensive description of important aspects of this study.

[3] This theory has been explicated in *New Patterns of Management* (3). Our description paraphrases this work, as well as Seashore and Bower's (9) synopsis of the theory.

ductivity and member satisfaction and decreases absenteeism, turnover, and waste. Likert explains the effects of the participative approach in terms of a system of interpersonal relationships that comprise what he calls the "inter-action-influence system." The present analysis is designed to examine this aspect of Likert's theory.

The experiment

The site

The Banner Company manufactures a great variety of plastic bags and other flexible containers. Although the company has numerous small plants from coast to coast, the study was done in the headquarters city at its main complex of plants, which employs about 700 persons.

At the time the research began, in 1958, the company was experiencing considerable difficulties. Since its founding in the 1920s, management had actively sought to maintain close and responsible relationships with employees. The result was a highly informal and paternalistic organization that was known for the high quality of its craftsmanship and for industrial leadership in new products and processes. However, by the 1950s small competitors had begun picking off technologically simple and standardized product lines that threw the company into a price-cost squeeze. The owners then began a program of rationalization, while at the same time striving to preserve the friendly informality for which Banner was known. Against this background, the company requested The University of Michigan Survey Research Center to study ways of increasing participative management, which was viewed as one means of coping with the difficulties besetting the company.

Objectives of change

Certain aspects of Likert's theory were selected as the objectives of the change program. "Our objective in the Banner study is to create an organizational structure in which . . . an extremely important set of human motive-sources, namely, the desire for status, recognition, approval, acceptance, etc. (the ego motives) might emerge" (9, p. 17). This structure, which was to be created experimentally, implied an organization in which (1) the basic unit in the organization is the work group, consisting of a single supervisor and his immediate subordinates. Ideally, the supervisor directs his subordinates on a group rather than on an individual basis. These groups form at all levels within the organization; for example, a plant superintendent and the department heads in a plant are a work group, as are a department head and his foremen, or a foreman and his crew. (2) High mutual influence is provided through group meetings and as a result of norms regarding the legitimacy of peer influence about work conditions. Influence is accepted on its merits regardless of source, and this influence may include reasonable pressure toward conformance with group standards, including high performance standards. (3) Psychological support is provided to all organization members. This support may take two forms: first, the support for achievement in terms of encouraging high goals, encouraging effective means of reaching them, and helping the organization member to do a better job; second, the support of an affiliative nature in terms of recognition of good work, the correction of mistakes, and the resolution of disputes in an atmosphere of positive effect. The sources of this support include supervisors and peers. (4) Groups are decision-making bodies, so that influence is not confined simply to eliciting conformity to goals, means, and norms but is brought to bear on changes in the goals, means, and norms that are of concern to the group. Groups may also suggest changes relevant to other groups and to the organization as a whole. (5) These groups are linked together by reason that, except at the very lowest and very highest echelons in the organization, each person in the organization is a member of two groups: one consisting of himself and his subordinates and another of himself, his peers, and his supervisor. Thus the supervisor is no longer part of a transmission belt of information and influence from upper to lower levels. Rather, he is a member of two decision-making groups, and he functions to convey the influence of each group to the other.

These were the states towards which the change agents sought to guide the experimental (but not the control) departments. However, during the experiment all groups throughout the plant were organized in linking-pin fashion, so that the fifth item drops out of the experimental design; the first four remain as independent-variable categories.

The change program

After initial planning, shortened through pressures of the worsening competitive position of the company, the experimental change program began in one department. Changes were to be instituted by the line management with the Survey Research Center agent acting as teacher, guide, and counselor. The means through which changes were attempted included supervisory seminars and discussion sessions, individual counseling sessions conducted by the Survey Research Center agent, and meetings of employees conducted by line supervisors. Results of the survey questionnaires were reported in some of the above sessions, and changes designed to improve supervisory practice consistent with the experimental design were considered.

Questionnaires were administered in August and December of 1958, prior to the introduction of any change, and in July of 1959, during the course of the change program. At the time of the 1959 measurement two departments were added as experimental departments and two as control departments. The change agent's services were continued through September of 1960, at which time the Survey Research Center judged that his services had reached a point of diminishing returns. Nonetheless, upper management and the line organization of the three experimental departments continued to apply the principles of the experiment. A final (after) questionnaire measurement was taken in December of 1961. This was complemented by interviews with management officials and union officers in May of 1962.

The initial research design envisioned a clear difference in treatments between the experimental and control departments and provided insulation against contamination of the control units by the change agent's activities in the experimental units. Circumstances prevented the complete execution of this design. As Seashore and Bowers (9, p. 70) put it,

> The designation of departments as experimental or control was therefore not in accordance with a predetermined experimental plan, but rather a designation that developed by a self-selection process as the work proceeded. The designation was made, however, before the terminal measurements were taken, and before it was known whether there would or would not be any measurable, significant differences between the experimental and control departments. While this deviation from proper experimental design should be noted, and considered in the interpretation of results, it should also be noted that this hazard of population control is probably an inherent feature of any field experiment in which control is relaxed in favor of observation of natural processes.

Independent and criterion variable changes

The results concerning the independent variables that Seashore and Bowers (9) developed are presented in Table 1.[4] The results concerning the criterion (dependent) variables, which include measures of satisfaction, productivity in terms of the percentage standard of machine efficiency achieved by the several departments, and absenteeism are shown in Table 2.[5]

When we examine the findings in Table 1, the 1958 column indicates that at the beginning of the experiment the control departments were generally superior to the experimental on the independent variables. The relative-change column shows that seven of the eleven variables changed in the predicted direction, six of them significantly. None of the negative changes reach near significance. A look at the two change columns reveals that, in general, the relative changes are a function of negative trends in the control departments coupled with positive trends in the experimental departments. When one examines the content of the variables, the striking fact emerges that all

[4] Our assessment of the data in terms of relative change implies that both kinds of departments are expected to change as a result of company-wide circumstances external to the experiment itself. However, any differential changes between these departments are assumed to be traceable to the experimental manipulations.

[5] Comparison of departments on productivity are based on the extent to which each department reached standards of machine efficiency set by industrial engineers. Although the absence rates for 1961 and 1958 are comparable, the methods of tabulating them vary between years in such a way that variances cannot be compared; consequently, tests of significance cannot be made.

TABLE 1 The Manipulated (Independent) Variables[a]

Variable	Difference[b] between control and experimental groups in		Change[c] between 1958 and 1961 in		Relative change[d]
	1958 (1)	1961 (2)	Control groups (3)	Experimental groups (4)	(4) minus (3) (5)
1. Emphasis on work group:					
Foreman's use of group approach	+.40†	+1.23†	+.03	+.85†	+.83†
Belong to a team	−.63†	+.18	−.24*	+.57†	+.80†
2. Supportive behavior:					
Foreman supportiveness—achievement	−.09	+.38†	−.25*	+.22†	+.47†
Foreman supportiveness—affiliation	+.11	+.44†	−.28*	+.05	+.33†
Peer supportiveness—achievement	−.03	−.03	+.02	+.02	−.01
Peer supportiveness—affiliation	+.09	−.03	−.10	−.22	−.13
3. Employee participation in decision making:					
Employee influence in department (actual influence of employees)	−.02	+.20	−.28	−.06	+.22
Foreman accepts influence from employee	−.29†	+.18	−.17	+.30†	+.46†
4. Peer interaction and influence:					
Peer influence among employees	−.73†	+.02	−.35†	+.41†	+.75†
Peer pressure for productivity	+.04	−.02	+.03	−.03	−.06
Peer pressure for waste reduction	−.10*	−.08	+.05	+.08	+.03

[a] Tests in columns 1 and 3 are two-tailed; those in columns 2, 4, and 5 one-tailed: * $p < .05$; † $p < .01$.

[b] A plus sign means experimental department is more participative than control departments.

[c] A plus sign means 1961 score is more participative than 1958 score.

[d] The significance of the relative change is derived from standard tables of critical values of (Student's) t. The generalized formulas can be found in Walker and Lev (20, p. 159), formulas (7.28) and (7.29).

four variables dealing with the interaction of foremen with workers show significant relative changes, but only two of the seven dealing with peer interaction do so.

In Table 2, the satisfaction variables show patterns somewhat similar to those of the independent variables. The relative changes in satisfaction in the expected direction are more striking than the changes in manipulated variables. Similarly, the relative changes in machine efficiency and absenteeism are consistently in favor of the experimental departments. In general, these results conform to Likert's theory.

In presenting this background, we have drawn heavily on the descriptions and analyses of Seashore and Bowers (9). We now turn to an assessment of the data describing the interaction-influence system.

THEORY AND HYPOTHESES

The major hypothesis of this investigation is that changes in the independent variables were accompanied by changes in the organization processes of interaction and influence, which the theory conceptualizes as a system, and that these processes intervene between the independent-variable changes and changes in the criterion variables. This assumes that changes in the independent variables create changes in the interaction-influence system.

In terms of the theory, the independent-variable conditions may be expected to affect aspects of the interaction-influence system in the following manner. The integration of superiors and subordinates into cohesive groups lowers barriers to accurate communication. In contrast, the competitive nature of the man-to-man system of organization encourages the withholding of information from competing peers and also the filtering and distortion of information. Support also reduces the threats involved in multidirectional communications flow. Group decision making elicits widespread communication for which the linking-pin articulation of the organization provides channels. The supportiveness of supervisors and peers, the cohesiveness of work groups, the expectancies of influence acceptance, and the articulation provided by the linking-pin form of organization also enhance the exercise of influence upward and laterally, as well as downward in the organization. A number of studies suggest that such a system of high mutual influence and multidirectional communication is conducive to effective organizational performance (2, 3, 11).

The theory holds that "decision points," like communication and interaction, occur at all levels in the organization. Decisions are made largely through groups. The high volume of information and influence, plus the fact that decisions are made by those most concerned with their execution, should result in informed and effective decisions. The linking-pin pattern of organization is hypothesized to reduce conflict of interests and to orient decisions to the larger goals of the organization, and participation in the making of decisions

TABLE 2 The Criterion (Dependent) Variables[a]

Variable	Difference between control and experimental groups in		Change between 1958 and 1961 in		
	1958 (1)	1961 (2)	Control groups (3)	Experimental groups (4)	Relative change (4) minus (3) (5)
1. Employee satisfaction with (in 5 units scale)					
a. Foreman	−.14	+.46†	−.40†	+.19†	+.59†
b. Company	+.07	+.27†	−.15	+.04†	+.20*
c. Work group	−.91†	−.19†	−.08	+.64†	+.72†
d. Pay	+.31†	+.53†	+.08	+.30†	+.22
e. Working conditions	+.03	+.37†	−.06	+.28†	+.34*
f. Job security	−.03	+.21*	−.05	+.19†	+.24*
g. Promotional opportunity	+.04	+.33*	−.50†	−.21*	+.29
2. Machine efficiency (in percentage of standard)[b]					
a. Depts. ABC—Depts. DE[a]	+13.2	+26.0	−1.7	+11.1	+12.8
b. Depts. AB—Depts. DE[a]	+18.1	+27.9	−1.7	+ 8.1	+ 9.8
3. Absences (rates per half year 1961 minus 1958)[c]					
a. Instances of absence	−1.32	−.34	−1.23	−.25	+ .98
b. Days absent	−2.00	+.13	−2.49	−.36	+2.13
c. Instances late	− .66	−.54	− .69	−.47	+ .12
d. Instances early departure	− .76	−.46	− .84	−.54	+ .30

[a] See footnotes, Table 1.

[b] Test of significance 2a involves comparison of three experimental departments (ABC) with two control departments (DE). However, increases in department C may have been artifactual, because of a new product line and changes in machine standards. Test of significance 2b deletes this experimental department.

[c] Significance tests not feasible.

minimizes resistance to their execution. Previous research suggests resultant high levels of member satisfaction and organization performance (6, 7, 11).

The theory further anticipates that an intense system of communication, interaction, and influence generates common perceptions and common attitudes that coalesce into widely accepted norms. These norms provide a framework that patterns the processes of communication, influence, and decision making. Indeed, an effective normative system was postulated to be a central aspect of the change program, as specified in the original design, taking the form of "near criterion variables" (9). Such a system of norms in other settings has been shown to represent more organization, as well as a more effective organization (10, 14, 16).

In short, it is hypothesized that, when the conditions denoted here as independent variables reach a high state of development, they set the conditions for an interaction-influence system characterized by a large flow of multidirectional communication, a high rate of mutual influence, and a pattern of group decision making throughout the organization that fosters, and in turn is supported by, a strong normative structure. This system, in turn, contributes to the effectiveness of the organization and to the satisfaction of its members.

The above theory concerning the role of the interaction-influence system as an intervening mechanism in the experiment leads us to predict that the experimental departments change differentially in relation to the control departments toward:

1. More two-way communication
2. More adequate communication
3. A greater total amount of influence or control
4. Greater increments of influence or control exerted at lower echelons relative to the increments exerted at higher echelons
5. More decentralized decision making, including an increase in the number and importance of decisions made at lower echelons relative to those made at higher echelons
6. More decisions made by groups than those made by individuals
7. More uniformity in perceptions of organizational structure and process

MEASUREMENTS

The data forming the basis of the present analysis are confined to comparisons of responses of rank-and-file personnel to the combined 1958 questionnaires and those administered in 1961. These yielded N's of 321 in the experimental departments and 143 in the control departments for the 1958 data, and N's of 251 and 97 in these departments for the terminal period.[6]

Aspects of the interaction-influence system were assessed in a number of

[6] The procedure of deriving data from respondents who were employed throughout the course of the experiment permitted greater comparability in assessing changes due to such continuity of personnel. The attrition in numbers between 1958 and 1961 is due to an actual decline in the labor force over the three-year period.

ways. Communication was measured on dimensions of "manner," "effort," "receptivity," and "adequacy."

The question measuring manner was "How do you feel about the way each of the following people keep you informed?" Four response categories were provided, ranging from "very pleased" to "objectionable" relative to the respondent's group leader, foreman, and supervisor.

The question measuring effort was "How much effort do you feel the following people make to keep you informed?" The four response categories ranged from "a great deal of effort" to "no effort at all."

The question measuring receptivity to communication was "To what degree can you get the following people to listen and act upon your proposals, suggestions, and ideas?" The four response categories ranged from "to a great extent" to "to no extent at all."

The question measuring adequacy of information was "How adequate is the information you have about the following items?" The four response categories ranged from "very adequate information" to "very inadequate information." The scores on five items were added to produce an index of adequacy of information regarding the company. The items were "the company's plans for expansion," "proposed new products," "what the industrial engineers do," "what other departments do," and "what the union's activities are." Similarly, an index of adequacy of information regarding the job was constructed from the three questions, "How I am doing," "What my foreman expects of me," and "Why my work is assigned or scheduled as it is."

Measures of organizational influence or control were developed and operationalized by employing the control-graph technique. These measures were derived from questions ascertaining actual general influence of the various echelons, the influence that respondents desired these echelons to have, and actual influence in specific areas of decision making.

Actual general influence was measured by the question, "In general, how much say or influence do you feel each of the following groups has on what goes on in your department?" The respondent was asked to check one of five response categories, ranging from "little or no influence" to a "very great deal of influence," for each of the following objects: "top manufacturing," "your foreman's supervisor," "your foreman," "your group leader," and "the employees in your department."

Desired general influence was measured by the question, "In general, how much say or influence do you think each of the following groups should have on what goes on in your department?" The same objects were used as in the previous question.

An index of specific influences was made by averaging the responses to influence questions about the following areas: "how pay raises should be set," "how employees are to be rotated on the different machines and which employees are to work together on these machines," "changes in the methods of work," and "how much an operator should produce per hour or how all such standards should be determined." Although the response categories were the same in these specific questions as in the actual and desired general influence questions, the referents were changed. They were "higher manufacturing managers," "people in staff departments, such as personnel, industrial engineering, scheduling, etc.," "the foreman," "the group leader," and "the hourly paid employees."

A "total-control" score was derived by summing each respondent's scale scores for all echelons and averaging these sums for all respondents.[7] "Slope" scores were derived by subtracting each respondent's scale score for the "employee" echelon from his score for the "management" echelon. The slope score is conceptualized graphically as a line drawn from the scale score attributing influence to the highest echelon in the hierarchy to the scale score for the lowest echelon. Past usage labels the slope "positive" when the influence at the lowest echelon is greater than at the highest and "negative" when the highest echelon is attributed the greater influence. All mean slope scores calculated in this study were negative, and hence a smaller score is designated as more positive than a larger score, in the sense that it is less negative.

Changes in the decision process were not measured quantitatively but must be inferred largely from the measures of communication and influence just described and from the qualitative information yielded by the interviews with management and union personnel mentioned above. Interviewees were asked to describe changes in decision-making processes from 1958 to 1961 and to differentiate between departments.[8] The interview protocol covered the following areas concerned with decision making; processes occurring in employee and higher-level meetings, frequency and kinds of suggestions obtained from employees, channels and levels of decision making, feedback on suggestions and decisions, and management decision patterns.

In order to measure consensus or uniformity, 84 items were selected from the questionnaire. These included (1) 43 items employed as questionnaire measures of the independent, intervening, and criterion variables; (2) 12 items measuring hierarchical role performance; (3) 20 items from which the "index of specific influences" was constructed; (4) indices of peer support, supervisory support, general satisfaction, and involvement; and (5) single questions on foreman pressure for productivity and decreased waste, actual and desired autonomy on the job, satisfaction with information about the company, and whether the foremen go to bat for their people. Before their uniformities were known, these variables were selected on the basis of high relevance to the organization and importance to individuals. Uniformity is said to

---

[7] Thus, these scores have about five times the magnitude of those from which the differences shown in Table 5 are derived. It should also be noted that the population on which all control measures were calculated for each of the three types of control was limited to those who answered for all levels and thus for whom total-control scores could be calculated.

[8] Only some of these respondents were able to provide information that discriminated between the control and experimental departments.

increase when the variance on an item decreases from 1958 to 1961.[9] Uniformity was compared statistically as follows. For each of the five departments a percentage was calculated of the number of variances that decreased between 1958 and 1961 relative to the 84 items on which variances were compared. These percentages were averaged for the three experimental and two control departments respectively, weighting the contribution of each department according to its average size over the experimental period. This method preserves within-department variances as the units of analysis. The difference between these weighted percentages was then calculated. The significance of this difference was determined, using a standard formula for the significance of the difference of proportions (4; formula 20, p. 60) treating the number of comparisons used in calculating the weighted percentages as the N of the respective samples.

RESULTS

Table 3 shows a clear improvement of the experimental departments over the control departments in communication. The relative changes are significant statistically and in the predicted direction for eight of eleven variables, pertaining both to downward (manner and effort) and upward (receptivity) communication, as well as to its adequacy. From the results of Table 1 (specifically the measure of peer influence among employees) together with information gained from interviewing management personnel, there is also some indirect evidence of improved lateral communication at all levels in the predicted direction. One notable finding in Table 3 is the consistent emergence of the foreman as a communicator in the experimental departments.

The results for influence and control are not so strong. On both the general and specific influence measures, influence as measured by the total-control statistic increased in the experimental and decreased in the control departments. However, only in the specific measures is the relative change significant.

Previous studies have shown that desired, or ideal, control is usually higher than, but follows the general pattern of, actual control (Smith and Tannenbaum, 12). These data show the same pattern (Table 4). Total control desired increased in the experimental departments and decreased in the control departments to produce a significant relative change. An examination of Table 5 indicates that the major changes in influence took place in the middle echelons of the organization, but little happened at the group-leader and employee levels.

[9] We do not believe variances were constricted by a "ceiling effect" by reason of means being at the extremes of the scales, because the means are within scores of 2.0 and 3.5 on five-point scales with standard deviations of less than 1.0. Examination of 2 × 2 tables for each department comparing changes in means over time with corresponding changes in variance indicates the relation between mean and variance changes is almost completely random. For a more detailed discussion of this point, see Tannenbaum and Bachman (16).

TABLE 3   The Intervening (Organization) Variables:^a Communication

Variable	Difference between control and experimental groups in		Change between 1958 and 1961 in		Relative change
	1958 (1)	1961 (2)	Control groups (3)	Experimental groups (4)	(4) minus (3) (5)
1. Communication manner					
a. Foreman's supervisor	+.14	+.29†	+.21*	+.37†	+.15†
b. Foreman	+.06	+.41†	−.08	+.27†	+.35
c. Group leader	+.14	+.18†	+.07	+.11†	+.04
2. Communication effort					
a. Foreman's supervisor	−.05	+.21*	+.21	+.47†	+.26†
b. Foreman	−.20	+.40†	−.21*	+.39†	+.60†
c. Group leader	+.04	+.00	+.07	+.03	−.04
3. Receptivity to opinion and ideas					
a. Foreman's supervisor	+.04	+.37†	+.13	+.45†	+.33*
b. Foreman	−.09	+.29†	−.01	+.37†	+.38†
c. Group leader	−.60†	+.00	+.03	+.63†	+.60†
4. Adequacy of communication					
a. Regarding job	−.18*	+.24†	−.11	+.30†	+.41†
b. Regarding company	−.31†	+.18*	−.36†	+.13*	+.49†

^a See footnotes, Table 1.

TABLE 4 The Intervening (Organization) Variables:[a] Control and Influence (Summary of Slope and Total Control)

| Variable | Difference between control and experimental groups in | | Change between 1958 and 1961 in | | Relative change (4) minus (3) |
	1958 (1)	1961 (2)	Control groups (3)	Experimental groups (4)	(5)
1. (Actual) general influence					
a. Positive slope[b]	−.17	+.16	−.64†	−.31	+ .33
b. Total amount of control	−.18	+.56	−.54	+.20	+ .74
2. Index of specific influences—work standards, rotation, raises, and methods					
a. Positive slope[b]	−.35†	−.30	−.84†	−.79	+ .05
b. Total amount of control	+.01	+.96†	−.46	+.49*	+ .95*
3. (Desired) general influence					
a. Positive slope[b]	−.21	+.05	−.66†	−.40	+ .26
b. Total amount of control	−.29	+.82	−.48	+.63*	+1.11*

[a] See footnotes, Table 1.
[b] The derivation of slope is explained in the text. Since the theory predicts less slope than calculated here, the signs of the actual differences have been reversed, so that plus (+) means in the direction predicted by the theory as in previous tables.

TABLE 5 The Intervening (Organization) Variables:ᵃ Control and Influence

| Variable | Difference between control and experimental groups in | | Change between 1958 and 1961 in | | Relative change (4) minus (3) |
	1958 (1)	1961 (2)	Control groups (3)	Experimental groups (4)	(5)
1. (Actual) general influence					
a. Top management	+.09	−.06	+.49†	+.34*	+.15
b. Foreman's supervisor	−.14	+.10	−.15	−.01	+.14
c. Foreman	−.10	+.23	−.38†	−.05	+.33*
d. Group leader	+.07	+.13	−.17	−.11	+.06
e. Employees	−.09	+.13	−.19	+.03	+.22
2. Index specific influences—work standards, rotation, raises, and methods					
a. High manufacturing management	+.28†	+.34†	+.81†	+.87†	+.06
b. Staff	−.10	+.21	−.80†	−.48	+.31*
c. Foreman	−.16	+.33†	−.46†	+.02	+.48†
d. Group leader	+.05	+.06	−.02	+.01	+.16
e. Employees	−.07	+.05	−.02	+.10	+.12
3. Desired general influence					
a. Top management	−.01	+.04	+.29	+.34†	+.05
b. Foreman's supervisor	−.12	+.22*	−.02	+.32†	+.34*
c. Foreman	+.04	+.32†	−.22	+.06	+.28*
d. Group leader	+.02	+.16	−.16	−.02	+.14
e. Employees	−.22	+.08	−.37*	−.07	+.30*

ᵃ See footnotes, Table 1.

Briefly, then, the findings concerning influence and control provide weak support for predictions of greater total control, but they do not support predictions for a more positive slope at all. The findings indicate that changes in influence took place at upper and middle but not at lower levels in the organization. Such changes support the view that participative management is a means of increasing management's influence, as well as, if not more than, that of the rank-and-file employees (See, for example, March and Simon, 5, p. 54, and Tannenbaum, 15).

These results suggest that, because of the apparent deficiencies of the organization and its weakening competitive position at the outset of the experiment, management attempted to tighten up the organization. In the control departments, they did so within a traditional management framework, increasing the control exercised by top echelons at the expense of control by middle and lower echelons. In the experimental departments, however, management was committed to a participative approach through which control by the top echelons was enhanced without decreasing control by lower levels. The result was a somewhat greater total amount of control.

The changes in control as measured are not very great, perhaps because the experiment did not proceed so far toward the participative model as originally intended and because the measures are not so sensitive as they should be.[10] The measures, for example, do not seem to reflect the increased influence that the employees report themselves to have on the foremen in the experimental departments, as indicated in Table 1. Nonetheless, some detectable changes did occur in the total amount of control consistent with theory.

Although rank-and-file members in response to questionnaire items did not indicate very great change in the distribution of control, management personnel reported through personal interviews that in the experimental departments more people were involved in decisions; that decisions were being given consideration, if not being made, at lower levels; and that they were based on more information and opinion than formerly.

One manager stated: "As a consequence of the (experimental) program, the emphasis is on decision-making. There's more decision-making by the department heads after sensing and getting group opinion. Now there's more decision-making at all levels."

The head of the staff unit stated: "[The three plant superintendents] make more decisions independent of [the manufacturing vice-president] than they did four years ago. And [the department heads] make more decisions. The level of decision-making is coming down. This is different from four years ago. It's a lot easier to make suggestions and decisions at lower levels and more acceptable."

However, it should be noted that the levels being discussed are department heads (supervisors) and sublevels of top manufacturing management.

---

[10] Specific measures may be more sensitive than global ones, as suggested by Patchen's findings (8).

A department head said: "More decisions are made by groups than by individuals now. We do more of our work in groups."

Another indicated: "There has not been much of a change in who makes decisions, [but] people have more say in decisions which affect them. In all manufacturing, there's been a change."

These responses suggest confirmation of the increased communications reported above and of the inference that decisions are made on the basis of wider consultation and a broader range of facts. However, although they imply some increased influence for rank-and-file employees, they appear more explicit in pointing to enhanced influence at upper levels. These responses suggest that the change program attempted at the managerial level was more effective than that attempted at lower levels, even though there is some evidence that lower participants were consulted more in the process of arriving at decisions.

The results of the analysis concerning uniformity are consistent with the expectation that variances in perceptions and attitudes would decrease in the experimental departments. In these departments 57.4 percent of the items showed an increase in uniformity, as compared with 43.9 percent of the items in the control departments. The relative difference between departments is significant at the .01 level of confidence. Hence, we are inclined to believe that interaction and influence in the experimental departments resulted in a better-defined social system, which, in turn, provided a more stable framework for communications and influence.

SUMMARY AND CONCLUSIONS

The first two predictions—that the experimental departments would change differentially in the direction of more two-way communication and more adequate communications—are substantially confirmed. This reflects employee perceptions of improvement on the independent variables, particularly the increased receptivity on the part of foremen to the ideas and suggestions of the employees. Furthermore, the interview data suggest increments over time in the extent of efficient and planned communication at higher supervisory levels. We should expect that these changes in communications would not only have positive motivational effects for the employees and increase their satisfactions but that they would also provide the basis for more effective decisions and actions resulting in higher productivity.

The third prediction, of a greater total amount of control, is supported only weakly. In general, those in the control departments see influence declining at every level but management, and those in the experimental departments see influence holding its own everywhere but at the management level, where, for all departments, it goes up. One assumption of the experiment is that, without the manipulations, changes in the experimental departments would have resembled those in the control departments. It may be that some factors unaccounted for by either theory or data were diminishing influence or control at all levels except management and that pressure was particularly strong on foremen. Of course, such factors might add up simply to the fact that change per se was having a disorganizing effect in these departments.

The fourth prediction, of an increase in influence at lower levels relative to that at higher levels, is not substantiated. These findings are consistent with those of previous research that suggest that predictions about slope as either a cause or effect are usually tenuous. Except in voluntary organizations, its behavior is far less consistent than the total control variable (12).

Results were inconsistent concerning the fifth prediction, of an increase in number and importance of decisions made at lower echelons compared with those at higher echelons. The managers interviewed were nearly unanimous in thinking that decision making had become more decentralized in the experimental departments. However, employees in the experimental departments saw an increase in decisions by management and, compared with the control departments, an increase by foremen. They reported no increased decision making farther down in the organization.

The sixth prediction, of more group decisions, cannot be confirmed or disconfirmed. Given the success of manipulations in increasing the foreman's group approach, in increasing the sense of belonging to a team, and in increasing peer interaction and influence and given the increased satisfactions with foreman and work group, one might extrapolate to an intervening group decision process in the experimental departments. Testimony from the interviews indicates this is generally true, especially at higher echelons, but data are unavailable to confirm the prediction with any confidence.

The seventh prediction, of greater uniformities of attitudes and perceptions in the experimental departments, is confirmed. We see this increased uniformity as a consequence of the increased communication, influence, and decision making in the experimental groups. Insofar as these uniformities represent norms, we see them as providing structure for organizational processes and as partly underlying the increased productivity and satisfaction in the experimental departments.

Our major conclusion is that a number of the (intervening) variables in the interaction-influence system changed in the directions predicted by the theory. Knowing that these changes as well as those found in the criterion variables may have been due to other factors, we examined eighteen measures of characteristics that lay outside the scope of the theory. They related to personal characteristics of the workers, characteristics of jobs (including technology and task interdependence), and characteristics of the formal organization. Although the details of the analysis are beyond the scope of this paper,[11] none of the differences between the experimental and control departments on these measures, either singly or in combination, offers an explanation

---

[11] At this writing, this examination is set out in a longer mimeographed draft on which this paper is based, Smith and Jones (13).

for the effects reported above. This exploration has increased our confidence in the predictive power of the theory.

However, we also need to explain why the experiment failed to yield some of the predicted results. One strong possibility is that the change agents spent more time with supervisory than with rank-and-file personnel and that, as a consequence, in the experimental departments rank-and-file persons have more a feeling of belonging to a team; they influence each other more; they communicate more; they are more uniform in their opinions and attitudes; they are more satisfied; they are comparatively better about getting to work; and they produce more. But they do not support one another more or encourage one another toward higher standards of performance; they do not have more power; and they do not make more decisions. The positive gains are easily attributable to the increase in group and supportive supervision that they receive, including support by the supervisor for higher standards of performance; the failures may be attributed to a lack of direct training of the workers in effective participation.

However, the failure of certain aspects of rank-and-file behavior to change in predicted directions may also indicate weakness in the theory itself. For example, one explanation for the failure of workers to gain more influence relative to levels above them in the hierarchy may lie with systems which have transactions with the organization but which lie outside its boundaries. It could be argued that such systems as stockholders, unions, or the larger society place severe restraints on the degree to which the organization is permitted to delegate effective power to the rank and file. A second explanation is that those independent variables which failed to respond to the manipulations are crucial antecedents to the increase of rank-and-file influence.

The difficulty with which we are faced at this point, from the standpoint of the theory, is that one of the above explanations is about as good (or bad) as another. The causal–intervening–end result relationships are stated in the theory in a way that gives us considerable power, as we have seen. But the intra- and extrasystem relationships between variables are defined so generally that, when the predictions fail, we cannot diagnose these failures in terms of the theory with any precision. The general relation between the intrasystem variables is derived from the way in which "management systems" are defined (3, Table 14–1, pp. 223–233). The variables that, in combination, constitute such a system tend to increase or decrease together. When they are at the low end of the scale we have exploitative-authoritative management (system 1) and at the high end participative-group management (system 4). In order to increase or decrease together, variables must bear a similar relation to one another; specifically they must be related monotonically. Although a good many examples of empirical relations between variables are to be found, this inference derived from the management systems is the closest the theory comes to specifying a set of functions. Similarly, although a number of conditions outside the organization system to which managements must adapt are described empirically, the effects of these conditions are not incorporated into the theory, so that the theory tends to treat the organization as a closed system. A closed system, in which all factors change in the same direction, provides an imprecise model for an organization, even when the causal–intervening–end result relations among the factors have been articulated. In fact, a real prototype of such a system could probably not maintain itself. Although such a model has general predictive power, it cannot generate specific predictions.

What we can do is to use the four systems and particularly system 4 as ideal models, as Likert suggests using an ideal model of the interaction-influence system as a tool to analyze organizations (3, pp. 184–185). Such applications do not provide precise tests of the model, but, as in the study reported here, they do allow one to construct a general framework of empirically based propositions that structure data a good deal more efficiently than, say, a set of predictions derived from a half dozen related hypotheses usually do.

BIBLIOGRAPHY

1. Coch, L., and French, J. R. P., Jr. (1948). Overcoming resistance to change. *Human Relat.*, **1**, 512–532.
2. Donald, Marjorie N. (1959). Some concomitants of varying patterns of communication in a large organization. Unpublished doctoral dissertation, The University of Michigan.
3. Likert, R. (1961). *New patterns of management.* New York: McGraw-Hill.
4. McNemar, Q. (1955). *Psychological statistics.* New York: Wiley.
5. March, J. G., and Simon, H. A. (1958). *Organizations.* New York: Wiley.
6. Morse, Nancy C., and Reimer, E. E. (1956). The experimental change of a major organizational variable. *J. abnorm. soc. Psychol.*, **52**, 120–129.
7. Mulder, M. (1960). Communication structure and decision structure and group performance. *Sociometry*, **23**, 1–14.
8. Patchen, M. (1963). Alternative questionnaire approaches to the measurement of influence in organizations. *Amer. J. Sociol.*, **49**, 41–52.
9. Seashore, S. E., and Bowers, D. G. (1963). *Changing the structure and functioning of an organization: report of a field experiment.* Ann Arbor, Mich.: Institute for Social Research, The University of Michigan.
10. Smith, C. G., and Ari, O. (1964). Organizational control structure and member consensus. *Amer. J. Sociol.*, **69**, 623–638 (in this book, Chap. 10).
11. Smith, C. G., and Brown, M. (1964). Communication structure and control structure in a voluntary association. *Sociometry*, **69**, 401–410 (in this book, Chap. 9).
12. Smith, C. G., and Tannenbaum, A. S. (1963). Organizational control structure: a comparative analysis. *Human Relat.*, **16**, 299–316 (in this book, Chap. 5).
13. Smith, C. G., and Jones, G. (1964). Organizational process and organizational change: a field experiment. Unpublished mimeograph, Institute for Social Research, The University of Michigan.
14. Tannenbaum, A. S. (1956). Control structure and union functions. *Amer. J. Sociol.*, **61**, 536–545 (in this book, Chap. 2).

15. Tannenbaum, A. S. (1962). Control in organizations: individual adjustment and organizational performance. *Admin. Sci. quart.*, **7,** 236–257.
16. Tannenbaum, A. S., and Bachman, J. G. (1966). Attitude uniformity and role in a voluntary organization. *Human Relat.*, **19,** 309–322 (in this book, Chap. 18).
17. Tannenbaum, A. S., and Kahn, R. L. (1958). *Participation in union locals.* New York: Harper & Row.
18. Tannenbaum, A. S., and Smith, C. G. (1964). The effects of member influence in an organization: phenomenology versus organizational structure. *J. abnorm. soc. Psychol.*, **69,** 401–410 (in this book, Chap. 13).
19. Tannenbaum, A. S. (1966). *Social psychology of the work organization.* Belmont, Calif.: Wadsworth Publishing Co.
20. Walker, Helen M., and Lev, J. (1953). *Statistical inference.* New York: Holt.

12

STRUCTURAL VERSUS
INDIVIDUAL EFFECTS*

Arnold S. Tannenbaum
Jerald G. Bachman[1]

One may define structural constructs as opposed to purely individual variables for purposes of group or organization theory. However, the frequent reliance, in empirical studies, on measures based on individual member responses often creates some operational ambiguity. Do the relationships observed when employing measures based on individual responses truly represent the effects of structural variables, or are they simply reflections of individual-level relationships?

Blau has suggested one approach to this problem. He proposes an analytic technique which provides, in effect, an operational definition of structure.[2] Davis, Spaeth, and Huson also provide an approach through the measurement of what they refer to as "compositional" effects.[3] These approaches overlap in several essential respects, and both represent significant contributions toward the solution of a difficult problem of sociological analysis. It is our intention to explore further the meaning of these methods, to consider some of their assumptions which appear to impose limitations on their applicability as presently formulated, and to suggest several means which may be helpful in reducing (if not overcoming) the effects of these limitations. Since Blau's approach is simpler in format, it will be easier to introduce the issues of the present paper primarily through reference to that approach. We shall then indicate their relevance to the method of Davis, Spaeth, and Huson.

Blau's strategy for determining structural effects may be summarized in three steps:[4]

1. An empirical measure, Z, is obtained that pertains to some characteristic of individual group members that has direct or indirect bearing upon the members' relations to each other (e.g., group identification, sociometric choices, initiation of interaction, rate of communication, or promotions).

* Reprinted from *American Journal of Sociology*, May 1964, Vol. LXIX, No. 6, with permission of The University of Chicago Press and the authors.

[1] We are indebted to the following friends and colleagues who kindly read an earlier draft and offered suggestions: David Bowers, Bruce Hill, Leslie Kish, Bernard Indik, John Kirscht, Philip Marcus, James Morgan, Frank Neff, Donald Pelz, Clagett Smith, and John Sonquist.

[2] Peter M. Blau, "Formal Organization: Dimensions cf Analysis," *American Journal of Sociology*, LXIII (1957), 58–69, and his "Structural Effects," *American Sociological Review*, XXV (1960), 178–93.

[3] James A. Davis, Joe L. Spaeth, and Carolyn Huson, "A Technique for Analyzing the Effects of Group Composition," *American Sociological Review*, XXVI (1961), 215–25.

[4] The following section closely paraphrases Blau, "Formal Organization . . . ," *op. cit.*, p. 63.

TABLE 1 Performance Scores by Rate and Frequency of Discussion (Hypothetical Example)*

Individuals who discuss their problems	Groups most of whose members discuss their problems	
	Rarely	Often
Often	0.65 (1)	0.85 (2)
Rarely	0.40 (4)	0.70 (3)

* Adapted from Blau, "Formal Organization . . . ," *op. cit.*, p. 64.

2. The scores for measure Z, which describes individuals, are combined into one index for each group, and this index no longer refers to any characteristic of individuals but to a characteristic of the group. The value of this index is presumed to vary across groups; we will define this variable as Z_{gp}. Thus any individual may now be characterized in terms of his *own* score along variable Z and his *group's* score along variable Z_{gp}.[5]

3. To isolate a structural effect, the relationship between the group attribute (Z_{gp}) and some dependent variable, W, is determined while the corresponding characteristic of individuals (Z) is held constant. The structural effect thus refers to the effect of Z_{gp} on W.

This method is illustrated by Blau through the hypothetical data of Table 1 in which five hundred persons are assumed to be arranged in fifty groups of about ten members each. We have numbered the cells for convenience from 1 to 4. Blau suggests that a structural effect is demonstrated by the differences in average performance scores between the two columns in Table 1. "This finding would show that, even when the effect of the individual's discussion rate of his problems on his performance is eliminated, just to be in a group where communication flows freely improves performance—other things being equal."[6] This statement, however, is based on an assumption which we must question.

The assumption of constancy within rows is asserted frequently by social researchers in relation to the type of analysis represented in Table 1. It can, however, lead to serious misinterpretations of data. It is important to recognize first of all that continuums underlie each of the axes in Table 1, even

---

[5] Lazarsfeld and Menzel would define the Z_{gp} variable in this usage as a "contextual property" of individuals, i.e., a property which stems from the individual's membership in a group (Paul F. Lazarsfeld and Herbert Menzel, "On the Relation between Individual and Collective Properties" in Amitai Etzioni [ed.], *Complex Organizations* [New York: Holt, Rinehart & Winston, 1961], pp. 422–40; see also Hannan C. Selvin and Warren O. Hagstrom, "The Empirical Classification of Formal Groups," *American Sociological Review*, XXVIII [1963], 399–411).

[6] Blau, "Formal Organization . . . ," *op. cit.*, p. 64.

though dichotomous categories are employed. Individuals (and groups) are not simply "often" or "rarely" communicators, but are likely to differ along a broad continuum of frequency of discussion. With this in mind, let us assume that all distributions within groups are normal (although almost any type of continuous distribution would lead to the same conclusion). The effects of this assumption can be seen in Figure 1. The points Z_1–Z_4 represent the average individual discussion scores of individuals in cells 1–4 of Table 1. Several facts of importance are apparent from Figure 1:

1. In comparing individuals in cell 1 of Table 1 with those in cell 2, we are comparing individuals who have relatively low (Z_1) discussion scores with those having higher (Z_2) scores. We are not, in other words, holding the individual independent variable (Z) constant, and cannot say that the difference between the two cells on the dependent variable represents the effects of social structure. The same problem applies to the comparison of the remaining two cells.

2. The failure to hold Z strictly constant within rows has its counterpart in the failure to hold Z_{gp} constant within columns when more than two groups are being analyzed. The reader can see for himself how this unfortunate state of affairs develops by adding two normal frequency distributions, representing two additional groups, to the curves drawn in Figure 1. The pair of curves on the right would be labeled "High Discussion Groups." However, the one furthest to the right would contribute more members toward the computation of the mean in cell 2 than would the second group in that pair, while it would contribute fewer to the computation of the mean in cell 3 than would the second group. We would therefore be contaminating the individual-level (i.e., within-column) comparison with group effects.

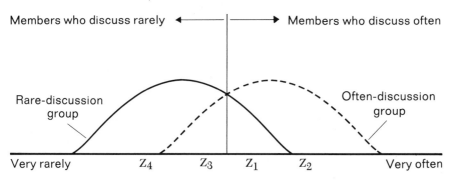

Z_1 = Average discussion score for individuals high on frequency of discussion in low-discussion group

Z_2 = Average for high-discussion individuals in high group

Z_3 = Average for low individuals in high group

Z_4 = Average for low individuals in low group

FIGURE 1 *Hypothetical frequency distributions of members within two groups on a scale of frequency with which member discusses problems.*

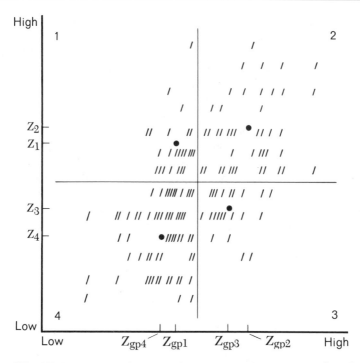

FIGURE 2   *Scatter diagram showing Z and Z_{gp} scores based on Monte Carlo data.*

Figure 1 implies a positive correlation between the Z scores of individuals and the Z_{gp} scores assigned these individuals according to the groups in which they are located. A more detailed and concrete illustration of this relationship and of the problems it creates can be seen from data which we have obtained employing Monte Carlo (random) techniques as follows: (*a*) A random sample of 150 individuals was drawn from a population which is normally distributed on individual variable Z. (*b*) This sample was randomly divided into fifty groups of three members each, and a Z_{gp} score (equal to the mean Z for the three members) was derived for each group. Figure 2 presents the data obtained in this way. Each of the 150 "statistical individuals" is located in the matrix according to his own Z score and the Z_{gp} score assigned to his group.

Let us define for these data a perfect linear relationship between the individual variable Z and the dependent variable W.[7] Table 2 analyzes these data

---

[7] For the sake of clarity we have assumed a linear correlation of 1.00 between Z and W. It is important to note, however, that the general observations which we will illustrate with these data apply equally well when there is *any* direct positive relationship between Z and W. The use of a perfect correlation in our illustration simply serves to rule out random variation or "noise." Individual-level, curvilinear relationships between Z and W might lead spuriously to "contingency" or "inverse" type structural relationships described by Blau, depending upon the shape of the individual-level relationships. We are illustrating here a spurious "direct" type structural effect (see *ibid.*).

by the Blau method. According to this method the results would be interpreted as showing a strong individual-level effect coupled with a moderate (but quite definite) direct structural effect. However, we have defined dependent variable W as being perfectly related to individual variable Z and have assigned members randomly to groups, thus effectively ruling out any

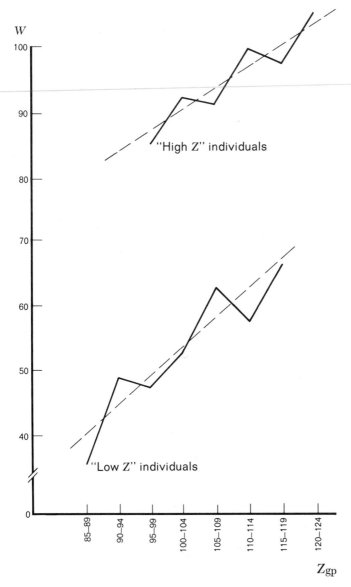

FIGURE 3 *Dependent variable W as related to individual variable Z and group variable Z_{gp} (hypothetical example—Davis et al. technique).*

possibility of a genuine structural effect. The spurious structural effect indicated in Table 2 reflects the failure to hold the individual characteristic strictly constant within rows.

The processes underlying the problems noted above can be seen more clearly by returning to Figure 2. The intersecting lines in the diagram correspond to the dichotomies employed in deriving Table 2, and the four quadrants match the four cells in that table. The solid black circle in each cell indicates the mean Z and Z_{gp} for those cases falling within the cell. It is apparent that the level of Z for individuals in cell 1 is, on the average, lower than that for individuals in cell 2. In other words, individual effects are not held strictly constant across the "high Z" individuals. And, of course, the same problem appears for the "low Z" individuals in cells 3 and 4.

The failure to hold group effects constant within columns can also be seen readily from this figure. "Low Z_{gp}" individuals in cell 4 come, on the average, from groups with *lower* Z_{gp} scores than do individuals in cell 1; and Z_{gp} scores are lower for "high Z_{gp}" individuals in cell 3 than for those in cell 2.

The strategy used by Davis, Spaeth, and Huson is similar in several respects to that proposed by Blau. However, the former dichotomizes only on the Z variable and not the Z_{gp}. The groups are spread out along the horizontal axis according to their Z_{gp} scores. This eliminates the problem of contaminating within-column differences with group effects. However, the problem of eliminating individual effects in the intergroup comparisons remains. A limited solution to this problem, implicit in the Davis, Spaeth and Huson method, is its restriction to individual characteristics that are dichotomous: "Within each population, individuals may be characterized by the presence or absence of a given *independent* attribute (A or $\bar{A}$)."[8] To the extent that the individual variables involved are truly dichotomous, neither the Blau method nor that of Davis, Spaeth, and Huson need be concerned about the problem of controlling for individual effects. However, most variables of interest to social scientists (including some of those discussed by Davis *et al.*) are continuous, and the problem remains for these. In Figure 3 we apply the method of Davis, Spaeth, and Huson to our Monte Carlo data and see demonstrated (spuriously) a "Type IIIA" compositional effect: "a constant individual difference, along with a linear effect of group composition."[9]

STRATEGIES FOR HOLDING CONSTANT INDIVIDUAL AND GROUP CHARACTERISTICS

The problems we have discussed stem from the assumptions that individual variables are held constant within rows and that group variables are held constant within columns. It is possible to reduce, if not to overcome, these problems through several modifications of the Blau or the Davis *et al.* methods.

[8] Davis *et al.*, *op. cit.*, p. 216 (italics as in original).

[9] *Ibid.*, p. 220.

However, it is worth noting that the two problems may not be equally important in all situations. For example, a researcher who is interested primarily in determining the presence of a structural effect may not be especially interested in whether a spurious individual-level effect appears as a result of his failure to hold group characteristics strictly constant. He will, on the other hand, be seriously concerned as to whether the structural effect he isolates is a spurious one caused by failure to hold individual characteristics constant. The techniques outlined below are not exhaustive, nor are they spelled out in fine detail. Our purpose is to open a number of avenues which may be useful in dealing with the problems raised above.

More precise matching of the individual variable

The need for holding individual effects constant when comparing "high Z_{gp}" and "low Z_{gp}" groups suggests that individuals be matched more closely on the individual independent variable (Z). It should be noted that the fairly crude matching achieved when Z is dichotomized represents a very great improvement over the situation which would exist if no attempt whatever were made to match individuals according to Z. However, as we have demonstrated, the dichotomy may not be sufficient. The larger the number of categories, of course, the greater the accuracy in matching; however, a "point of diminishing returns" is soon reached as the matching becomes more precise and as the number of cases falling within each category is reduced. The optimum number of categories to be used in any particular situation must be determined by the researcher.

Once the researcher has determined the number of categories into which to divide variable Z, he can proceed as in the Blau technique; he will, however, use an $N \times 2$ rather than Blau's 2×2 table. Certain of the cells in such a table might be empty; these, as well as their counterparts in the opposite column, would have to be abandoned. The remaining cells will provide an esti-

TABLE 2 Dependent Variable W as Related to Individual Variable Z and Group Variable Z_{gp} (Hypothetical Example—Blau Technique)*

	Groups	
Individuals	Low Z_{gp}	High Z_{gp}
High Z	93.3	100.4
	(1)	(2)
Low Z	49.5	61.4
	(4)	(3)

* Cell entries indicate mean W (for all individuals in the cell).

mate of structural effects with individual effects held (more or less) strictly constant. Returning to our random data, the application of this modification (using a 7×2 table rather than a 2×2 one) completely eliminates the spurious structural effect shown in Table 2. It may not, however, eliminate spurious individual effects.

The modified technique described above can be extended further so as to cover a broader range of scale points along the horizontal axis (Z_{gp}) in a manner suggested by Davis et al. This is preferable to the dichotomous analysis for several reasons. First, the dichotomy is usually inefficient statistically. Second, the use of a sufficient number of categories along the horizontal (Z_{gp}) dimension would hold group characteristics strictly constant and thus avoid the problem of spurious individual effects. Finally, the broader range of cases along the horizontal axis may lead to richer possibilities of analysis, increasing the likelihood of detecting the direct, inverse, and contingency effects discussed by Blau, or the various relationships in the typology outlined by Davis et al. Returning once again to our random data, the use of a 7×8 table rather than a 2×8 table would convert Figure 3 into a series of seven essentially horizontal lines, correctly indicating the presence of an individual, but not a structural, effect. However, the use of such a large number of cells drastically reduces the number of cases within each cell, so this variation will be appropriate only when the over-all number of cases is quite large.

Correlational methods

Given a breakdown into N levels of the individual variable (Z) as described in the preceding section, it would be possible to determine the presence of structural effects by correlating Z_{gp} and W at each of the N levels of Z. This requires that each individual be assigned a Z_{gp} score according to the group in which he is located as well as his own individual W score. In the case of our Monte Carlo data, we would have seven separate correlation coefficients (corresponding to the seven levels of individual variable Z). These correlations would not provide information about individual-level effects. Such effects might be detected through the use of intragroup correlations, that is, by correlating Z and W separately within each group (thereby holding group effects constant).

Each of the above correlational procedures involves holding one variable constant while measuring the relationship between two others. If the particular data to be analyzed meet the necessary statistical requirements, the technique of partial correlation might achieve the same result. This could have the advantage of simplicity and precision. A structural effect could be measured in terms of the correlation between Z_{gp} and W with Z partialed out. An individual effect would be determined by the correlation of Z and W with Z_{gp} partialed out.[10]

---

[10] Thanks are due to Peter Blau for suggesting this possibility. Hubert M. Blalock, Jr., explains that "the partial correlation coefficient can be interpreted as a *weighted average* of the correlation coefficients that would

A more thorough analysis of the dependent variable W using Z and Z_{gp} as the independent variables could be carried out through multiple-regression techniques. In such an approach, the change in W expected with a unit change in Z_{gp} provides a measure of the structural effect, and the change in W expected with a unit change in Z provides a measure of the individual effect. It is very important in applying either this technique or that of partial correlation to remember the assumption of linearity upon which they are based. Unless the relationships between Z, Z_{gp}, and W are linear, the results of these analyses can be very misleading. However, it may sometimes be possible when the relationships are curvilinear to employ transformations, such as Z^2, log W, $(Z_{gp})^2$, and the like, to achieve the necessary linearity.[11]

The correlational techniques described thus far are all concerned with predicting the dependent variable (W) at the individual level. Another approach to detecting structural effects makes use of aggregate data such as those in the $N \times M$ table described in the preceding section. Given such a table, the correlations between Z_{gp} and *mean* W can be determined at each of the N levels of Z. In the case of the 7×8 table derived from our Monte Carlo data, we would have seven correlation coefficients (corresponding to the seven levels of individual variable Z). Each correlation would be based upon eight cells, with each cell referring to a certain level of Z_{gp} and the *mean* of the dependent variable W for all individuals located in that cell.

Several cautions should be borne in mind in applying this method. First, while correlations based upon *mean* data can provide information about the overall presence or absence of a structural effect, they cannot be used to estimate how much of the variance in *individual-level* W can be related to Z_{gp}. Second, correlations based upon aggregate data are not directly comparable to intragroup correlations, since different N's and different groupings of the data are used; accordingly, their relative magnitudes do not indicate a relative strength of structural as compared to individual effects. Third, a correlation based upon a small number of data points (eight in our illustration) is subject to a great deal of variation due to chance, although this may be somewhat reduced when each of the points is based upon averages. Accordingly, any conclusion concerning the presence or absence of a structural effect should probably be based upon the overall pattern of correlations.[12] On

---

have been obtained had the control variable been divided into very small intervals and separate correlations computed within each of these categories" (*Social Statistics* [New York: McGraw-Hill Book Co., 1960], p. 332).

[11] The multiple regression approach is somewhat related to L. A. Goodman's "Some Alternatives to Ecological Correlation," *American Journal of Sociology*, LXIV (1959), 610–25 (see esp. pp. 623–25); and Dean Harper's Ph.D. dissertation ("Some New Applications of Dichotomous Algebra to Survey Analysis and Latent Structure Analysis" [Columbia University, 1961]).

[12] A weighted average correlation combining all of the correlations for each Z level may sometimes be justified as a summary measure. In some cases it may be reasonable to derive a weighted average regression curve from the 7 (or N) curves, and a single, more stable correlation may be computed from this (see, e.g., A. S. Tannenbaum and C. G. Smith, "The Effects of Member Influence in an Organization: Phenomenology versus Organization Structure," *Journal of Abnormal and Social Psychology*, 69 [1964], 401–410 (in this book, Chap. 13). While a single correlation obscures distinctions between the types of group compositional effects suggested by Davis *et al.* (*op. cit.*, p. 219), it can indicate a general overriding trend of the data.

the positive side, the use of aggregative instead of individual data may provide a more stable and accurate estimate of the true effect across groups, since each data point represents the observation of a number of individuals, thus eliminating a large portion of the random variance which occurs at the individual level.[13]

SOME FURTHER CONSIDERATIONS

A number of problems remain which apply to the original methods of Blau and of Davis *et al.* as well as to the modifications outlined in the preceding section.

The problem of overlap

It can be seen through examination of Figure 1 and Table 1 that the N's in the four cells of the table are likely to be unequal, depending upon the extent to which the distributions of individual scores within the respective groups overlap. The N's in the four cells approach equality as the two distributions approach each other. But as this statistically desirable condition is approached, the data become meaningless as a basis for demonstrating structural effects; that is, structurally the groups are the same (on the independent variable) when the distributions coincide exactly. On the other hand, as the groups become more and more distinct, it is less and less possible to tell whether or not group effects are present. The N's in cells 1 and 3 become zero when the two distributions do not overlap at all. This implies, in terms of the scatter diagram of Figure 2, a correlation between Z and Z_{gp} approaching 1.00. It is ironic that this situation, which seems conceptually most felicitous for the discovery of structural effects, precludes their detection by the methods under consideration.

Deviants

A further qualification can be seen from Figure 1 and Table 1. Individuals in cells 1 and 3 are deviants within their respective groups (at least with respect to their scores on the independent variable), and their responses may be influenced by that fact alone. Thus, when we compare individuals in cell 2 with those in cell 1 we may be comparing "average" members in one group with "deviant" members in another. The same problem applies in the comparison of cells 3 and 4. The importance of this problem cannot be ascertained easily. One can hope that it is not a serious source of contamination in most cases, although we know that deviants are likely to be affected differently by group experiences than are average members. The researcher would probably do well to consider its possible effects in terms of the particular variables being analyzed.

[13] Selvin and Hagstrom, *op. cit.*

Selection

The manner in which members are selected into groups may influence the relationship between Z_{gp} and W and may create in this way a spurious structural effect. For example, members of fraternities with high average intelligence (Z_{gp}) may have higher grade-point averages (W) than members of low average intelligence fraternities, even when individual intelligence (Z) is held strictly constant. This finding might be interpreted as indicating that being in a group of intelligent students creates better performance. Suppose, however, that certain fraternities maintain a policy of stressing high academic standing. Such a policy could lead to the selection of members directly on the basis of grades. Since intelligence and grades tend to be related, fraternities with such policies would be relatively high in average intelligence, thus producing the spurious structural relationship between average intelligence (Z_{gp}) and grade-point average (W), while holding individual intelligence (Z) constant.

It is probably worth keeping this problem in mind when interpreting group effects, since selection is a common phenomenon in social life. It is not unusual for individuals to join groups whose members are like themselves. Furthermore, even if selection *into* a group is random, selection *out* may be systematic, leaving a non-random selection behind. The various bases for selection may differ from case to case, and the corresponding interpretation of group effects would have to differ accordingly. Obviously, the problem can be completely eliminated in laboratory studies where groups are constructed by random procedures. Many field situations too would seem reasonably safe. The selection processes employed in creating formal work groups in industry, for example, are in many cases irrelevant to the particular variables under study, and these groups can be considered reasonably free of the problem. Certain informal and voluntary groups, however, may be more problematic, but this would depend again upon the variables under investigation.

Structural effects, operations versus concepts

There is some conceptual haziness about variables which somehow are characterizations of both the organization and the individual. Research in group or organization functioning would do well to distinguish effects which are uniquely structural. While it may be easy enough to denote *conceptually* some variables that apply uniquely to structure and have no meaningful counterparts on the individual level, the fact that much social research must fall back upon measures based on individual responses creates a difficulty. While the concepts may be structural, the measures may be contaminated by individual effects. It is for this reason that the Blau method and that of Davis *et al.* are important approaches to the discovery of structural effects.

It is interesting to note, however, that Blau's original method, which is an operational approach to the definition of structural effects (and consequently structural characteristics), precludes from consideration, according to Blau, "those aspects of social structure which are not manifestations of frequency distributions, such as the form of government in the community."[14] This type of variable, however, is obviously of great interest to the social researcher. Furthermore, the Blau method *can* be helpful in approaching this type of variable if this method is employed not simply as a means of operationally defining structural variables and effects, but as a means of helping to ascertain whether the instrument chosen to measure a structural variable is in fact measuring such a characteristic.

We would like, therefore, to maintain the important distinction between a structural concept and a structural measure. While the concept, for example, may refer to aspects of the organization such as "chain of command," "flexibility," or "distribution of control," which are not manifestations of frequency distributions, the measures may very well be based on distributions, that is, on the responses of individual members.[15] Measures of these structural concepts would be subsumed under Kendall and Lazersfeld's unit datum of Type V where "the unit item characterized the group only" and where "no information is introduced about a single individual."[16] We add simply that, while no information may be introduced about a single individual, information may be introduced *by* individuals. It is for this reason that the Blau method and that of Davis *et al.* can prove helpful.

Structural variables should be chosen first on the basis of their theoretical meaningfulness. Measurement is a second step, and tests of relationships between these variables and others are a third. Measurement of a pure structural effect in this sense might then be gauged by the occurrence of a difference between groups according to one of the above methods and a zero difference within groups. This is, with some modification, the Type II effect described by Davis *et al.* Conceptually, we would attempt to approach in this way the effect of a structural variable which has no meaningful counterpart on the individual level—although all of our measures are obtained at that level.

SUMMARY AND CONCLUSIONS

Since measures of group and organization variables are often based on responses of individuals, it is sometimes difficult to know whether the effects observed are due to structure or due simply to individual characteristics.

[14] Blau, "Structural Effects," *op. cit.*, p. 192.

[15] See, e.g., Ellis L. Scott, who is concerned with the causes of error in the perception of the "chain of command" (*Leadership and Perceptions of Organizations* [Research Monograph No. 82 (Ohio State University, Columbus: Bureau of Business Research, Ohio State University, 1956)]). Basil Georgopolous and Arnold S. Tannenbaum measure organizational flexibility by averaging responses of organization members to questions designed to provide estimates of this variable ("A Study of Organizational Effectiveness," *American Sociological Review*, XXII [October, 1957], 534–40). Martin Patchen is concerned with the validity of measures, based on member responses, of distribution of control in organizations ("Alternative Questionnaire Approaches to the Measurement of Influence in Organizations," *American Journal of Sociology*, LXIX [July, 1963], 41–52).

[16] Patricia L. Kendall and Paul F. Lazarsfeld, "Problems of Survey Analysis," in Robert K. Merton and Paul F. Lazarsfeld (eds.), *Continuities in Social Research* (Glencoe, Ill.: Free Press, 1950), pp. 133–96. See also Selvin and Hagstrom's discussion (*op. cit.*) of aggregative and integral properties of groups and their distinction between members as respondents and as informants.

Blau has suggested a useful approach to this difficulty, but one that appears to contain two problems: (1) it fails to hold individual characteristics strictly constant and thereby makes it possible to obtain spurious structural effects; (2) it fails to hold group characteristics strictly constant, making possible the occurrence of spurious individual-level effects. A technique similar in some respects to Blau's has been developed by Davis *et al.;* this method is susceptible only to problem (1).

We have proposed several modifications of the Blau and the Davis *et al.* methods, making use of more precise matching and correlational techniques. Each of these modified methods involves certain advantages and limitations, and the researcher may want to employ them in combination or modify them further to suit his particular purposes.

Several additional problems have been considered including the effect of deviants, overlap of distributions among groups, and selection. We were also concerned about the purpose of the original methods discussed here, namely, defining structural or compositional effects (and, by implication, structural variables) *operationally.* In the authors' opinion this is not an adequate substitute for the conceptual definition of structural variables; conceptualization should come first. The application of the above techniques could then serve the very useful function of determining whether or not the operations employed can be justified as measures of structural characteristics and effects.

13

EFFECTS OF MEMBER INFLUENCE IN AN ORGANIZATION: PHENOMENOLOGY VERSUS ORGANIZATION STRUCTURE*

Arnold S. Tannenbaum
Clagett G. Smith[1]

Phenomenology has had an important impact in social psychology. Analyses of behavior are often preceded by the question: "How does the social situation seem to the actor?" rather than: "What are the objective facts about the situation?" More specifically, one finds, in the notion of "psychological participation," the feeling that one is exercising influence through contributing to decisions—whether or not one is in fact (French, Israel, & Ås, 1960; Vroom, 1960). Sills' (1957) explanation of member loyalty and activity in a large voluntary organization illustrates the application of this notion. Sustained volunteer interest in the National Foundation for Infantile Paralysis is explained by the fact that nearly half the members *believe* that the organization is "democratic" even though it is not.

> As far as these volunteers are concerned, the Foundation has a democratic structure [p. 219].

March and Simon (1958) offer a general appraisal of this view:

> . . . most students of the subject argue that (providing the deception is successful) the perception of individual participation in goal setting is equivalent in many respects to actual participation [p. 54].

However, as Fenichel (1945) has pointed out:

> social psychology is by no means limited to the study of what is going on in individual minds when groups are formed . . . it must likewise face and solve problems of an entirely different nature, namely, not only that of subjective but also of objective groups, of the similar effects that similar external stimuli have on different individuals [p. 87].

* Reprinted from *Journal of Abnormal and Social Psychology*, Oct. 1964, Vol. 69, No. 4, 401–410, with permission of the publisher and the authors. (This article has been edited to eliminate overlap and to bring it into a consistent format with the other articles in this book. Certain portions have therefore been deleted or reworded. Ed.)

[1] We would like to acknowledge the help and suggestions of Jerald G. Bachman, Michael E. Brown, Dora Cafagna, and Marijana Benesh in the analysis and preparation of the material presented here.

The exercise of influence in a group or organization, for example, has important implications, quite apart from how this influence is perceived. The role a member plays in the influence structure bears on what he must and must not do, the areas of freedom and choice which he has, the level of rewards he will receive and the deprivations he may suffer, whether his group or organization moves in directions congenial to him or in directions to which he is opposed. The exercise of influence within a group or organization can be seen as part of a structure which, in simplest terms, redounds to the advantage or disadvantage of members. It is in terms of these implications that members might be expected to be satisfied or dissatisfied, express loyalty or disloyalty, or be energetic or apathetic on behalf of their organization. We shall refer to this view as the structural hypothesis by way of contrast with the phenomenological described earlier.[2]

In a recent study, Tannenbaum (1961) shows variations among 104 leagues of the League of Women Voters of the United States in their effectiveness and in their levels of member activity, corresponding to differences in patterns of influence as reported by the members. Leagues in which members report that the membership as a group is high in influence relative to the president tend to have relatively active and loyal members (according to self-reports by members) and these leagues are also judged to be relatively effective by a group of raters chosen by the National Office. The results are consistent with a body of theory and research concerning the relationships between the exercise of control or influence and indices of satisfaction, loyalty, identification, and motivation in group and organizational settings (Blau, 1956; Blauner, 1960; Coch & French, 1948; Likert, 1961; Morse & Reimer, 1956; Mulder, 1960a, 1960b). The analysis to be reported here is concerned with the relative tenability of the above two views as explanations of the findings in the League. Does it seem reasonable to explain the relatively high level of member loyalty and activity in some leagues in terms of members' perceptions that their leagues are controlled by the membership, or is it more reasonable to explain these relationships in terms of the control which the membership actually exercises?

This article reports a secondary analysis of data from the above study. Although objective measures of influence patterns in leagues are not available (since all of our measures are based on member reports) the present analysis

---

[2] We use these terms for the sake of simplicity and convenience although we recognize considerable variation in view among psychologists who, in a dichotomous scheme, might be classified either as phenomenologists or structuralists. Snygg (1941), for example, in expounding the need for pure phenomenology, criticizes the Gestaltists for incorporating objective, as well as phenomenological, elements. Allport (1955) questions Lewinian theory by pointing out

that physicalistic considerations have been brought into the theory, surreptitiously and without raising the question of how they are to be articulated with the prevailing phenomenological scheme [p. 156].

We do not pretend to test, below, the general validity of the broad (and, to some extent, ambiguous) theories which these terms may imply. The hypotheses which we shall investigate are more limited and the reader is asked to keep in mind the particular operational definitions which we employ.

can provide some evidence relative to those contrasting interpretations. Essentially, the analysis involves two major comparisons. The first compares within each of the 104 leagues separately the levels of loyalty and activity of members who differ in their perceptions of membership influence relative to the president's influence. The phenomenological hypothesis would suggest a preponderance of positive relationships in this analysis. The second compares the levels of loyalty and activity of individuals from leagues which differ in amount of relative membership influence as reported by their average members. However, perceptions of influence patterns are held constant in this analysis by comparing the loyalty and activity only of those members who report identical perceptions of relative membership influence. The phenomenological hypothesis would suggest zero relationships in this instance since perceptions are held constant; significant positive relationships here would be more consistent with a structural interpretation.

METHOD

The data of this study come from a survey conducted within the League of Women Voters of the United States. The design of the study and some of the measures of influence employed in this analysis are described on pages 60 to 64.

The index to be explored here is designed to represent the slope of a best fit straight line on the control graph. Slope is approximated operationally by subtracting the amount of influence reported to be exercised by the president from that reported to be exercised by the membership. A value of slope is computed for each league by averaging the responses of members within each league. This index is found to correlate .31 with ratings of league effectiveness (p .001).[3] Each member can also be characterized in terms of her individual perception of the influence pattern in her league, i.e., slope as she sees it. A positive slope for a league means that the membership is reported to have more influence in determining the policies and actions of that league than is the president. This index might be taken to represent what is popularly referred to as degree of "democratic control." Of the 112 leagues in our sample, 88% are found to have negative slopes.[4]

Each respondent was also asked to answer on a five point scale (from 1, "no influence" to 5 "a very great deal of influence") the question, "How much influence do you think [you personally] have in determining the policies and actions of your local league?" These data do not form part of the index of slope, but they provide useful supplementary information.

---

[3] Effectiveness scores for each of the leagues were obtained from a group of 29 raters familiar with the work of most of the leagues. These raters were chosen by the National Office and are not members of the leagues in question. For a more detailed description, see Tannenbaum (1961). The correlation reported above is a partial correlation in which size of league is controlled. The first-order correlation is .33. However, since size of league varies so widely (from 25 to about 3,000), and since it has been found in an earlier study to have important effects, we follow the practice of controlling for the effect of size, where this is possible, through the method of partial correlation. Furthermore, the effect of size is found to be more adequately represented by a logarithmic rather than a linear function (Tannenbaum, 1961, 1962a). We therefore employ log size in all correlations involving size. However, it should be noted that the primary advantage of using partials here is that the results presented will be consistent with those in earlier reports where partialing proved important. Actually, partialing makes relatively little difference in the present analysis.

[4] We shall employ henceforth the term "slope" as a shorthand for the amount of influence exercised by the membership as a group compared to that exercised by the president. We shall also refer to perceptions of slope, although subjects were never asked to estimate slope as such. Perception of slope is to be understood then as the amount of influence perceived to be exercised by the membership minus the amount of influence perceived to be exercised by the president.

Dependent variables

Two dependent variables, amount of member activity and of loyalty, are to be considered. Amount of activity is measured in terms of two questions, the responses to which are averaged to form an index:

> 1. How many of the following types of meetings have you attended during the past year? (A list of six types of meetings was provided in tabular form and respondents were asked to check boxes for each indicating the number of meetings attended.)
>
> 2. How much time would you say you spend *during the course of an average month* on league affairs? Include everything such as telephone calls, traveling time, reading league materials, attending meetings, etc. If you do not spend any time in connection with the league, place a zero in the space provided. Do not leave it blank.
>
> _____hours

Member loyalty is also measured in terms of two questions, the responses to which are averaged to form an index:

> 1. Suppose that as a result of strong opposition to the league within your community your local league were in real danger of folding up. How much effort would you be willing to spend in order to prevent this?
>
> 2. Suppose as a result of general member disinterest your local league were in real danger of folding up. How much effort would you be willing to spend in order to prevent this? (Each of these questions is answered in terms of a 5-point scale from 1, "none," to 5, "a very great deal.")[5]

RESULTS

The first pair of correlations in Table 1 represents averages of product-moment correlations within each of the 112 leagues between members' perceptions of slope in their league and their personal loyalty and activity. The averages of the intraleague correlations are quite small. Individual members who judge their leagues to be relatively high in degree of positive slope are not, in general, more active than their co-members who "see" a less positive slope ($\bar{r} = .00$) nor are they on the average very much more loyal ($\bar{r} = .12$). If individual perceptions of slope determined loyalty and activity one might expect more substantial relationships. The second pair of correlations is based on average scores for each league: each league is assigned scores computed by averaging members' reports of slope, loyalty, and activity, respectively; the average dependent variable scores are then correlated with the independent variable scores. These correlations suggest that leagues which are judged on the average to be relatively high in degree of positive slope have relatively active and loyal members (r's = .39 and .28, p's < .01). This pair of correlations taken by itself is agreeable to either a phenomenological or structural interpretation, i.e., leagues in which members "see" positive slope might tend to be more active and loyal *or* leagues which actually have more positively

These questions are posed in a manner consistent with Allport's (1955) notion of "negative causation."

TABLE 1   Inter- and Average Intraleague Correlations between Member Reports of Influence, and Their Responses of Loyalty and Activity

Influence variable and type of correlation	Results relative to	
	Loyalty	Activity
Degree of positive slope		
1. Averages of 112 intraleague correlations	.12	.00
2. Interleague correlations	.27	.38
3. Interleague correlations (rank order, holding individual perception constant)	.45	.55
Personal influence of respondent		
4. Averages of 112 intraleague correlations	.34	.39
5. Interleague correlations	.41	.45

sloped influence patterns (reported more or less accurately by members) might tend to have more active and loyal members.

The third pair represents correlations between league average slope scores (as in Pair 2) and each of the dependent variables *when individual perceptions of slope are held constant.* These correlations were computed as follows: Nine categories of perception of slope were formed representing each of the scale points from -4 to $+4$ in the index of slope. Individuals whose perceptions fall within any one of these categories are assumed to be matched on their perceptions of slope regardless of the league to which they belong. For example, an individual whose perception for her league is -3 is considered matched to all other individuals whose perception of slope for their leagues is -3, even though the average perceptions for these leagues may vary considerably. Nine curves were then plotted, one for each perception category, describing the relationship between league average slope score and the dependent variable in question. An average of these curves was then formed by weighting each curve as a whole (i.e., all the points on the curve) according to the total number of persons upon which it is based. Since slope scores for all leagues fall within 21 categories, the average curve has 21 points. Rank-order correlations were then computed from these points ($\bar{N} = 21$) representing the relationship between slope scores for each league and the dependent variables holding individual perceptions of slope constant. These correlations, .55 and .45, are significant at the .03 level or better.[6] It would

---

[6] The reader should note that some cells are empty in the 9 × 21 matrix implied by the above analysis. These blanks tend to occur in two corners of the matrix where the cells represent high slope perceivers in low average slope leagues or low slope perceivers in high average slope leagues. This means that the effect of individual perception (phenomenology) may not be entirely eliminated by the averaging process described above, since the effects of high slope perceivers will tend to contribute somewhat more to one end of the derived average curve while the low slope perceivers will contribute more to the other end of the curve, and it is possible according to the phenomenological hypothesis that high slope perceivers are more active and loyal than the low perceivers. This effect was eliminated by adding a different constant to each of the nine curves for the nine perception categories so that all of the nine curves have precisely the same average height (representing the same average loyalty or activity). Averaging the nine curves as described above, *after* equating their heights, has the effect of eliminating this possible effect of individual perceptions; i.e., the average scores on the dependent variables for persons in the different perception categories are made identical. This adjustment turns out to have practically no effect on the magnitudes of the derived correlations.

seem that the relationships between league average slope scores and the levels of activity and loyalty of members are not simply a function of member perceptions as measured through our questionnaire since perceptions now are being held constant.

While the three pairs of correlations discussed here are not strictly comparable since they are necessarily based on different methods, groupings of the data, and on different N's, it is nevertheless clear that the loyalty and activity of members vary significantly with average reported slope in their leagues when the members being compared report the same slope pattern. We thus have essentially what Blau (1957) calls a "structural effect" and what Davis, Spaeth, and Huson (1961) refer to as a "group compositional effect." These data offer some support for the structural hypothesis.

We should note a distinction, however, between the results when the dependent variable is loyalty and when it is activity. In the former case a small, but statistically significant average intraleague correlation is observed ($\bar{r} = .12$). While this does not offer strong support for the phenomenological interpretation, it does suggest, as we shall see below, that variations in individual member loyalty may correspond in at least some leagues to perceptions of influence processes suggested by the phenomenological interpretation.

It is interesting to contrast the correlations that occur when the independent variable refers to a characteristic of the league, with the results when the influence variable refers to the individual respondent herself. The fourth pair of correlations in Table 1 represents averages of product-moment correlations within each of the 112 leagues between members' reports of their own personal influence and their personal loyalty and activity. They suggest that individuals who exercise (or think they exercise) influence within a league tend to be more active ($\bar{r} = .39$) and more loyal ($\bar{r} = .34$) than individuals who do not exercise (or do not think they exercise) influence. The fifth pair of correlations is based on average scores for each league. These correlations suggest that leagues in which individual members are (or think they are) on the average high in influence, have more active ($r = .45$) and more loyal ($r = .41$) members. All of these correlations are significant beyond the .01 level but each is conducive to either a phenomenological or structural interpretation. However, Pair 4 demonstrates highly significant intraleague correlations where these might reasonably be expected structurally or phenomenologically as contrasted to the very small correlations of Pair 1 where significant correlations would be expected only under the phenomenological hypothesis.[7]

[7] Meltzer (1963) distinguishes between variables for which the referent is individualistic and those for which the referent is an aspect of group process. Although our analysis does not replicate Meltzer's, the relatively high correlations of Pairs 2 and 4 are partly consistent with his suggestion that individualistic variables will tend to show better relationships when the unit of analysis is the individual, while group process variables will tend to do better when group averages are employed. The relatively high correlations of Pair 5, however, do not fit this pattern. One might want to consider the possibility of a response set explaining some of the correlations dealing with personal influence. However, this is not a reasonable interpretation of any of the correlations when the independent variable is slope, since slope is an index constructed by subtracting one score from another.

Figure 1 shows the distributions of intraleague correlations between members' reports of their amount of activity and loyalty and their reports of slope and of personal influence. A number of facts are evident from these distributions. A contrast can be seen between the distributions of correlations when the influence data refer to the individual respondent and when they refer to the distribution of influence within the league (slope). This is especially apparent when the dependent variable is activity. The correlations involving slope and activity are distributed fairly symmetrically with a mode close to zero while the distribution involving personal influence includes many large positive correlations. Figure 1 indicates another distinction, that between leagues. While the average or modal intraleague correlation between slope and loyalty is very small, a number of the individual intraleague correlations

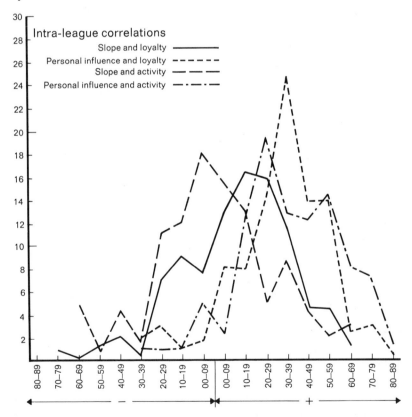

FIGURE 1　*Distributions of intraleague correlations when the independent variable measures refer to slope and personal influence and the dependent variable measures are member activity and loyalty.*

are sizable, suggesting that the phenomenological hypothesis may be appropriate in some leagues at least if not in all. This possibility is clarified by considering the probable deviations of the above distributions from chance. Seventy-seven of the correlations between individual perception of slope and loyalty are positive; 35 are negative. This diverges from what we might expect by chance ($p < .01$) if the true correlations were zero (Siegel, 1956, p. 72). Furthermore, when the confidence levels of each of the 112 correlations are considered individually, 16 are found to be significant at the .05 level or better. This number would occur fewer than 1 in 100 times by pure chance if the null hypothesis were true (Siegel, 1956, p. 40). The picture is different, however, when the dependent variable is amount of member activity. Approximately half (55) of the correlations between slope and activity are positive, indicating a result that could easily occur by chance. Furthermore, only 8 of these correlations out of 112 prove significant at the .05 level. This would occur about 20 times out of 100 by chance, and we cannot reject the null hypothesis with any confidence. The results at the individual level are very clear in demonstrating the existence of large numbers of significant intraleague correlations. When the dependent variable is loyalty, 101 of the correlations are positive, and 49 of these are significant at the .05 level. When the dependent variable is activity, 101 are positive and 54 are significant at the .05 level. However, these correlations are agreeable, as we have pointed out, to either a structural or phenomenological interpretation.

DISCUSSION

The greater loyalty and activity of members in leagues judged to have relatively high positive slope cannot be explained easily in terms of the reported perceptions of members. It does not seem reasonable to attribute these interleague correlations to differences in the way members "see" the patterns of control in their leagues since members within a league who see a relatively positively sloped distribution of control are not likely to be more active than their co-members who see a less positively sloped distribution, nor are they likely in general to be very much more loyal. Furthermore, the interleague correlations are significant even when individual perceptions of slope are held constant. Members in leagues reported on the average to have high positive slopes are, in general, more active and loyal than members in leagues reported to have less positive slopes, when the members being compared do not differ in their perceptions of slope. It seems reasonable to conclude that leagues actually differ in slope, that these differences correspond to differences in activity and loyalty, and that *perception* of slope itself does not explain these relationships. It seems a reasonable inference, furthermore, that differences among leagues in average member reports of slope reflect actual differences in slope. While we cannot be certain about the direction of causality between slope and the dependent variables, it is significant that these results are in essential agreement with the experimental study by Morse and Reimer (1956) who found that lowering the locus of control along the hierarchy in a clerical organization led to increases in members' motivation to produce, identification with, and involvement in the organization. We therefore see some evidence for the structural hypothesis as we have defined it. However, the significant intraleague correlations when the dependent variable is loyalty suggest that a phenomenological effect may be occurring too.

There is no need to assume that the phenomenological and structural hypotheses as we have defined them are mutually exclusive in their operation. It is entirely possible that each represents a partial explanation of behavior, or that one hypothesis may be appropriate under one set of conditions while the second may be more appropriate under another. Further studies of the possible circumstances under which the respective hypotheses most adequately explain behavior represent a fruitful avenue of exploration. One might want to consider, for example, the possibility that certain populations lend themselves differently to each of the hypotheses. Some authors argue that individuals who are relatively intelligent (and presumably more sophisticated about social issues) are not as likely as less intelligent persons to be affected by propaganda (Krech, Crutchfield, & Ballachey, 1962, pp. 220–221). Thus, sophisticated persons are less likely than others to be "taken in" by any "deceit" that may be involved in creating perceptions of "psychological participation." Similarly, some persons may be less affected by "appearances" and are more concerned with the pragmatic effects of social processes. Such persons may not be uninterested in whether or not their organization is "democratic," but they may be more concerned with their own personal adjustment to the organization—whether it is rewarding in terms of the many needs which they bring to it. Union members, for example, are probably *more* interested in what their union can do for them than in how control is distributed within it.[8] At the same time, what the union does for them may very well depend on the distribution of control in it. In a laboratory study, Levinger (1959) shows, contrary to his phenomenological prediction, that mere self-perceptions of power do not lead to power relevant behavior but rather ". . . trial-to-trial fluctuations in such behavior *were reflected* significantly ($p < .01$) in subjects' immediately following estimates of their perceived power [p. 92]." Perception of power in this case was an effect, not a cause, of behavior. Furthermore, creating a feeling in subjects that they are superior to others in power resources such as experience, education, and knowledge relative to an experimental task affected self-perceptions of power only slightly. On the other

---

[8] Lipset, Trow, and Coleman (1956) argue:

> By itself the existence of oligarchy in voluntary organizations rarely leads to great concern even in democratic societies and organizations. In most cases where men have forcefully and actively opposed oligarchy, their concern has usually arisen from disagreement with the policies of a specific oligarchy.

hand, whether or not experimenters acceded to subjects' influence attempts had a very marked effect on subjects' perceptions of their own power (Levinger, 1959).

Many individuals may be more "hard-headed" and more realistic about control in their organizations than is commonly believed. League members in particular comprise a relatively intelligent, critical, and sophisticated group. This is illustrated by their responses to our questions dealing with influence. Eighty-eight percent of the leagues studied are reported to have negative slopes. This represents a distinct contrast to the stereotype which is frequently applied to that organization, and it is further emphasized by member responses to questions dealing with how control *should be* distributed in their local league. Only 10% of leagues have members who, on the average, propose a negatively sloped distribution of control. In all leagues the "actual" distribution as reported by members is more negative than the "ideal." Members do not appear to be answering these questions lightly or in stereotyped ways (Smith & Tannenbaum, 1963). It is possible that organizations with memberships like that in the league may tend to provide conditions relatively more favorable to a structural than to a phenomenological interpretation.

Several other hypotheses consistent with the findings of this study might also help explain the conditions under which the phenomenological or structural views may be more appropriate:

1. The phenomenological hypothesis may be more appropriate in relation to a highly subjective dependent variable such as loyalty, but not to a more objective and behavioristic one such as amount of activity. The converse may be true for the structural hypothesis.

2. The phenomenological hypothesis may be more appropriate in relation to a relatively "distant" and ambiguous independent variable referent, such as influence in a national organization, as compared to a less "distant" referent such as influence in a local organization of which the observer is a member. The converse may be true for the structural hypothesis.

This hypothesis was suggested by an analysis of data concerning the influence of all the leagues in the national organization (as contrasted to the analysis involving slope). The question in this case is "In general, how much influence do you think . . . all the leagues as a group . . . actually have in determining the policies and actions of the League of Women Voters of the United States?" Individual member responses to this question yield significant intraleague correlations, consistent with a phenomenological interpretation. The average correlations in this case are .08 and .21 when the dependent variables are activity and loyalty, respectively. Although these correlations are small, they differ significantly from zero. Again, the larger of the two correlations occurs for loyalty as the dependent variable.

3. The phenomenological hypothesis may be more appropriate in some social situations or organizations (for example, some leagues) but not in others. The converse may be true for the structural hypothesis.

It has been possible to investigate several relationships in connection with the latter hypothesis on the assumption that the phenomenological hypothesis would be more appropriate within those leagues where influence processes are relatively complex or ambiguous, or where the members are less familiar with how their leagues work. These conditions presumably would be more conducive to autistic processes.[9] The sizes of intraleague correlations between loyalty and degree of positive slope and between loyalty and influence of all local leagues were taken as criteria of the extent to which the phenomenological hypothesis is appropriate within the respective leagues. Large positive correlations imply a relative appropriateness of the phenomenological hypothesis; small or negative correlations imply its relative inappropriateness. The following are the criteria chosen to measure ambiguity or complexity of influence process, or member knowledge about how the league works:

1. Size of league (larger leagues—more ambiguity and less knowledge by members).
2. Number of respondents within each league who answered the relevant questions, divided by size of sample within each league (lower response rate—greater ambiguity and lower knowledge).
3. Intraleague variance in response to relevant influence questions (greater variance—greater ambiguity).
4. Average amount of activity of members (lower activity—lower knowledge).
5. Average length of membership in league (greater length—more knowledge).

None of these variables yields significant correlations ($p < .05$) with the intraleague correlations between loyalty and slope or between loyalty and influence of all local leagues. We therefore cannot explain in terms of these characteristics why sizable and significant correlations occur within some leagues but not in others. It is nevertheless worth noting that differences in intraleague variance on the measures of slope and of influence of all local leagues as a group do not explain differences in the size of the intraleague correlations. We can thus rule out the argument that variance differences within leagues in the independent variable measure represent a possible statistical artifact contributing to the intraleague correlations. We are therefore left with the general hypothesis that the phenomenological explanation may be more appropriate in some situations and not in others. We shall want to pursue in further studies the factors which may contribute to these differences.

The two hypotheses that we have defined and tested represent only a very special and limited treatment of a number of broader theories under the phenomenological and structural headings. The present hypotheses are nonetheless significant for psychological theory and practice. Psychologists should understand whether the major effects of social structure are mediated through perceptions of that structure or through some of its other implications, including, perhaps, perceptions of these other implications. And those who are concerned with applying psychological theory in organizations ought to consider whether their efforts should be addressed primarily to creating images and perceptions of social structure or to creating actual changes in that structure.

REFERENCES

Allport, F. H. *Theories of perception and the concept of structure.* New York: Wiley, 1955.

Blau, P. H. *Bureaucracy in modern society.* New York: Random House, 1956.

Blau, P. H. Formal organization: Dimensions of analyses. *Amer. J. Sociol.,* 1957, **63,** 58–69.

Blauner, R. Work satisfaction and industrial trends in modern society. In W. Galenson & S. M. Lipset (Eds.), *Labor and trade unionism.* New York: Wiley, 1960. Pp. 339–360.

Coch, L., & French, J. R. P., Jr. Overcoming resistance to change. *Hum. Relat.,* 1948, **1,** 512–532.

Davis, J. A., Spaeth, J. L., & Huson, C. A technique for analyzing the effects of group composition. *Amer. sociol. Rev.,* 1961, **26,** 215–225.

Fenichel, O. *The psychoanalytic theory of neurosis.* New York: Norton, 1945.

French, J. R. P., Jr., Israel, J., & Ås, D. An experiment in participation in a Norwegian factory. *Hum. Relat.,* 1960, **13,** 3–19.

Krech, D., Crutchfield, R. S., & Ballachey, E. L. *Individual in society.* New York: McGraw-Hill, 1962.

Levinger, G. The development of perceptions and behavior in newly formed social power relationships. In D. Cartwright (Ed.), *Studies in social power.* Ann Arbor, Mich.: Institute for Social Research, 1959. Pp. 83–98.

Likert, R. Influence and national sovereignty. In J. G. Peatman & E. L. Hartley (Eds.), *Festschrift for Gardner Murphy.* New York: Harper, 1960. Pp. 214–227.

Likert, R. *New patterns of management.* New York: McGraw-Hill, 1961.

Lipset, S. M., Trow, M., & Coleman, J. *Union democracy: The inside politics of the International Typographical Union.* Glencoe, Ill.: Free Press, 1956.

Mann, F. C., & Hoffman, L. R. *Automation and the worker: A study of social change in power plants.* New York: Holt, 1960.

March, J., & Simon, H. *Organizations.* New York: Wiley, 1958.

Meltzer, L. Comparing relationships of individuals and average variables to individual responses. *Amer. sociol. Rev.,* 1963, **28,** 117–123.

Morse, Nancy, & Reimer, E. The experimental change of a major organizational variable. *J. abnorm. soc. Psychol.,* 1956, **52,** 120–129.

Mulder, M. The power variable in communication experiments. *Hum. Relat.,* 1960, *Sociometry,* 1960, **23,** 1–14. (a)

Mulder, M. The power variable in communication experiments. *Hum. Relat.,* 1960, **13,** 241–257. (b)

Siegel, S. *Nonparametric statistics for the behavioral sciences.* New York: McGraw-Hill, 1956.

Sills, D. L. *The volunteers.* Glencoe, Ill.: Free Press, 1957.

Smith, C. G. Autism, realism, and system balance in a student group. Unpublished doctoral dissertation, University of Michigan, 1961.

Smith, C. G., & Tannenbaum, A. S. Organizational control structure: a comparative analysis. *Hum. Relat.*, 1963, **16**, 299–316 (in this book, Chap. 5).

Snygg, D. The need for a phenomenological system of psychology. *Psychol. Rev.*, 1941, **48**, 404–424.

Tannenbaum, A. S. The concept of organizational control. *Journal of Social Issues*, 1956, **12**, 50–60 (a).

Tannenbaum, A. S. Control structure and union functions. *Amer. J. Sociol.*, 1956, **61**, 536–545 (b) (in this book, Chap. 2).

Tannenbaum, A. S. Control and effectiveness in a voluntary organization. *Amer. J. Sociol.*, 1961, **67**, 33–46 (in this book, Chap. 4).

Tannenbaum, A. S. Reactions of members of voluntary groups: a logarithmic function of size of group. *Psychol. Rep.*, 1962, **10**, 113–114. (b)

Tannenbaum, A. S., and Georgopoulos, B. The distribution of control in formal organizations. *Soc. Forces*, 1957, **36**, 44–50 (in this book, Chap. 3).

Tannenbaum, A. S., & Kahn, R. L. Organizational control structure: A general descriptive technique as applied to four local unions. *Hum. Relat.*, 1957, **10**, 127–140.

Tannenbaum, A. S., & Kahn, R. L. *Participation in union locals.* Evanston, Ill.: Row, Peterson, 1958.

Vroom, V. Some personality determinants of the effects of participation. Englewood Cliffs, N. J.: Prentice-Hall, 1960.

Williams, L., Hoffman, L., & Mann, F. C. An investigation of the control graph: Influence in a staff organization. *Soc. Forces*, 1959, **37**, 189–195.

14

CONTROL, PERFORMANCE, AND SATISFACTION: AN ANALYSIS OF STRUCTURAL AND INDIVIDUAL EFFECTS*

Jerald G. Bachman
Clagett G. Smith
Jonathan A. Slesinger[1]

The present investigation is concerned with the relationship between organizational effectiveness and social control in organizations. In particular, it is designed to explore two aspects of control: the *distribution* of control among organizational levels, and the *bases* for this control.

In many discussions of organizational life there appears to be a serious dilemma concerning control. On the one hand, hierarchical control is said to be necessary to insure efficient administration and coordination of effort. On the other hand, decentralization of control and decision making is said to lead to higher rank-and-file motivation. Recent research has suggested that this may not really be a dilemma. It has been argued that increased control at the lower levels need not, and should not, involve any sort of proportionate decrease in control at some other level. A number of studies indicate that relatively high amounts of control exercised by members at *all* organizational echelons is associated with higher performance and increased satisfaction (Bowers, 1964; Smith & Tannenbaum, 1963; Tannenbaum, 1962). Tannenbaum (1961) and Likert (1961) have argued that this pattern of high total control is successful because it involves members at all levels of the organization, leading to more effective decisions and also to higher motivation.

A related question concerns the bases of control in organizations, and how these may be associated with performance, satisfaction, and total amount of control. French and Raven (1960) describe five bases for the social power which an agent, O, can exert over a person, P:

> (a) *Reward power*, based on P's perception that O has the ability to mediate rewards for him; (b) *coercive power*, based on P's perception that O has the ability to mediate punishments for him; (c) *legitimate power*, based on the perception by P that O has a legitimate right to prescribe behavior for him;

* Reprinted from *Journal of Personality and Social Psychology*, 1966, Vol. 4, No. 2, 127–136, with permission of the publisher and the authors. (This article has been edited to eliminate overlap and to bring it into a consistent format with the other articles in this book. Certain portions have therefore been deleted or reworded. Ed.)

[1] We wish to thank the following colleagues who read an earlier draft and offered suggestions: Frank M. Andrews, David G. Bowers, Judith A. Long, Philip M. Marcus, Stanley E. Seashore, and Arnold S. Tannenbaum.

(d) *referent power, based on P's identification with O;* (e) *expert power, based on the perception that O has some special knowledge or expertness* [pp. 612–613].

In the present research we have attempted to measure these five bases of power (or social control) and relate them to the total amount of control as well as to performance and satisfaction.

Likert (1961) and Tannenbaum (1962) have suggested that the processes underlying a system of high control and its effects derive essentially from the satisfaction of the ego motives of the individuals, such as the desire for status, achievement, and acceptance. If their interpretation is correct, then we would expect reward, referent, and expert power to be the more important bases underlying total control and its implications. In contrast, if the more traditional Weberian view is indeed correct, then the more important bases of control and its effects would be legitimate authority and the manipulation of rewards and sanctions.

The setting for the present study has certain features which make it especially attractive for our purposes. It involves subjects in responsible positions, with fairly high levels of skill and income. Thus we have an opportunity to see whether earlier findings obtained largely from rank-and-file workers can be generalized to persons at higher organizational levels. Another important advantage is the availability of accurate individual performance data, which permits us to study factors affecting performance at individual as well as group levels. Finally, the subjects are located in 36 branch offices, each under the supervision of an office manager. We are thus able to study a fairly large number of distinct organizational units, each with basically the same tasks and the same criteria of success.

Some methodological considerations

Frequently, quantitative studies of organizations depend upon members' perceptions to provide measures of organizational characteristics, particularly administrative characteristics. Indeed, most of the research mentioned above falls into this category. The traditional procedure for handling such data is to characterize each organizational unit in terms of average ratings by all respondents in that unit. Thus, for example, if a researcher found that organizational units with high mean ratings of total amount of control also have relatively high mean satisfaction ratings, he might well conclude that total control and satisfaction are positively related at the organizational level. More specifically, he might view the pattern of influence as a part of the objective *structure* of the organizational environment which has real-life consequences for its members.

While organizational studies using this traditional form of analysis have been valuable, they continue to be subject to a serious weakness: what appears to be an objective structure effect may in fact be spurious—merely a reflection of purely individual-level relationship (Blau, 1957, 1960; Davis, Spaeth, & Huson, 1961; Tannenbaum & Bachman, 1964). Returning to our example, a positive correlation between mean satisfaction and mean ratings of total control might indicate only that persons who *perceive* a high degree of total control tend also to be satisfied persons. Such an individual-level relationship would be consistent with a *phenomenological* interpretation of the control-satisfaction findings.

Tannenbaum and Smith (1964) studied the problem of structural versus phenomenological effects using several analytic techniques in addition to the correlation of group mean data. They concluded that both types of effect occurred in their study, depending upon the criterion used to measure organizational effectiveness. When the criterion was the amount of time spent in organizational affairs, a structural relationship with patterns of control was observed. But in the case of loyalty, a more subjective dimension, a phenomenological effect appeared.

The analysis strategy used in the present study, following the same basic approach as Tannenbaum and Smith (1964), makes an operational distinction between office-level effects (including structural effects) and individual-level effects (including phenomenological effects). We assume that the criterion scores (performance and satisfaction) *for each individual* are influenced in part by aspects of the organizational environment which are common to most or all of his office colleagues, and we refer to these influences as *office-level effects*. Such effects include, but are by no means limited to, the impact of administrative characteristics such as control and bases of power.[2] We assume that the criterion scores are also influenced by a host of idiosyncratic factors which differ from person to person, and we refer to these influences as *individual-level effects*. This definition includes so-called phenomenological effects, but it also includes such spurious relationships as halo effects and simple response biases. (Indeed, while the present study deals only with the correlates of perceptions, our definition of individual-level effects encompasses the effects of all individual differences—ability, motivation, etc.). Note that the same *individual* criterion scores are used to assess both office-level and individual-level effects; we are thus exploring the extent to which each subject's performance and satisfaction are affected by office-level versus individual-level variables.

Ideally, of course, office-level variables should be manipulated experimentally, measured by observers, or assessed through other methods which are independent of the persons directly involved. In the present study, however, it was necessary to rely on the subjects' own perceptions. Nevertheless, we have been able to maintain the distinction between office-level and individual-level

---

[2] The term office level is somewhat specific to the present study. We might speak more broadly of these relationships as group-level effects, since the analysis could equally well be applied to any group or organization that provides some sort of common climate for most or all members.

effects in the analysis of our results. Our basic strategy is to partial out the individual's own perception of office characteristics and compare his performance and satisfaction with the perceptual measures of the other group members. And we consider this distinction to be an important advance over the traditional correlation of group mean data.

METHOD

Research site

The data used in the present study were obtained in 36 branch offices of a national firm selling intangibles. Each branch office is managed by a single office manager, who has sole responsibility for the conduct of his office. His functions include supervision, on-the-job training of employees, and enforcement of home-office policies.

Directly under each office manager are a number of salesmen. The salesman's functions include soliciting and opening new accounts, and servicing existing accounts; he may also serve as the client's main source of information and expertise for decisions leading to sales. Since the firm derives its income largely from commissions on the sale of intangibles, the salesman is the basic producer in any branch office. The salaries of salesmen are indirectly related to individual productivity; most are within a range from $10,000 to $25,000 per year.

The remaining employees in each branch office serve in essentially a supporting or staff capacity. They provide necessary technical information, secretarial and clerical services, and the like, which help the salesmen provide service to their clients. In the present study we will not deal directly with these staff functions; instead, we will concentrate on the line side of the branch office: the office manager and his salesmen.

The branch offices used in the analysis were divided into two groups for separate analysis. The 18 offices in Group A are all located in areas judged to have high business potential, and yet they vary widely in actual office performance. Offices in Group B are all located in areas rated as having lower business potential, and yet some are high on actual performance, others relatively low. Ratings of business potential were derived from the pooled judgment of 10 high-level members of the home-office staff who had personal knowledge of the business conditions. The 18 offices in Group A were selected from among those offices which at least 8 of the 10 raters placed in the top quartile for business potential. The 18 offices in Group B were selected from among those offices which at least 8 raters placed *below* the top quartile. Thus in terms of business potential, the Group A offices may be more homogeneous than the Group B offices.

In order to restrict the sample to those offices having continuity of operations and leadership, no office was included which had been established within the 5-year period preceding the study, or which had experienced a change of manager within the 2 years preceding the study.

Measures

The data for this study consist of sales performance measures and salesmen's questionnaire responses. The number of salesmen in Group A offices ranged from 10 to 35, with a mean of 23.4 and median of 22.5. In Group B the number ranged from 8 to 17, with a mean of 13.1 and median of 14. The total number of respondents was 656, with 421 in Group A offices and 235 in Group B offices.

Virtually every salesman in each of the 36 offices filled out an extensive questionnaire dealing with many aspects of his work and his adjustment to it.[3]

The administrative variables of interest in the present study include control, and the bases of the office manager's power. The criterion variables consist of salesmen's performance, and their satisfaction with their office manager.

Control

Two closely related measures of control were used. They have been treated separately because they involved somewhat different "influence receivers." The measures of *control over the office* dealt with the general amount of influence over the way the office is run. The *interpersonal control* measures dealt strictly with influence patterns between the office manager and his salesmen (with respect to office-relevant matters).

The following questionnaire item was used as a measure of the office manager's control over the office: "In general, how much say or influence do you feel [the office manager] has on how your office is run?" The extent of salesmen's control over the office was measured by a similar item: "In general, how much say or influence do you feel [the salesmen as a group] have on how your office is run?" Response categories for both items ranged from 1, "little or no influence," to 5, "a great deal of influence." A measure of *total control over the office* was derived by combining the responses to these two items.

The following items were used to measure the amount of interpersonal control between the office manager and his salesmen: "How much say or influence does your office manager have with [the salesmen in your office] when it comes to activities and decisions that affect the performance of your office? Now, thinking in the other direction, how much say or influence [do the salesmen] in your office have on your office manager when it comes to his activities and decisions that affect the performance of your office?" Both items used response categories ranging from 1, "no influence at all," to 5, "a great deal of influence." A measure of *total interpersonal control* was derived by adding the responses to the two items.

Bases of Power

A single questionnaire item was used to assess five bases of the office manager's power or influence over the salesman respondent: referent, expert, reward, coercive, and legitimate power.

Listed below are five reasons generally given by people when they are asked *why* they do the things their superiors suggest or want them to do. Please read all five carefully. Then number them according to their importance to you as reasons for doing the things your office manager suggests or wants you to do. *Give rank "1" to the most important factor, "2" to the next, etc.* "I do the things my office manager suggests or wants me to do because:

A. "I admire him for his personal qualities, and want to act in a way that merits his respect and admiration;

B. "I respect his competence and good judgment about things with which he is more experienced than I;

C. "He can give special help and benefits to those who cooperate with him;

D. "He can apply pressure or penalize those who do not cooperate;

E. "He has a legitimate right, considering his position, to expect that his suggestions will be carried out."

---

[3] Since it was necessary to identify respondents, conditions of complete anonymity could not be maintained; however, respondents were assured that the information they provided would be kept in strictest confidence, and would be available only to the research team.

In order to simplify analysis and interpretation of results, the rank values for this item were later reversed so that a value of 5 indicates maximum importance, 1 indicates minimum importance. The measures of the five bases of power are not independent, because of the ranking procedure involved; in a sense, any single base of power can be given prominence only at the expense of the other bases.[4]

Satisfaction with office manager

Each salesman's satisfaction with his office manager was assessed by the following item: "All things considered, how satisfied are you with the way your office manager is doing his job?" Response categories ranged from 1, "very dissatisfied," to 5, "very satisfied."

Standardized salesman performance

The measure of salesmen's performance was designed to rule out the effects of length of service upon dollar productivity, thus permitting a fair comparison of younger men with more experienced men. This was accomplished by separating salesmen into the following subgrouping based on years of experience: less than 1 year, 1–2 years, 2–3 years, 3–4 years, 4–5 years, 5–10 years, and more than 10 years. Within each of these subgroups, the distribution of dollar productivity was sharply skewed toward the high end. A logarithmic transformation applied to the dimension of dollar productivity yielded distributions that were approximately normal. Moreover, although the means of each of the seven subgroups were different, the standard deviations of the transformed distributions were almost identical. Each salesman was assigned a score corresponding to his position within the transformed productivity distribution for his subgroup. The standard performance scores which resulted from these operations were independent of length of service and approximated the normal distribution. (To facilitate computation, this distribution was given a mean value of 50, with a standard deviation of 10.)

Significance level

Because many of the relationships examined in this study were not specifically predicted in advance, two-tailed tests were used with the .05 minimum criterion for significance. (Although all subjects completed questionnaires, a small proportion of nonresponses occurred for some questions. Accordingly, a consistent 10% nonresponse rate was assumed for each pair of variables when computing degrees of freedom. This was slightly conservative; the actual frequency of nonresponse was usually smaller.)

RESULTS

Because of the differences between Group A and Group B offices outlined above, it seemed appropriate to carry out separate analyses for the two groups of offices, thereby controlling most effects of differences in business potential. The separate analyses produced very similar results, thus indicating a high degree of reliability for the data. It then appeared that reporting these findings separately would be an unnecessary duplication; therefore, the data were combined, and weighted means of Group A and Group B findings were used throughout the present paper.[5]

---

[4] The ranking procedure has the advantage of forcing the respondent to discriminate among all of the bases of power, rather than giving prominence to only one or two. Moreover, it may in this case help the respondent to avoid confusing the *extent* to which he does what the office manager asks and the *reason* for doing so.

[5] When the office was the unit of analysis (see Table 2) results for Group A ($N = 18$ offices) and Group B ($N = 18$ offices) were weighted equally. When the unit of analysis was the individual, the results for Group A ($N = 421$ salesmen) received proportionately more weight than those for Group B ($N = 235$ salesmen). Mean correlations were obtained using the z transformation procedure described in Table 4 (Johnson, 1949).

TABLE 1 Administrative and Criterion Variables: Means and Standard Deviations

| | M rating[a] | SD among: | |
		Individuals	Offices
Control over office			
Exercised by office manager	4.57	0.81	0.36
Exercised by salesmen	3.01	1.05	0.45
Total control	7.58	1.40	0.63
Interpersonal control			
Office manager's influence on salesmen	4.30	0.91	0.43
Salesmen's influence on office manager	3.00	1.03	0.42
Total interpersonal control	7.30	1.55	0.72
Bases of office manager's power			
Referent	2.93	1.30	0.57
Expert	3.46	1.35	0.61
Reward	2.70	1.09	0.42
Coercive	1.90	1.23	0.48
Legitimate	4.02	1.11	0.39
Criterion variables			
Standardized performance	50.43	9.70	2.78
Satisfaction with office manager	3.78	1.09	0.58

[a] Possible scores range from 1.0 (lowesf) to 5.0 (highest), except for total control measures (ranging from 2.0 to to 10.0) and standardized performance (described in text).

Statistical analysis and rationale

Our analysis explores the effects of several administrative characteristics upon two criterion variables, performance and satisfaction. The mean responses and standard deviations for all measures are presented in Table 1. Tables 2, 3, and 4 present the results of several types of correlational analyses, as described below.

We make the assumption that the best available estimate of organizational structure in our data is a composite of perceptions within a given organizational unit. Thus our measure of each administrative characteristic consists of the mean rating by all salesmen in a given office. These mean ratings are correlated with performance and satisfaction at two distinct levels of analysis: office mean criterion scores and individual criterion scores.

Office mean criterion scores

The first level of analysis involves what we have called the traditional comparison of office mean data. The correlations between administrative characteristics and office mean criterion scores are presented in Table 2.[6] This form

[6] The correlations in Table 2 are based upon office mean scores, with each office weighted equally. An alternative procedure weighting each office according to its number of salesmen produced almost identical results. As a further check, Spearman rank correlations were computed for all relationships shown in the table. The results were essentially the same as the product-moment correlations.

TABLE 2 Administrative Characteristics Correlated with Office Mean Criterion Scores (N = 36 Offices)

Office mean ratings	Office mean criterion scores	
	Standardized performance	Satisfaction with office manager
Control over office		
Exercised by office manager	.22	.60**
Exercised by salesmen	.39*	.60**
Total control	.39*	.79**
Interpersonal control		
Office manager's influence over salesmen	.35*	.82**
Salesmen's influence over office manager	.39*	.75**
Total interpersonal control	.41*	.88**
Bases of office manager's power		
Referent	.40*	.75**
Expert	.36*	.69**
Reward	—.55**	—.51**
Coercive	—.31	—.71**
Legitimate	—.17	—.57**

Note.—Cell entries are product-moment correlations.
* $p < .05$, two-tailed.
** $p < .01$, two-tailed.

of analysis often highlights office-level effects, since many kinds of individual-level effects may be canceled by the use of mean criterion data. We noted earlier, however, that *systematic* individual-level effects, including some phenomenological effects, are not canceled, and the danger that they will be misinterpreted as genuine office-level effects remains a major weakness of the traditional method. Thus the analysis in Table 2 cannot stand alone as a demonstration of office-level effects; further evidence is necessary.

Individual criterion scores

The second level of analysis deals with individual salesmen; Table 3 presents correlations computed between administrative characteristics (still based on office mean perceptions) and the individual criterion ratings ($N = 656$ salesmen).[7] This form of analysis deals with the question: Given the many causes of an individual's performance and satisfaction, what is the relative importance of administrative characteristics such as the distribution and bases of control? It is clear at a glance that the correlations in Table 3 are, on the whole, much smaller than those in Table 2. The office administrative charac-

---

[7] These correlations were obtained by simply treating the office mean perceptions as if they were individual data. Each salesman was characterized by the administrative ratings for his office (based on mean perceptions), as well as his own personal criterion scores; then these two kinds of variables were correlated for all salesmen.

teristics have a sort of monopoly in Table 2, whereas in Table 3 their impact is shared with the many causes that may be different for each individual, another instance of aggregate correlations showing higher values than individual correlations.

Isolation of office-level effects

The individual level of analysis has an additional advantage; it can tell us something about the *way* in which administrative characteristics have their influence on individual performance and satisfaction. Early in this paper we

TABLE 3 Administrative Characteristics Correlated with Individual Criterion Scores ($N = 656$ Salesmen)

	Individual criterion scores	
Office mean ratings	**Standardized performance**	**Satisfaction with office manager**
Control over office		
Exercised by office manager	.06	.31**
	.07	**.19****
Exercised by salesmen	.11**	.28**
	.13**	**.14****
Total control	.11**	.38**
	.12**	**.21****
Interpersonal control		
Office manager's influence over salesmen	.06	.41**
	.10*	**.25****
Salesmen's influence over office manager	.10*	.33**
	.12**	**.22****
Total interpersonal control	.11**	.43**
	.14**	**.25****
Bases of office manager's power		
Referent	.11**	.36**
	.09*	**.22****
Expert	.10*	.33**
	.13**	**.17****
Reward	—.14**	—.25**
	—.12**	**—.16****
Coercive	—.09*	—.33**
	—.09*	**—.19****
Legitimate	—.07	—.31**
	—.08	**—.24****

Note.—The upper entry in each cell presents the zero-order product-moment correlation, r_{Ab}; the lower boldface entry presents the partial correlation, $r_{Ab.a}$; where A = office mean ratings of administrative characteristics, b = individual criterion scores, a = individual ratings of administrative characteristics.
* $p < .05$, two-tailed.
** $p < .01$, two-tailed.

raised the question: Is it merely the *perception* of these characteristics which affects the criterion variables (or perhaps vice versa)? In order to deal with this issue, the relationships in Table 3 are presented in two forms: zero-order correlations and partial correlations. The partial correlations rule out the effects of each salesman's own perception of the office administrative characteristics, thereby removing that portion of the relationships, which might be attributed to individual-level effects. The relationships that remain are office-level effects. (For a further discussion of the background and rationale for this form of analysis, see Tannenbaum & Bachman, 1964.) We interpret these office-level relationships as being specific structural effects of control and bases of power, since these are the office-level variables we have attempted to measure. It must be noted, however, that this particular interpretation does not follow necessarily from the logic of our analysis. It is possible, for example, that our measures have actually tapped some cultural stereotype common to the office as a whole, rather than the actual behaviors assumed to be associated with control and bases of power.

Effects of office administration characteristics

Control

Measures of control over the office and interpersonal control correlated positively with both criterion measures (Tables 2 and 3). These positive relationships appeared no matter who exercised the control—the office manager, the salesmen, or both. Moreover, there is a strong positive relationship between the amount of interpersonal control exercised by the office manager and that exercised by the salesmen ($N = 36$ offices, $r = .50$, $p < .01$, two-tailed). These findings seem inconsistent with the position that the total amount of control in any situation remains a fixed quantity; on the contrary, they support the view that the total amount of control or influence is variable.

Bases of power

For the average salesman, the most important basis of the office manager's control was legitimate power (Table 1); nevertheless, in offices relatively high on this dimension, respondents indicated significantly less satisfaction with their office manager, and there was a tendency for performance to be lower (Tables 2 and 3).

The second and third most important dimensions were expert and referent power. Offices in which the office manager was rated relatively high on these bases of power were also high on performance and satisfaction with the office manager.

Reward and coercive power were rated the least important reasons for complying with the office manager's wishes, and both were negatively related to the criterion variables.

It is important to note that the five bases of power related to the overall amount of control in much the same way as they related to performance and satisfaction: Correlations with total control were .66 and .58 for expert and referent power; −.48, −.49, and −.58 for legitimate, reward, and coercive power, respectively. Nearly identical correlations were obtained with the measure of total interpersonal control. (All were product-moment correlations, $p \leq .01$, two-tailed.)

Some caution must be exercised in interpreting correlations with the bases of power. The ranking method used in obtaining the data makes it impossible for all five bases of power to be correlated in the same direction with any single criterion variable. Thus, it may be that positive correlations with expert and referent power are responsible for negative correlations with the other bases of power, or vice versa.

Office-level versus individual-level effects

A comparison of the zero-order and partial correlations in Table 3 indicates the presence of office-level relationships between the administrative characteristics and both criterion variables. When the effects of the individual's perception of administrative characteristics are removed, the small but significant correlations with performance are not reduced. On the other hand, the same partial correlation procedure does lead to a substantial reduction in the correlations between administrative characteristics and satisfaction with the office manager. This suggests that a portion of the zero-order relationship with satisfaction is attributable to individual-level effects.

Isolation of individual effects

In order to isolate individual-level effects, it is necessary to reverse the strategy employed earlier; we now rule out any possibility of an office-level effect, thus leaving only those relationships which we have defined as individual effects. This is accomplished by treating each office separately, and correlating individual perceptions of administrative characteristics with individual criterion scores. Since we are considering objective administrative characteristics to be identical for all persons within a given office, these intraoffice correlations provide a measure of pure individual-level effects.

Table 4 presents the means of the intraoffice correlations, weighted according to the number of respondents in each office. The pattern of relationships is clear and highly consistent. Individual performance is unrelated to individual perceptions of office administrative characteristics. On the other hand, an individual salesman's satisfaction with his office manager is significantly related to his personal appraisal of administrative characteristics in his office, and the pattern of individual-level relationships parallels very closely the pattern of office-level effects isolated earlier.[8]

---

[8] The mean intra-office variance is, of course, smaller than the variance for all individuals grouped together. But the reduction is too small to have much effect on Table 4. (For most variables, including performance and satisfaction, the mean intraoffice SD is only about 10% smaller than the SD among individuals shown in Table 1.)

TABLE 4 Intraoffice Correlations between Individual Ratings of Administrative Characteristics and Individual Criterion Scores

	Individual criterion scores	
Individual ratings	Standardized performance	Satisfaction with office manager
Control over office		
Exercised by office manager	−.03	.21**
Exercised by salesmen	−.06	.36**
Total control	−.07	.42**
Interpersonal control		
Office manager's influence over salesmen	−.05	.33**
Salesmen's influence over office manager	−.06	.38**
Total interpersonal control	−.07	.46**
Bases of office manager's power		
Referent	.02	.41**
Expert	−.08	.40**
Reward	−.01	−.30**
Coercive	.02	−.40**
Legitimate	.02	−.21**

Note.—Cell entries present the weighted means of 36 intra-office product-moment correlations. The weighted means were obtained by using the z transformation ($z = \tan h^{-1}r$) in the following formula (Johnson, 1949, pp. 52–53):

$$\bar{z} = \frac{(n_1 - 3)z_1 + (n_2 - 3)z_2 + \cdots}{(n_1 - 3) + (n_2 - 3) + \cdots}$$

$\bar{z}$ values were then transformed to the $\bar{r}$ values which appear in the table.
** $p < .01$, two-tailed.

Relationship between performance and satisfaction

On the whole, our criterion variables—performance and satisfaction with the office manager—have shown fairly similar patterns of correlation with administrative characteristics. This finding might indicate that high performance causes a salesman to be satisfied with his office manager; or perhaps such satisfaction is a cause of high performance. If either of these explanations were correct, we should find that an *individual's* performance is correlated with his personal satisfaction with the manager. But in fact, when the possibility of office-level effects is removed, no such relationship is evident; the mean intra-office correlation between performance and satisfaction is −.02 (using the procedures described in Table 4). However, the correlation between office mean performance and office mean satisfaction is .35, $p < .05$ (using the procedures described in Table 2). In other words, our criterion measures covary at the office mean level of analysis, but are entirely independent at the intraoffice level, and these findings are fully consistent with the view that performance and satisfaction are subject to similar but separate *structural* relationships, with the administrative characteristics under study.

DISCUSSION

The present findings again illustrate the importance of total control as a factor in organizational effectiveness: the overall amount of influence in the organization correlated substantially with performance and satisfaction. Moreover, the generality of this relationship has been extended to include highly skilled persons performing a variety of complex tasks. It may be that the branch offices under study are especially conducive to the patterns of influence and power reported above. An office manager's success is largely dependent upon the performance of the salesmen in his office; thus he has a strong incentive toward management practices which support and encourage high productivity.

It is of particular interest to note that the degree of control exercised by an office manager over his subordinates was positively related to the control they exercise over him. These findings clearly imply that control at one level is not exercised at the expense of another level.[9] On the contrary, the data indicate that any increase in control—by office manager, subordinates, or both —should be associated with higher satisfaction and performance.

The comparison of bases of power further illuminates the processes which underlie a pattern of high total control. Total control, performance, and satisfaction with the office manager were all relatively high for the office manager whose leadership was perceived as resting largely upon his skill and expertise (expert power) and upon his personal attractiveness (referent power). Conversely, the less effective office manager was one who appeared to rely more heavily upon the use of rewards and sanctions (reward power and coercive power) and upon the formal authority of his position (legitimate power)—as a formal description of his role might indicate. At the level of interoffice comparison, this overall relationship was substantial and highly consistent (see Table 2).

The negative relationship between the use of reward power and our measures of effectiveness requires further explanation. We stated earlier that reward power might be associated with supportive or ego-enhancing practices of management (Likert, 1961). However, it may well be that many employees are ambivalent about the use of reward power by their superiors. It may be well to reward someone for a job well done, but rewards may also be perceived as bribes, payoffs, favoritism, and the like. The phrase used in the pres-

[9] Although the data have not been reported in the present paper, it should be noted that an index of *relative* control (derived by subtracting the office manager's control from that exercised by his subordinates) showed no clear relationship with criteria of satisfaction or performance.

ent study, "He can give special help and benefits to those who cooperate with him," may have implied the latter type of reward.

The relationship between control, bases of power, satisfaction, and performance are still far from clear; nevertheless, the present findings suggest two tentative conclusions. First, it appears that the most effective offices can be characterized by the following high total control syndrome: high levels of interpersonal control, and control over the office, by both office manager and salesmen; relatively greater reliance by the office manager on expert and referent power (as opposed to legitimate, reward, and coercive power); and high mean levels of performance and satisfaction with the office manager. Second, since an individual salesman's satisfaction with his office manager is not correlated with his performance (at the intra-office level of analysis), it seems clear in the present setting that neither variable is the direct cause of the other. A more likely explanation is that they are both caused in part by the high total control syndrome.

The present comparison of office-level versus individual-level effects yielded results largely consistent with those of Tannenbaum and Smith (1964). Satisfaction with the office manager was associated to a considerable degree with each salesman's personal perception of the office administrative pattern, but after this relationship was removed, an individual's satisfaction was also substantially related to a more objective measure of administration—the mean of all perceptions by those in his office. Performance, on the other hand, was not at all related to individual perceptions of control and bases of power, but it did show small correlations with the more objective office mean perceptions. We interpret these findings as indicating that satisfaction was subject to both structural and individual-level effects, whereas performance was subject only to structural effects.

It is of interest that administrative characteristics proved to be weak predictors of individual performance (Table 3), yet fairly good predictors of performance on the average (Table 2). This relationship, which may be a very common phenomenon in organizations, would have gone entirely unnoticed had we limited our analysis to the traditional correlations among office means (as in Table 2). This observation highlights the differences between grouped data and individual data, and it points to the importance of both forms of analysis in studying the impact of organizations upon their members.[10]

One final conclusion is in order. This paper has stressed very strongly the distinction between office-level and individual-level effects. We have noted the difficulties that attend the use of perceptual measures, particularly when the analysis is limited to the usual practice of correlating mean data. Our strat-

---

[10] It is worth mentioning that for "practical" purposes the small relationship with individual performance shown in Table 3 would be fully as useful as the larger correlation with mean performance in Table 2; in either case a change in office characteristics would lead to essentially the same overall *predicted effect* (using ordinary regression equations).

egy of partialing out the individual's own perceptions eliminates the possibility of a halo effect, since a halo must exist in individuals rather than in groups. We have no guarantee that our measures tapped exactly the structural dimensions we intended, but the evidence is clear that they tapped something that exists in the organization—something that influences an individual's performance and satisfaction, quite apart from his perception of it.

REFERENCES

Blau, P. M. Formal organization: Dimensions of analysis. *American Journal of Sociology*, 1957, **63**, 58–69.

Blau, P. M. Structural effects. *American Sociological Review*, 1960, **25**, 178–193.

Bowers, D. G. Organizational control in an insurance company. *Sociometry*, 1964, **27**, 230–244 (in this book, Chap. 7).

Davis, J. A., Spaeth, J. L., & Huson, C. A technique for analyzing the effects of group composition. *American Sociological Review*, 1961, **26**, 215–225.

French, J. R. P., Jr., & Raven, B. The bases of social power. In D. Cartwright & A. Zander (Eds.), *Group dynamics: Research and theory.* (2nd ed.) Evanston, Ill.: Row, Peterson, 1960. Pp. 607–623.

Johnson, P. O. *Statistical methods in research.* New York: Prentice-Hall, 1949.

Likert, R. *New patterns of management.* New York: McGraw-Hill, 1961.

March, J., & Simon, H. *Organizations.* New York: Wiley, 1958.

Smith, C. G., & Tannenbaum, A. S. Organizational control structure: A comparative analysis. *Human Relations*, 1963, **16**, 299–316 (in this book, Chap. 5).

Tannenbaum, A. S. Control and effectiveness in a voluntary organization. *American Journal of Sociology*, 1961, **67**, 33–46 (in this book, Chap. 4).

Tannenbaum, A. S. Control in organizations: Individual adjustment and organizational performance. *Administrative Science Quarterly*, 1962, **7**, 236–257 (in this book, Chaps. 1 and 21).

Tannenbaum, A. S., & Bachman, J. G. Structural versus individual effects. *American Journal of Sociology*, 1964, **69**, 585–595 (in this book, Chap. 12).

Tannenbaum, A. S., & Smith, C. G. The effects of member influence in an organization: Phenomenology versus organization structure. *Journal of Abnormal and Social Psychology*, 1964, **69**, 401–410 (in this book, Chap. 13).

15

BASES OF SUPERVISORY POWER: A COMPARATIVE STUDY IN FIVE ORGANIZATIONAL SETTINGS*

Jerald G. Bachman
David G. Bowers
Philip M. Marcus[1]

This paper deals with two interrelated problems: Why do people comply with the requests of organizational "superiors"? And how are these various reasons related to the total amount of control and to organizational effectiveness? Stated another way, we are interested in the bases of supervisory power and its effects.

French and Raven (1960, pp. 612–613) describe five bases for the social power which an agent O can exert over a person P:

(1) Reward power, based on P's perception that O has the ability to mediate rewards for him; (2) coercive power, based on P's perception that O has the ability to mediate punishments for him; (3) legitimate power, based on the perception by P that O has a legitimate right to prescribe behavior for him; (4) referent power, based on P's identification with O; (5) expert power, based on the perception that O has some special knowledge or expertness.

These five bases of power represent a useful framework for studying supervisory power over subordinates. It should be noted that each basis of power depends on some perception or cognition on the part of the person P. Thus one approach to measuring bases of supervisory power is to ask the subordinates why they comply with supervisory wishes. This approach has been used in a number of studies recently carried out by the Survey Research Center. The present paper summarizes the findings from five of these studies.

METHOD

Respondents and organizational settings

The organizational settings for this research are described below and summarized in Table 1. Data were obtained from a total of 2,840 respondents in 148 different organizational units.

* Adapted from a paper delivered at the American Psychological Association Convention, 1965, and appearing here with permission of the authors.

[1] Most of the data were obtained through several larger projects conducted at the Survey Research Center and supported by the participating companies. The collection of data in colleges was supported by a grant from the Carnegie Corporation.

TABLE 1 Summary of Organizational Settings

	Organization				
	1 **Branch offices**	**2** **Colleges**	**3** **Insurance agencies**	**4** **Production work units**	**5** **Utility company work groups**
Number of units	36	12	40	40	20
Supervisory role	Office manager	Academic dean	Regional manager	Production foreman	First-line foreman
Respondent's role	Salesman (opening and servicing accounts; providing expert information)	Faculty member (teaching and related activities)	Insurance agent (selling and servicing insurance policies)	Production worker (routine production of electric appliances)	Semiskilled worker (installing and maintaining equipment)
Number of respondents	656	658	860	486	180
Response rate, %	95	60	83	66	99

1. Salesmen in branch offices

Respondents were 656 salesmen in 36 branch offices of a national firm selling intangibles. These salesmen solicit and open new accounts, service existing accounts, and provide clients with information and expertise. The salesmen work under the supervision of an office manager, who has sole responsibility for the conduct of the office (for a more extensive description see Bachman, Smith, and Slesinger, 1966).

2. Faculty in liberal arts colleges

Respondents were 658 full-time faculty members in 12 liberal arts colleges belonging to a regional association of colleges. Faculty are not ordinarily considered supervised in the same sense as other subjects in this study; nevertheless, the relationship between faculty and the academic dean may usefully be studied in this manner. In many respects the academic dean's role is similar to middle-management positions; he represents the faculty viewpoint to the president and trustees and also represents higher administration to the faculty (see Bachman, 1965, for a detailed description of the study of college faculty).

3. Agents in life insurance agencies

Respondents were 860 full-time agents in 40 agencies of a life insurance mutual company. Agents work under the general supervision of regional managers, selling policies and maintaining the insurance programs of clients (a more detailed description of these agencies appears in Bowers, 1964).

4. Production workers in an appliance firm

Respondents were 486 production workers in 40 work groups of a firm manufacturing electric appliances. Each work group is supervised by a production foreman and performs either line assembly or parts-fabricating tasks.

5. Workers in a utility company

Respondents were 180 semiskilled workers in 21 work groups of a large middle western utility company. These workers install and repair new equipment in customers' homes and maintain service in several plants.

To summarize, our subjects are drawn from a variety of occupations, ranging from college professor to factory worker. Yet they all do their work in organizational settings, and they all are subject to some degree of influence by others in the organization.

Measures

Five questionnaires were used, each tailored to fit the organizational setting in which it was used. Among the items that all the questionnaires had in common were a measure of the five bases of power, one or more measures of satisfaction with the supervisor (or with the job as a whole), and measures of total control.

Bases of power

The salesmen in branch offices were asked why they do what their office manager asks or suggests. They ranked the importance of the following five reasons:

Legitimate power: "He has a legitimate right, considering his position, to expect that his suggestions will be carried out."

Expert power: "I respect his competence and good judgment about things with which he is more experienced than I."

Referent power: "I admire him for his personal qualities, and want to act in a way that merits his respect and admiration."

Reward power: "He can give special help and benefits to those who cooperate with him."

Coercive power: "He can apply pressure or penalize those who do not cooperate."

The college faculty ranked a nearly identical list of reasons to indicate why they do what their academic dean suggests or wants them to do.

The workers in the utility company used a very similar set of items to rank their reasons for complying with the wishes of their foreman.

Similar items were also used by the insurance agents and by the appliance production workers in rating their immediate supervisors. A major difference, however, was that these respondents did not rank the five different reasons; they made an independent rating of importance for each, using a five-point response scale.[2]

Satisfaction

In four of the organizational settings the respondents were asked to indicate their general level of satisfaction with the way their supervisor was "doing the job." Workers in the utility company were asked a series of questions that were combined to yield an overall job-satisfaction index.

[2] It should be noted that both the ranking and the rating procedures for assessing bases of power have special advantages. The ranking procedure forces the respondent to discriminate among all the bases of power, rather than giving prominence to only one or two. Moreover, it may help the respondent to avoid confusing the extent of his compliance with the reasons for doing so. The rating procedure, on the other hand, has the advantage of permitting each basis of power to be independent of the others (whereas the ranking procedure is relative and permits the emphasis of one basis of power only at the expense of the others). Because both forms of assessment are included in the present paper, we are in a position to use the advantages of both.

Total control

Total control was measured in each of the five sites by adding the control exercised by the rank-and-file level to that exercised by the supervisory level.

Performance

Measures of performance are available only in three of the organizations. The measure of performance by salesmen was based on dollar productivity, with a correction for length of service in the company (Bachman et al., 1966). The overall performance effectiveness of insurance agencies was ranked by company officials on the basis of objective measures modified by subjective judgment. Performance in the appliance-manufacturing firm was assessed using four objective measures: indirect labor costs, supplies costs, quality of output, and scrap rate.

RESULTS

Relative importance of the five bases of power

Table 2 presents the mean rating of the five bases of power for each kind of organization. The most important reasons for complying with organizational superiors were legitimate and expert power. Of lesser importance were referent and reward power. In every case coercive power was the least likely reason for compliance.

Bases of power, total control, and criteria of organizational effectiveness

The correlations presented below treat the organizational unit (a single work group, office, or college) as the basic unit of analysis. Some performance measures were originally collected for the organizational unit as a whole. In all other cases, the score for a unit consisted of the mean of the scores for all respondents in that unit.

Bases of power and satisfaction

Table 3 presents the correlations between the five bases of power and measures of satisfaction with the supervisor or with the job as a whole. Expert and referent power provide the strongest and most consistently positive correlations with satisfaction, coercive power the most negative.

The pattern for legitimate and reward power is less clear; correlations with satisfaction are negative when we consider the data for the salesmen and college faculty, but predominantly positive when the insurance agents and production workers are considered. This finding is less puzzling when we note that the ranking method used by the salesmen and college faculty makes it

TABLE 2   Mean Ratings of Bases of Power*

	Organization				
	1	2	3	4	5
Bases of power	Branch offices	Colleges	Insurance agencies	Production work units	Utility company work groups
Legitimate	4.1	3.6	3.3	3.4	4.7
Expert	3.5	4.1	3.8	3.4	3.0
Referent	2.9	3.5	2.5	2.7	2.1
Reward	2.7	2.3	2.8	2.8	2.7
Coercive	1.9	1.6	1.8	2.3	2.5

* All ratings have been adjusted so that a value of 5.0 represents the highest possible rating, 1.0 represents the lowest possible rating. Respondents in organizational settings 1, 2, and 5 used a ranking procedure; those in settings 3 and 4 used a procedure that permitted independent ratings of the five bases of power.

impossible for all five bases of power to be correlated in the same direction with any single criterion variable. It seems likely that the positive correlations with expert and referent power caused negative correlations with the other bases of power, particularly legitimate and reward power.[3]

Bases of power and performance

The correlations between the bases of power and measures of performance, available in three of the five organizational settings, are presented in Table 4. Expert power again shows the most consistently positive correlations with this second criterion variable. Referent power is positively related to performance in two cases and unrelated to it in the third case. The correlations between reward power and performance are predominantly positive, particularly if we note that the one negative correlation may be due largely to the ranking method used by the salesmen. Legitimate and coercive power show no clear relationship, positive or negative, with performance criteria.

Bases and total amount of power

Correlations between bases of power and total amount of control are not entirely consistent in magnitude and direction in all five organizational sites. Correlations between total control and expertness present the most positive picture; these correlations fall between .22 and .66, and two are significant at

[3] Of course, the reverse explanation (that the negative correlations caused the positive ones) is also possible, but it is much less compelling in the light of the overall pattern of findings.

TABLE 3 Correlations with Satisfaction Measures

	Organization				
	1	**2**	**3**	**4**	**5**
Bases of power	**Branch offices (N = 36)**	**Colleges (N = 12)**	**Insurance agencies (N = 40)**	**Production work units (N = 40)**	**Utility company work groups (N = 20)**
Legitimate	−.57*	−.52	.04	.40†	−.35
Expert	.69*	.75*	.88*	.67*	.30
Referent	.75*	.67†	.43†	.57*	.11
Reward	−.57*	−.80*	.48*	.27	−.12
Coercive	−.31	−.70†	−.52*	.01	−.23

* $p < .01$, two-tailed.
† $p < .05$, two-tailed.

the .01 level of confidence. Referent power is the basis next most positively related to total control, with two correlations (.30 and .58) significant at the .05 and .01 levels respectively. One of the five correlations is in the negative direction (−.12), although it is not significant. The other bases present quite mixed pictures with the exception of coercion, which shows two significant

TABLE 4 Correlations with Performance Measures

	Organization		
	1	**3**	**4**
Bases of power	**Branch offices (N = 36)**	**Insurance agencies (N = 34)***	**Production work units (N = 40)†**
Legitimate	−.17	.26	.06
Expert	.36‡	.48§	.22
Referent	.41‡	−.19	.31‡
Reward	−.55§	.54§	.21
Coercive	−.31	.03	.08

* Six of the 40 insurance agencies were considered too new to permit accurate ratings of performance effectiveness; thus the correlations in this table are based on the remaining 34.
† Each cell in this column reports the mean (using the Z transformation) of four correlations, corresponding to the four objective measures of performance in the appliance manufacturing firm (see text).
‡ $p < .05$, two-tailed.
§ $p < .01$, two-tailed.

negative correlations ($-.58$ and $-.64$) with total control. Only one correlation here is positive, but it is not statistically significant. Although these data do not provide strong evidence, they are consistent with arguments for the organic-participative models discussed in Chapter 1.

DISCUSSION

This summary of data obtained in five organizational studies has provided a number of fairly consistent findings. (1) Legitimate power was rated one of the two most important bases of power; however, it did not seem a consistent factor in organizational effectiveness, nor was it related significantly to total amount of control. (2) Expert power was the other very prominent basis of power, and it was strongly and consistently correlated with satisfaction and performance. Of the five bases, expert power was most positively related to total amount of control. (3) Referent power was of intermediate importance as a reason for complying with a supervisor's wishes, but in most cases it was positively correlated with criteria of organizational effectiveness. In two sites it was significantly and positively related to total amount of control. (4) Reward power was also of intermediate importance; in this case the correlations with organizational effectiveness and with total control were not consistent. (5) Coercive power was clearly the least prominent reason for compliance; moreover, this basis of power was often negatively related to criteria of effectiveness and in two cases negatively related to total amount of control.[4]

We have been concerned primarily with the relationships of bases of power to organizational performance and to the satisfactions of members. It is of interest to consider also the relationship between the total amount of power (or control) and these criteria of organizational effectiveness. Tannenbaum and his colleagues have found that relatively high control is associated with higher performance and increased satisfaction (Tannenbaum, 1962; Smith and Tannenbaum, 1963; Marcus and Cafagna, 1965). Similar findings relating total amount of control to satisfaction were obtained in four of the five organizations studied in this paper and relating it to criteria of performance in the three organizations (see Table 4) for which performance measures are available (Bachman, Smith, and Slesinger, 1966; Bachman, 1965; Bowers, 1964).

One limitation of the results reported here is that they are based heavily, although not exclusively, on relationships between questionnaire responses. Such relationships might indicate simply that persons who do a good job and are satisfied in their work tend to favor the "nice" bases of power when rating their reasons for compliance in the organization. This problem of "phenomenological effects" has been discussed in detail elsewhere (see especially Tan-

---

[4] These findings, no doubt, reflect the influence of fairly pervasive cultural values. For example, there may be a widespread value in the United States that supervisors should, whenever possible, avoid coercion in dealing with subordinates. This may actually lead supervisors to avoid coercion. However, it may also make subordinates unwilling to admit compliance based on a fear of sanctions; if so, our data may underestimate the actual use of coercive power.

nenbaum and Smith, 1964, and Tannenbaum and Bachman, 1964). It is sufficient for our present purposes to note that extensive analyses have dealt directly with this issue in the branch offices and the colleges; these analyses indicate that our present findings cannot be explained simply in terms of phenomenological effects (Bachman, Smith, and Slesinger, 1966, and Bachman, 1968).

Given a comparative study based on five different organizational settings, it is tempting to look for more subtle differences, as well as overall similarities, in the use and effects of power. Such differences must certainly exist; for example, our findings imply that college faculty and insurance agents are somewhat more impressed by expertise than by sheer legitimacy of authority, whereas the opposite seems true for salesmen and utility workers. Unfortunately, our data are not adequate to support many such distinctions. Our example of organizations is varied but far too small; our measures are fairly consistent from study to study, but the differences remain a problem.

At this stage of our efforts, then, we must limit our conclusions to those findings which appear to have some generality in the organizations studied. These findings provide the following tentative answers to the questions with which we began. People say that they comply with the requests of organizational superiors primarily because of legitimate and expert power and least of all because of coercive power. Criteria of organizational effectiveness, including the satisfactions of organization members with these organizations, seem related positively to expert power and to referent power and negatively to coercive power. The total amount of control seems also to be related positively to expert and referent bases, and negatively to coercive bases in at least a couple of the organizations studied.

REFERENCES

Bachman, J. G. (1968). Faculty satisfaction and the dean's influence: an organizational study of twelve liberal arts colleges. *J. appl. Psychol.*, **52** (1), 55–61.

———, Smith, C. G., and Slesinger, J. A. (1966). Control, performance, and satisfaction: an analysis of structural and individual effects. *J. Pers. soc. Psychol.*, **4** (2), 127–136 (in this book, Chap. 14).

Bowers, D. G. (1964). Organizational control in an insurance company. *Sociometry*, **27** (2), 230–244 (in this book, Chap. 7).

French, J. R. P., Jr., and Raven, B. (1960). The bases of social power. In D. Cartwright and A. Zander (Eds.), *Group dynamics.* New York: Harper & Row.

Marcus, P. M., and Cafagna, Dora (1965). Control in modern organizations. *Publ. Administration Rev.*, **25**, 121–127.

Smith, C. G., and Tannenbaum, A. S. (1963). Organizational control structure: a comparative analysis. *Human Relat.*, **16**, 299–316 (in this book, Chap. 5).

Tannenbaum, A. S. (1962). Control in organizations: individual adjustment and organizational performance. *Administrative Sci. quart.*, **7** (2), 236–57 (in this book, Chaps. 1 and 21).

————, and Bachman, J. G. (1964). Structural versus individual effects. *Amer. J. Sociol.*, **LXIX** (6), 585–95 (in this book, Chap. 12).

————, and Smith, C. G. (1964). The effects of member influence in an organization: phenomenology versus organizational structure. *J. abnorm. soc. Psychol.*, **69** (4), 401–410 (in this book, Chap. 13).

PART 3

This section presents several analyses that focus on reactions and adjustments of organization members. Research has generally shown that those workers who exercise relatively high control in their job situations are likely to be more satisfied with their jobs than those who exercise little control. In Chapter 16, Bachman and Tannenbaum extend this principle by showing that a worker may exercise different degrees of control relative to different aspects of his work situation and that his satisfaction with these aspects corresponds to the amount of control exercised in them. Chapter 17 explores a little studied effect of control, that on personality change. Although the detected effects are slight, there is some indication of a tendency for personality to change toward a better "fit" with the control structure. In Chapter 18, Tannenbaum and Bachman study conformity by members in a voluntary organization. They find that the more active and influential members are also the more controlled members.

16

THE CONTROL-SATISFACTION RELATIONSHIP
ACROSS VARIED AREAS OF EXPERIENCE*

Jerald G. Bachman
Arnold S. Tannenbaum[1]

The relationship between control and satisfaction in job or task situations has been the subject of considerable study by social scientists. In summarizing some of the sociological literature, Blauner (1, p. 346) reached the following conclusion: *"It is possible to generalize on the basis of the evidence that the greater the degree of control that a worker has (either in a single dimension or as a total composite) the greater his job satisfaction."* (Italicized in the original.)

The most consistent correlate of the control or influence variables reported in the literature has been satisfaction with the job or task, as reflected by attitude measures and sometimes also by "harder" criteria of satisfaction such as turnover and absenteeism (3, 8, 9, 13, 14, 15). Much of the research which has been done was designed to examine variations in control and in satisfaction across a number of individuals while holding constant the situation or area of experience (usually the present job or task). Thus a typical conclusion is that individuals who have relatively high control over their jobs are more satisfied with their jobs than individuals with lower control. However, little is known from this research about how a given individual may experience different degrees of satisfaction in different areas of activity as a function of differing amounts of control which he may exercise in the respective areas. Furthermore, most studies have been restricted to job or task situations, and we know relatively little about the control-satisfaction relationship in other areas of experience. Is it possible to infer that those experiences which offer the greatest opportunity for the exercise of control by an individual whether on the job or off are also the ones which provide the greatest satisfaction to him?

The research reported in the present paper consists of two studies intended to deal with these questions. In each study the relationship between control and satisfaction is examined for the *same* individuals in *different areas* of experience. Both studies bear directly upon the following hypothesis: *Across areas of experience, satisfaction will be a positive function of control.*

* Reprinted from *The Delta Pi Epsilon Journal*, May 1966, Vol. VIII, No. 2, 16–25, with permission of the publisher and the authors. (This article has been edited to eliminate overlap and to bring it into a consistent format with the other articles in this book. Certain portions have therefore been deleted or reworded. Ed.)

1 We wish to thank those of our colleagues who served as judges in this study. We also gratefully acknowledge the valuable suggestions of John R. P. French, Jr., Gerald Gurin, Glenn Jones, Philip M. Marcus, and Clagett G. Smith, and the assistance of Roberta Levenbach.

STUDY I

Method

The data used in Study I were gathered in a clerical department of a large insurance company where a systematic attempt was made to increase the control exerted by rank and file workers in a number of areas of their work.

The following description of the study is excerpted from a research report by Morse and Tannenbaum.

> The time span was one and one-half years: a before measurement, one-half year of training of supervisors to create the experimental conditions, one year under the experimental conditions, and then remeasurement. . . .
>
> The rank and file employees were women, mostly young and unmarried, with high school education. The usual clerk's plans were for marriage and a family rather than a career. The population used in the analysis . . . is a subgroup of the clerks . . . [who] were present throughout the one and one-half year period, and [for whom] before and after questionnaires were individually matched. While they comprise somewhat less than half of the clerks present in these divisions at any one time, they are comparable to the total group, except on such expected variables as length of time in the division, in the work section, and on the job . . . .
>
> The experiment was carried out within the larger framework of company operations. . . . First, there were formal structure changes to create a new organizational environment for the divisions; . . . authority was delegated by upper management to lower levels in the hierarchy with the understanding that they would redelegate it to the clerical work groups. . . . Second, there were training programs for the supervisors of the divisions to ensure that the formal changes would result in actual changes in relations between people (2, 4, 5, 10, 12).

The questionnaire administered before and after the experiment included several items about "systems"—areas of activity within the work situation which are subject to some regulation and control. For twenty of these systems (listed in Table 1), separate measures of control and satisfaction are available.

A measure of control for each system was derived from three pairs of questions. Each pair applies to a different aspect of control. The aspects of control treated by the three pairs of questions are (a) decisions regarding ". . . the policies, rules, procedures of methods of the ――――System;" (b) ". . . instructions, advice, . . . suggestions or help . . . with regard to the――――System;" and (c) the administration of sanctions in the event that someone would "deliberately disregard the established methods, policies, rules or procedures of the ――――System." One question in each pair concerns the degree to which the clerks exercise control; and the other question in the pair measures the control exercised by higher ranking persons. For each question pair, the *ratio* of rank and file control to higher level control was computed,

TABLE 1   Study I. Control and Satisfaction Ratings: Initial Levels and Positive Change (Ranked)

System	Initial level		Positive change	
	(1) Control	(2) Satisfaction	(3) Control	(4) Satisfaction*
Absence	2.5	1	15	19
Borrow and loan	6	17	12	20
Closing time (deadline)	9	16	19	14
Overtime	7	14	10	17
Section meetings	4	6	5	6
Recess	10	10	2	4
Starting and stopping hours	16	4	17	12.5
Tardiness	17	12	3	15
Vacation	5	5	18	11
Work assignment	2.5	13	8	7.5
Work	1	2	13	12.5
Error report	15	11	11	7.5
Lunch	20	3	16	18
Planning	11	8	6	2.5
Cost allocation	12	19	14	9
Staffing control	14	20	4	1
Training	8	7	7	10
Transfer	19	18	9	16
Field office	13	9	20	5
Office conduct rules	18	15	1	2.5

Note: A rank of 1 indicates the highest or most positive value; a rank of 20 indicates the lowest value.
* Not all changes in satisfaction were in the positive direction; thus the rank of 20 indicates the largest change in the negative direction (i.e., the "least positive" change).

and the mean of these three ratios formed an index measuring *relative* control by clerks over each of the twenty systems.[2] Column 1 in Table 1 presents these control ratings (based on the means of the 114 respondents).

The measure of satisfaction is obtained from the following open-ended question: "How do you feel about this system in general?" Written responses were coded on a five point scale ranging from high positive affect to high negative affect. The mean satisfaction ratings for each system are presented in column 2 of Table 1.

Before-After shifts in relative control and satisfaction were derived by comparing mean Before questionnaire responses with mean After questionnaire responses. These shifts are presented in the last two columns of Table 1.

[2] See (4, 5) for a more detailed description of the measures of control.

Results

Across the twenty systems, the rank correlation between Before ratings of satisfaction and relative control is .30. While this relationship falls short of statistical significance, it may indicate the presence of a moderate positive relationship between control and satisfaction before the introduction of experimental treatment.

Of greater importance, however, is the effect of the experimental treatment designed to increase control by rank and file workers. The over-all effect of the manipulation was to increase substantially the degree of decision-making by the clerks, with a corresponding increase in their general satisfaction with the company and with supervisory personnel. The increase in control did not occur equally within all systems, however. For example, there was a considerable increase in control over the "Office-conduct-rules System," but no appreciable increase in control over the "Vacation System." Given these differences, our hypothesis would lead us to predict the greatest increases in satisfaction with those systems providing the greatest increase in control. And this is what happened. The Before-After *changes* in satisfaction were significantly correlated with *changes* in relative control; the rank correlation is .46, significant at the .05 level (two-tailed).

The relationship between Before-After changes is especially noteworthy, because it is the direct result of a series of experimental manipulations designed to increase control. These manipulations led to more extensive changes in some systems than in others (because not all systems were equally amenable to change in control); and in those systems where rank-and-file control showed the greatest increases, the resulting positive changes in satisfaction also tended to be greatest.

STUDY II

Method

Study II made use of satisfaction data derived from the Weitz (16) General Satisfaction Test. This test consists of items which respondents check according to the degree of their satisfaction. The complete list of items used in the present study is reproduced in Table 2.[3]

Two samples are employed in this study. The first includes 489 workers in a Canadian oil refinery. A number of the items in the Weitz General Satisfaction Test had been included in a questionnaire administered to this group. The data consist of the percentages of respondents who indicated that they were satisfied, dissatisfied, or neither satisfied nor dissatisfied with each of the items.[4]

---

[3] Two items were added to the original list in the Weitz test: "Your health" and "the way things are going at home."

[4] We are indebted to Edwin Blakelock for providing these data. The original data collection was carried out by the Survey Research Center and directed by Carol Slater.

TABLE 2 Study II. Mean Control and Satisfaction Data

Item	Mean ratings of control	Mean reported satisfaction*	
		Refinery	Auto mfg.
Food prices	1.0	2.5	2.2
Automobile prices	1.0		2.3
Income tax	1.0		2.3
Sales tax	1.0		2.5
Public transportation	1.0		2.5
The way local traffic is handled	1.0		2.7
The way people drive	1.0	3.0	
Our foreign policy	1.0		2.8
The movies being produced nowadays	1.0	3.4	2.9
National political situation	1.0	3.4	
Local political situation	1.0	3.6	2.9
Advertising methods	1.0	3.4	3.0
Restaurant food	1.0	3.5	3.0
Local newspapers	1.0	3.5	3.6
Women's clothing styles	1.0		3.6
Popular music	1.0	3.5	3.9
Today's automobiles	1.0	3.3	4.1
Television programs	1.0	3.7	
The way you were raised	1.0	3.9	4.2
Your first name	1.2	3.9	3.9
Telephone service	1.2	3.9	4.1
Your telephone number	1.4		3.8
The climate where you live	1.6	3.7	3.4
The last school you attended	1.6	3.9	4.2
Your last job	1.8		3.7
Your last boss	1.8		3.9
The city in which you live	1.8	3.8	3.9
Your present job	1.8		4.2
The amount of time you have for recreation	2.0		3.1
Opportunities to get ahead	2.0		4.0
Yourself	2.0	3.7	
Your health	2.0	3.9	
The people you know	2.2	3.9	3.0
The way things are going at home	2.2	3.9	
The house or apartment in which you live	2.4		4.0
The last suit you bought	3.0	3.8	

* The data from both sources were originally presented in terms of the percentage of respondents who chose each category along a scale of satisfaction. Means were computed by assigning values to each of the categories (equal intervals were assumed). The data in column 3 were derived from a five-point scale by assigning from 1 (most dissatisfied) to 5 (most satisfied). The data in column 2 were derived from a three-point scale; in order to facilitate comparison between the two samples, values were assigned from 2 (dissatisfied) to 4 (satisfied).

A second and independent sample includes 4,199 persons, the majority of whom were employed by a large automobile manufacturing corporation in the United States. The group also includes some subsamples from other companies, as well as some luncheon club members, university groups, and others. Most of the respondents in this sample indicated their satisfaction with each of the items by checking one of five "faces" ranging from a broad smile to a deep frown; other respondents used a five-point adjectival response scale. These data were provided by investigators outside the Survey Research Center; further details are not available about the nature of the sample or the proportion of the respondents using each kind of response scale.[5]

The heterogeneity of this "sample" and the mixture of procedures may raise questions as to the reliability of the second set of ratings. On the other hand, the data seemed worth including as a cross-validation sample. At best such data could replicate the findings for the first sample and could prove some indication as to the generality of our results. At worst, the true relationship would be weakened or obscured. Since any lack of reliability would usually lead to an underestimate of a relationship, our use of this cross-validation sample is essentially conservative.

Satisfaction data for both samples are summarized in Table 2. Of the total set of items in the Weitz scale, the first sample provides data for 22, and the second sample provides data for 29. Of these, 15 items are common to the two samples. Considering only these common items, the rank correlation between the mean ratings by the two groups is .53, indicating a moderate level of consistency.

The data from the sample described above are limited to the mean of satisfaction ratings. Since respondents' estimates of control are not available, estimates of control are based upon judgments made by social scientists (none of whom was familiar with the nature and purpose of the project or with any of the available data). It may be argued that judges' ratings of control are less appropriate than workers' responses; however, this possible limitation seems less severe when we note that our present concern is with the "average worker" rather than with individuals. Moreover, the use of judges' ratings may actually be preferable from a methodological standpoint, since they provide measures of control which are completely independent of the workers' estimates of satisfaction, thus ruling out a spurious relationship based on response set or "halo effect."

Five judges rated control according to the following instructions: "Please estimate the *amount of control* which the *average worker* has over each of these items. In making your estimates, consider the control ordinarily available to an *individual* average worker (not workers as a group or bloc)." The judges used a three-point scale: high, medium, low. They were instructed to "judge each item separately, paying no attention to how your responses are

[5] We wish to thank Joseph Weitz, Chester Evans, and R. D. Boynton for making these data available.

distributed" (across the three categories). Since the resulting judgments were markedly skewed, interjudge reliability was measured using a nonparametric technique: Kendall's coefficient of concordance, W (7). For the five judges' ratings, W = .86, $r_{s_{av}}$ (average Spearman rank correlation) = .82. This indicates a high degree of reliability for these ratings.[6]

Results

In the case of both samples, satisfaction is highly correlated with the ratings of control (rank correlations are .71 and .53). The fact that this relationship is consistent across two somewhat different sets of respondents may indicate that this relationship between control and satisfaction is a fairly general one. The fact that the data provided by the automobile manufacturing corporation yield a slightly weaker correlation may be attributable to the previously stated limitations of the sample.

CONCLUSION

The findings presented above are consistent with those reported in the literature concerning job satisfaction. They also support the view that the positive control satisfaction relationship holds across a range of areas within the scope of an individual's experience. Individuals tend to be more satisfied with those aspects of life or of their jobs over which they have some control than with those over which they have none.

Although in general the data conform to our hypothesis, two matters may require further comment. First, we find a somewhat stronger correlation between *changes* in control and satisfaction than appeared in the "before only" part of Study I. Satisfaction in the "before only" stage was no doubt a complex function of many factors, thus allowing us to account at best for only a portion of it in terms of control. This limitation, which occurs in most studies of the control-satisfaction relationship, makes it difficult to determine what it is that *causes* the relationship. Even in experimental studies, the manipulations often include changes in such human relations variables as supervisory consideration, group cohesiveness, and the like. Thus it is difficult to pinpoint changes in satisfaction which are attributable to changes in control. In Study I, however, specific changes in satisfaction were related to specific changes in control across twenty systems of experience which were affected in varying degrees by the over-all manipulation. The use of such a procedure may have avoided the above problems to some extent. Although the over-all experimental manipulation may have changed such things as group attractiveness or supervisory

---

[6] Unfortunately, the Spearman-Brown prophecy formula, which can be used to estimate reliability from average interjudge correlations, was designed for use with product-moment correlations. Thus it may not be directly applicable to the present rank-correlation data. Nevertheless, it may be helpful in assessing the reliability of the present scale to note that an average *product-moment* correlation of .82 among five judges would yield an estimated reliability coefficient of .97.

behavior, in addition to the pattern of control, these general factors are not likely to vary across the twenty systems in such a way as to confound the relationship between changes in control and changes in satisfaction. Thus, in effect, we tend to "hold constant" or randomize the extraneous variables.

Second, we find that the control-satisfaction correlations which appeared in Study II are substantially higher than the analogous "before only" correlation in Study I. This may be attributable to the differences in the items in the two studies. One of the strengths of the present analysis may be the use of a variety of items including elements from a person's private life, his work experience, and his general political, social, and cultural environment. Compared with Study I, it seems safe to say that variance along the control dimension was far greater in Study II, thus permitting the relationship to be seen more clearly.

The studies reported in the present paper dealt with the "average" respondent rather than a single person; however, in principle they could have been carried out separately for each respondent. An analysis of this sort might reveal individual differences in the control-satisfaction relationship which would be of interest to personality theorists. Control may matter a great deal in determining the satisfaction (high or low) of some persons, while for others it may have at best a minor effect. And although the control-satisfaction relationship seems positive for most persons (judging from the average data derived from this and other research), there may be a minority for whom satisfaction is negatively related to control. Studies by Sanford, Tannenbaum and Allport, and Vroom have already indicated that dimensions of personality such as authoritarianism or the need for independence affect the relationship between control and satisfaction (6, 12, 15). An exploration of the relationship among individuals across a variety of areas of experience would be a logical extension of the present study.

REFERENCES

1. Blauner, R. Work Satisfaction and Industrial Trends in Modern Society. In Galenson, W., and S. Lipset (Eds.), *Labor and Trade Unionism.* New York: Wiley, 1960.

2. Kaye, C. The Effect on Organizational Goal Achievement of a Change in the Structure of Roles. Ann Arbor: Survey Research Center, University of Michigan, 1954 (mimeo).

3. Likert, R. *New Patterns of Management.* New York: McGraw-Hill, 1961.

4. Morse, N., Reimer, E., and Tannenbaum, A. Regulation and Control in Hierarchical Organizations. *Journal of Social Issues,* 1951, **7** (3), pp. 41–48.

5. Morse, N., and Reimer, E. The Experimental Change of a Major Organizational Variable. *Journal of Abnormal and Social Psychology,* 1956, **52** (1), pp. 120–129.

6. Sanford, F. *Authoritarianism and Leadership.* Philadelphia: Institute for Research in Human Relations, 1950.

7.   Siegel, S. *Nonparametric Statistics for the Behavioral Sciences*. New York: McGraw-Hill, 1956.

8.   Smith, C. G., and Tannenbaum, A. Organizational Control Structure: A Comparative Analysis. *Human Relations*, Fall 1963, **16**, pp. 299–316 (in this book, Chap. 5).

9.   Tannenbaum, A. Control in Organizations: Individual Adjustment and Organizational Performance. *Administrative Science Quarterly*, 1962, **7** (2), pp. 236–257 (in this book, Chaps. 1 and 21).

10. Tannenbaum, A. Personality Change as a Result of an Experimental Change of Environmental Conditions. *Journal of Abnormal and Social Psychology*, 1957, **55** (3), pp. 404–406 (in this book, Chap. 17).

11. Tannenbaum, A. *Social Psychology of the Work Organization*. Belmont, Calif.: Wadsworth, 1966.

12. Tannenbaum, A., and Allport, F. H. Personality Structure and Group Structure: An Interpretative Study of their Relationship through an Event-Structure Hypothesis. *Journal of Abnormal and Social Psychology*, 1956, **53** (3), pp. 272–280.

13. Viteles, M. *Motivation and Morale in Industry*. New York: Norton, 1953.

14. Vroom, V. *Some Personality Determinants of the Effects of Participation*. Englewood Cliffs, New Jersey: Prentice-Hall, 1960.

15. Vroom, V. *Work and Motivation*. New York: Wiley, 1964.

16. Weitz, J. A Neglected Concept in the Study of Job Satisfaction. *Personnel Psychology*, 1952, **5**, pp. 201–205.

17

PERSONALITY CHANGE
AS A RESULT OF
AN EXPERIMENTAL CHANGE
OF ENVIRONMENTAL CONDITIONS*

Arnold S. Tannenbaum

The question of the consistency of adult personality is a continuing problem in the field of personality theory. Kelly, in his longitudinal study of marital adjustment, found evidence of a remarkable degree of consistency as well as some evidence of significant changes over a 20-year period (2). One of the questions that remains is the extent to which personality change, when it occurs, can be understood in terms of the effect of specific environmental conditions. The present note is intended to report results bearing on this question from an experimental study in a large clerical organization. Other aspects of this study have been reported earlier (4, 5, 7).

Two experimental groups were created that differed in their distribution of control. In one, called the autonomous program, the amount of control exercised by lower-level employees was increased and that of the upper hierarchical levels decreased. In the other, called the hierarchical program, the amount of control exercised by the rank and file was decreased and that of the upper levels increased. The program for each group of approximately 200 female employees continued for over a year. A paper-and-pencil questionnaire designed to measure 26 personality trends to which each of the programs had some degree of relevance was administered near the beginning of the experimental period, and about a year later at the end. Results reported earlier (7) indicated that subjects' reactions to the work programs can be understood partly in terms of the relationships between their personality structures and the nature of the program in which they were located.

It was initially assumed that personality trends are quite stable and would be unlikely to change as a result of experimental treatment.[1] Nevertheless, the two programs were seen to have profound effects on the subjects' attitudes toward the company and satisfactions in it. In addition, the duration of the experiment, as well as the seriousness with which the subjects reacted to it, raised the question of its possible effects on the relevant personality variables. A number of hypotheses regarding change in personality trends were therefore formulated on the basis of the assumption that environmental conditions

* Reprinted from *Journal of Abnormal and Social Psychology*, Nov. 1957, Vol. 55, No. 3, with permission of the publisher. (This article has been edited to eliminate overlap and to bring it into a consistent format with the other articles in this book. Certain portions have therefore been deleted or reworded. Ed.)

[1] For the conception of personality used, see Allport, F. H. (1).

TABLE 1 Before-After Correlations and Incidence of Change
(Change in the predicted direction significant at the .05 level is indicated by +; change in a direction opposite to that predicted by —)

	Before-after r ($N = 195$)[a]	Autonomous program ($N = 115$)[a]	Hierarchical program ($N = 80$)[a]
Autonomous trends			
1. Assume responsibility (anticipating, preparing for, and accepting the consequences of one's activities)	.59	n.s.	n.s.
2. Be creative (develop new patterns; to use one's imagination; to think up new and original ways of doing things)	.56	n.s.	n.s.
3. Increase the variety (number of types) of satisfactions in any given situation (to enjoy as many different things as possible in the same situation, e.g., to "mix business with pleasure")	.41	n.s.	n.s.
4. Understand and explain the reasons for one's behavior and opinions (to understand and explain one's feelings)	.48	n.s.	n.s.
5. Help others	.59	n.s.	n.s.
6. Understand others' viewpoints and feelings (to know why people feel or act as they do; to understand the reasons for others' behavior)	.60	n.s.	+
7. Be independent of control figures (to be free of direction and control of persons in authority)	.54	n.s.	+
8. Express one's considered judgments (to think things through carefully and state one's opinions)	.78	n.s	+
9. Base one's actions on one's own critical judgments and evaluations (to carefully evaluate and decide things for oneself)	.38	—	+
10. Act on the same level as others (to treat and be treated by others as an equal)	.52	n.s.	n.s.
11. Understand relations between and reasons for things (to understand the basis for things; to figure things out; to know "why")	.72	—	+
12. Do one's own thinking (not be suggestible; to decide things for oneself; to draw one's own conclusions)	.40	n.s.	+
13. Take the initiative with others (to start things; to organize things)	.42	n.s.	—

Hierarchical trends

14.	Avoid emotional involvements (to avoid the expression and reception of emotional acceptance; to keep emotionally distant from others; to avoid being "warm" in relationships with others; to avoid affection)	.65	n.s.	n.s.
15.	Conform to the wishes of control figures (to please persons in authority)	.60	n.s.	n.s.
16.	Adhere rigidly to specific rules or directions (to follow rules to the letter; to be given directions for doing things)	.58	n.s.	n.s.
17.	Act inferior to control figures (to be humble in relation to persons in authority)	.60	+	n.s.
18.	Avoid committing oneself (to keep one's opinions to oneself; to keep from getting oneself "out on a limb"; to keep people from knowing where one stands on controversial questions)	.40	n.s.	n.s.
19.	Keep one's roles (behavior categories, relationships) at any given time distinct from other roles (to keep various parts of one's life separated)	.40	n.s.	+
20.	Admire or respect control figures or symbols (to look up to persons in, or symbols of, authority)	.68	n.s.	n.s.
21.	Be superior to others (to be better than others; to be more outstanding than others)	.69	+	—
22.	Be efficient (not waste time or effort)	.58	+	—
23.	Be submissive to control figures (to submit to dominant leaders; to obey strong and forceful authority figures)	.45	n.s.	+
24.	Show self-discipline (to show self control; to keep one's behavior disciplined)	.42	+	—
25.	Depend on others (to receive direction from others)	.48	n.s.	n.s.
26.	Obey rules and follow directions	.58	n.s.	n.s.

[a] In some cases the N's are slightly less than this value due to a very small proportion of NA's—never more than 4%.

may increase or decrease the characteristic energic (homeostatic) level of trends on the basis of a simple reward-and-punishment principle: characteristics that are given opportunities for expression tend to increase in potency; trends that are given only minimal opportunities for expression tend to decrease.

The 26 trends measured by the personality questionnaire were divided into two groups of thirteen: "autonomous trends," which were likely to be given opportunities for expression in the autonomous program (and not in the hierarchical), and "hierarchical trends," which were likely to be given opportunities for expression in the hierarchical program (and not in the autonomous). It was hypothesized that (a) in the autonomous program, autonomous trends should tend to increase in potency and hierarchical trends tend to decrease; (b) in the hierarchical program, hierarchical trends should tend to increase in potency and autonomous trends tend to decrease.

Care was taken in framing the questions used to measure the personality trends to make them as general as possible and distinct from the company situation. Responses to these questions are therefore not likely to reflect the subjects' changing attitudes toward the experimental programs or toward the company. Five questions were employed to measure each trend. For example, one of the questions for the trend, "trying to be independent of control figures," was "How much do you believe that people generally require someone to tell them what to do?" For the trend, "trying to understand others' viewpoints and feelings," we asked, "How much does it bother you when you do not understand the viewpoints and feelings of people you associate with?" For the trend, "trying to keep one's role at any given time distinct from other roles," we asked, "Generally, how good an idea do you think it is to choose very close friends from among persons you work with?" For the trend, "trying to do one's own thinking," we asked, "How hard do you find it to disagree with others even in your own thinking?" For the trend, "trying to act inferior to control figures," we asked, "Do you think that people who have reached high office in government have a right to feel that they are better than most people?" For the trend, "trying to be submissive to control figures," we asked, "Do you think that for a truly happy marriage that in major issues the husband should tell the wife what to do?"

RESULTS

Table 1 shows the before-after correlations (test-retest reliabilities) for each of the trends, and the direction of changes significant at the .05 level or less. A plus sign indicates that the change is in the direction predicted; a minus sign, a change in the opposite direction. Although all of the predictions are directional, two-tailed rather than one-tailed tests are employed to permit ascribing levels of confidence to changes contrary to hypothesis.[2]

---

[2] The following statistical formula, designed specifically to test the significance of change, was employed: $t = (A - D - 1/\sqrt{A + D})$ (3, p. 207).

Twelve changes in the predicted direction prove significant at the .05 level of confidence. Six changes, significant at the .05 level occur in a direction opposite to that predicted.[3] The *combined* results cannot be assessed statistically since the trend measures are not independent, but it seems reasonable to conclude that some change has occurred and that it is predominantly in the predicted direction.

The preponderance of changes in the direction of decreasing trend potency is hard to explain. Most of the "correct" changes involve the *decrease* of autonomous trends in the hierarchical program or the *decrease* of hierarchical trends in the autonomous program. Likewise, five of the six "incorrect" changes involve the *decrease* of autonomous trends in the autonomous program or hierarchical trends in the hierarchical program. No single trend is found to change significantly in the predicted direction in *both* programs.

Although somewhat ambiguous, the data seem to indicate that measurable change can be effected by a persisting change in environmental conditions. Furthermore, the change seems partly explicable in terms of the movement of personality toward equilibrium with its environment. A type of organism-environment reciprocity is suggested in which the organism selects, reacts, and adjusts to its environment, so as to optimize personality "closure" while at the same time modifying itself within limits so as to further increase trend expression. This integral character of inner needs and outer conditions, as a general psychological principle is consistent with the position taken by Murphy: "A personality is a structured organism-environment field, each aspect of which stands in dynamic relation to each other aspect. There is organization within the organism and organization within the environment, but it is the cross-organization of the two that is investigated in personality research" (6, p. 8).

REFERENCES

1. Allport, F. H. Teleonomic description in the study of personality. *Charact. Pers.*, 1937, **5**, 202–214.
2. Kelly, E. L. Consistency of the adult personality. *Amer. Psychologist*, 1955, **10**, 659–681.
3. McNemar, Q. *Psychological statistics*. New York: Wiley, 1949.
4. Morse, Nancy, & Reimer, E. The experimental change of a major organizational variable. *J. abnorm. soc. Psychol.*, 1956, **52**, 120–129.
5. Morse, Nancy, Reimer, E., & Tannenbaum, A. S. Regulation and control in hierarchical organizations, *J. soc. Issues*, 1951, **7**, (3), 41–48.
6. Murphy, G. *Personality, a biosocial approach to origins and structure*. New York: Harper 1947.
7. Tannenbaum, A. S., & Allport, F. H. Personality structure and group structure: an interpretative study of their relationship through an event structure hypothesis. *J. abnorm. soc. Psychol.*, 1956, **53**, 272–280.

---

[3] The pattern of results remains essentially the same when evaluated in terms of the .01 level of confidence. In this case, eight changes prove "correct" and four "incorrect."

18

ATTITUDE UNIFORMITY AND ROLE
IN A VOLUNTARY ORGANIZATION*

Arnold S. Tannenbaum
Jerald G. Bachman[1]

A number of years ago F. H. Allport (1934) illustrated an approach to the objectification and measurement of institutional behavior. In the years since Allport's first J-curve measurements, social psychologists have become increasingly concerned with the dynamics of conformity in social settings. Group and organizational life are premised on certain uniformities of attitude, value, and behavior. These are the very 'groupness' of a group, according to Sherif and Sherif (1956). Uniformities help to preserve the group; and the group in turn, or rather its importance to members, provides the basis for members' implicit or explicit insistence on uniformity (Allport, 1962).

This paper is concerned with attitudinal uniformities among members in 104 local League of Women Voters' organizations. We focus here on the degree to which these uniformities manifest themselves among members playing three types of role: (a) Officers, including the president and the board of directors; (b) Actives, including minor leaders, such as committee chairmen and discussion leaders, as well as non-leaders who are frequent meeting-attenders; and (c) Inactives, consisting primarily of members who attend meetings rarely or not at all. We predict uniformities to be a function of these roles, with greatest uniformities occurring among the Officers, and least among the Inactives.[2]

A number of studies have been conducted in organizations and in laboratory groups concerning aspects of the above roles and conformity, but these studies are not entirely consistent in their conclusions. The relevant research and theories can be grouped under three headings broadly defined: Status; Cohesiveness—Potency of Involvement; and Activity. We assume that these characteristics are highly related in voluntary organizations.

* Reprinted from *Human Relations*, 1966, Vol. 19, No. 3, 309–322, with permission of the publisher and the authors. (This article has been edited to eliminate overlap and to bring it into a consistent format with the other articles in this book. Certain portions have therefore been deleted or reworded. Ed.)

[1] The authors are indebted to a number of colleagues for their helpful criticisms of an earlier draft and for their suggestions which are incorporated in this one: Frank Andrews, John R. P. French, Jr., Robert L. Kahn, Martin Patchen, and Clagett G. Smith.

[2] We define role in terms of the predictable and unique things members do, or the functions they perform. Although the differences between some Actives and Inactives may be a matter of degree (e.g. some Actives attend only a few more meetings than some Inactives), in general the distinctions between Inactives, Actives, and Officers are sufficiently clear to justify their being defined as separate role categories.

Status

Homans has proposed the hypothesis that 'the higher the rank of a person within a group, the more nearly his activities conform to the norms of the group' (1950, p. 141). Although Homans did not test this hypothesis methodically, he saw evidence for it in the results of the Hawthorne studies. Since then the Merei (1949) research and several other studies have been cited as providing some evidence for the special pressures on leaders to conform to group norms and of the resulting tendency for leaders to be more conformant than rank-and-file members. On the other hand, Dittes and Kelley (1956) have suggested that conformity, particularly relative to publicly expressed views, may be a function of *low* status. Hollander (1958), in reviewing some of the research on this subject, makes a special point of the developmental aspects of leadership and conformity in groups. At early stages, conformity by a member may be instrumental in gaining status (e.g. leadership or hierarchical rank). Having achieved status, however, the member may then be free to behave more idiosyncratically. Hence Officers (and Actives to a lesser extent) may sometimes exercise their prerogative to act deviantly, spending, in this way, what Hollander calls their "idiosyncracy credit." Blau (1960), in a study of deviancy in social work agencies, propounds a similar view.[3]

Cohesiveness—potency of involvement

A number of studies have been concerned with the effects of cohesiveness and related variables on uniformity. Festinger (1950) suggests that a member's attraction to the group will have a positive influence upon his tendencies to communicate with other members, to conform to group demands for opinion change, and to reject non-conformers. Essentially, the same predictions may be derived from balance theory (Cartwright and Harary, 1956; Newcomb, 1953, 1959). In the process of seeking balance and avoiding imbalance, individuals who are positively oriented toward a group will tend to be attracted to each other; and, alternatively, members attracted to each other will tend to develop similar orientations toward relevant objects (such as the group). Basically, the processes implied by these models involve a number of interrelated variables which, in concert, lead to uniformity: attraction to the group, inter-action-communication, and the tendency to send and receive influence or "pressure."[4]

Allport has proposed *potency of involvement* as the equivalent of cohesive-

---

[3] Blau suggests that this tendency may be more prevalent in some groups than in others. In groups where members have relatively little free choice as to membership (such as some work groups), this tendency might be important. The low-status member has to conform to be accepted. In groups where members are relatively free to belong or to leave, such as neighborhoods (or voluntary organizations), the low-status member does not have to conform. He can quit.

[4] For support of the Festinger hypotheses see Festinger, Schachter, and Back (1950); Back (1951); Schachter (1951). Some of this research has been done in field settings but almost none in organizations. An exception is Seashore's (1954) study of work groups. For another model under the cohesiveness heading, which leads to the same prediction, see French (1956). French employs graph theory in a formal model of social power. The "disconnected" and "weakly connected" graphs describe social relations among Inactives in an organization while the "strongly connected" and "complete" graphs more nearly describe relations among Actives and Officers.

ness in his event-structure theory. Allport's measurement of "involvement," which we have adopted in this research, is designed to represent 'the individual's "net investment" in, or tendency to maintain, the *collective structure* concerned' (Allport, 1962, p. 29). The event-structure prediction is that individuals high on this variable would manifest in their behavior high total "effort for consonance" in the collective structure (Allport, 1962, p. 29). Uniformities on "relevant" attitudes should result.

Activity

Activity is a third major dimension which appears to be related to uniformity within organizations. March (1954) found some support for his hypothesis that "the more active members of an organization will tend to exhibit a higher degree of conformity to group norms than will the less active members." Tannenbaum and Kahn (1958), in a study of four local unions, found that union Actives were more uniform (i.e. lower in variance) than Inactives in certain of their relevant views and behaviors. These studies in organizations are the most direct antecedents of the present research. However, March's study was based on a single group, and Tannenbaum and Kahn were limited to four unions. The present research affords an opportunity to investigate the hypothesis in a relatively large number of organizational units, and it extends the hypothesis to a consideration of Officers as a separate category.

The literature to which we have just referred is concerned in part with group norms; and we believe the present research is pertinent to this issue. However, a distinction is necessary in order to clarify what we are doing here:

A specific organizational norm may be defined in either of two ways, formally or operationally. The former implies an official position for the organization which is recognizable through formal statements or official documents, or it is inferred from knowledge about organizational policy. A norm, defined in this way, represents an official ideal. The researcher knows this ideal in advance and measures the degree to which members' behaviors conform to it.

The second approach makes no assumptions about what the norm should be. It measures members' attitudes along a relevant dimension and infers from observed uniformities the degree to which a norm is manifest. Norms of this kind may represent ideals too, but they are not necessarily *official* ideals; they are the ideals expressed by members. This approach implies that there may be as many norms along a given dimension as there are categories of members that the researcher chooses to define. Whether or not norms do in fact exist for these groups or, more exactly, to what degree norms are manifest, is an empirical question. One might therefore want to leave open the possibility that officers as one group conform to one norm position, while members as a second group conform to another. Then the question arises as to how much these persons conform to the norms of their respective subgroups. We think that this is a meaningful approach to the study of norms in organizations and have premised our research on this conception.

We shall therefore look separately within each of the three subgroups that we have defined and ascertain the degree to which uniformities occur around whatever the mean position for the respective groups may be. This avoids one problem which is implicit in some of the research and thinking on norm formation in groups. If officers are compared with members in their conformity to a single norm based on a total distribution, the former are in danger of being deviant simply by virtue of their minority status. While officers may be a relatively deviant group when they are measured against an overall group standard, they may nevertheless manifest a high degree of uniformity (i.e. normness) within their own category of membership.

METHOD

Research site and design

The data for the present study were obtained from 104 local leagues within the League of Women Voters of the United States.[5] The League of Women Voters of the United States includes over 100,000 members organized into about 1,000 relatively autonomous local leagues around the country. These local leagues vary in size from about 25 to 3,000 members. A probability sample of 104 leagues was drawn from a complete list of all leagues in the country. A stratification procedure by state and by size of league was employed so as to increase the accuracy of the sample. Each league was assigned a probability of falling into the sample proportional to its size.[6]

A questionnaire was mailed to approximately twenty-five randomly chosen members in each of the sample leagues. The mail questionnaire was considered feasible in view of the high educational level of the members and their expected high interest and motivation to cooperate. A final response rate of 77 per cent was obtained after an elaborate set of follow-up procedures including letters and phone calls by members of the research staff.[7] (Tannenbaum, 1961, pp. 36–39; Tannenbaum and Smith, 1964). In addition to this random sample, a supplementary sample of Officers was drawn from each local league to insure a minimum number of Officers for analysis in each league. Over 95 per cent of these respondents returned their questionnaires completed (Tannenbaum and Donald, 1957).

Subjects

Within each of the 104 local leagues, respondents were classified into three categories. The first, Officers, were selected on the basis of their responses to a questionnaire indicating membership on the board of directors or being the

[5] For a more detailed description of the League of Women Voters and of the larger study within which the present analysis has been performed, see Tannenbaum (1961).

[6] We are indebted to Leslie Kish and Irene Hess for the technical design of the sample.

[7] We are indebted to Charles Cannell and Sharon Summers for their contribution to this phase of the research.

local president. The remaining members were divided into Actives and Inactives according to their responses to the following questions:

How many of the following types of league meeting have you attended during the past year? (The types of meeting that the respondent could check included: study or resource committee meetings; board meetings; other committee meetings; general meetings; unit meetings; county, state, or national meetings.)

How much time would you say you spend *during the course of an average month* on league affairs? Include everything, such as telephone calls, travelling time, reading league materials, attending meetings, etc.

These two items were formed into a single index. Members classified as Actives were those whose score on the index was above the mean for all non-officers *in their league;* those below the mean were designated Inactives. The numbers of Officers, Actives, and Inactives fluctuate somewhat from league to league; the median numbers of respondents in each category in each league are eight, seven, and ten respectively.[8]

Measures

Twenty-five questions concerned with opinions about and attitudes toward the league were chosen from a large questionnaire as the basis for the measures of uniformity. These items were selected (prior to any analysis) on the basis of their judged relevance to the organization. Each of the items is described in *Table 2.*

Analysis

The following procedure was carried out separately for each of the twenty-five questionnaire items used:

Within each of the local leagues, the responses of the Officers, Actives, and Inactives were compared using the variance estimate (S^2) as an inverse measure of uniformity.[9] The hypothesis that uniformity will be greater among the more active members of an organization can be stated operationally as follows:

$$S^2 \text{ for Officers} < S^2 \text{ for Actives}$$
$$S^2 \text{ for Officers} < S^2 \text{ for Inactives}$$
$$S^2 \text{ for Actives} < S^2 \text{ for Inactives}$$

[8] Actives and Inactives were selected in this way so as to obtain nearly equal numbers in each category. Selection of Actives on the basis of minor leadership roles would result in so few Actives in some leagues as to preclude comparisons. There were usually more Inactives than Actives by the method of selection employed, since the distribution of activity scores is skewed.

[9] It is important that the distinction between the variance (σ^2) and the variance *estimate* (S^2) be clear, since the variance estimate may be used to compare samples of different size. The distinction may be expressed as follows:

$$S^2 = \sigma^2 \left(\frac{N}{N-1} \right).$$

Each of the above forms of the hypothesis was tested across the 104 leagues separately for each of the twenty-five items using the sign test. A plus was assigned to each league in which the results conformed to the hypothesis; a minus was assigned to those with contrary results; ties were disregarded.

The problem of bias

A serious possible source of bias stems from the relationship between variances and means of response distributions. The variance of the distribution will tend to diminish as the mean value approaches either the upper or lower limit of the scale because these limits restrict the range of responses. In order to determine the effects of this bias, its direction was ascertained for each comparison of variance estimates (i.e. Officers versus Actives, Officers versus Inactives, and Actives versus Inactives). For example, if the mean of the Actives' responses on a particular item was closer to one of the extremes of the scale than the mean of the Inactives' responses, the bias would be favorable to our hypothesis. Analysis did indicate, in fact, a greater tendency for the hypothesis to be supported in those cases where the bias was favorable to it than where it was unfavorable. We shall take this bias into account in the analyses that follow.

RESULTS

We have implied in the introductory rationale that differences exist between Officers, Actives, and Inactives on a number of variables which, we assume, partly underlie the predicted differences in variances. Table 1 presents the mean scores for Officers, Actives, and Inactives on some of these underlying characteristics as measured through responses to questionnaire items. We see in this table some documentation for the assumption that active members are more likely than inactive members to be high in attraction to the group or potency of involvement, to exercise influence, to exert pressures and to have pressure exerted over them, and to communicate and be communicated to. All of the differences are clearly significant beyond the .01 level, using the sign test.

Table 2 presents the results of the sign test applied to the comparison of variance estimates. The cell entries indicate the percentage of local leagues in which the results are in the predicted direction. The proportion expected by chance is 50 per cent. Fifty-seven of the seventy-five comparisons are favorable to the hypothesis; thirty-four of these, indicated by an asterisk, are significant at the .05 level (two-tailed sign test). Only one of the seventy-five comparisons proves significant in a direction opposite to that predicted.[10] A number of comparisons, however, are subject to the problem of bias.

---

[10] Although directional predictions were made, it was not clear that the effect would in fact occur for each of the twenty-five items used. The two-tailed test was applied in order to permit a statistical evaluation of any differences that might occur in a direction opposite to that predicted. When the individual items were combined to form an index (see below), a one-tailed test was applied.

TABLE 1   Mean Scores for Officers, Actives, and Inactives on Influence, Attraction to the Group, Pressures, and Communication Variables

	Mean responses[a]		
Question content	Officers	Actives	Inactives
Cohesiveness—Potency of Involvement			
(a) Suppose that as a result of strong opposition your local league were in real danger of folding up. How much effort would you be willing to spend in order to prevent that? (1, a very great deal; 5, none)	1.59	<1.99	<2.65
(b) Suppose that as a result of general member disinterest your local league were in real danger of folding up. How much effort would you be willing to spend to prevent this? (1, a very great deal; 5, none)	1.85	<2.31	<3.00
Influence			
(a) How much influence do you personally have in determining policies and actions of your local league? (1, no influence; 5, a great deal of influence)	2.57	>2.06	>1.51
(b) In general, how much influence do you personally have on what the following groups or persons do in your local league? (1, no influence; 5, a very great deal)			
On what the president does	2.43	>1.55	>1.23
On what the board of directors does	2.70	>1.60	>1.25
On what the members as a whole do	2.39	>1.70	>1.30
Pressure			
(a) If you were not to participate in league affairs, how likely is it that a league member would let you know that you should? (1, some would certainly let me know; 5, no one would let me know)	2.08	<2.39	<2.92
(b) If you knew a member who did not participate in league affairs, how likely is it that you would let her know that she should? (1, I would certainly let her know; 5, I would not let her know)	2.71	<2.99	<3.73
Communication—Interaction			
(a) How often do you give information concerning league matters to the following persons? (1, never; 5, several times a month or more often)			
Your local president	4.12	>2.52	>1.39
Members of your board	4.08	>2.67	>1.67
Other members	3.65	>3.10	>1.96
(b) How often do the following persons give you information concerning league matters? (1, never; 5, several times a month or more often)			
Your local president	4.32	>3.00	>2.36
Members of your board	4.26	>3.17	>2.44
Other members	3.54	>3.37	>2.61

[a] For all questions the Officers, Actives, and Inactives differ from each other significantly ($p < \cdot 01$; sign test, two-tailed).

TABLE 2   Comparisons of Uniformity among Officers, Actives, and Inactives

	Variance comparison[a]		
Question content	Officers vs. Actives	Officers vs. Inactives	Actives vs. Inactives
How much effort would you be willing to spend to prevent your local league from folding up as a result of:[b]			
Strong opposition within your community?	(71*)	(85*)	(76*)
General member disinterest?	(63*)	(74*)	(71*)
How much opportunity do you think the league should provide for sociability among the members?[c]	64*	73*	60*
How important do you think it is that your local league should avoid doing things which bring it into conflict with the following?			
Certain other organizations in your community[c]	58	63*	56
Certain influential persons in your community[c]	61*	66*	52
Your community at large	62*	(67*)	64*
Your state league	(60*)	(67*)	(57)
The national league	(60*)	(66*)	(62*)
To what extent should the league emphasize its study functions, and to what extent its functions as an action or pressure group?[c]	57	67*	58
How serious a loss to your community, your state, your nation (respectively) do you personally think it would be if:			
Your local league ceased to function?	54	(65*)	(61*)
Your state league ceased to function?[c]	48	60*	63*
The League of Women Voters of the United States ceased to function?	(55)	(67*)	(62*)
How much care do you personally think a league board member should exercise in keeping out of partisan politics?	[50]	[57]	[55]
In your opinion, how much influence do you think each of these groups should have in determining the policies and actions of your local league?			
Your local president	53	55	(67*)
Your local board as a group	(62*)	(59)	48
Your local membership as a whole[c]	54	55	59
The state board[c]	61*	50	47
The national board[c]	51	59	48
You, personally	50	[65*]	[67*]

Table 2   continued

Question content	Variance comparison[a]		
	Officers vs. Actives	Officers vs. Inactives	Actives vs. Inactives
In general, how much influence do you think the following groups should have in determining the policies and actions of the League of Women Voters of the United States?			
The national board[c]	54	50	40*
Your state league[c]	46	48	46
Your local league[c]	55	49	46
All the local leagues as a group	(61*)	(65*)	(57)
Do you personally agree or disagree with the choice of:			
Individual liberties as the first national agenda item?	48	(50)	50
Conservation as the second national agenda item?	51	(52)	45

[a] The cell entries indicate the percentage of local leagues in which the direction of results was consistent with our hypothesis. An asterisk indicates an effect significant at the .05 level (sign test, two-tailed). Those comparisons which are subject to consistent bias (greater than 60%) in favor of the hypothesis are enclosed in parentheses; those subject to bias against the hypothesis are enclosed in square brackets (see text).
[b] These items are included among the items of Table 1.
[c] These items were combined to make a single, essentially unbiased index (see text).

We have defined the problem of bias in terms of the possible relationship between mean and variance scores on an item. Operationally, a comparison is considered subject to bias if, for the item under consideration, one group (e.g. Actives) has more extreme scores than the other with which it is being compared in more than 60 per cent of the leagues. Parentheses designate these comparisons in Table 2 that are subject to bias favorable to the hypothesis; square brackets denote those comparisons that may be biased against the hypothesis. Twenty-six of the comparisons are subject to a favorable bias. All of these yield results in the predicted direction; and twenty are significant. Unfortunately, we cannot know whether this high rate of support for the hypothesis relative to these items is artifactual or legitimate.[11] However, all of the five comparisons that are subject to an "unfavorable" bias are also in the predicted direction; and two of these comparisons are significant. Of the remaining comparisons which are free of bias, twelve are significant in the predicted direction whereas only one is significant in the opposite direction. In so

[11] It is possible that those items that are subject to bias are those that are most relevant to the hypothesis in the first place. The more extreme scores for Actives on these items, which create the bias problem, may reflect the greater pressures relative to these items toward uniformity.

far as these unbiased items are concerned, it is unlikely that the variance differences are attributable to differences in mean scores.[12]

Although the results seem preponderantly favorable to the hypothesis, the twenty-five items presented in Table 2 are not independent. Because of this, a definite overall statistical evaluation cannot be made on the basis of the analyses presented so far. This problem of independence was overcome by reducing the eleven unbiased items to a single index. For each league a single score (plus or minus) was derived for each of the three comparisons: Officers versus Actives, Officers versus Inactives, and Actives versus Inactives. Taking each of the above comparisons separately, a plus indicates that a majority of the eleven items is favorable to the hypothesis; a minus indicates that a majority is unfavorable. Employing a one-tailed sign test, we find that Officers are more uniform in their responses than either Actives ($p < .01$) or Inactives ($p < .01$), and that Actives tend to be more uniform than Inactives ($p = .08$). Thus it appears that the data support the hypothesis even when we restrict ourselves to unbiased items.

DISCUSSION

The results of the above analysis are in general consistent with the proposed hypothesis: Officers appear to be most uniform on relevant attitudes and Inactives least uniform. At the same time, the data in Table 2 show that in twenty-six comparisons the more involved or active members take significantly more extreme positions on the attitude scales, while in only five comparisons are the less active members more extreme. Leaders in particular are more likely to be deviant relative to an overall group standard than are members. We thus see some support for two hypotheses which may have seemed contradictory, but need not be. Leaders are more likely to be deviant (or idiosyncratic) in the total group, while they are likely to be more conformant as a group within their own category of membership.

In Figure 1 we have idealized this relationship as suggested by our data. Two conditions are shown: those for which the correlation between the relevant attitude score and activity (or status or involvement) is negative (dashed line), and those for which it is positive (solid line). In either case, leaders as a subgroup are more extreme and deviant, while at the same time they are more uniform among themselves.

Since we are employing a cross-sectional survey design, we are faced with the usual limitations of that method relative to drawing inferences about causality. It seems safe to conclude that the relationships we have observed may occur by either (or, perhaps more likely, by a combination) of the following general routes: (a) The attitudes of members may *change* in the direction of

[12] One might suspect an *incipient* bias among these 'unbiased' comparisons, i.e. they might all tend in the biased direction—although not so strongly as to meet our 60 per cent criterion. However, of the forty-four comparisons classified as unbiased, twenty-one show this 'incipient' bias favorable to the hypothesis, and twenty-one are unfavorable (with the remaining two cases tied). Thus the results cannot be attributed to this sort of bias.

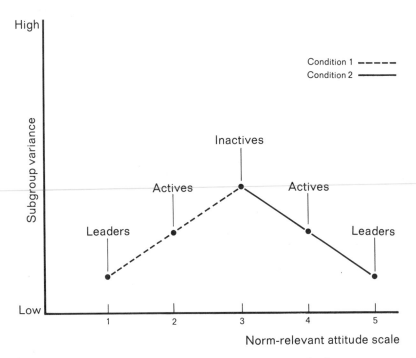

FIGURE 1 *Variance and attitude scale positions for leaders, actives, and inactives under two conditions.*

greater uniformity as a result of activity in the organization. (b) Members may be selected into and out of the organization—or an active role in the organization—because of their attitudes. Most theoretical statements about conformity or about norms propose some combination of these processes (e.g. group cohesiveness is said to involve greater pressures toward conformity along with a greater likelihood of rejecting deviates).[13]

The relationships observed in this study, while consistent with the initial hypothesis, are not sharp. There may be several theoretical reasons for this apart from possible methodological limitations:

1. We have already mentioned the arguments of Hollander (1958) and of Blau (1960), which suggest greater deviance among higher-status group members. Tendencies of this kind may occur in sufficient strength to weaken the relationships we predicted but not to eliminate them completely or to reverse them.

2. We have assumed the existence of a standard represented by a point on our attitude scale around which uniformity becomes established as a norm. This implies an optimum position on the scale for Actives (or Inactives). Po-

---

[13] A longitudinal study might make it possible to determine the extent to which the greater uniformity among Actives was caused by changes in individuals' views, or by loss or rejection of individuals holding discrepant views.

sitions above or below this point imply some degree of deviancy. March (1964) refers to this as a "preferred value norm." However, on some issues attitudinal deviance may be tolerated or even rewarded on one side of the modal point but not on the other. "Attainable-ideal" and "unattainable-ideal" norms have this characteristic (March, 1954).[14] Actives may be more likely than Inactives to deviate toward unattainable goals or to exceed attainable ones, contributing variance in this way to their distribution of attitudes.

3.   The items of Table 2 were chosen because they were judged to refer to issues around which norms are most likely to develop. However, the basis for this choice is not always clear, and it is possible that the items chosen were not, after all, the best ones. This problem illustrates a general weakness in theories of norms, none of which is explicit about the criteria that distinguish those issues concerning which norms are likely to develop and all others. Norms are said to develop about "anything and everything which is of shared interest . . ." (Newcomb, 1951), or norms develop around issues which are somehow "relevant" to the group (Festinger, 1957).

In defining the notion of relevance for the purposes of this study we accepted the view of Allport (1962) that norms serve the function of helping to preserve the group or to maintain for members relationships that are important to them. Items were selected on the basis of our judgement that uniformity among members on the items was necessary for the continued existence of the group. Our judgement was a dichotomous one; an item was either relevant or not relevant. Perhaps we can learn something about the dimension of "relevance" by observing which kinds of issues yield the largest differences in variance between Actives and Inactives. This assumes that Actives are, in fact, more uniform than Inactives and that the uniformity differences are greater for the more relevant issues.

The items in Table 2 are arranged roughly in the order of their success in supporting the initial hypothesis. This ordering is very crude because of the bias problem; nevertheless, the arrangement may be revealing. Items near the top of the list are presumably the most relevant. These appear to be issues concerning which shared views are most important to the maintenance and success of the local league as an organization. The first pair of items concerns the willingness of members to stand behind their local organization in the face of a threat to it. The second item concerns the question of the league's basic purpose; in effect, whether it is to be a social club or a (non-partisan) political organization. Disagreement on these issues among members (particularly among Officers and Actives) could be damaging to the group's continued existence. The third set of items concerns conflicts which might be considered a threat to the existence of the local league. Shared views regarding the issues near the bottom of the list, however, may not be so essential to the maintenance of the group. This is probably most evident for the question concerning agree-

---

[14] A man cannot be too saintly (unattainable goal) for a priestly group. A halfback need run with the ball only as far as the goal line (attainable); running further is acceptable but not necessary (March, 1954).

ment with individual liberties and conservation as agenda items. These are ephemeral issues for the organization, which are the subject of legitimate debate. Agenda items change every couple of years and disagreement about them does not imply a threat to the organization in general.

Implications for the theory of groups

The data of this study, we believe, have some general implications for the theory of groups (and of organizations). The definitional criteria of a group suggest that groups may vary in their degree of "groupness" or structuredness. The important elements of group life which contribute to the group's coherence, to its orderliness and predictability, to the effective coordination of individual behaviors into some form of concerted or integrated action, vary from one group to another.

But a group itself may be heterogeneous with respect to the qualities that imply groupness. Regions within a group, when construed in field theoretical terms, can be seen to differ in the intensity or density of those characteristics that define the group as a social entity. Some regions are more organized, structured, predictable, and more information-laden and higher in negative entropy than others.[15] More specifically, as we move through the field along a dimension defined in terms of activity level of members, we go from regions that are low in indicia of groupness to regions that are high. We have seen in the data of this study some evidence of these gradients, and propose that others exist as well. Thus the group is more "cohesive" in the more active regions, more dense in interactions among members, higher in influences and "pressures" on and by members relative to defining and achieving "group goals." The higher levels of influence, pressure, and communication imply a greater degree of interdependence and feedback in the active region and a greater manifestation of coordinated, "goal-directed" behavior. We have, in *graph theory* terms, more "connectedness" (French, 1956) and this is reflected in the relative uniformity which characterizes the active region. More group things get done here, and they get done with more certainty. There is less randomness (entropy) in relevant attitudes and probably in relevant behaviors too.

One can extend this field theory analysis to encompass the group's environment of potential members. Some members are members only nominally and cannot easily be distinguished from many non-members who endorse the league's goals, give financial support, and feel some sense of identification with the league. Thus, where the group picks up and where it leaves off are not clear dynamically, although they may be clear pheno-typically when the group is defined simply in terms of card-carrying members. If we were to measure the relevant attitudes of "fellow-traveling" non-members, we would expect

---

[15] See Tannenbaum and Kahn (1958, pp. 203–4) for a brief discussion of uniformity in groups in relation to the concepts of entropy and information.

some resemblance to those of formal members. But we would also expect less uniformity among these potential members than that found within our least active region. Thus the group looks more like a group in certain regions, less like a group in others, and it may even manifest some semblance of groupness in regions that, formally speaking, are not part of the group.

The narrowed variance implicit in Allport's J-curve is a characteristic of institutionalized behavior. In organizations or in groups it reflects one aspect of degree of organization, or of "groupness." We have taken attitudinal uniformities on "relevant" issues as one index of this groupness and have noted one way in which it might vary within a group. It would be interesting to learn more about the gradients of groupness that apply within groups as well as the variations in groupness between them.

REFERENCES

Allport, F. H. (1934). The J-curve hypothesis of conforming behavior. *J. soc. Psychol.* **5,** 141–83.

Allport, F. H. (1954). The structuring of events: outline of a general theory with applications to psychology. *Psychol. Rev.* **61,** 281–303.

Allport, F. H. (1962). A structuronomic conception of behavior: individual and collective I. Structural theory and the master problem of social psychology. *J. abnorm. soc. Psychol.* **64,** 3–30.

Back, K. (1951). Influence through social communication. *J. abnorm. soc. Psychol.* **46,** 9–23.

Blau, P. (1960). Patterns of deviation in work groups. *Sociometry* **23,** 245–61.

Cartwright, D. & Harary, F. (1956). Structural balance: a generalization of Heider's theory. *Psychol. Rev.* **63,** 277–93.

Dittes, A. & Kelley, H. (1956). Effects of different conditions of acceptance upon conformity to group norms. *J. abnorm. soc. Psychol.* **53,** No. 1, 100–7.

Festinger, L. (1950). Informal social communication. *Psychol. Rev.* **57,** 271–82.

Festinger, L. (1957). *A theory of cognitive dissonance.* Evanston, Ill.: Row-Peterson. Reissued 1962, Stanford: Stanford University Press; London: Tavistock Publications.

Festinger, L., Schachter, S. & Back, K. (1950). *Social pressures in informal groups: a study of human factors in housing.* New York: Harper. Reissued 1963, Stanford: Stanford University Press; London: Tavistock Publications.

French, J. R. P., Jr. (1956). A formal theory of social power. *Psychol. Rev.* **63,** 181–94.

Hollander, E. P. (1958). Conformity, status and idiosyncrasy credit. *Psychol. Rev.* **65,** 117–27.

Homans, G. C. (1950). *The human group.* New York: Harcourt, Brace.

Kelley, H. H. & Thibaut, J. W. (1954). Experimental studies of group problem solving process. In G. Lindzey (Ed.), *Handbook of social psychology.* Cambridge: Addison-Wesley.

March, J. G. (1954). Group norms and the active minority. *Amer. sociol. Rev.* **19,** 733–41.

Merei, F. (1949). Group leadership and institutionalization. *Hum. Relat.* **2**, 23–39.

Newcomb, T. M. (1951). Social psychological theory: integrating individual and social approaches. In J. Rohrer and M. Sherif (Eds.), *Social psychology at the crossroads*, Chapter 2. New York: Harper.

Newcomb, T. M. (1953). An approach to the study of communicative acts. *Psychol. Rev.* **60**, 393–404.

Newcomb, T. M. (1959). Individual systems of orientation. In S. Koch (Ed.), *Psychology: a study of a science*, Study I. *Conceptual and systematic*, Vol. 3. New York: McGraw-Hill.

Schachter, S. (1951). Deviation, rejection, and communication. *J. abnorm. soc. Psychol.* **46**, 190–207.

Seashore, S. E. (1954). *Group cohesiveness in the industrial work group.* Ann Arbor, Michigan: Institute for Social Research.

Sherif, M. & Sherif, Carolyn W. (1956). *An outline of social psychology.* New York: Harper & Row.

Tannenbaum, A. S. (1961). Control and effectiveness in a voluntary organization. *Amer. J. Sociol.* **67**, 33–46 (in this book, Chap. 4).

Tannenbaum, A. S. & Donald, Marjorie N. (1957). *A study of the League of Women Voters in the United States, Report IV: Factors in league functioning.* Ann Arbor, Michigan: Survey Research Center, Institute for Social Research.

Tannenbaum, A. S. & Kahn, R. L. (1958). *Participation in union locals.* Evanston, Ill.: Row Peterson.

Tannenbaum, A. S. & Smith, C. G. (1964). The effects of member influence in an organization: phenomenology versus organization structure. *J. abnorm. soc. Psychol.* **69**, 401–10 (in this book, Chap. 13).

PART 4

This concluding section presents three papers. In Chapter 19 we consider a number of formal and informal means by which union members may exercise control in their locals. The data of this chapter also help explain what union members mean by control when they respond to questions about it. The development of measures consistent with definitions remains a serious problem in the study of control. In Chapter 20, Whisler, Meyer, Baum, and Sorensen study several alternate concepts and measures of centralization of control, including a measure based on questions employed earlier in this text. Although the work described in this chapter was done independently of the programmatic effort presented earlier, we include it here because it is illustrative of much needed research concerning the meaning and measurement of control. The last chapter summarizes some of what we have learned about the effects of control on the reactions and adjustments of organization members and on the performance of organizations. If this research helps answer some questions about control, it also raises questions, some of which imply dilemmas of serious proportions.

19

MECHANISMS OF CONTROL
IN LOCAL TRADE UNIONS*

Arnold S. Tannenbaum[1]

We discuss data here that describe some of the means by which members of union locals may exercise control in their organizations. The data also point to aspects of control that figure prominently in the thinking of members when they are asked to evaluate the control process in their organizations. Four union locals have been studied. All are industrial, ranging from 350 to 850 members. None of the officers is employed by the unions on a paid basis. Two kinds of data are presented: responses to a number of questions asked in a paper-and-pencil questionnaire and illustrative quotations from interviews conducted with a small number of members. Although the locals differ in their level of membership participation and in certain aspects of their control structure, the tabular data presented below are derived by averaging the results for the four locals.[2] These data are based on a representative sample of members and officers in each local. The total N is about 700. Although the data from these locals may not be typical of American unions, they nevertheless illustrate some of the mechanisms through which union members may exercise control, and they provide some insight into the way control in these unions is evaluated by members.

Control in a union, as in any organization, may be exerted through several categories or phases of activity.[3] One of these is the *legislative* or decision-making phase, which involves the process of deciding upon the rules, policies, and general actions of the organization. Another is the *administrative* phase which involves the day-to-day interpretating, expediting, and carrying out of legislative decisions. There is also the *sanctions* phase, which entails the met-

* From *The British Journal of Sociology*, December 1956, **VII**, 306–313, by permission of the publisher. (This article has been edited to eliminate overlap and to bring it into a consistent format with the other articles in this book. Certain portions have therefore been deleted or reworded. Ed.)

[1] The material presented here is partly adapted from a larger report written by the present author in collaboration with Robert L. Kahn. This study was supported by a grant from the Rockefeller Foundation. I should like to thank Irwin Goffman and Robert Kahn for their helpful discussions in the development of the material presented here. Marjorie N. Donald and Basil Georgopoulos have made useful suggestions with regard to the write-up.

[2] The reader is referred to two articles that discuss differences in control structure among these locals: A. S. Tannenbaum, Control structure and union functions, *Amer. J. Sociol.*, **61** (6), May 1956, 536–545 (in this book, Chap. 2), and A. S. Tannenbaum and Robert L. Kahn, Control structure in organizations: a general descriptive technique as applied to four union locals, *Human Relat.*, **10** (2), 1957, 127–140.

[3] N. C. Morse, E. Reimer, and A. S. Tannenbaum, Regulation and control in hierarchical organizations, *J. soc. Issues*, **VII** (3), 1951, 41–48.

ing out or withholding of rewards and punishments in the process of enforcing rules and standards.

Although each of these phases of control may occur either formally or informally, legislative control occurs largely at meetings or through other formally defined union structures. Administrative and sanctions control, however, frequently occur outside meetings and may be oriented relative to either formal or informal union standards. For example, informal sanctions may be instituted against a member who fails to play a formal role such as helping out during a strike or attending a union meeting.

The relationship among these phases of control is often complex; the same persons need not be involved equally in all three. As in government, some persons may be primarily charged with the responsibility of legislating, others with administering, and still others with the sanctions process. In large organizations specialization among these phases of control is necessary while in smaller organizations it is possible for the same persons to be involved in all three. An interesting and not uncommon arrangement involves "administrators" administering law over "legislators" who originally made it. The former exercise a degree of control over the latter, but this control is within a framework initially formulated by the latter. This process is illustrated experimentally by the Merei research with children in which a dominant, leader-type child is placed in an ongoing group which has an established set of traditions, customs, and rules. In some cases, this "leader" may continue to play a leadership role by ordering the other children to do *precisely those things which they were already doing* and which were a part of the rules evolved prior to his entry into the group.[4] He becomes an administrator of law over those who made the law, and he performs significant control functions to the extent that the group becomes dependent on him for some degree of law enforcement.

In certain respects this arrangement is characteristic of the large, democratic organization. General law and organizational policy are decided by a broad segment of the membership, and the administrative function and the authority to initiate formal sanctions are delegated to a few. The administrative and order-giving power of the leaders is relatively narrow and specific and is subsumed under general legislative decisions made elsewhere. Furthermore, the leaders may be chosen by the followers, thus complicating the task of evaluating who controls whom.

The issue of control in unions is further complicated by the fact that control is exercised with regard to many issues which vary in their importance to the membership. A few outstanding areas of decision-making, for example, include whether or not certain money expenditures are to be made, what the union will ask in its bargaining with management, or whether or not the union will go out on strike. Decisions with regard to these issues are made only infrequently but they are of the utmost importance to most members. On the other hand, there

---

[4] Ferenc Merei, Group leadership and institutionalization, in Guy E. Swanson, T. M. Newcomb, and Eugene L. Hartley (Eds.), *Readings in social psychology*, New York: Holt, 1952, 318–328.

is a large body of decisions which are made almost daily and which are of little concern to most members: how a particular grievance should be handled, who should be appointed to this or that *ad hoc* committee, which member is to be sent to a national training conference. Obviously these issues arouse differential interest. By and large the members are not concerned with the minute details of the ongoing organization although their interest may reach fever pitch when it comes to deciding about bargaining demands or going out on strike.

Union members view the control processes of their organization in predominantly pragmatic terms; they view control in terms of issues that are important to them. It is therefore necessary to make the distinction between decisions which are crucial to the members and those which are of less importance. One worker who felt that the rank and file had a high level of control in his local put it this way:

"Speaking frankly, most issues are cut and dried before you get there [to meetings]—that is, except the important ones."

Table I illustrates the differences in involvement which members indicate relative to three important areas of decision making: going out on strike, bargaining demands, and money expenditures. These data are based on the following questions: "Who do you think has the most to say in deciding whether or not the union will go out on strike over an issue?", "Who do you think has most to say about what kinds of things the union will ask for in negotiations?", and "Who do you think has the most to say in deciding whether or not the union will spend money out of its treasury?" The possible alternatives which were provided in response to these questions are indicated in Table 1.

On the issue of strike action, 72 per cent of the members agree that the membership as a whole has the most say. On the other hand, less than a majority consider the membership to have the most say in deciding money expenditures or bargaining demands. What is true of the rank and file very likely applies to other groups within the local. Officer groups may have different amounts of influence relative to different issues. The bargaining committee probably exerts more influence over negotiation demands than it does over money expenditures. The executive board may (in some locals) have a greater say in the area of money expenditures than it does with regard to the question of strike action.

Informal sanctions instituted by the members likewise appear to follow a gradient with regard to different issues. This is illustrated by data in response to the following questions: "If someone in this local did not attend a local meeting, would you let him know that he should have?", "If you found out that someone in this local had not voted in a union election, would you let him know that he should have?", and "If this local was having a strike and someone did not help out, would you let him know that he should have?" Table 2 presents the responses to these questions as averaged for the four locals.

Sanctions are more likely to be instituted by the members against those who fail to help out during a strike than against those who fail to attend a

TABLE 1 Proportion of Members Who Indicate That the Membership or Other Groups in the Local Have the Most Say in Deciding Strike Action, Bargaining Demands, and Money Expenditures

	Proportion of members who indicate:					
	Membership as a whole has most say	Active members have most say	Bargaining committee has most say	Executive Board has most say	Others* have most say	Total per cent
In deciding strike action	72	14	5	2	7	100
In deciding money expenditures	46	29	5	17	3	100
In deciding bargaining demands	40	23	18	6	13	100

* Stewards and committeemen, the president, and the international field representative.

TABLE 2 Likelihood of Sanctions by Members

	Likelihood member would tell another that he should have taken part in activity:					
Activity	Would certainly let him know	Would probably let him know	Might let him know	Would probably not let him know	Would not let him know	Total per cent
Helping out on strike	57	17	15	5	6	100
Voting in union election	46	22	15	7	10	100
Attending a union meeting	26	22	22	13	17	100

union meeting. The members express much interest in and exercise a great deal of sanctions control relative to the former issue; it is an issue which has an important bearing on the welfare of the average member. On the other hand they exercise relatively little sanctions control in connection with regular union meetings. These meetings, generally concerned with the minutiæ of running the union, interest the members but little, and their control over attendance is correspondingly less.

Member participation in union meetings is often considered a criterion of union democracy. However, there is a growing realization that attendance at union meetings is but one means through which the members might exercise some influence in their union. The rank and file has recourse to devices of control in addition to those exercised at regular meetings. Among these are informal and representational mechanisms of control,[5] and election and recall power over leaders. They may also have a broad potentiality of control where they may not actively and explicitly exercise it, but this too has important implications for the way in which the union is run and serves as an indirect form of control which the members implicitly exercise. This should not be construed as attempting to negate the importance of the union meeting as *one* channel through which control may be exercised. The union meeting is an obvious *locus* of decision making. Many of the members who attend do so largely because they want to have a say in what the union is doing. Especially by attendance at *special* meetings, members exercise control when important issues are at stake. Generally speaking, it might be expected that the level of membership control will be partly reflected in the level of meeting attendance. This will be true not only because the meeting is on possible channel for decision-making, but also because attendance is likely to reflect a general level of interest and activity on the part of the membership in the various affairs, formal and informal, decision making and non-decision-making, of the local. Thus we find that among the four locals studied there is a relationship between amount of formal participation and the level of control exercised by the members in the affairs of the union.

Direct attendance at meetings, however, is not an absolute requisite to control. The member does not have to be physically present at a meeting for his voice to be heard. One vehicle for the informal decision-making process is the discussion which takes place outside the meeting hall:

"It's always talked around all over. It's talked around the shop and down at the meeting."

Members may influence the course of any prospective decision by what they say at these informal sessions. Furthermore, many members can rely on others to represent them at the meetings. One worker felt:

"There are a couple of stewards that I can depend on pretty well. They speak for me very often. That's what they're stewards for."

[5] See, for example, Joseph Kovner and Herbert J. Lahne, for a detailed discussion of this point. Shop society and the union, *Ind. & Lab. Rel. Rev.*, 7 (1), October, 1953, 3–14.

Or:

"The steward is supposed to—that's his job. The steward has done this for me occasionally—once or twice a year. It depends on how you feel. You have to represent yourself on some things."

Or as one active member put it:

"Usually if I'm not at a meeting and I know that some points should be brought up, I usually tell a committeeman to bring it up."

In addition to representation along organizational lines (through the steward or officers) informal representation may occur among groups of friends:

"Sometimes we get together and talk it over before. We elect someone to speak for us. We can't all do it."

Even though many members fail to attend meetings, and many abstain from this process of informal representation, they may nevertheless exercise a degree of control in more subtle ways. Their mere membership in the local makes a difference and their presence must be taken into account by the decision-makers. These members may remain inert only so long as matters go their way or do not get too seriously out of hand. The decision-makers know this and guide their actions accordingly. They cannot persist in decisions which contravene the interests of this quiescent element without arousing it to action. Members who feel this way frequently explain their failure to attend meetings on the grounds that "Things will be decided the way I like them anyway." Why should such a member exert himself when he gets what he wants without effort? But let an important decision arise which he fears will "go the wrong way," and he may try to have a more direct effect on its course. We have here a latent force which has an important bearing on the manifest actions of the local; it represents what we have called the potentiality of control.

Closely related is the power of ratification. Legislative or decision-making control can be seen as consisting of at least two kinds of behaviour. One is the process of initiating and influencing the passage of legislative decisions. The other involves the function of ratifying, or legitimizing these decisions. Legislative control thus includes two aspects—one relatively prolonged and the other relatively concise. The prolonged aspect involves the political and psychological interplay of forces—argument, compromise, persuasion. The second aspect involves a simple yes-or-no decision. Will or will not the union be committed to a particular policy; will it or will it not follow a given course of action? The former is a long and complex process. The latter is relatively short and simple. This distinction is especially important in labour unions, where relatively few members take the initiative in raising legislative issues, and few have the time or ability to "sell" their point of view. Ratification control while highly important requires relatively little effort. It is in this way that a large segment of the membership may step in to accept or reject the effort of others. Thus, members see the "Body" as being subject to the persuasion of various persons. "Men who are good talkers and good salesmen," for example, may have considerably more influence at union meetings. "They get across their point." But it is clear that many in these locals see the Body as ratifying all important decisions. "Officers have a lot to say—but it's still up to the Body." An issue may be settled only after long and arduous effort on the part of interested parties but if it is an important issue the Body makes the final decision: "If they vote it in, it's in—if they vote it out, it's out." While members recognize the influence of leaders, they tend to stress their own power of ratification. When asked about going out on strike, for example, one member said: "The officials have more say. They call the strike meetings in the first place. The Body decides though."

One further aspect of membership control is made apparent in talking to union members. We have touched before on the sensitivity of union leaders to the desires of a relatively inert membership. One important determinant of this sensitivity is the fact that the leaders are elected and depend upon the support of the rank and file for their continuance in office. Even inactive members may carefully watch what their officers do and stand ready to remove them at the time of election. A much higher proportion of members vote in union elections than regularly attend meetings. One worker when asked whether or not it were possible for the president and executive board to have *all* of the say in deciding things in the local, put it this way:

"No, you wouldn't have a union then, you'd have a dictator board. All have a vote when it comes down to brass tacks. *It wouldn't last long because the people would rise up against them.* These things should be done open and above board. The laws of the land are made that way, why not this?"

Another member who saw the officers as a powerful group in the local had this to say in response to the same question:

"It would be possible. They could do it by rigging meetings through parliamentary tactics. They probably have. *They couldn't get away with it often —there'd be a recall vote.*"

Although the members may not be highly involved in the day-to-day decisions of the local, they appear to have a measure of control over those who are.

SUMMARY

Control in a local union is a complex process. It is exercised through various phases of activity: legislative, administrative, and sanctions; and relative to many issues which differ in their importance to the membership. Different persons may be differentially involved in the various phases of control. Furthermore, the members often view control of their union in pragmatic terms, in terms of those issues which make a difference to them.

The above descriptions help explain what members mean by control, and how membership control may be maintained at a fairly high level without a corresponding involvement of the rank and file in the regular formal meetings of the union. Members exercise control through meetings, but also through other channels. Informal discussions and representational arrangements, ratification power and the power of election and recall, all represent possible mechanisms of control at the disposal of the membership.

20

CENTRALIZATION OF ORGANIZATIONAL CONTROL: AN EMPIRICAL STUDY OF ITS MEANING AND MEASUREMENT*

Thomas L. Whisler
Harald Meyer
Bernard H. Baum
Peter F. Sorensen Jr.[1]

This study is aimed at clarifying the meaning of a key variable in theories and models of organizations—*centralization of organizational control.* To do so, it is necessary to first examine the concept of control. The study is empirical as well as analytical. We compare certain proposed measures of control, the comparison being designed both to test our inferences about the control concept underlying each of the measures and to assess the degree to which the concepts and measures are interrelated.

Study of the growing literature of organizations makes one aware that, until recently, the centralization variable has usually been lamely handled in empirical research. The probable explanation is that both *control* and *centralization* have always been ambiguous concepts. In view of the importance of the concepts of control and centralization in theory and the growing emphasis on empirical research for the purpose of testing and refining theory, empirical exploration of the meaning and measurement of centralization of control appears urgently required.

The study focuses upon three measures of control already suggested in organizational literature: (1) individual compensation,[2] (2) perceptions of interpersonal influence recorded on a questionnaire,[3] and (3) the span of control in the formal organization.[4]

* Reprinted from *Journal of Business*, Jan. 1967, Vol. 40, No. 1, 10–26, with permission of The University of Chicago Press and the authors.

[1] This study was jointly planned. Baum and Sorensen are responsible for data collection and for the task analysis and ranking described on p. 293. Whisler and Meyer are responsible for the analysis and preparation of the manuscript. Responsibility for the article is shared jointly. Support for the research was provided by NASA grant NSG-370.

[2] Thomas L. Whisler, "Measuring Centralization of Control in Business Organizations," in W. W. Cooper, H. J. Leavitt, and M. W. Shelly II (eds.), *New Perspectives in Organization Research* (New York: John Wiley & Sons, 1964).

[3] Arnold S. Tannenbaum and Basil S. Georgopoulos, "The Distribution of Control in Formal Organizations," *Social Forces*, 36, No. 1 (1957), 44–50 (in this book, Chap. 3).

[4] A. Janger, "Analyzing the Span of Control: How Many Subordinates Should Report to a Single Manager?" *Management Record*, XXII (July–August, 1960), 7–10, and Peter M. Blau and Richard D. Scott, *Formal Organizations* (San Francisco: Chandler Publishing Co., 1962), pp. 168–69.

TABLE 1 **Measures and Concepts of Control**

Measure of control	Related concept of control
A. Individual compensation	A. Control over system output (system control)
B. Scaled perceptions of individual influence	B. Perceived interpersonal control
C. Span of control	C. Formally defined (or intended) interpersonal control

It appears to us not only that these three measures are based upon different concepts of the process of control in organizations but also that the concepts themselves represent different orders of explanation, with the compensation-related concept being broader than the other two.

The *first* concept, upon which the compensation measure is based, is that of individual control over system (organizational) output, either by influencing other members or by direct personal task inputs. The *second* concept, underlying the questionnaire measure of control, defines control as perceived interpersonal influence—the perceived influence of members upon each other. The *third* concept is that of control as the formally planned influence of organization members upon one another in their roles as superiors and subordinates.

These relationships of concept and measure are summarized in Table 1.

Discussion of concepts and measures of control

A.   Individual compensation

In our view the concept of system control, upon which this measure is based, is the broadest of the three considered in this study. Each member of the organization provides inputs which, in various ways, influence the outcome of the total effort of the organization. These inputs can be applied either through *direct personal task effort* (commonly, "work" or "problem-solving" at various levels of sophistication) or *through other members* (commonly, "direction" or "supervision"), or both. This concept we define as system control, the "system" being the totality of resources and procedures constituting the organization.

One expects, in any hierarchical organization with specialization of tasks, that there will be differences among individuals in the amount of control they exert over system output. Von Bertalanffy, in a discourse on what he calls "general system theory," argues the universal existence of a principle of centralization, meaning that some elements (individuals) in a system (organization) function as "triggers," because a small change in energy input by those elements results in large (disproportionate) changes in system output.[5] This

---

[5] L. Von Bertalanffy, "An Outline of General System Theory," *British Journal for the Philosophy of Science*, I, No. 2 (1950), 150–51.

disproportion results from the design characteristics of the system. The present concept closely parallels this idea.

The measure of control based on this concept is the compensation paid the individual by the organization. Compensation is the "inducement"; control is the "contribution" (expressed in terms of effect upon organizational output) in the terminology used by March and Simon.[6] As these writers point out, the organization seeks always to maintain a balance between contributions and inducements.

The way in which an organization's "role" or job structure and performance-evaluation procedures tie together with market prices to make individual compensation a reflection of individual control has been analyzed in detail elsewhere.[7] But the argument may be briefly restated here:

In the bureaucratic organization, roles are formally structured and control explicitly assigned to them by those in top leadership positions (their own roles included). It seems reasonable to assume that control can be assigned in a variety of alternative patterns at the discretion of leadership, with technology, organization size, and other factors undoubtedly influencing their choices as they seek an effective pattern.

The pattern of control that is established determines a homologous pattern of role demands made upon the individuals who fill these roles (or, in traditional managerial language, a grant of authority carries a corresponding measure of responsibility). These role demands can be expressed in terms of individual attributes: innate intelligence, acquired special or general knowledge, energy, sensitivity and insight, daring—any attribute associated with individual contribution and commitment to organization goals based upon *his present activity and upon past investment in himself.*

These attributes are unevenly distributed in the general population, with individuals who possess them in high degree, singly or in combination, being relatively scarce. Given that organizations generally prefer those who possess more, rather than fewer, of these attributes, we have the determinants of a structure of labor prices in any society in which individuals sell their services to organizations.

If we assume the existence of broad, reasonably competitive labor markets, then the organization paying monetary compensation to those who participate in its activities will not be able to influence prices significantly but must regard them as constraints on its choice of control structure. In other words, the leadership of the organization will establish what it conceives to be a satisfactory pattern of control in the role structure, given the prices it must then pay to staff these roles adequately. Given the structure of prices in the market, alternative control patterns will produce different compensation patterns.

In practice, rational bureaucratic organizations act just about this way, devising job-analysis and job-evaluation schemes in order to assess role de-

[6] James G. March and Herbert A. Simon, *Organizations* (New York: John Wiley & Sons, 1958), chap. iv.
[7] Whisler, *op. cit.*

mands, with this job structure then determining the compensation structure. The official structure of compensation in an organization is periodically examined in light of market and other changes, and discrepancies (evidenced through difficulties in finding people to fill jobs or by the existence of maneuvering and bargaining to obtain overvalued jobs) tend to be rectified. Every organization also has some scheme for assessing individuals that is a counterpart to the one used in assessing jobs. Discrepancies between the control structure and the compensation structure can occur not only because of market changes but also because of changes in individuals and because of initial imperfections in analysis of the control or compensation structures. Those discrepancies may be rectified by adjusting *any* of the variables—the role, role occupant, or the compensation. This process tends to be continuous, consisting of marginal adjustments throughout the organization. It thus becomes possible to infer the control structure of the organization from its compensation structure and to compare organizations with one another at the same or different points in time.

B.   Perceived interpersonal control

A more restricted concept of control than that just discussed has been used in organization research by investigators at the University of Michigan. In this case, control is defined as a process of interpersonal influence. Control is exerted *by* members, *on* members in accomplishment of the organization task. Further, control is exerted only to the extent that it is perceived as being exerted by members of the organization. Those individuals who work in relative isolation from most other members of the organization, therefore, will likely be seen as having relatively little influence (control) over others. Research personnel and staff analysts would be examples, as would presidents.[8] For that matter, anyone in the organization lying beyond the perceptual range of respondents would also be likely to have little influence attributed to him.

The measure of control is provided by asking all members of an organizational unit to indicate on a scale the amount of influence that other members of the organization—identified by hierarchical levels—exert upon individuals at each level of the hierarchy. (This questionnaire is described in detail on pp. 291–292.) These attributions are then summed and averaged by hierarchical level.[9]

C.   Span of control

The literature of classical organization theory has given a prominent place to the span of control. It has been argued occasionally that a large span of control (a high subordinate-to-superior ratio) indicates a high degree of decentraliza-

---

[8] A recurring phenomenon in empirical studies using the "control graph" is the perception of the top man in the organization as having less influence than his immediate subordinates.

[9] This aggregation greatly reduces the precision of the measure for purposes of the present study. Later, we deal with the problem it created for us—that of inferring the influence or control of the individual.

tion: "If the manager practices close supervision, if he is constantly checking the work of subordinates, and if he insists upon prior approval of all decisions . . . made by the subordinate, then he is decreasing the number of people he can supervise. He broadens his span by granting them more authority to take action without checking back with him on all details. On a company-wide basis, this is analogous to centralized vs. decentralized operations."[10] The costs of queuing time set limits on the span of control, if nothing else does.

The concept of control is again that of interpersonal influence, or control, in this case between a superior and his subordinates. The span of control becomes a visible map of the formally planned or intended pattern of interpersonal control. The span of control defines a two-level work group, with control shared between the two levels, among the superior and his subordinates. The average individual share is inversely proportional to the number-sharing. Thus, increasing the span of control reduces the relative control of the superior, *ceteris paribus.*

Concepts and indexes of centralization of control

Discussion up to this point has been restricted to different concepts of the process of control and to the measures associated with them. We need to give consideration now to concepts and measures of centralization. Starting with the three concepts of control, we can develop concepts of centralization and viable measures of centralization associated with them.

If, as Von Bertalanffy states, centralization is an attribute of a system or structure, to study centralization we need first to specify the structure to which it applies. Our interest centers on control, considered up to this point as a dimension of individual behavior. To get an analogue that is a dimension of organizational behavior we must define the control structure. Given a definition of control structure, we can then derive a concept of centralization related to it as well as an index of centralization based upon this concept.

These concepts and measures of control structure and centralization are spelled out below for each of the three concepts of individual control.

A. System control

The structure of control can be defined as the array of individual valences (relative amounts) of control (as reflected in individual compensation) for the entire membership of the organization. Centralization is a condition of concentration of control in the hands of a few members. The limiting case of centralization is the assignment of all control to one member. The limiting case of decentralization is the peer group, with all members assigned equal control.

Appropriate indexes of centralization are measures of inequality of distribution of individual compensation.

---

[10] Janger, *op. cit.*

B.   Perceived interpersonal control

The structure of control again can be defined as an array—in this case, of perceived individual valences (relative amounts) of influence or control over others (as reflected by questionnaire responses). Centralization is the concentration of interpersonal control in a few members, with the extreme case of centralization (approached as a limit) being that where one member has all the perceived control and the others none. The limiting case of decentralization is that where all members have equal perceived control (a peer group).

Again, appropriate indexes of centralization are measures of inequality of distribution of individual influence.

C.   Span of control

The structure of control is the network of interconnected spans of control as mapped on a typical organization chart. In this case, following the arguments of Janger and others, we define centralization as a condition where the spans of control are relatively narrow, with the limiting case of centralization being a chain of one-for-one superior-subordinate relationships and the limiting case of decentralization being a single superior for the whole organization.

An appropriate index of centralization is the average span of control for the entire organization, or for such part of it as one chooses for study.

In Table 2 we summarize the concepts and measures just discussed and add them to those presented in Table 1.

Congruence of concepts and measures

We indicated earlier that it appears to us that the concepts underlying the three measures we have chosen to study represent different orders of explanatory power. System control encompasses both interpersonal control and direct task control and is thus broader than either perceived interpersonal control or formally defined interpersonal control.

However, since the broader concept includes the other two, we expect that overlap or congruence would always exist in indexes of centralization developed from them. Furthermore, we believe that it is possible to specify the organizational conditions under which the congruence would be high and those under which it would be low. Specifying these conditions makes it possible to test our earlier inferences about the differences in the control concepts.

The conditions to which we refer relate to the degree of routineness of organization activities and to the derivative standardization of individual tasks and rationalization of the authority and communication structures. There are, on the one hand, organizations, usually operating under stable conditions, with rather narrowly defined goals and detailed programs for achieving these goals. Many production departments fall under this heading. There are, on the

TABLE 2 Measures and Concepts of Control, Control Structure, and Centralization of Control

Control as it pertains to individuals		Control as it pertains to organizations		
Concept of control	Measure of control	Structure of control	Concept of centralization of control	Index(es) of centralization of control
A. System control	A. Individual compensation	A. Array of individual valences of control (individual compensation)	A. Concentration of individual control	A. Measures of inequality of distribution of individual compensation
B. Perceived interpersonal control	B. Scaled perceptions of individual influence	B. Array of individual valences of control (questionnaire responses)	B. Concentration of individual control	B. Measures of inequality of distribution of control valences from questionnaire
C. Formally defined interpersonal control	C. Span of control	C. Network of interconnected individual spans of control	C. Narrowness of spans of control	C. Average span of control

other hand, organizations with more broadly defined goals, organizations that not only must devise solutions to problems but often have the responsibility for defining the problems in the first place. A variety of "staff" departments in a modern corporation would fit this description.

In the first kind of organization (routine) we expect a substantial congruence among indexes of centralization based upon the three concepts of control. System control will be exercised largely *through* other members (an operating hierarchy) with only those at the bottom exerting the direct personal-effort kind of control through their work. We would expect continuous efforts at rationalization of tasks to remove ambiguities in the supervisor-subordinate relationship with a consequent reinforcement of formal influence relationships. Perceived influence should reflect this reinforcement. Real differences in concepts should, in this case, have little empirical significance.

In the second kind of organization (problem-solving), low congruence should be expected. Many members of the organization will be working individually and independently for much of the time. Interpersonal influence, whether formally defined or perceived, will describe only part of the behavior of such an organization. Formally defined influence will also describe a smaller subset of behaviors than in the first case, since influence relationships should shift from problem to problem (on the assumption that authority of knowledge dominates and some specialization of knowledge is present). Perceived influence may well be at odds with the formal map.

Our empirical test will involve correlation of indexes of centralization under the different conditions. In a set of organizational units that perform routine tasks, variance should reflect largely errors of measurement, and correlations should be substantial. In a set of problem-solving organizational units, variance should reflect both errors of measurement and the disparity in concepts. Correlations should be low.

THE EMPIRICAL STUDY

Design

The empirical study was designed to get answers to two questions: (1) What is the degree of congruence or overlap of the three concepts when indexes of centralization derived from them are applied to a set of organizations? (2) Can we substantiate our inferences about the differences among the control concepts?

To answer the first question, we obtained compensation, perceived-influence, and span-of-control data for a set of departments. Using these data in the indexes of centralization we generated three series of index numbers for the departments and computed their intercorrelations.

To answer the second question, we obtained a rank ordering of the departments in terms of the degree of routinization of tasks. We then compared size-matched subsets of the departments, subsets chosen from different parts of the continuum. We expected correlations among the index-numbers series to be higher in the more routinized subset than in the size-matched less-routinized subset. We were able to make this comparison twice, for two pairs of samples.

Research site and data

Data were gathered on seventy-three departments within a large insurance firm, each with its own head and formal structure. This group of departments includes thirty in the home office performing a variety of functions (personnel, organization analysis, legal, reinsurance, etc.) and forty-three branch claims offices performing an identical function in different locations throughout the United States. The size range of these departments in terms of number of individuals is shown in Table 3. Four kinds of data were collected on these departments:

1. Individual compensation

Monthly salaries were obtained for every individual in each department for the pay period during which the influence questionnaire was completed within the particular department. These salaries were used as compensation data, fringe items being ignored. No bonuses or incentive payments were involved.

2. Influence-questionnaire responses

The questionnaire, a portion of which is shown in Figure 1, was used to gather perceptions of influence. It is quite similar to those used by Tannenbaum and others in studies of organizational control. The data used in this study were the responses to the question shown in Figure 1, in which respondents are asked to indicate by check marks their estimate of the influence exerted by each identified group in the department on every other group in that depart-

TABLE 3   Size of Departments Used in the Study

Size	Thirty home-office departments	Forty-three branch claims offices	All seventy-three departments
Smallest	3	2	2
Largest	44	75	75
Median	9	7	8
Mean	10.4	11.1	10.8
Standard deviation	8.1	14.5	12.2

In general, how much influence do the people in group one* have on what the following individuals or groups do in the company?					
	Little or no influence	Some influence	Quite a bit of influence	A great deal of influence	A very great deal of influence
The individuals in group two					
The individuals in group three					
The individuals in group four					
The individuals in group five					
The individuals in group six					

Job groups
A & H branch claim personnel

Group one   Divisional claim supervisor
Group two   District manager
Group three   District supervisors
Group four   Clerical supervisors
Group five   Adjusting personnel
                 (Adjusters, examiners, etc.)
Group six   Clerical

*Question repeated for each group, one through six.

FIGURE 1   *Sample question on influence questionnaire.*

ment. Responses were given values from one to five, left to right. The influence of each level or group is the mean value of responses of all members in the department.

3. Reporting relationships

A review of reporting relationships and a classification of organizational levels were made jointly by corporate staff personnel and individual department heads at the same time that other data were gathered. We could thus pinpoint each superior and his span of control.

4. Ranking on a task continuum

Three staff members of the company (organization and job analysts) made a joint ranking of the seventy-three departments in order, from that with the least routinized tasks to the most routinized. (These analysts have no connection, formal or otherwise, with those who establish wage and salary structure.) All forty-three branch offices, which performed the same task and thus received the same ranking, fell below eighteen less routinized home-office departments and above twelve more routinized home-office departments.

Index construction

For each of the three definitions of centralization of control we sought indexes of centralization that could be applied to whole organizations or to parts of them, with a minimum of data transformation necessary to their application. It turned out that the only transformation involved was made necessary by the nature of the questionnaire data available to us. (See Section A, below.)

A.   Indexes of inequality of distribution of compensation

Several indexes were devised, all derived from cumulative frequency distributions expressed in percentages (Lorenz distributions). The items in these distributions were individual compensation figures.

As a global index of centralization we used a modified Gini ratio of concentration (see Appendix I). Portions of the total compensation distribution in each department also were examined and indexes calculated. These indexes were the percentages of total compensation earned by the highest paid 20, 30, 40, and 50 per cent of the members.

A data transformation was necessary. The reason lies in the fact that the influence-questionnaire data, with which we wish to compare compensation data, are averages computed from questionnaire responses focused on groups. Since true individual compensation figures are available, true individual influence ratings would be desirable.

Because it was not possible to get such individual ratings,[11] we reduced compensation data to the same level of imprecision as the influence data *for purposes of comparing perceived influence and compensation indexes, only.*[12] That is, we computed the average compensation for each member of each group in each department (the groups being identical to those used in measuring perceived influence). This figure was used to compute indexes of con-

---

[11] Questionnaire data had already been gathered by corporate personnel for other purposes. We borrowed the data in the only form in which they were available—expressing the influence of groups.

[12] Had we not done so, we would have incorporated an error of measurement substantially reducing correlation coefficients.

centration of *adjusted* (average) compensation in the same fashion as indexes of concentration of *true* compensation were computed.

Indexes based upon true compensation were used for comparison with span of control. Indexes based upon adjusted compensation were used for comparison with perceived influence.

B.   Indexes of inequality of distribution of perceived influence

Indexes similar to those described in Section A were computed. In this case, items in the distributions were individual influence valences.

A problem of data interpretation arose in connection with these indexes. The reason lay, once again, in the fact that questionnaire responses pertained to *groups* and we wanted *individual* valences. The number representing the influence exerted by a group is a mean of individual responses. A critical question arises as to what the respondent intends when he assigns an influence valence to a group. Does this number represent the combined influence of all those in the group or the influence of an average member of the group? Either response could follow logically from the wording of the question; the respondent is given no further guidance by the questionnaire.

As far as we know, those who have used this questionnaire have not attempted to answer the question raised. Tannenbaum and Kahn, in describing scaling problems associated with this technique, do not raise the issue.[13]

We asked a sample of the respondents in the company (after a time lapse of three months) to tell us what they meant when they made their responses. They were unable to answer the question with any certainty, except to say that their rating was *not* influenced by the number of people at each level.

Therefore, we made a preliminary comparison of influence and compensation data to get some clue to aid us in interpreting the responses. This procedure is described in Appendix II. On the basis of the two tests described there, we decided to calculate the index of perceived influence on the assumption that respondents were actually describing the influence exerted by the average member in a given group.

C.   Index of concentration of formally assigned control

We used the simplest global index we could devise, the average span of control. Its computation is simply $(N - 1)/S$, where S is the number of department members who have at least one subordinate, N is the total membership, and $N - 1$ is the number who are subordinates in the department.

---

[13] Arnold S. Tannenbaum and Robert L. Kahn, "Organizational Control Structure: A General Descriptive Technique as Applied to Four Local Unions," *Human Relations*, X, No. 2 (1957), 127–40.

Correlation

In Table 4 we show correlations among the indexes for the seventy-three departments and for the subsamples of thirty home-office departments and forty-three branch claims offices. Where the average span of control is used as an index the sign is negative as expected, since greater centralization is associated with a larger ratio of concentration and a smaller span of control.

To get at the effects of the degree of task-programing on correlations among the indexes of centralization, we used the forty-three branch offices as a reference group. Performing an identical departmental task, these units had been placed on the task continuum just behind the eighteenth and ahead of the nineteenth home-office departments by the organization analysts who functioned as judges. (The farther down the ranks a department is placed, the more routine and programed its activities are; see Fig. 2.)

Thus the branch offices came close to being in the middle of the distribution on the task continuum. Taking advantage of the large number of units performing an identical job, we tested the task-effect hypothesis twice.

First of all, we compared the correlations among eighteen home-office departments at the "least programed" end of the task continuum with the correlations among the forty-three branch offices and the latter, in turn, with the

TABLE 4 Simple Correlation Coefficients among Various Indexes of Centralization for Thirty Home-office Departments, Forty-three Claims Offices, and All Seventy-three Departments

Correlations between:	Home-office departments ($N = 30$)	Branch offices ($N = 43$)	All departments ($N = 73$)
Concentration of compensation* (adjusted) and concentration of influence*	.62	.48	.53
Concentration of compensation* (true) and average span of control	—.68	—.52	—.60
Average span of control and concentration of influence*	—.66	—.55	—.56
Proportion of total compensation and proportion of total influence held by i per cent of department members, where $i =$ top:			
20 per cent	.36	.26	.24
30 per cent	.47	.21	.31
40 per cent	.58	.19	.40
50 per cent	.60	.20	.41

* Modified Gini ratios of concentration.

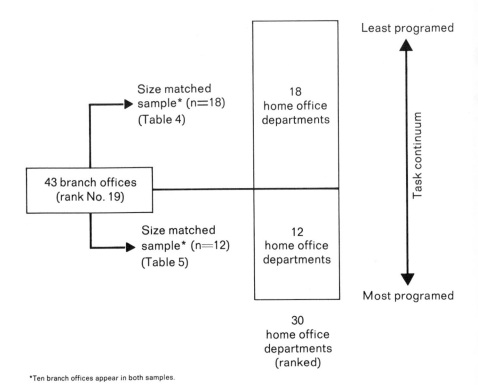

*Ten branch offices appear in both samples.

FIGURE 2 *Schematic illustration of method of drawing size-matched samples to show task effects.*

correlations among the twelve home-office departments at the "most programed" end. The results are shown in Table 5.

Our second test was performed only because we noticed that the smallest home-office departments were concentrated in the least programed end of the continuum. While we know of no reason a priori to expect departmental size to affect the correlations we are examining, the existence of the branch offices permitted us to control for size by a sample-matching technique.

We matched as closely as possible, on the basis of size (see Table 6), the eighteen departments ranked ahead of the branch offices (toward the least programed end of the continuum) with eighteen of the branch offices. Thus we had two subgroups between which correlations were run as before. Similarly, we compared the twelve departments ranked below the branch offices (more routine) with a size-matched sample of twelve branch offices. Correlations for these two comparisons are shown in Tables 7 and 8. Figure 2 shows, schematically, how these comparisons were made.

TABLE 5 Simple Correlation Coefficients for the Control-structure Measures in the Eighteen Least Programed Home-office Departments, the Forty-three Branch Offices, and the Twelve Most Programed Home-office Departments

Correlations between:	Least programed home-office departments ($N = 18$)	Branch offices ($N = 43$)	Most programed home-office departments ($N = 12$)
Concentration of compensation* (adjusted) and concentration of influence*	.16	.48	.86
Concentration of compensation* (true) and average span of control	−.31	−.52	−.75
Average span of control and concentration of influence*	−.38	−.55	−.64
Proportion of total compensation and proportion of total influence held by i per cent of department members, where $i =$ top:			
20 per cent	.19	.26	.65
30 per cent	.15	.21	.86
40 per cent	.14	.19	.91
50 per cent	.01	.20	.90

* Modified Gini ratios of concentration.

ANALYSIS AND DISCUSSION

Over-all relationships

The three independent indexes of centralization exhibit varying degrees of correlation, in the expected direction, in these seventy-three departments (Table 4). The global indexes (indexes describing centralization in a department as a whole) correlate more highly than do those measuring the relative control exercised by parts of these units (what we have called partial indexes).

The rather low coefficients obtained for fractions of these units could result from discontinuities and errors of measurement in very small groups. A fifth or a third of, say, a nine-person department gives one very little to work with. Our purpose in considering such partial indexes comes from the fact that, especially in large organizations, one often is interested in changes in segments of the control structure. One example would be an assessment of the effectiveness of divisionalization as a device for decentralizing corporate top managerial control. Another would be testing the notion that installation of computer systems tends to shift control from middle to upper levels of management.

TABLE 6   Pairings of Departments from the Home-office and Branch-office Groups, Showing Actual Department Sizes

Department sizes in the pairing of twelve branch and twelve home-office departments		Department sizes in the pairing of eighteen branch and eighteen home-office departments	
Branch*	Home office	Branch*	Home office
6	5	3	3
11	11	9	9
12	12	9	9
9	9	12	12
9	8	3	3
7	8	2	3
19	18	10	10
7	8	5	5
9	9	6	6
23	24	5	5
14	13	7	7
36	44	14	14
		4	3
		11	12
		6	6
		19	20
		9	9
		7	8

* Ten branch claims offices are common to both samples.

Furthermore, a global index may conceal as much as it reveals. Conceivably, shifts in concentration of control from one part of the organization to another could occur without any consequent change in the modified Gini ratio appearing. And a change in the global index simply tells one that a change in concentration of control has occurred without pinpointing its location. Hence our emphasis upon partial indexes.

The low coefficients yielded for the smallest fractions of these small departments would make one cautious about accepting these indexes as effective substitutes for one another under such conditions. In larger organizations, errors of measurement arising out of the discontinuities of small size should be a lesser problem, making partial indexes more reliable and the substitution of one of the three indexes for another more acceptable.

The data in Table 4 provide a tentative answer to the first question the study sought to answer. Were we able to get more precise data we would hope that the correlation among the indexes would be somewhat higher, perhaps by another ten points on the average. But, in any event, the remaining variance is sufficiently large to make tenable our assumptions of differences in basic concepts of control.

Control for degree of task-programing

The second question in the study related to our ability to demonstrate empirically the differences imputed analytically to the different concepts of control. Our prediction was that in more highly programed task situations the control concepts would tend toward congruence and that indexes developed from them would show higher correlations.

Tables 6, 7, and 8 show that, on two trials, both the global indexes and the partial indexes behaved as predicted.[14] We believe this behavior to reinforce strongly our assumption that we have identified three basically different ways of defining organizational control and that these indexes give cognizance to them.

General conclusions

This study must be classified as criteria research. We started with three proposed criteria of an organizational variable—centralization of control—that seemed to us not only to use different organizational data but to have distinctive conceptual underpinnings.

We sought to test empirically the degree to which they yielded comparable results in comparing a group of organizations. In this respect we were motivated by a practical concern. The researcher cannot always get the sort of data in one organization that he can in another. Hence, we hoped that it might turn out that alternative measures would correlate to a degree that would permit free substitution.

We also sought evidence to support our belief that these criteria were based upon different concepts of control and control structure—differences that could be defined formally and operationally. Our interest here was both theoretical and practical. The structure of control has always been a muddy concept and attempts to measure it usually abortive.

We think we have found evidence to support two conclusions: (1) The three measures analyzed do not relate to a common construct or concept but to three different constructs that are closely related under certain specifiable conditions in an organization and that are quite unrelated under others. These "conditions" appear to be summed under the heading of the degree of routinization or programing of the organizational task. Where the organizational task is highly programed, the shape of the formal structure, the distribution of individual control over organizational achievement, and the perception of interpersonal authority and influence relationships will be highly correlated. We found that, with highly programed tasks, correlations varied from $|.64|$ to $|.86|$. Where the organizational task is relatively unprogramed, they will tend to diverge. In this situation, we found correlation coefficients to range from

---

[14] The correlation coefficient between compensation and span of control in the second column of Table 8 takes on a positive sign. In the population of forty-three branch offices, correlation between these two measures is —.52. We found, from examination of the appropriate scatter diagram, that the twelve offices we chose for size-matching purposes unfortunately happened to yield observations producing this small but positive correlation.

TABLE 7 Simple Correlation Coefficients for the Control-structure Measures in the Eighteen Least Programed Home-office Departments and Eighteen Size-matched Branch Offices

Correlations between:	Least programed home-office departments (N = 18)	Size-matched branch offices (N = 18)
Concentration of compensation* (adjusted) and concentration of influence*	.16	.70
Concentration of compensation* (true) and average span of control	−.31	−.37
Average span of control and concentration of influence*	−.38	−.68
Proportion of total compensation and proportion of total influence held by i per cent of department members, where i = top:		
20 per cent	.19	.23
30 per cent	.15	.32
40 per cent	.14	.41
50 per cent	.01	.42

* Modified Gini ratios of concentration.

|.16| to |.38|. (2) Except in studies confined to organizations characterized by loosely structured and unprogramed tasks, the three indexes of centralization may be used empirically as substitutes for one another. For our total group of seventy-three departments, with no control for degree of task-programing, coefficients ranged from |.48| to |.68|.

In our judgment, those engaged in empirical research would select one of these measures of centralization of control on the basis of the following considerations:

1. The control construct most relevant to other variables studied

System control is likely to be most relevant where other variables relate to the organization as a whole, for example, cultural or demographic differences in the environment, technological change, changes in size or dispersion. The same is true of span of control, especially when the other variables are "internal" in nature, such as technology and task complexity. Perceived control is apt to be most relevant when psychological variables are studied.

TABLE 8   Simple Correlation Coefficients for the Control-structure Measures in the Twelve "Routine" Home-office Departments and Twelve Size-matched Branch Offices

Correlations between:	Most programed home-office departments ($N = 12$)	Size-matched branch offices ($N = 12$)
Concentration of compensation* (adjusted) and concentration of influence*	.86	.49
Concentration of compensation* (true) and average span of control	−.75	.26
Average span of control and concentration of influence*	−.64	−.28
Proportion of total compensation and proportion of total influence held by i per cent of department members, where $i =$ top		
20 per cent	.65	.52
30 per cent	.86	.59
40 per cent	.91	.55
50 per cent	.90	.36

* Modified Gini ratios of concentration.

2.   The ease of use

In this regard, one can see appreciable qualitative differences in these measures. Questionnaire data are costly and difficult to gather. Compensation data, already generated, are often treated as confidential in private business, although they frequently are freely available elsewhere. Formal organization structures are there for the asking, provided one has a reliable and knowledgeable informant or provided that the organization maintains and preserves charts. The availability of various kinds of data is often related to the industry or local research site within which research is carried out.

3.   The research design

Two considerations are important here. One concerns specifically the use of a longitudinal (before-and-after) design. If one seeks to compare the present with the past, the influence-questionnaire measure is unfeasible (unless one can find a situation in which the questionnaire had for some reason been administered earlier). It would be necessary to use either the span of control or compensation measures. Second, when one encounters informally organized groups, or organizations that do not use monetary compensation, the influence questionnaire or some variation on it may be the only feasible measure among the three.

APPENDIX I

CONSTRUCTION OF CENTRALIZATION INDEXES FROM CUMULATIVE
FREQUENCY DISTRIBUTIONS

Global index (modified Gini ratio of concentration)

To measure centralization, using compensation data and influence-questionnaire data in the seventy-three departments, we selected the Gini ratio of
concentration. This measure has been widely used by others, especially by
economists studying income distribution.

The Gini ratio, based upon Lorenz distributions, has some inherent limitations[15] but seemed the best measure available for our purposes where the departments (and distributions) are quite small. However, the very fact of
small size made a modification of the Gini ratio necessary.

Consider the Lorenz diagram shown in Figure 3. The side AB represents
the cumulative number of members in the department, the side BC the cumulative compensation or influence in the department, and the curve AEC the
cumulative frequency distribution of either salaries or influence ratings,
ranked from the lowest to the highest.

Normally, the Gini ratio of concentration is computed as the ratio of the area
$AECA$ to the area $ABCA$, supposedly the ratio of the observed area of deviation from equality to the largest possible area of deviation. But, strictly speaking, the maximum area of deviation is not $ABCA$ but $AFCA$, where AF is the
total membership less one, a situation where all compensation or interpersonal
influence is held by one member, while the others hold none. In many applications of the ratio (e.g., large labor markets), it does not matter greatly that
$ABCA$ is substituted for $AFCA$. When numbers are large, the area $FCBF$ is
very small. But in our case $FCBF$ can be quite large (e.g., in a five-member
department $FCBF$ comprises one fifth and in a two-member department one-
half, of $ABCA$). Therefore, in order to adhere to a strict interpretation of the
rationale of the Gini index of concentration, it was necessary to use the ratio
of area $AECA$ to the area $AFCA$.

In addition, to compute indexes of concentration of compensation and perceived influence at various points of the compensation or perceived-influence
distributions, we calculated the second, third, fourth, and fifth decile deviation
in each of the seventy-three departments. For instance, the second decile deviation indicates the percentage of control (compensation or perceived influence) held by the top 20 per cent of the department's members. In terms of
the Lorenz diagram above, this is equal to the ratio of DE to CB, assuming that
FB comprises the department's 20 per cent top employees. These decile devia-

[15] See Mary Jean Bowman, "A Graphical Analysis of Personal Measure Distribution in the United States,"
American Economic Review, XXV, No. 4 (1945), 607–28, and "The Analysis of Inequality Patterns: A Methodological Contribution," *Metron*, XVIII, Nos. 1–2 (1956), 2 ff.

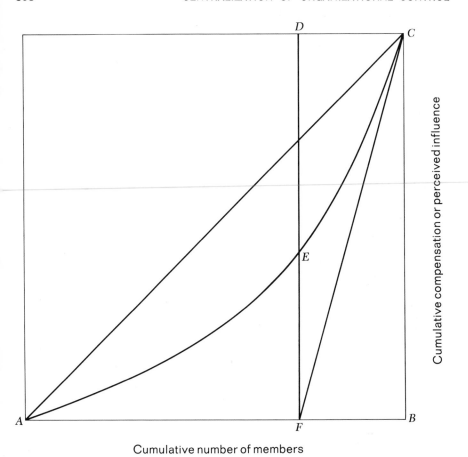

FIGURE 3   *Lorenz diagram, illustrating the modification of the Gini ratio.*

tions are relatively easy to understand and compute and have been discussed and used in this context in an earlier study.[16]

APPENDIX II

INTERPRETATION OF INFLUENCE-QUESTIONNAIRE RATINGS

In order to calculate indexes of centralization of perceived influence for each department, it was necessary to determine whether the influence-questionnaire ratings made by each member for each level of a department represented the perceived influence of the total level or of the average member at that level. To illustrate the point, consider the first four columns in Table 9. These columns contain information obtained from a sample department. If the in-

[16] Whisler, *op. cit.*

TABLE 9 Salaries and Influence Ratings for a Nine-member Department, Showing Proportionate Shares for Each Level under Different Assumptions

| | Obtained from company | | | | Computed | |
| | | | | | Per cent of total influence for group under assumption | |
Group (level)	No. of members (1)	Salaries received (dollars) (2)	Influence rating (3)	Per cent of total salary received by group (4)	A* (5)	B† (6)
1	1	$775	3.52	20.4	18.7	48.0
2	4	467, 550, 500, 425	2.30	51.1	48.9	31.3
3	4	280, 275, 275, 255	1.52	28.5	32.4	20.7
Total	9	3,802	A*: 18.80 B†: 7.34	100.0	100.0	100.0

* Assumption A: The influence rating represents influence of the average member of the group.
† Assumption B: The influence rating represents the influence of the group as a whole.

fluence ratings in column (3) are assumed to pertain to the average member at the given level (assumption A), then the total perceived influence exerted in that department is 18.80; if the ratings denote the total control of all members at a level, then the departmental total is 7.34.

Several months after administration of the questionnaire, we asked a sample of respondents what they meant when they made their responses. They were unable to answer the question with certainty, except to say that they did not adjust their answer to the number of people at each level.

Since this direct approach proved fruitless, we engaged in two calculations. First, for every department we computed the relative share of total salaries paid to each level and the relative share of total perceived influence for each level under both assumptions [columns (4)–(6)]. These computations were made for all 273 levels in the seventy-three departments, and correlations between influence and compensation shares were calculated. When assuming the perceived-influence ratings [as in column (3)] to pertain to the average member of the level, then the simple correlation coefficient between the relative share of salaries (column 4) of the 243 levels and the corresponding influence shares [column (5)] was +.93. When assuming the perceived-influence ratings to express the control of the entire level, then the corresponding correlation coefficient is +.27.

We made a second and different kind of test. Choosing the clerical (fourth) level from a random sample of twenty branch claims offices (all performing the same task), we correlated the number of members in each department at this level with the total perceived influence of the level in each department under both assumptions. Under assumption A, the simple correlation coefficient is +.90; assuming the rating reflects the total influence of the level, the correlation coefficient is +.16.

On the basis of the outcome of these two tests, and the rater statements referred to earlier, we assumed the questionnaire ratings to represent ratings of the perceived influence of the average member at a given level.

21

CONTROL IN ORGANIZATIONS: INDIVIDUAL ADJUSTMENT AND ORGANIZATIONAL PERFORMANCE*

Arnold S. Tannenbaum[1]

Research suggests that the manner in which control is exercised, or the amount that is exercised, has significant effects on the adjustments of organization members and on the performance of the organization. A number of general propositions help explain some of these effects.

CONTROL AND ADJUSTMENT

First, every act of control has both pragmatic and symbolic implications. Pragmatically, control implies something about *what* an individual must or must not do, the restrictions to which he is subject, and the areas of choice or freedom that he has—whether, for example, a worker is transferred to a new machine or stays on the old, whether he is classified into a $2.50 or a $2.75 wage category, whether he is free to talk, smoke, rest, slow down, or speed up while on the job. These pragmatic implications are often of vital importance to the controlled individual as well as to the individual exercising power. Symbolically control has special meaning or significance to the individuals involved. It may imply superiority, inferiority, dominance, submission, guidance, help, criticism, reprimand. It may imply (as some students of control argue) something about the manliness and virility of the individuals involved. The exercise of control, in other words, is charged emotionally.

Second, the exercise of control is a positive value for most organization members. While individual differences certainly exist, organization members generally prefer exercising influence to being powerless. Research consistently shows that the average organization member (as well as the average officer) is more likely to feel that he has too little authority in his work than too much (Katz, 1954; Porter, 1962; Smith and Tannenbaum, 1963). This desirability of control may be attributed to the psychological or symbolic satisfactions that come from exercising control, *or* it may derive from the pragmatic implications of power—being able to affect the work situation in ways favorable to one's personal interests as the individual sees them. But for whatever reasons, persons generally want to exercise some control in their work situations

* This chapter draws in part from the article Control in organizations: Individual adjustment and organizational performance, published in *Admin. Sci. Quart.*, 1962, 7 (2), 236–257, and appears here with permission of the publisher.

[1] I would like to thank Robert Kahn for his helpful suggestions.

and they experience more satisfaction when they do exercise this control than when they do not (Blauner, 1960, 1964; Bachman and Tannenbaum, 1966).

√Third, the exercise of control is a major basis for the psychological integration of the member into the system. Because the exercise of control implies affecting the system in a manner consistent with the intents of the controller, the system is more fully instrumental in meeting the needs of one who exercises some control than of one who does not exercise control. This instrumentality is the basis for the increased involvement in and identification with the system that are found to accompany the exercise of control. Psychologically, the system is an extension of the person who exercises control more than of one who does not. Hence, the person who exercises control is less alienated from the system than his uninfluential counterparts.

Fourth, the exercise of control has frustrating as well as satisfying consequences. Individuals who are not able to exercise control are, in general, less satisfied with their work situations than those who have some power, but their dissatisfaction often has the alienated quality of apathy and disinvolvement. For individuals who exercise control, added dimensions of personality come into play contributing to the energies that they put into their work and to the problems they may encounter. The responsibility that devolves upon persons in control creates a sense of personal involvement and concern over the success or failure of the decisions taken. This can be a satisfying, even an exhilarating, experience, but it can also lead to sleepless nights.

Fifth, increases in the control which persons exercise in organizations may sometimes be accompanied by increases in the extent to which these persons *are* controlled in the organization. Paradoxically, one of the costs to the influential organization member for the influence he exercises may be the increased control to which he may be subject. The loyalty and identification which he feels for the organization may lead him to accept organizational requirements and to conform to organizational norms which he might not otherwise do. We found evidence of this in the behavior of members of effective unions with high total control (see Chapter 2). Members here were more amenable to control because of their greater loyalty to and identification with their unions; they were also subject to norms and pressures toward conformity which were lacking in the less effective unions. Consequently the behaviors of members in these unions were more uniform than the behaviors of members in the less effective, laissez-faire unions. An analysis in the thirty-one departments of the industrial service organization described in Chapter 10 revealed a similar phenomenon. Norms, measured in terms of uniformity in the attitudes of workers, were somewhat more apparent in the departments having high total control than in those having low control. In these "better" departments, influence by the men as a group was greater, morale was more favorable, productive effort was higher, and so was uniformity. Similarly, while the active members in the voluntary organization discussed in Chapter 4 exercised more influence than the inactive members, the former were also *subject* to greater influence and "pressure"—and their behavior as a group was more uniform. The exercise of control does not necessarily spare the controller from being controlled. The contrary may be true in effective organizations with high total control, where influence tends to be reciprocal.

CONTROL AND ORGANIZATIONAL PERFORMANCE

Variations in control patterns within organizations have important—and in some cases quite predictable—effects on the reactions, satisfactions and frustrations, feelings of tension, self-actualization, or well-being of members. They may also have implications for the performance of the organization. Although these implications have been subject to controversy,[2] we can nonetheless make a number of statements with some confidence based on research.[3]

First, it seems safe on the basis of available evidence to assert that organizations with influential rank-and-file memberships *can be* as effective as organizations with relatively uninfluential members. This statement, though conservative in the context of contemporary arguments for participative approaches to organization, is a clear departure from traditional bureaucratic and administrative arguments.

Second, it seems equally safe on the basis of the available evidence to assert that organizations with powerful officers *can be* as effective as organizations in which the officers are less influential. This statement, though conservative in the context of traditional views, is not entirely in accord with many contemporary arguments for democratic, participative organization.

Third, it seems a reasonable inference from the evidence presented in this book that organizations with influential rank-and-file memberships are likely to be more effective than those with uninfluential memberships *providing* the officers are not less influential in the first than in the second group of organizations. This statement flatly contradicts traditional theories.

Fourth, it seems a reasonable inference that organizations with powerful officers are likely to be more effective than those with less powerful officers *providing* the memberships are not less influential in the first than in the second group of organizations. This statement is not entirely consistent with participative arguments.

Fifth, data from a variety of organizations support the contention that organizations with influential leaders *and* members are likely to be more effective than organizations with less influential members and/or leaders. This inference clearly contradicts traditional views and many conventional participative arguments. It assumes, as do the previous two statements, a variable

---

[2] See, for example, Strauss, G. (1963).
[3] In so doing we assume that the measures reported in this text are reasonably valid measures of control objectively defined. We feel supported in this assumption by the analyses concerning structural and phenomenological effects reported in Chaps. 13 and 14. If the reader cannot accept our assumption, he may nonetheless find our inferences worth thinking about, even though they may connote for him inferences concerning organizational performance and control *as perceived* by organization members.

total amount of control within organizations—an assumption that until recently has had no place in theories of organization.

Finally, within "normal" ranges, variations in power differentials (differences in power between persons of different rank) are *not* likely to be associated with criteria of performance.[4] This statement sharply contradicts some arguments for participative organization to the extent that these arguments identify participation with "power equalization." Similarly it contradicts some traditional views that attach primary importance to a fixed system of power differentials. The research presented in this text suggests that the preoccupation by researchers with "power equalization" may be misplaced in that this preoccupation has detracted from a consideration of the *total amount* of power as a possible explanation of organizational functioning.

CONCLUSION

Organizations in a democratic society present a seeming dilemma. As Geoffrey Vickers (1957, pp. 1–8) put it,

> *We are forever oscillating between two alternatives which seem mutually exclusive—on the one hand, collective efficiency won at the price of individual freedom; on the other, individual freedom equally frustrated by collective anarchy. Those who believe in a middle way which is more than a compromise do so in the faith that human beings are capable or can become capable of social organization which is both individually satisfying and collectively effective; and they have plenty of evidence for their faith. On the other hand, our knowledge of the laws involved is still rudimentary.*

"Middle ways" are sprouting up around the globe today. The workers' council systems in Yugoslavia, Germany, France, Belgium, England, though differing radically in character and effectiveness, are, within their respective cultures, experiments in the middle way. We have our Scanlon Plans, profit sharing, and suggestion schemes, as well as varying degrees of participative management. However, our knowledge of the effects of these systems is, as Vickers says, rudimentary.

If the clues provided by our research so far are substantiated, the "middle way" will have to take into account the important facts about control: how control is distributed within an organization and how much it all amounts to. Patterns of control—as they are perceived by organization members at least—are often tied significantly to the performance of the organization and to the

---

[4] An exception to this statement can be found in the research on the voluntary organization reported in Chap. 4. The research by Morse and Reimer (1956) in a clerical organization also appears to contradict this statement. However, the Morse and Reimer research (and the research of others dealing with participative approaches) provides information about power differentials without offering data about the *total amount* of power. We have no way of knowing therefore whether the results of these researches are best explained by variations in power differentials per se, or by accompanying variations in *total amount* of power.

adjustments and satisfactions of members. If our research leads are correct, some of the significant improvements in the human side of enterprise are going to come through changes in the size of the "influence pie." This middle way leans on the assumption that influential workers do not imply uninfluential supervisors or managers. This is a relatively novel assumption for many managers who have been weaned on the all-or-none law of power; one either leads or is led, is strong or is weak, controls or is controlled. However, managers who in their behavior question the all-or-none principle do not seem less influential for it.

Our middle way assumes further that the organization member who exercises some influence over matters of interest to him in the work situation acquires a sense of self-respect which the powerless individual may lack. He can also elicit the respect and high regard of others. This is the key to good human relations. Supervisory training alone cannot achieve this any more than good intentions in bad organization can achieve it. The pattern of control in an organization, however, is likely to have a direct and profound effect on the organization's human-relations climate. Workers who have some sense of control in most of the organizations we have studied are in general more, not less, positively disposed toward their supervisors and managers. And their managers are more positively disposed toward them.

We assume further, with some support from research, that increasing and distributing the exercise of control more broadly in an organization helps to distribute an important sense of involvement in the organization. Members become more ego-involved. Aspects of personality that ordinarily do not find expression now contribute to the motivation of the members. The organization provides members with a fuller range of experiences. In doing this, however, it creates its own dilemmas, similar in some respects to those described by Vickers, yet in some respects different.

A first dilemma arises out of the increased involvement and motivation that are likely to accompany the exercise of control. While we see greater opportunity for human satisfaction in the middle way, the result is not simple felicity. Whenever man is highly motivated, he may experience the pangs of failure as well as the joys of success. He will know some of the satisfactions that come from a challenge met and a responsibility fulfilled. He may also feel frustration from the development of goals that are not easily reached.

A second dilemma concerns the increased control to which the influential organization member may be subject. While he controls more, he may not be controlled less. Contemporary participative models of organization illustrate the seeming paradox of providing members new freedom while requiring of them additional discipline. This discipline is founded not so much on attention to orders and concern for formal sanctions as on the sensitivity of members to each other and on their commitment to the larger purposes of the organization. Control under these circumstances is more subtle than in traditional systems because it is less unilateral—and it may occur between peers who are not distinguished by the signs and symbols that ordinarily distinguish the controller and the controlled. Nor is control here characterized by the overt conflicts and the surveillance that frequently mark the exercise of control. Hence, while control may be more subtle, compliance may be "all the more absolute when [as in the organic system] it is made voluntarily, even enthusiastically" (Burns and Stalker, 1961, p. 11).

The subtlety of control in the participative-organic system derives in part from the complexity of the system. The organic organization compromises the principle of simplification upon which traditional mechanistic systems are premised. Complexity, however, creates confusion unless those who cope with the more complex system are somehow more knowledgeable about and skilled in using it. The organic system therefore requires the employment of skills and the exercise of intelligence to a degree not otherwise called for—and these are the bases of the enhanced freedom characteristic of the organic system. However, while members in the organic system may be more fully active in shaping the organization, they are also more "totally included" in it. The lines of demarcation between the member as an individual and the member as a member are less sharply drawn than in the mechanistic organization. Thus the redefinition of organization from mechanistic to organic implies a redefinition of the organization member himself, for as Allport has said, organizations "are not merely our instruments; they are a part of ourselves."

REFERENCES

Allport, F. H. (1933). *Institutional behavior*. Chapel Hill, N.C.: University of North Carolina Press.

Bachman, J., & Tannenbaum, A. (May 1966). The control-satisfaction relationship across varied areas of experience. *Delta Pi Epsilon Journal*, **7** (2), 16–25 (in this book, Chap. 16).

Blauner, R. (1960). Work satisfaction and industrial trends in modern society. In W. Galenson and S. Lipset (Eds.), *Labor and trade unionism*. New York: Wiley.

Blauner, R. (1964). *Alienation and freedom*. Chicago: The University of Chicago Press.

Burns, T., & Stalker, G. M. (1961). *The management of innovation*. London: Tavistock Publishing Company.

Katz, D. (1954). Satisfactions and deprivations in industrial life. In A. Kornhauser, R. Dubin, & A. Ross (Eds.), *Industrial conflict*. New York: McGraw-Hill, pp. 86–106.

Morse, Nancy, & Reimer, E. (1956). The experimental change of a major organizational variable. *J. abnorm. soc. Psychol.*, **52**, 120–129.

Porter, L. W. (1962). Job attitudes in management: I. Perceived deficiencies in need fulfillment as a function of job level. *J. appl. Psychol.*, **46** (6), 375–384.

Smith, C. G., & Tannenbaum, A. (1963). Organization control structure: A comparative analysis. *Human Relat.*, **16** (4), 299–316 (in this book, Chap. 5).

Tannenbaum, A. (1961). Control and effectiveness in a voluntary organization. *Amer. J. Sociol.*, **67** (1), 33–46 (in this book, Chap. 4).

Strauss, G. (1963). Some notes on power-equalization. In H. Leavitt (Ed.), *The social science of organizations: Four perspectives.* Englewood Cliffs, N.J.: Prentice-Hall, 41–84.

Vickers, G. Control stability and choice. Ninth Wallberg Memorial Lecture, University of Toronto, October 30, 1956. Reprinted in *General systems, yearbook of the society for general systems*, Vol. II, 1957, 1–8.

NAME INDEX

Abel, T., 31n.
Allen, S., 21n., 26
Allport, F., v, x, 5n., 7n., 16, 17, 26, 147n., 151n., 200n., 202n., 210, 248, 249, 251n., 255, 257–259, 268, 270, 312
Andrews, F., 128, 213n., 257n.
Arensberg, C., 28
Argyris, C., 22, 26
Ari, O., 111, 145–163, 183
Aristotle, 8
As, D., 56n., 74, 88, 165n., 199, 210

Bachman, J., 112, 129n., 175n., 184, 185–197, 199n., 213–227, 229–239, 241–249, 257–271, 308, 312
Back, K., 15n., 27, 258n., 270
Ballachey, E., 207, 210
Barkin, S., 28
Barnard, C., 4, 26
Barnes, L., 22, 26
Barrett, D., 129
Barton, A., 88, 151n.
Baum, B., 23n., 273, 283–305
Baumgartel, H., 45n.

Bavelas, A., 129
Becker, W., 41n.
Bell, D., 7, 26
Bendix, R., 7n., 8, 26
Benesh, Marijana, 199n.
Benne, K., 22, 26
Bennis, W., 9n., 22, 26
Berger, M., 31n.
Berkowitz, L., 28
Berle, A., 4, 26
Bidwell, A., 22, 26
Blake, R., 21, 22, 26, 28
Blakelock, E., 244n.
Blalock, H. M., 128, 192n.
Blau, P., 15, 26, 56n., 57, 69n., 73, 88, 91n., 112, 185, 186n., 188n., 189–192n., 194–197, 200, 204, 210, 215, 227, 258, 267, 270, 283n.
Blauner, R., 200, 210, 241, 248, 308, 312
Borgatta, E., 59n.
Bowers, D., 73n., 75, 89, 111–123, 125, 126n., 127–129n., 165n., 168, 170, 183, 185n., 213, 227, 229–238
Bowman, Mary Jean, 302n.

SUBJECT INDEX